THE CINEMA OF NORTH AFRICA
AND THE MIDDLE EAST

First published in Great Britain in 2007 by
Wallflower Press
6a Middleton Place, Langham Street, London W1W 7TE
www.wallflowerpress.co.uk

A catalogue record for this book is available from the British Library

ISBN 978-1-905674-10-7 (paperback)
ISBN 978-1-905674-11-4 (hardback)

Printed by Replika Press Pvt Ltd. (India)

THE CINEMA OF
NORTH AFRICA
AND THE MIDDLE EAST

EDITED BY

GÖNÜL DÖNMEZ-COLIN

WALLFLOWER PRESS LONDON & NEW YORK

24 FRAMES is a major new series focusing on national and regional cinemas from around the world. Rather than offering a 'best of' selection, the feature films and documentaries selected in each volume serve to highlight the specific elements of that territory's cinema, elucidating the historical and industrial context of production, the key genres and modes of representation, and foregrounding the work of the most important directors and their exemplary films. In taking an explicitly text-centred approach, the titles in this list offer 24 diverse entry-points into each national and regional cinema, and thus contribute to the appreciation of the rich traditions of global cinema.

Series Editors: Yoram Allon & Ian Haydn Smith

OTHER TITLES IN THE **24 FRAMES** SERIES:

THE CINEMA OF LATIN AMERICA *edited by Alberto Elena and Marina Díaz López*

THE CINEMA OF THE LOW COUNTRIES *edited by Ernest Mathijs*

THE CINEMA OF ITALY *edited by Giorgio Bertellini*

THE CINEMA OF JAPAN & KOREA *edited by Justin Bowyer*

THE CINEMA OF CENTRAL EUROPE *edited by Peter Hames*

THE CINEMA OF SPAIN & PORTUGAL *edited by Alberto Mira*

THE CINEMA OF SCANDINAVIA *edited by Tytti Soila*

THE CINEMA OF BRITAIN & IRELAND *edited by Brian McFarlane*

THE CINEMA OF FRANCE *edited by Phil Powrie*

THE CINEMA OF CANADA *edited by Jerry White*

THE CINEMA OF THE BALKANS *edited by Dina Iordanova*

THE CINEMA OF AUSTRALIA & NEW ZEALAND *edited by Geoff Mayer and Keith Beattie*

THE CINEMA OF RUSSIA & THE FORMER SOVIET UNION *edited by Birgit Beumers*

FORTHCOMING TITLES:

THE CINEMA OF INDIA *edited by Lalitha Gopalan*

THE CINEMA OF GERMANY *edited by Joseph Garncarz*

THE CINEMA OF CHINA & SOUTH-EAST ASIA *edited by Ian Haydn Smith*

THE CINEMA OF SOUTHERN AFRICA *edited by Jacqueline Maingard*

CONTENTS

NOTES ON CONTRIBUTORS

ROY ARMES is Emeritus Professor of Film at Middlesex University, London. He has written widely on the cinema for the past forty years, most recently with a focus on African film. His latest books are *Postcolonial Images: Studies in North African Film* (2004) and *African Filmmaking: North and South of the Sahara* (2006). His current project is a dictionary of African filmmakers.

NITZAN BEN-SHAUL is Senior Lecturer at the Film and Television Department in Tel Aviv University. He is the author of *Mythical Expressions of Siege in Israeli Films* (1997), *Introduction to Film Theories* (2000), *A Violent World: TV News Images of Middle Eastern Terror and War* (2006) and *Film: The Key Concepts* (2007). He has published articles on television, film theory, new media and Israeli cinema in *Third Text*, *Film Quarterly*, *New Cinemas Journal*, *Journal of Modern Jewish Studies*, *Zmanim* and others.

HAIM BRESHEETH is Professor of Media and Cultural Studies at the University of East London. He is the co-editor of *Khamsin: Palestine – A Profile of an Occupation* (1989), *The Gulf War and the New World Order* (1992), *Cinema and Memory: Dangerous Liaisons* (1994), *The Holocaust for Beginners* (1994) and *Introducing the Holocaust* (1997). He was also the co-editor of the special double-issue *Third Text: The Conflict and Contemporary Visual Culture in Palestine & Israel* (2006). He has also produced and directed a number of documentary films, amongst which are *The Crumbling Ivory Tower* (1975), *Dinosaurs in the Playground* (1977), *The Options* (1981) and *A State of Danger* (1988), and is currently completing the video installation *A Civilised Clash*.

HAMID DABASHI is Hagop Kevorkian Professor of Iranian Studies and Comparative Literature at Columbia University. Among his publications are *Close Up: Iranian Cinema, Past, Present, Future* (2001), *Staging a Revolution: The Art of Persuasion in the Islamic Republic of Iran* (with Peter Chelkowski, 1999), *Dreams of a Nation: On Palestinian Cinema* (2007) and *Masters and Masterpieces of Iranian Cinema* (2007).

MONA DEELEY is the Director of Zenith Foundation, a London-based organisation dedicated to contemporary Arab culture. She was the commissioning editor of the Arab Art Workshop held at the Barbican Centre in London in June 2004, and she curated the Arab Film Season at the National Film Theatre in London in August 2004. She has extensive experience in the media business including her work at BBC Worldwide for the last four years.

KAY DICKINSON is Lecturer in media at Goldsmiths College, University of London. She has edited two collections: *Movie Music: The Film Reader* (2002) and *Teen TV: Genre, Consumption and Identity* (with Glyn Davis, 2003) and is currently completing a monograph entitled *Off Key: When Film and Music Won't Work Together*.

GÖNÜL DÖNMEZ-COLIN is a writer, researcher and lecturer. She has taught in Montreal and Hong Kong and has done field research in Iran, Turkey, India and Central Asia. Among her books are: *Women, Islam and Cinema* (2004), *Cinemas of the Other: A Personal Journey with Filmmakers from the Middle East and Central Asia* (2006) and *Turkish Cinema and Identity* (2007). She has written the Central Asia section of *The Companion Encyclopedia of Middle Eastern and North African Film* (2001), Turkey and Greece sections of *Die Siebte Kunst Auf Dem Pulverfass: Balkan Film* (1996) and the Cinema section of *The World of Islam* (2007). She has been a regular contributor to *Le Monde Diplomatique*, *Central Asian Survey*, *Cinemaya Asian Film Quarterly*, *Blimp*, *Kinema: A Journal for Film and Audiovisual Media* and the Turkish national daily, *Cumhuriyet*.

NEZIH ERDOĞAN is Dean of the Faculty of Communication at the Bilgi University, Istanbul and lecturer in film theory, semiotics and sound at Bahçeşehir University, Istanbul. He has mainly published on Turkish popular cinema and Hollywood in Turkey. He is the co-author of the Turkish cinema section of *The Companion Encyclopedia of Middle Eastern and North African Film* (2001). Currently, he is working on the early years of cinema in Turkey.

IMAN HAMAM is Professor of Film Studies at the American University in Cairo and writer for *Al-Ahram Weekly* newspaper. She has taught film, literary theory and cultural studies at Middlesex, Exeter and Sussex universities. She is currently working on Egyptian popular culture and Palestinian documentary film.

AYLA KANBUR is Assistant Professor in the Department of Radio, Television and Cinema at the Yeditepe University, Istanbul. She has contributed regularly to several Turkish publications as a film critic and feature writer and worked as a member of the editorial board of the journal *Antrakt*. She is also on the editorial board of the journal *Yeni Sinema* (*New Cinema*) and the editor of a book on Lütfi O. Akad (2004).

LINA KHATIB is Lecturer in World Cinema at the Department of Media Arts at Royal Holloway, University of London. She is the author of *Filming the Modern Middle East: Politics in the Cinemas of Hollywood and the Arab World* (2006) and is currently writing a book titled *Lebanese Cinema: Imagining the Civil War and Beyond*. She is also the editor of the *Journal of Media Practice*, and a founding editor of the *Middle East Journal of Culture and Communication*.

SHOSHANA MADMONI-GERBER is Lecturer in journalism and media at Suffolk University in Boston. She has worked as a journalist in Israel for *Yediot Aharonot*, *Shishi*, *Hadashot* and *Hapatish* newspapers and as a researcher and diversity trainer at Adva Centre for Equality of Israeli Society.

FLORENCE MARTIN is a Professor of French and Francophone Literatures and Film at Goucher College, Baltimore. She is the author of *Bessie Smith* (1996), the co-author of *De la Guyane à la diaspora africaine: écrits du silence* (with Isabelle Favre, 2002), and has widely published articles on cinema, literature and music. Her most recent research has focused on Tunisian women's films, and she is currently working on a book on North African women filmmakers entitled *Veils and Screens: Maghrebi Women's Cinema*.

YEHUDA JUDD NE'EMAN is Professor in the Department of Film and Television at Tel Aviv University. He is the author of the Israel section of *The Companion Encyclopedia of Middle Eastern and North African Film* (2001), and has published articles, co-written and co-edited books on Israeli cinema and war and cinema. He has also produced and directed feature films and documentaries for cinema and television; his films *Maasa Alunkot* (*Paratroopers*, 1977), *Mered Hayamaim* (*Seamen's Strike*, 1981), *Fellow Travellers* (1984) and *Streets of Yesterday* (1989) have been invited to festivals and shown on TV in many countries. He has recently directed and produced a feature documentary, *Scheherazade's Tears* (2006), and a feature film, *Nuzhat al-Fuad* (2007).

S. RUKEN ÖZTÜRK is Associate Professor in the Radio, Television and Cinema Department at Ankara University. Among her published work are *Postmodernizm ve Sinema* (*Postmodernism* *and Cinema*, 1997), which she co-translated and co-edited; *Sinemada Kadın Olmak* (*Being a Woman in Cinema*, 2000) and *Sinemanın Dişil Yüzü: Türkiye'de Kadın Yönetmenler* (*Female Side of Cinema: Women Filmmakers in Turkey*, 2004). She is one of the five contributors to *Çok Tuhaf Çok Tanıdık: 'Vesikalı Yarim' Üzerine* (*Strangely Familiar, Familiarly Strange: On 'My Licenced Beloved'*, 2005) about a classical Turkish melodrama.

MEHRNAZ SAEED-VAFA teaches film studies in the Department of Film and Video at Columbia College, Chicago. She is the author of numerous essays and articles on Iranian cinema and the co-author of *Abbas Kiarostami* (with Jonathan Rosenbaum, 2003). She is also a filmmaker whose work includes *The Silent Majority* (1987), *Ruins Within* (1992), *A Tajik Woman* (1994), *Saless: Far From Home* (1998) and *A Different Moon* (2007).

RASHA SALTI is an independent curator and writer, living and working between New York City and Beirut. She is the editor of *Insights into Syrian Cinema* (2006) and has published articles on culture, art and cinema in periodicals such as *Zawaya* (Lebanon), *Al-Ahram Weekly* (Egypt), *MERIP* (US) and *London Review of Books* (UK). She is currently the director of CinemaEast Film Festival held in New York, which focuses on the Middle East, North Africa and its Diasporas. She co-curated 'Image Quest' (1995), the first film and video festival in postwar Beirut, and was one of the chief organisers of the conference 'For a Critical Culture: A Tribute to Edward Saïd' (1997), also held in Beirut.

VIOLA SHAFIK teaches cinema studies at the American University in Cairo. She is the author of *Arab Cinema: History and Cultural Identity* (1989) and *Popular Egyptian Cinema: Gender, Class and Nation* (2007) and has contributed to the Egyptian and Palestinian cinema sections of *The Companion Encyclopedia of Middle Eastern and North African Film* (2001). She has also directed experimental films and documentaries, including *The Lemon Tree* (1993), *Planting of Girls* (1999) and *The Journey of a Queen* (2003).

RUTH TSOFFAR is Associate Professor of Comparative Literature and Women's Studies and Associate Adjunct in the Department of Anthropology at the University of Michigan, Ann Arbor. She is the author of *The Stains of Culture: An Ethno-Reading of Karaite Jewish Women* (2006). She is currently completing a monograph entitled *Cannibal Ideology: Sexuality, Ethnicity and Colonialism in Hebrew Cultures*.

PREFACE

The Hallucinations of a Filmmaker from the South

It's unbearably hot, a kind of heat that's only felt in the South. If Europeans had the misfortune to experience anything like it it would kill them. But in our country, the most destitute search out the shade of a tree near one of those open gutters (in Europe they are called gutters, here, streams) particular to our city or they set out for the nearest cinema (which is still fairly cheap) where they settle down peacefully and make the most of the air-conditioning. As for me, I wasn't in the mood to go home, no one was waiting for me there and the fridge had given me a dirty look the last time I'd fruitlessly tried to feed myself from it. So why not treat myself to an ice cream and a seat, not in the sun but in an air-conditioned cinema? Once installed, armed with my ice cream and spectacles, I noticed that the theatre was beautiful and full of spectators. Suddenly, as if by magic, surrounded by perfect strangers, I felt less alone and at the same time less hot. After a few air-conditioner advertisements that carry you away to a place where you believe you also were invited to a *déjeuner sur l'herbe* and refrigerators so prettily provisioned you end up believing you're looking at a work by Cézanne, the screening finally begins. I wondered what destiny would offer me to watch and what I might like to see myself. Only the day before, I had found myself in the middle of a discussion about the concept of magic realism in the context of cinema. I was told that this was a matter of making the 'strange' emerge at the heart of the everyday and rendering the 'inconceivable' acceptable. But isn't this the very definition of our everyday life? In fact, in the countries that those elsewhere so delicately dub 'the South' the strange and inconceivable is part and parcel of everyday life. Here, the acceptance of reality itself and its day-to-day integration frequently approaches the magical. Which is why I am often fond of quoting Foucault, changing only a word of his well-known phrase, 'to shake things up, shake up images' (Foucault wrote 'words'). Images pass before the spectators' eyes – nothing but pure realism, exact replicas, and yet they are troubling. Such is the magic of the 'seventh art', such is the power possessed by those modern-day sorcerers, the filmmakers. Which explains why, from time to time, somewhere in the South someone wants to burn them! In this heat…

Returning to the images unwinding before my eyes and which I have the privilege to share with all those who, through love of the cinema or to escape the heat, are gathered under the roof of this temple of modern religion. I love the cinema for the truths it reveals without worrying about upsetting some or pleasing others. Illusion fascinates and the truth has few followers and we know all too well that by the 'magic of cinema' even the most unbearable reality becomes conceivable. The image passes for the real thing and vice versa. Where is the frontier between reality and representation that the image offers? Does the child I see onscreen being struck by an enraged mother deserve such punishment? Is the mother herself an appalling hysteric who has fallen victim to another attack? And these spectators doing nothing to save the child … Am I the child? And the mother? Is she my mother? And the spectators? Are they in the film or are they really sitting with me in the cinema? It has become so hot again. What's happening to me? Don't they beat their kids in the North, in the West? One must absolutely avoid all forms of ostracism, exclusion and closure. Keeping one's eyes turned towards the other and all the while having one's feet firmly planted in our respective cultures. Eyes turned North and feet planted in the South! It's just too hot … And what if I opened this window? Which window? That of my convictions? Didn't Nietzsche compare our convictions to a strong and handsome donkey? What heat! Maybe I'm feverish. The air-conditioning isn't working in this cinema. And the child, what's become of him? Did he represent the people of the North's lost innocence and the people of the South's scorned honour, or simply a little rascal who deserved punishing?

If I manage to get out of this bed I'll open this wretched window, if only to let the breath of wisdom in. A bed? In a cinema? But I'm dreaming. It must be one of those celebrated cases of 'falling asleep while standing' or at least while sitting down! Such confusion. Such heat. Words and images unwind before my eyes, coming together and falling apart … Construction and deconstruction of images and words … Dream or reality? Always the same questions. And this heat only known in the South…

Filmmakers of the world, unite! Shake up images (and words) to shake things up! Upset them! Disturb them! And for pity's sake, open this window for me … and let me breathe.

Abbas Kiarostami
Tehran
April 2007

Translated by Chris Darke

INTRODUCTION

The aesthetic realm is autonomous and should never be confused with or reduced to politics, economics or history, even though every work of art is necessarily connected to its own time and place in society. The essence of criticism is of course to specify the nature of that connection, which is totally different for every work, given that the aesthetic artefact is utterly individual and irreducible.

– Edward Said (2000)

By its very title, a volume on the cinema, or rather cinemas, of North Africa and the Middle East presents a challenge. Where does North Africa start? Where does it become the Middle East? Morocco, Algeria, Tunisia and Libya (the Maghreb countries) are considered as North Africa. So are Egypt, Mauritania, Sudan and Western Sahara. The Azores, Canary Islands, Ethiopia, Eritrea and Madeira are sometimes also regarded as part of North Africa. But Egypt and Libya can also be included in the definitions of the Middle East, with the Sinai Peninsula of Egypt usually perceived as part of Asia.

The birthplace and spiritual centre of Judaism, Christianity, Zoroastrianism and Islam, the Middle East has been a strategically, economically, politically and culturally sensitive area that extends from the eastern Mediterranean Sea to the Persian Gulf. Cyprus, Egypt, Turkey, Iran, Iraq, Israel, Bahrain, Jordan, Kuwait, Lebanon, Oman, Qatar, Saudi Arabia, Syria, the United Arab Emirates, Yemen and the Palestinian Territories of the West Bank and the Gaza Strip are considered Middle Eastern countries. However, Afghanistan, parts of Central Asia and western Pakistan are also sometimes referred to as part of the Middle East. Armenia, Azerbaijan and Georgia, situated in the Caucasus, along the vague border between Europe and Asia, are often considered as Middle Eastern, but sometimes referred to as European – or Eurasian – from a historical or geographical perspective. Turkey, the majority of whose land (Anatolia) is in Asia, considers itself a European nation; in 2005 negotiations began for Turkey's entry into the European Union.

The term 'Middle East' has been disputed on several grounds and criticised for its alleged Eurocentrism. Countries such as India prefer 'Western Asia' as the region is only east from the

North American perspective. The description 'middle' has also been confusing. Before World War Two, 'Near East' was used in English for the Balkans and the Ottoman Empire, whereas the 'Middle East' referred to Persia, Afghanistan, the Caucasus region and Central Asia. With the demise of the Ottoman Empire, only the term 'Middle East' was retained. However, Germans still use *Naher Osten* (Near East) and the French divide the region between *Proche Orient* (Near East) and *Moyen Orient* (Middle East). Other terms such as 'MENA' (Middle East/North Africa) or Greater Middle East are intended to link the region with North Africa to evoke the common history of civilisations.

Neither North Africa nor the Middle East is a homogeneous identity, a label to group people. The two regions carry diverse histories, traditions and cultures that converge at certain points, such as the dominant religion (Muslim) and language (Arabic). However, in Israel the main religion is Judaism, along with Islam, and the main languages are Hebrew and Arabic. The dominant language in Iran is Farsi (Persian) and in Turkey, Turkish. There are Christian communities throughout North Africa and the Middle East, most notable being the Copts in Egypt. In the Middle East, Kurds are the largest ethnic minority. Almost all of the area was at one time occupied by the Ottoman Empire, colonised notably by the French in North Africa and the British and French in the Middle East. The American presence in the latter is indisputable today.

Colonialism, as Wimal Dissanayake informs us in 'Nationhood, History and Cinema', his introduction to *Colonialism and Nationalism in Asian Cinema*, 'is a form of violence and domination, a state of mind, a cultural practice, a multivalent discourse, and an ideology of expansion'. However, the relationship between colonialism and nationalism is complex and paradoxical. Nationalism, as Dissanayake points out, goes beyond the span and depth of colonialism, offers resistence to it, subverts its authority and serves 'to reproduce it in subtle and not so subtle ways'. Homi K. Bhabha, both in his *Nation and Narration* (1990) and *The Location of Culture* (1994) encourages a rigorous rethinking of nationalism, representation and resistence that stresses the 'hybridity' that characterises the site of colonial contestation – a 'liminal' space in which cultural differences manufacture 'imagined' constructions of cultural and national identity. Rather than homogenous, innate and historically continuous traditions, which erroneously delineate and warrant their subordinate status, nations are 'narrative' constructions that occur from the 'hybrid' interaction of competing cultural constituencies. The 'liminal' or 'interstitial' occupies a space between competing cultural traditions, historical periods and critical methodologies. Bhabha argues that neither the cultural identities can be attributed irreducible ahistorical cultural traits that define the conventions of ethnicity, nor can the 'coloniser' and the 'colonised' be viewed as separate independent identities. Filmmaking in both North Africa and the Middle East was generally initiated by colonial powers that subsequently used it to advance their colonial aims. In return, one may argue that cinemas of different nations carry the influences of their respective colonisers.

Film historians tell us that the screenings of the Lumières' *cinématographe* were organised in Algiers and Oran in Algeria in 1896 and in Tunis in 1897. The first reported feature film produced by an African was *Ain al-ghazal* (*La fille de Carthage*/ *The Girl from Carthage*, 1924) by Tunisian Albert Samama Chikli, which starred his daughter, Haydée Chikli. The Qajar Court of Iran is known to have made films as early as the 1890s. Mirza Ebrahim Khan Akkas Bashi, the official photographer of Mozaffar al-Din Shah, is regarded as the first Iranian film-maker. He bought a camera in Paris in 1900 and filmed the Shah's visit to Belgium. Cinema arrived in Turkey in 1896, a year after the first motion picture was screened in Paris. Alexandre Promio, the cameraman of the Lumière brothers shot short films about Turks in Istanbul. At the same time, a Frenchman named Bertrand was holding private screenings at the palace of Sultan Abdulhamit II. Egypt also produced its first motion picture that same year. By the 1950s, Middle Eastern cinema, with Egypt leading the way, became a vital counterpoint to Hollywood, ranking second in size to commercial Indian cinema.

Wars of independence, civil wars and wars with neighbours have torn North Africa and the Middle East apart, slowing economic growth and restricting or diverting cultural activities. This has not only resulted in the preservation of films and the establishment and maintenance of film archives suffering enormously, but film production has come to a halt in some countries, such as Algeria. Wars (civil or otherwise) continue to be fought in the Middle East. One would have liked to include in the present volume films from Afghanistan and Iraq, each with its own tradition of cinema. However, for the moment, it is a difficult task to unveil their rich cinematic heritage. A glimpse at films made in Afghanistan in the 1960s and 1970s (thanks to a retrospective at the Festival of 3 Continents in Nantes in 2004) reveals a rich cinematic tradition that the young generation today – many of them women – are attempting to revive. By the 1940s, Iraqis began making their own films – mostly romantic, pastoral stories – only to be silenced by the Baath Party in 1968, who endorsed just those films whose subject matter fitted the regime's message, the two safe subjects being Saddam Hussein and the historical Arab heroes he tried to emulate. The industry collapsed under United Nations sanctions. Both countries have resumed productions – in collaboration with foreign producers – and have begun hosting film-related events. On the other hand, some of the Gulf States have been creating artificial film industries by funding expensive film festivals instead of funding films.

To maintain a certain focus and clarity in this collection, films have been chosen from Algeria, Morocco, Tunisia, Turkey, Iran, Egypt, Israel, Lebanon, Syria and Palestine, countries that have been, and are actively involved in filmmaking. Each of the countries presented would have deserved at least 24 films of their own. As such, this volume does not claim to be comprehensive. Rather, it is an attempt to give only a taste of the rich cinematic heritage of the two regions and to stimulate curiosity for further exploration. Due to the constraints of space, only fiction work is considered, with one exception, *Forget Baghdad: Jews and Arabs – The Iraqi Connection* (2003), a documentary by Baghdadi Samir, who is now settled in Switzerland. It was felt that the choice would enhance the volume, as it consolidates issues underscored in some of the other chapters. With this film, Samir engages on an intimate level with Israeli ethnic identity politics (also the main theme of Beni Torati's *Kikar Hahalomot* (*Circle of Dreams*, 2000). 'Baghdad appears in the film as a place of origin, a cultural reference and a genealogy', Ruth Tsoffar informs us; 'The idea of "going back", therefore, is part of a wider discussion of discursive legitimacy and recently invented strategies to effectively participate in the public debates on ethnicities and cultures of origin.' This raises the question of 'home', a haunting question for the modern man. To be 'unhomed', Bhabha informs us, is not to be 'homeless'. When the borders between home and the world become confused, the world may expand immensely. Several films we have chosen explore this complex issue.

The relationship between the filmmaker and the urban space is another important aspect that finds parallels in a number of films explored here. In fact, four films included in this volume carry the name of a city in their title. Urban life may or may not be the explicit subject of these films and yet the spirit of the city saturates even the works that do not take it as their explicit subject. The urban experience seems to impose a specific vision as city life offers modes of experience from which one can fashion analytical means or stylistic values. The artists discover in the life of the city a mirroring – or doubling – of their own dispositions, attitudes or apprehensions. Both *Cairo Station* (Youssef Chahine, 1958) and *Umut* (*Hope*, Yılmaz Güney, 1970) describe in meticulous detail a central train station – a liminal space where only the homeless stay longer than they have to – where the dissonant chorus of the crowds drown the individual voice. In *Docharkheh Savar* aka *Bicycleran* (*The Cyclist*, Mohsen Makhmalbaf, 1988), an Afghan refugee and his son walk hurriedly through traffic in a world that is alien to them. In *Gelin* (*The Bride*, Lütfi Ö. Akad, 1973), the city is there but not seen; the characters are new arrivals and 'in-between' two worlds, at home in neither. In *Uzak* (*Distant*, Nuri Bilge Ceylan, 2002), the protagonist has made a niche for himself living in his corner of the world, in uptown Istanbul. His cousin, a new arrival from the country, begins his urban life in a different place, in cafés where men share tables without permission and where women normally do not enter. Ceylan's city, covered with fresh snow, evokes novelist Orhan Pamuk's Istanbul, the protagonist of his several books, a city akin to T. S. Eliot's *Waste Land*, where the inhabitants carry sadness like second skin.

The gaze, which is the core of cinema and an integral part of North African and Middle Eastern traditions, is a very important aspect of the films from the two regions manifesting cultural restrictions of modesty, especially when applied to women, who cannot voice their concerns. However, no matter how restricted it may be, the gaze – of a veiled woman or the lens of the camera – always finds a way of independence from the authorities. Language is often denied to women and particularly forbidden to servants and concubines as seen in *Samt al-qusur* (*Silences of the Palace*, Moufida Tlatli, 1994), where a young girl observes the rape of her mother by one of the *beys* and stays silent. Women's plight in patriarchal societies is central not only in *Silences of the Palace*, but also in *The Bride* and *Bab al-sama Maftouh* (*A Door to the Sky*, Farida Benlyazid, 1988). *Ten* (Abbas Kiarostami, 2002) offers a candid – and controversial – portrait of an Iranian woman caught between modernity and tradition, whose voice is heard only in confined spaces, like her car.

Hollywood endorses a certain stereotyping of the 'other'. Arabs are often shown as the dark enemy. In the early days of Hollywood, they were depicted as exotic and over-sexed, riding camels in the desert and lusting after white women. After the Arab/Israeli war of 1973 and the oil embargo, they emerged as the rich and corrupt oil sheikhs replacing the classic anti-Semitic Jewish banker stereotype of the 1920s. In the 1980s, Arabs were fanatical terrorists, but since 9/11, they have become fanatical Islamist fundamentalist terrorists. Iranians are forever chastised for the 1981 hostage crisis at the US Embassy in Tehran. How can we forget *Not Without My Daughter* (Brian Gilbert, 1991) and the astonishing courage displayed by Sally Fields as Betty Mahmoody (who wrote the eponymous 'autobiographical' novel) crossing impregnable mountains to escape her barbaric Iranian husband. When the Turks stopped wearing the fez they became the bad guys of international drug trafficking, sadists who skin cats alive or homosexuals by cultural inclination. In *Midnight Express* (Alan Parker, 1978), a popular and successful film, the protagonist claims that even the taxi drivers, the waiters and peddlers throw 'lecherous' glances at him. At the end, he pronounces Turkey 'a nation of pigs'.

The representation of Muslims in the Western media is mostly negative. They are not only anti-democratic but also anti-human and a threat to Western civilisation. Saddam Hussein, Ayatollah Khomeini, Osama bin Laden and company have been made household names through television coverage, but how many Westerners know about Omer Khayyam, Khalil Gibran, Forugh Farrokhzad or Yaşar Kemal? Cinema's role is very important as a more accessible medium than literature, but only a few distributors take a chance and choose to exhibit films of and by the 'other'. The aim of this volume is thus to open a dialogue through culture, or enhance existing dialogues, by presenting works that are representative of the cinemas of the North African and Middle Eastern countries and/or their important filmmakers.

We begin the anthology with Anwar Wagdi's *Ghazal al-banat* (*Candy Floss*, 1949), which is 'a consummate example of an enduring Egyptian studio film', according to Kay Dickinson. This film is very significant as Egyptian cinema has been the source of inspiration (and imitation) for the Arab world and beyond, not to mention its long hegemony over other national film industries. In the years after World War Two, Egyptian cinema was a 'dream factory', churning out farce or melodrama spiced with ample belly dancing to lure viewers away from the mundane realities of everyday life (not dissimilar to the Indian genre that eventually came to be known as Bollywood). The star-led industry quickly established its hegemony over the Arab world, particularly due to its accessible language, and from the post-war period into the 1990s Egypt was the major exporter of films throughout the African continent.

Not all Egyptian cinema features song and dance routines. Kemal Selim, Youssef Chahine, Salah Abu-Sayf and others began to make realistic films during a period when locally-produced Indian imitations were saturating the market and American box-office hits were a big success. The 'New Realism' used the melodramatic aspects of the commercial genre to expose new social evils, such as the increased materialism and the nouveau riche who profited from this trend. Chahine has successfully created works that are both popular and intellectual. A group of younger filmmakers have been trying to continue the artistic tradition, but censorship, commercialism, inflation, video piracy, lack of government sponsorship and also originality have had a detrimental effect on the Egyptian cinema that once earned Cairo the title, 'Hollywood on the Nile'. Today, Bollywood musical melodramas and Chinese kung-fu films occupy the position that Egyptian films once held in markets throughout Africa.

Arab cinema outside Egypt has generally developed as a resistance to colonialism. In 1972 the Alternative Cinema in Syria openly opposed the commercial cinema of Egypt and decided to focus on pan-Arab nationalism and social justice with the Palestinian question at the core, but following the Arab defeat in the Six Day War of 1967, official ideologies and political discourse took a different turn. Oussama Mohammad, one of the most prominent Syrian filmmakers, whose masterpiece *Nujum al-Nahar* (*Stars of the Day*, 1988) is included in this volume, has succeeded in maintaining an independent stance in an industry that since 1963 has been entirely run by the state. However, the film was never released in its own country. Nationalisation of the cinema sector resulted in a drainage that benefited television production. Since the 1970s Syria has produced one feature film per year but, after Egypt, it is the second most important producer of soap operas in the Middle East.

Palestinian cinema worked as a cultural arm of the Palestinian resistance, using cinema as a weapon to publicise their plight. During the early 1980s, when Lebanon was invaded by Israel, Palestinian filmmaking stopped. Several talented filmmakers, including Michel Khleifi, left for the West. Recent Palestinian cinematic and audiovisual production is concentrated on documentaries, made by young filmmakers with a desire to rectify the image of Palestinians as suicide bombers or martyrs, as is customarily presented by foreign media. Feature films are made with monetary assistance from foreign sources. Elia Sulieman, whose *Segell Ikhtifa* (*Chronicle of a Disappearance*, 1996) is included here, is one of the most prominent Palestinian filmmakers today.

As for Lebanon, the civil war and the subsequent Israeli occupation of southern Lebanon were detrimental to the film industry. Many Lebanese movie theatres were converted to boutiques or local shopping centres; several filmmakers emigrated, including Jocelyn Saab, director of *Once Upon a Time Beirut* (1994).

Filmmaking has been a constant and growing presence in Israel since the early years of the state, to document the development of Jewish communities and institutions but also to seek international support for the Zionist movement. After the founding of the state of Israel in 1948, filmmakers continued the efforts of nation building but were gradually compelled to adopt a more distanced stance from the state, aiming for a more reflective approach. Ideological conflicts, political instability and lack of sufficient official support have forced some filmmakers to work abroad. Whether Israeli cinema fully represents Israeli society has therefore been an ongoing debate.

Iranian cinema has had its roots in a popular art form called *pardeh-khani* – similar to the *benshi* of Japanese silent cinema – which involves a *pardeh-khan* (narrator) to uncover a painting as the story progresses. A similar art form, *nagali*, was performed in the *ghahve-khanes* (coffeehouses), the main venues for cultural interaction. A *nagal* (storyteller) would improvise stories inspired by images, usually painted on glass and hanging on the walls. In Turkish cinema, one may find influences of the traditional shadow play, *karagöz* or *gölge oyunu*. Several transnational elements are distinguishable in the evolution of the cinema of these neighbours. The early years were inundated with stories of prostitutes, vamps and 'fallen women'. In Iran, *film farsi* copied Indian commercial cinema, whereas the Turkish studio system, Yeşilçam, churned out rural melodramas produced by urbanites with little or no knowledge of the countryside. Forugh Farrokhzad, a leading female poet in contemporary Persian literature, wrote and directed the documentary *Khaneh Siah Ast* (*The House is Black*, 1963), which is considered a landmark for the emergence of New Iranian Cinema. The Institute for Intellectual Development of Children and Young Adults, which established its cinema department in 1969, was instrumental for launching the careers of many prominent contemporary Iranian filmmakers, such as Bahram Bayza'i, Amir Naderi, Abbas Kiarostami and Sohrab Shahid Saless. In 1970, when Dariush Mehrjui's *Gav* was heralded as the harbinger of *cinéma verité*, on the Turkish side, Yılmaz Güney made *Hope*, considered the first truly realist Turkish film. Just as the Islamic Revolution of 1979 was detrimental to independent cinema in Iran, several *coup d'états* forced many Turkish filmmakers into exile, or silence. Nevertheless, remarkable works found their way through the restrictions in both countries. Today Iranian cinema is considered as one of the best in the world and in Turkey, a new generation of filmmakers have emerged, determined to preserve the long filmic tradition of the country, but with their own stories.

Morocco, Algeria and Tunisia have also had a long film history. Although their films have not benefited from the same local popularity as Egypt, they are better known in European art houses. Algerian cinema, just like Syrian cinema, is rooted in using the medium as a resistance to colonisation, but subjects of social injustices of the post-colonial society, urban alienation, bureaucracy, emigration to France, the changing roles of women and Islamic fundamentalism have gradually gained ground with changes in society. Although the free market economy and the closure of all audiovisual institutions by the government were a blow to Algerian cinema, with the *Milénaire d'Alger* initiative of President Abdelaziz Boutefika, several films received public funding in 2005 and the Algerian cinemateque was transformed into a modern cinema museum with the necessary technology for the conservation of film. However, films that reach world audiences are still those funded by the ex-colonisers, such as the very successful *Indigènes* (*Days of Glory*, 2006) by Rachid Bouchareb, a co-production with France, Belgium and Morocco, which was nominated for an Academy Award in 2007 in the Best Foreign Language Film category.

In 1949 Tunisia had the largest number of film clubs on the continent and in 1966 launched the Carthage International Film Days film festival. The atmosphere was thus favourable to establishing quality filmmaking. In 1986 Nouri Bouzid's *Rih al-Sid* (*The Man of Ashes*, 1986) broke box-office records, out-performing Hollywood and Egyptian films. But the proliferation of cheap television, satellite dishes and piracy has been detrimental to the development of a national cinema and production has been reduced to only three films per year.

Morocco does not produce many films but it has good production facilities and many cinemas, although there is a lack of public and private funding. However, 2005 was a golden year: several Moroccan films were screened at prestigious international film festivals; both the Ministry of Communication and Moroccan TV announced increased funding; co-productions with France, Spain, Italy and Norway increased, with the possibility of co-productions with the Sub-Saharan countries; several film festivals, including the 5th Marrakech International Film Festival, presented ambitious programmes; and King Mohammed VI inaugurated the Dino de Laurentis CLA studios in Ouar zazate', opened in partnership with Cinecitta Roma. Encouraged by these developments, a new generation of filmmakers has emerged, which has considerably increased the film production. Algeria and Tunisia now consider Morocco as an emerging cinematographic power and try to emulate its strategies in terms of supporting the national cinema.

The 'New Cinema', which started in the Maghreb, spreading to Syria, Lebanon and Palestine, is a cinema that counterpoises escapist cinema that has not reflected the socio-political reality of the Arab world. A very important characteristic of the New Cinema is a break with the melodrama and musical genres of Egyptian cinema that have dominated Arab screens for much of the twentieth century. With due respect to Egyptian masters such as Youssef Chahine or Henri Barakat, who have influenced Maghrebi filmmakers to create a cinema that reflects reality, the New Cinema also diverges from the Egyptian model stylistically. An important aspect is that, contrary to dialogue-driven Egyptian cinema, the Maghrebi New Cinema gives priority to the image. Furthermore, the limited amount of studio backing forces the filmmakers to raise their own budgets, which allows them to be more independent. But the question is for whom are they making their films. Does the local audience recognise itself in these films?

This is a crucial issue for North African and Middle Eastern cinemas that, faced with production obstacles, lack of funding and distribution, censorship, satellite TV and piracy, rely on foreign backing. The majority of North African films are financed by former colonial powers, in particular France. It would be naïve to think that European dependence would not determine the direction and destination of the end product. The number of festivals that have increased also play a certain part in the proliferation of films that are supposed to be for a universal audience, but are in fact made for festival audiences with little to offer to their home audience.

The 'village films' are a case in point. Their exotic qualities seem to appeal to Western audiences and hence attract foreign finance. Some of these films are, no doubt, of exceptional quality, whereas others try to bank on a tried-and-tested formula and do not go further than reinforcing Orientalist thinking that assumes the East as the 'other' of the West, an 'othering' that underpins stereotypes and reduces whole cultures to one dimension. A case in point is the post-Islamic Revolution Iranian cinema, which, under the severe restrictions of a fanatical regime, has shifted to the countryside where the mandates of *hejab* (Islamic code of dress) are less severe. Iranian 'village films', some of which display remarkable qualities in the hands of master craftsmen, have begun winning international awards with their 'humanistic' stories. Naturally, the historical and social ambiguity of 'village films' that position their narrative outside history and outside time allow them to fall more easily within the abstraction of humanism implying that humanity is the same everywhere, which is an attractive notion in an age of globalisation.

But globalisation inevitably leads to conforming to standardised cinematic norms, based on the Hollywood model, which is a serious threat to national and regional cinemas that are already suffering under the worldwide hegemony of Hollywood. For a cinema to exist, it is imperative to engage in a productive dialogue with its own social context.

In Tamara Straus's essay, 'Telluride and the Power of World Cinema', Israeli filmmaker Amos Gitai points out that Hollywood fabricates and promotes 'the ideology of consumerism' and 'the aesthetics of the American living room'; 'I think cinema needs a context, social and political. Cinema is an extraordinarily powerful way to expose different situations', Gitai underlines. He does not presume that film is a revolutionary medium or even that it is capable of political transformation: 'You cannot convert reality through cinema. There is a limit. But you can expose it, you can mobilise it in the minds of people. That is its power.' Volumes such as this are our contribution to that kind of power.

Gönül Dönmez-Colin

REFERENCES

Bhabha, Homi K. (ed.) (1990) *Nation and Narration*. London and New York: Routledge.

____ (1994) *The Location of Culture*. London and New York: Routledge.

Dissanayake, Wimal (ed.) (1994) *Colonialism and Nationalism in Asian Cinema*. Bloomington and Indianapolis: Indiana University Press.

Said, Edward (2000) 'Cultural Politics', *al-Ahram Weekly*, 4–10 May. On-line; available at http://www.ahram.org.eg/weekly (accessed 15 December 2004).

Straus, Tamara (2000) 'Telluride and the Power of World Cinema'. On-line; available at http://www.alternet.org/story/1112 (accessed 15 September 2005).

GHAZAL AL-BANAT CANDY FLOSS

ANWAR WAGDI, EGYPT, 1949

Ghazal al-banat (*Candy Floss*, 1949) is a consummate example of the enduringly popular Egyptian studio-made film. It was originally released three years before the Free Officers' coup that eventually led to Gamal 'Abd al-Nasser's rise to power. Playing with one of the most persistent narrative themes of popular Egyptian cinema, it interlaces song, dance and a quick-fire comic script in a tale of love across different classes, featuring some of the biggest stars of the time: Layla Murad, Nagib al-Rihani, Anwar Wagdi (who also directed) and Mahmud al-Miliji, as well as theatre director and actor Yusuf Wahbi and esteemed musician Muhammad 'Abd al-Wahhab, both of whom play themselves. This criss-crossing between the realms of theatre, music and dance has been a staple practice, almost from the moment Egypt began producing synchronised-sound movies in the 1930s.

With its straightforward narrative and continuity editing, *Candy Floss* is like most 'mainstream' films. The script was written by Badi' Khayri, a playwright who had collaborated with al-Rihani on previous projects. The wordplay that features throughout the film often requires an appreciation of the diversity and dexterity of Arabic expression, frequently at the expense of characters who have not fully mastered their native tongue. Even the title has an open meaning and can be translated as 'candy floss' or 'the flirtation of girls'.

To stress the centrality of the film's main concern – fluency in Arabic – the plot revolves around Hamam (al-Rihani), a downtrodden, dishevelled and impecunious Arabic teacher who has been hired by the local Pasha (a member of the landed gentry) to coach his daughter Layla (Murad), who has failed her Arabic exams. The scenario raises questions about the regard with which Arabic as a language was then held by Egyptians of various backgrounds and how – and to what extent – Egyptians and other Arabs might be brought together through a shared cinematic, as well as spoken and written, language. *Candy Floss* indulges in the mishaps that arise from mistaken identities, most commonly the ones that relate to social status. The primary misinterpretation within the narrative occurs when Hamam overhears a telephone conversation Layla is having with her beau, erroneously believing that she has been making overtures towards him. Excited by reading romantic literature and misinterpreting the slushy, amorous song that Layla has been singing in her bedroom, he makes his feelings known to her in a scene that parodies his most recent reading material, *Romeo and Juliet*. He addresses her from below her balcony, only to climb into her room in order to avoid the aggravated family dogs. He ends up having to hide in Layla's shower, mimicking her dog's barking, so that her nurse and father will not discover his presence. Later, Layla invites Hamam to a nightclub, to act as a chaperone, so that she can meet her lover. However, the boyfriend only wants Layla's money and she is eventually rescued by Hamam and Wahid (Wagdi), a commercial pilot dragged into the fray as he is attempting to hail a taxi outside the nightclub. All three drive off together, only to stop by at the house of Yusuf Wahbi. There follows a surreal sequence in which the famous theatre practitioner offers the protagonists shrewd advice on matters of love and social position; a tongue-in-cheek exchange, with Wahbi parodically drawing on his stage persona. He then invites them to enjoy the music of the internationally acclaimed star, Muhammad 'Abd al-Wahhab, who 'just happens' to be rehearsing with a full orchestra and choir in the adjoining room. The contents of the song they hear and the homilies that Wahbi proffers to Hamam and Layla make her realise that Hamam is sincerely in love with her. He, on the other hand, is reminded of the impossibility of a poor man marrying a rich woman. As the three of them drive away from Wahbi's house, love begins to blossom between Layla and Wahid.

As unreal as some of this plot may seem, it should not preclude the film from analysis in terms of the social politics of Egypt at that time, particularly in relation to its exploration of the richness of Arab linguistic culture and the injustices of class hierarchies. At the time of its release, Egypt had been ruled by a rapid succession of weak coalition governments; the ineffectual King Faruq and, more crucially, the British who – although signing away their protectorate of the country in 1922 – legally retained control of trade interests, communications, defence, the status of Sudan and the Suez Canal. During World War Two, Egypt had been transformed into a battleground for what was essentially a European war. Outrage at this and other colonialist impositions had led to much unrest in the streets of Egypt in 1945–46. This anti-imperial struggle culminated, in 1952, in the Officers' Revolt, which eventually brought Gamal 'Abd al-Nasser to power. *Candy Floss*'s concern for class dynamics and the enriching qualities of the local language seem all the more pertinent against this backdrop.

The war had a positive impact on the indigenous film industry. The migration of people into urban areas (where work was more plentiful) increased cinema attendance and, because the import of foreign titles was hampered by military activity, Egyptian films faced less competition. The presence of British forces helped boost the economy and it is believed that film production was used as a means of laundering money earned through the black market. Building on a studio system that had been developed during the previous decade (the first and still the largest in the Arab world), Egypt produced scores of movies each year and exported them across the region.

As is typical of such modes of filmmaking, successful story themes (the cross-class romance) and genres (musical comedies) have a tendency to crop up repeatedly. From this perspective, *Candy Floss* offers an insight into the instances where formula and the fulfilment of narrative expectation rule supreme, often overriding the potential for diegetic surprises. Although these films are less inclined to deal with social injustice in any specifically revolutionary manner (as much of the cinema of the Nasser period attempted to do), they remain admirable examples of how such texts might subtly alert viewers to contentious topics within an environment of commercial and political restraint. *Candy Floss*, its title evoking something airy and pleasantly digestible, but hardly nourishing, teases the audience with its awareness of the public perception of popular cinema as 'disposable', when it could be read as something altogether more sophisticated and thoughtful.

This knowingness also pervades many of the intertextual jokes, elements that Walter Armbrust contends make the film infinitely richer (if one has the cultural knowledge to appreciate them) than many of the art films that have been produced in the Arab world for European audiences. Armbrust's essay 'The Golden Age Before the Golden Age: Commercial Egyptian Cinema Before the 1960s' unravels these complexities in great detail. He believed each actor played on their established star persona and previous professional relationships with the other cast members (most had previously worked together, and Murad and Wagdi were actually married). By playing themselves, 'Abd al-Wahhab and Wahbi not only reached out to us from other spheres of the entertainment world (thus encouraging us to contemplate their additional artistic commodities whilst we simultaneously consume this one), they also stood somewhat outside the traditional confines of conventional narrative. In this respect, they act as an omniscient chorus (they are aware of the story as it unfolds and provide solutions for unresolved matters), as well as highlighting the power of such artists to shape the destinies and emotions of people who live beyond this fictional world. It is the subtle interjections of Wahbi and 'Abd al-Wahhab, and the way they draw on tropes familiar from Arabic theatre, literature and music, that reinstates order to the filmic world.

As already noted, one of the regular formulae for popular Egyptian movies is the imposition of a class divide that separates a couple from union. One overarching joke *Candy Floss* plays at the expense of more earnest versions of this narrative archetype is that Layla is ignorant to and later uncompelled by the affections of Hamam, who, although sympathetic, is middle-aged, unkempt and maladroit; in no way the typical romantic hero. The impossibility of cross-class relationships within this era is evoked by the movie. It seems to mock the cautious hopefulness of other, more optimistic films, adding a bitter-sweet dimension to the comedy. On a historical level, post-war Egypt was marked by a ruthlessly rigid class system, with the majority of the wealth lying in the hands of local land owners (as represented by Layla's family) and foreign and Egyptian investors in the commercial sector. Rapid industrialisation over the preceding century had been accompanied by little concern for workers' conditions, which, by this period, had led to various strikes, demands for land reforms and mass mobilisation, the likes of which are worth considering, not only in terms of the class debates within the film, but also in its concern for the delicacies of the Arabic language.

Candy Floss may appear reactionary in its conclusions about social mixing. Hamam is ultimately chided by Wahbi and 'Abd al-Wahhab for dreaming of rising above his station, achieved through a number of direct, literary and allegorical comments. Throughout 'Abd al-Wahhab's performance, a portrait of King Faruq – a symbol of class hierarchy – dominates the orchestra. However, as Viola Shafik points out, the film was daring for its time. In one of the early scenes, Hamam meets the Pasha. Because he is dressed in gardening clothes, Hamam assumes him to be a servant and ridicules him. 'Correct' decorum is soon reinstated, but this is one of the many 'mistaken identities' throughout the film. It allows for a degree of 'social fluidity' that is both tolerated and enjoyed, precisely because it is tempered with an easily recognisable comedy that derives from the everyday impossibility of class mobility and the immediate recognition of class status. When Hamam misconstrues Layla's telephone conversation, he identifies himself with his literary heroes, *Romeo and Juliet,* and their Arabic counterparts, *Madjnun and Layla* (otherwise known as *Qais and Layla*). 'Abd al-Wahhab had previously written an operetta based on this story and, whilst Layla can be envisioned as her namesake, the moniker of Hamam's assumed fictional foil translates into English as 'mad'. Hamam is not the only character who incorrectly perceives others' intentions. The man Layla believes loves her turns out to be a gold-digger. Even Wahid enters the story because Hamam wrongly identifies him to a police officer who could legally intervene and remove Layla from the nightclub that Hamam has also been thrown out of. The entrance of Wahbi and 'Abd al-Wahhab, playing themselves, emphasises the poignancy of what they have to say to their visitors.

The confusion of identity (particularly class and national identity) is manifest in the behaviour of many of the characters. In his first scene, we see Hamam failing to keep order in a class full of young girls at the school he is shortly to be dismissed from. It is insinuated that the girls' attitude stems from the fact that he is a pure Egyptian (his southern accent creeps in sporadically) whereas they are of mixed Turkish roots (and thus the remnants of the ruling Turko-Circassian élites of the past). This comes through in their poor command of Arabic and their lack of respect for it as a language (it was common for the Egyptian upper classes of previous decades to deliberately neglect their Arab heritage). However, Hamam also clings onto the legacy of the Ottoman Empire, most notably in his adoption of the Turkish fez. The only characters wearing what they believe to be an emblem (or affectation) of superiority are Hamam and his head teacher, whereas the Pasha and the 'true' upper classes who frequent the nightclub wear Western attire. There is a fracas at the nightclub when Hamam refuses to hand over his *tarbush* to the cloakroom attendant. The scene reinforces his dependency on reactionary symbols of status that are inscribed with a history of colonial subordination.

Hamam is not the only archetype of the Egyptian class system ridiculed in the film. His deference to and comic misreading of the Pasha's values are all the more ridiculous when we see that the nightclub the rich frequent is a dissolute and louche environment, filled with women in revealing, frequently see-through, outfits. Moreover, these people – if we take Layla and her father as examples – are in no way versed in the higher levels of expression of their native tongue and have little desire to improve their use of the language.

The only characters who escape ridicule are 'Abd al-Wahhab and Wahid. He speaks French and is educated, but is not a member of the land-owning classes. He is deemed respectable through his chosen profession and thus an example of the future Egyptian role model. It is these negotiations of ideal citizenship and how they are drawn up in respect to contemporary international relations that *Candy Floss*, by looking into the impact of Arabic upon its speakers, seeks to explore.

Although Turkish and French references can be found in the film (most notably through younger members of the upper classes who throw the odd French word into their conversations), no direct allusion is made to the British colonial force, either linguistically or through characterisation. In many other ways, *Candy Floss* is very much an 'international' film. It blends Hollywood techniques into an Egyptian theatrical tradition that itself bears the traces of older Napoleonic art forms in its hybrid make-up. The music is distinctly multicultural, from the mambo inflections of the 'Abgad Hawiz' (alphabet) song that Layla sings with her female friends, through to the infusion of European, North African and Asian musical styles and orchestrations that distinguish 'Abd al-Wahhab's finale to the film.

'Abd al-Wahhab's oeuvre, through its mingling of classical and modern linguistic idioms, was widely acclaimed for heralding a new sense of pride in Arab traditions. This dimension of *Candy Floss* – along with the religious plurality of its cast (Murad was a Jew who had converted to Islam, Wagdi a Muslim and al-Rihani a Christian) – reveals the extent to which the movie was helping to construct a new brand of Egyptian identity within a climate of complex exchanges between global regions, not all of them sharing equal political power. In a way, by laughing at some people and not others, *Candy Floss* is a film about the fabrication of a worthy national character and whether to found such notions on the shared language of Arabic (which, as explained below, is not such a common tongue as one might imagine).

The dissemination of mass-produced media – particularly music and film – across the Arabic-speaking world in the twentieth century is often cited as something that helped galvanise otherwise disparate groups who just happened to speak (almost) the same language. Such a development is best understood in parallel with the mass movement of class and anti-colonial struggle that was growing in influence during this period. However, to assess the extent to which *Candy Floss* was a portent of the Arab nationalism that was to come with the rise of Nasser, further detailing of the historical context from which the film arose becomes necessary.

Nationalism, of either the Egyptian or the pan-Arab variety, was considered an anomalous concept by many Arabs prior to the twentieth century. As a mode of categorisation, it was associated with Europe (and consequently with colonial oppression) and regarded as antithetical to stronger family or kinship ties. However, groups such as the Muslim Brotherhood, who gained momentum as a movement for reform and independence in the 1930s and sought to bring together those sharing their faith, revered the Koranic language and were sympathetic to elevating the importance of Arabic, which *Candy Floss* also attempts to do. This turn towards Arabic as a unifying factor can also be positioned within a gradual decrease in the influence of the Turko-Circassian elite after the 1919 'Urabi revolt and the simultaneous rise of a mainly Arabic-speaking (rather than Turkish or French) middle class who were beginning to gain more control over the media and education systems.

One key figure, who also helped to consolidate these newer notions of what it was to be Egyptian, was Tal'at Harb. An influential writer, he proposed – and throughout the 1920s and 1930s organised – a cooperative banking system, as well as a web of collectivised industrial concerns that would compete with foreign interests in Egypt, eventually becoming figureheads of national pride. Notably, his Misr Company ('Misr' means 'Egypt') also set up the first major film studio in the country. Thus, cinematic culture was not only incorporated into the fight against the overseas divestment of Egyptian resources, but also helped to frame this struggle as a national one.

A sense of Arab solidarity grew during and after World War Two, as the various countries of the region formed new and interconnected means of resisting colonial subjugation and exploitation. The Arab League was formed in Alexandria in 1944–45 to protect Arab interests; trade reforms and foreign policies in Egypt in the mid- to late 1940s began to safeguard local markets more vehemently; boycotts of foreign goods began (including Yusuf Wahbi's plea for cinemagoers to avoid American movies); and, in 1947, Egypt made a (largely ignored) formal request for self-governance to the United Nations Security Council.

Although Arab groups began to see common goals emerging in their political agendas, the various nations were still factionalised and consumed with rivalry. However, one important and devastating event took place just prior to the release of *Candy Floss*, which brought the various Arab nations together: the transformation of an area of British-mandated Palestine into the state of Israel and the ensuing war of 1948, resulting in the creation of a vast Palestinian refugee population. The bordering Arab countries entered into this war to varying degrees and for diverse political motives. It may have been a desire to bolster Arab morale after their defeat in this campaign that motivated the celebration of Arabic that is so central to *Candy Floss*.

No film is able to draw upon a generic Arabic language, because there is not one singular spoken language of that name. Each region has its own dialect (some almost entirely incomprehensible to Arabs from elsewhere) and the only universal modes of communication are written and very strict, including the Quranic variants, which were only accessible to the few who could read at the time. Layla is incompetent at written Arabic; she is only fluent in her spoken dialect and displays little interest in the classical forms that would identify her with her Arab heritage. Hamam's efforts to impart such traditions to both Layla and the school pupils (whom he is teaching to read the eleventh-century Arabic classic, *Kalila and Dumna*) are laughably unsuccessful. Jokes about these inadequacies propel the first quarter of the film. The most amusing linguistic jokes centre on the fact that short vowels are not included in written Arabic and must be deduced by the knowledgeable reader, a skill that none of the school pupils have succeeded in.

From another perspective, it is Hamam's rigid dedication to the written variant – like his insistence on wearing a *tarbush* – that make him too unyielding to fit into contemporary

Egyptian society. More amusingly, even he cannot maintain consistent Arabic and many of the film's gags revolve around his lapses from formal expression into supposedly 'coarser' colloquialisms which display his poor, rural, Upper Egyptian accent. Although many Arabs fall foul of these linguistic mistakes, his are rendered all the more stark by the contradistinction of his sporadic formal Arabic and its backdrop of vernacular scripting, which has become the convention for Egyptian film dialogue delivery.

The members of the Pasha's family are more at home with the colloquial dialect, but their lack of regard for Arabic is derided through a variety of wordplay, which reveal their lack of command of the language, and thus even less capacity to commune with fellow Arabs across international borders. Their lack of regard for such skills is evident in their paying the guardian of their pet dog a higher salary than the Arabic teacher.

Although both these sections of society are presented as stunted by their recourse to singular modes of articulation, Wahbi and 'Abd al-Wahhab effortlessly glide between registers to fabricate an enriched mosaic of Arabics – a hallmark of popular music, theatre and, to a lesser extent, cinema. The fact that Wahbi and 'Abd al-Wahhab have the final word and resolve the dilemmas of the narrative carries the implication that the linguistic fusion disseminated by the modern popular media is the one best equipped for communication with large groups of Arabic speakers.

Such a notion is reaffirmed by the songs that are interspersed throughout the film. Like popular Arabic music, they maintain a classical form, but frequently break its rules, slipping into colloquial modes. As Walter Armbrust points out, 'Abd al-Wahhab's final song wafts between the classical and the spoken Egyptian, preserving a nexus of populist and classical, local and regional, common to many popular songs of the area. The split between different Arabics, ocurring throughout the film, opens spaces for both national and pan-Arab affiliations, sentiments that were to dominate the politics of the immediate post-colonial period.

Very little of the class politics of the era to come are evident in the film's dénouement and its recourse to Arabic. Wahbi quotes the book Hamam has been reading in order to curb Hamam's feelings for Layla: 'All I would ever want is for her to be happy and content, even if I've had to give up the light of my life. If the love of your life is happy, you should be happy for them.' From within a very modern context, classical Arabic literature here reaffirms the implacability of the Egyptian class system.

There are other hierarchies manifest in the uses of Arabic in *Candy Floss*. Most pointedly, there is an assertion of the Egyptian way of speaking. Although classical Arabic is used throughout the film, it is delivered with Egyptian accents and inflections. For instance, pronouncing a 'j' as a 'g' and a 'q' as a glottal stop are particular to this country and alien to classical delivery, yet these errors are preserved throughout. This can be seen to reveal a certain current within contemporary Egyptian politics. In various ways, most notably with respect to Egyptian quasi-imperialist aspirations over the destiny of Sudan and its desire for an economically preferential relationship with Israel, it has been contended that Egypt was angling for a particular arrangement of pan-Arabism that simultaneously acknowledged its own dominance. Whilst it seems unlikely that this was a mood prevalent in Egyptian movies, it is supported by the promotion of a particular type of Arabic in the popular films that the country exported. It might be argued that the most recognised Arabic *lingua franca* is now the Egyptian dialect, precisely because of the successful marketing and selling of Egyptian movies around the region. As such, this is Arab unification of a specific, modern, populist and *Egyptian* breed; although variety and slippage inform its structure, there are definite limitations and ideological priorities shaping its construction.

With films like *Candy Floss*, we witness not so much the dismissal or re-inscription of foreign popular culture but a wholehearted attempt to instate an enriching and specifically Egyptian reworking of art and communication; a form of interaction whose organisation and influence stretches well beyond the film text. It is hardly surprising, when the more deliberate Arab nationalism of Nasser became orthodoxy, that he not only courted Muhammad 'Abd al-Wahhab, but also nationalised the Egyptian film industry. It displayed the potential of the mechanisms of mass and popular communication to enable Arabs to reconfigure their relations to each other. *Candy Floss* was thus a timely precursor to a series of crucial national and international debates that grew in relevance and importance.

Kay Dickinson

REFERENCES

Armbrust, Walter (2000) 'The Golden Age Before the Golden Age: Commercial Egyptian Cinema Before the 1960s', in Walter Armbrust (ed.) *Mass Mediations: New Approaches to Popular Culture in the Middle East and Beyond*. Berkeley: University of California Press, 292–327.

Shafik, Viola (1998) *Arab Cinema: History and Cultural Identity*. Cairo: American University in Cairo Press.

BAB EL-HADID CAIRO STATION

YOUSSEF CHAHINE, EGYPT, 1958

Bab el-Hadid (*Cairo Station*, 1958) is regarded as one of Youssef Chahine's masterpieces. Chahine is arguably Egypt's most well-known director, with a career spanning over five decades; he received the Cannes Film Festival's 50th Anniversary Award for Lifetime Achievement in 1997 and has continued to direct films. *Cairo Station* links the personal and social struggle among working-class Egyptians, and revealed Chahine as a director with a distinct style that set him aside from other Egyptian filmmakers working around the same time. It was his eleventh film and the first in which he appears; he plays the cripple Kenaoui and delivers a powerful performance that has left its mark on the development of characterisation within Egyptian cinema. Contrary to the vast majority of Egyptian films produced both before and after, *Cairo Station* relies more on visuals than dialogue to convey the stories, emotions and struggles of the characters. It is considered one of the finest representations of Chahine's work, and cemented his unique position in the history of Egyptian cinema.

At the time of its domestic release, the film sparked controversy for its bleak portrayal of Egyptian society. It was also rejected by audiences due to its casting, against type, of Hind Rustum and Farid Chaouqi. Rustum was famous for her glamorous, seductive roles, and was considered the Marilyn Monroe of the Arab world. Chaouqi was known for his portrayal of a positive hyper-masculinity. He plays Abu Seri', a labourers' union activist with an oppressive and violent personality, often directed at his fiancée, Hanouma (Rustum), a poor soft-drinks seller working on the trains. However, what was initially considered a negative representation of Egypt later became a symbol of protest against the harsh conditions of life among the poor. The film marked Chahine's entry into a socio-political cinema which has continued throughout his career; his stance on the struggle for independence in Algeria was portrayed in *Djamilah* (*Jamila*, 1958); his respect for the ideals of Gamal 'Abd al-Nasser, the Egyptian president of the time, was communicated in *El Naser Salah el Dine* (*Saladin*, 1963); his nationalism revealed in, among others, *al-Nass wal Nil* (*Those People of the Nile*, 1968) and *Hadduta misrija* (*An Egyptian Story*, 1982); and his compassion for the poor continued in *Al-Ard* (*The Land*, 1969).

Walid Chmeit has pointed out that Chahine's career began at a time of change in Egypt, with Nasser's revolution in 1952, the Suez Crisis in 1956 and the rise of socialism. Such events reinforced Chahine's 'commitment' to social causes. However, it would be wrong to regard Chahine's cinema merely in terms of social causes. His work is unique because of his ability to link this broader context with personal issues. In almost all of his films, it is possible to find an element of Chahine himself. Sometimes this representation of the self is more obvious, such as the frustrated director Yehya in *Iskanderija... lih?* (*Alexandria... Why?*, 1978). At other times, it is allegorical. In *Al-Massir* (*Destiny*, 1997), Chahine used the struggles faced by the philosopher Averroes, whose interpretation of the Koran outraged religious extremists, as a vehicle for his own struggle with Islamic fundamentalists. It was a reaction to being accused of blasphemy, following the release of *Al-Muhagir* (*The Emigrant* (1994), which took as its inspiration the story of Joseph. In *Cairo Station*, Chahine's role is more oblique in terms of his own persona. He plays a cripple so convincingly that, according to Ibrahim Fawal, the jury at the Berlin Film Festival, where the film screened, assumed that he was a cripple playing himself.

In an interview with Walid Chmeit in 1977, Chahine confessed that *Cairo Station* was an outlet for him to represent himself on the screen, after a series of difficult experiences employing actors as his on-screen persona. He also admitted that his initial calling, when studying film in Pasadena in 1946, was as an actor. However, he soon realised that he did not have the look of a movie star and decided to concentrate on directing. It could be argued that Kenaoui's longing to be part of the world he is dislocated from reflects Chahine's desire to 'belong'.

The film constructs Kenaoui's world as a microcosm of the society around him, with his repression, sense of injustice and yearning for a better life. It is set in one of Cairo's biggest and busiest train stations, Bab el-Hadid (which lends its name to the film's title). Chahine makes great use of the grand setting of the station, using the architecture to dwarf the people who use it everyday. As Martin Stollery observes, Bab el-Hadid is a haven for people from all walks of life; from youth dancing to music to religious men, from peasants to middle-class train passengers. These groups never come together in the film, instead moving in different directions. But the film does not merely use the randomness of these groups to comment on society's lack of cohesion. Those who are well off occupy a transient status at the station, but for the poor workers, the station is their everyday reality. The film's relationship with movement is twofold: the direction of the travellers indicates a society without a core to hold it together, but their movement is a painful reminder of the immobility of the poor workers. What links the people mired to the station is not just their social exclusion, but also their dream of a better life. Outside the station lies the realm of possibility. The film avoids sentimentality by exposing the difficulties those people face in their struggle.

Cairo Station presents a subtle yet powerful criticism of governmental authority. The police, in particular, are not pathologised but are depicted as either absent or indirectly contributing to the continuation of the station people's poverty. The absence of the police is most notably felt in the subplot about the workers union. Abu Seri' is a well-respected railway porter with dreams of establishing a union of rail workers. He succeeds in rallying a group of porters around him, who all agree with his political vision. However, establishing a union would challenge the authority of the local *za'im* (gangster), Abu Gaber, who is running the station as he pleases in the absence of official authority. The confrontation between Abu Seri' and Abu Gaber is one of the several incidents in the film that suggest that life at Bab el-Hadid is survival of the fittest. While Abu Seri' eventually succeeds in opposing Abu Gaber, his fiancée, Hanouma, fails to improve her lot. She makes little money selling soft drinks from a bucket on trains prior to their departure. She is also pursued by the police who are always on the lookout for illegal sellers; often having to abandon her trade and run for cover along the tracks, even though the train passengers are shown to enjoy her services – a brief respite from the heat of the city.

Chahine goes further, adding an element of irony to one of Hanouma's sequences by staging a feminist protest at the train station, led by a woman lecturing through a loud speaker about the abysmal condition of women in rural areas. Chahine subtly introduces a rural woman who passes by, carrying a basket on her head, completely oblivious to the speech. At the same time, Hanouma seems uninterested in the feminist statements; her sole concern is selling her soft-drink bottles to the crowd. Another contrast appears in this sequence, when we compare Hanouma's disinterest in the feminist speech with her own relationship with men. She is a woman struggling to make a living in a man's world, who remains subject to patriarcharchal attitudes. In particular, she is constructed as an object of desire. She is engaged to Abu Seri', who regards her as his possession, and is obsessed over – from afar – by Kenaoui, who dreams of being with her. Hanouma's harsh living conditions mean that her relationship with men is based on material gain. She therefore accepts Abu Seri' and his promises of a better life, while she mocks Kenaoui's marriage proposal, telling him that he has no money, only big dreams.

In one scene, Hanouma boards a train to sell drinks to a group of dancing young people. For a moment, she seems to forget herself and joins in the dancing, although she still uses the dancing to sell more bottles. However, she is unaware of Kenaoui watching her from outside the carriage, mirroring her dance movements. Abu Seri also catches a glimpse of her dancing.

Kenaoui's presence outside the carriage reflects his inability to join Hanouma's world. When Hanouma eventually sees him, with only his head visible from the train window as she looks outside, she leans over and offers him a bottle through the window; a metaphorical bridge, inviting Kenaoui into her world. At the same time, Hanouma does not simply give Kenaoui the bottle, but points it at him in a phallic way. Hanouma's gesture can be seen as an attempt at self-empowerment, which is halted when she sees Abu Seri watching her. Fearing his anger, she attempts to run away. Abu Seri' catches up with her in a warehouse and beats her. Hanouma seduces him into stopping and, with Chahine employing another phallic metaphor, she sprays him with the fizzy drink she was selling. Abu Seri's violence slowly transforms into lovemaking, although his anger is not completely extinguished. Watching Hanouma and Abu Seri' playing hide and seek in the warehouse, our expectations of a harmonious union are confused by Abu Seri's standing on Hanouma's knee as she lies down in the hay. Thus, Abu Seri' is marked out, amongst other things, as a sexual predator.

Abu Seri's beating of Hanouma and its confusion with lovemaking is not the only incident in the film when the line between sex and violence is blurred. Just as Abu Seri's masculinity establishes itself in violence, so does Kenaoui's. However, while Abu Seri's violence is presented as a manifestation of hyper-masculinity, Kenaoui's descent into violence stems from sexual repression and the resulting sense of failure as a man. His sexual repression is made clear from the beginning, and his descent into violence is built up slowly and skilfully by Chahine.

We are first introduced to Kenaoui as he lies on the ground of the station. Chahine does not allow us to see him fully at first, only offering a partial view of his body. The camera pans to reveal his crippled leg, moving slowly to show his partially hidden face. His face is later seen from behind a shattered pane of glass. This expressive use of space highlighted the difference between *Cairo Station* and the mainstream productions of Egyptian cinema at that time, where stories were told rather than shown. Kenaoui's temporarily hidden physiognomy is one of ways Chahine's links Kenaoui's personal exclusion with his social exclusion from those surrounding him. He does not seem to belong to the space he occupies; he is, metaphorically, an intruder into the world around him, which fights to obscure his presence.

Kenaoui's relationship with space is further explored on the only ocassion he steps out of Bab el-Hadid. Having understood Hanouma's high regard for material goods, Kenaoui saves enough money to buy her a gold necklace. On his suggestion, she accompanies him to a park where they sit by a fountain. As Hanouma humours Kenaoui's marriage proposal, we cannot help but feel his character shrink in pain and frustration. Chahine emphasises this feeling of insignificance by seating Kenaoui and Hanouma under a statue of Ramses II. The huge statue seems to gaze down at Kenaoui disapprovingly, dwarfing him the way he is dwarfed by the enormity of Bab el-Hadid. In this subtle way, we witness the shattering of Kenaoui's dream of a better life outside of the station. His destiny is one of rejection and escalating repression. Thus, he finds himself back in his kiosk at the station, a tiny wooden construction that serves as a cocoon, protecting him from the harshness of the outside world.

As Kenaoui fails to fully participate in the world around him, he seeks solace in observing. Chahine uses of point-of-view shots to show the forbidden fruits that Kenaoui desires but cannot have. He is a voyeur, gazing at women who are unaware of his presence. From the moment we are introduced to Kenaoui – lying on the ground, his crippled leg extended but partially hidden – the camera moves to show us Kenaoui's gaze. This establishes one of the subplots in the film, about a young woman who is eager to meet her lover at the station to say goodbye as he and his parents depart for Europe. Hidden from the woman's view, Kenaoui eavesdrops on her telephone conversation with her lover, as they plan to meet. Kenaoui's eavesdropping is another way of establishing his exclusion and his jealousy. The idea of two lovers meeting stirs him into examining his own loveless condition, and his infatuation with Hanouma.

Chahine allows us to gaze at Hanouma as she changes her clothes, capitalising on the allure of Hind Rustum to hint at Hanouma's status in the film. The camera's view of Hanouma is then established as that of Kenaoui, hiding in her kiosk and staring at her exposed body. It is a good example of what Laura Mulvey terms 'scopophilia', which refers to the way women in cinema are often represented as objects of the gaze of men. This gaze is not only that of the male characters in a film, but also of those in the audience. In this sense, cinema functions as an outlet for the expression of repressed desires, which are projected onto the female character. The on-screen female then is presented as a spectacle inducing pleasure in looking in the gazing male. Mulvey also argues that this pleasure in looking is divided between representing the male as active and female as passive and this dichotomy affects films' narrative structures, whereby the male is the protagonist who is absolved from the burden of objectification. *Cairo Station* initially exemplifies Mulvey's theory. However, the film complicates her last point, on male objectification. Kenaoui is indeed the bearer of an active gaze, yet he is also the object of the audience's gaze as well. The extreme close-ups of Kenaoui's body and face used by Chahine throughout the film confirm this, and almost serve to fetishise his physical existence.

Kenaoui does attempt to exercise power through his position as 'gazer'. When he hides in Hanouma's kiosk as she undresses, he wants to touch her, to grab her hand. She sees him and pulls away. All he can do is leave, dragging his crippled leg across the train tracks, as Hanouma's female friends throw stones at him. This sense of frustration is a constant in the film. At first, after the kiosk incident, Kenaoui finds solace on an immobile, empty train, where he hides from Hanouma's friends and finds a collection of pictures featuring scantily-clad models. Unable to consummate his 'relationship' with Hanouma, Kenaoui resorts to staring at the pictures. He hangs them on the wall of his kiosk. This time, he is alone with the women, and he can do with them as he pleases; in one of the pictures he draws a handbag around a woman's arm.

Kenaoui's unfulfilled desire is further stirred by another encounter with the young woman and her lover. This time, his frustration grows stronger as the woman succeeds in meeting her lover. Shots of Kenaoui looking from his kiosk at the couple are intercut with shots of them together, another representation of the pleasure he is denied. Again, he channels his desire by gazing hard at an unsuspecting woman's breasts, emphasised by an extreme close-up of his eyes. This incident motivates Kenaoui to propose to Hanouma in the park, but her rejection fuels his frustration. He channels it the only way he can, this time by cutting the contour of a woman from one of his pictures. As he is doing so, he hears about the details of the murder of a woman, and reacts by suddenly hurrying away and leaving the woman's picture beheaded and her arms cut, just like the murder described. The sexy women in the pictures are the only ones that do not fight against Kenaoui's gaze, and are his only successful attempt at exercising power; he can draw on them, or even destroy them.

This metaphorical killing soon paves the way for a real one. When Hanouma is trapped by Abu Seri' in the warehouse, Kenaoui is also there, lurking outside, listening to the events unfolding inside. His frustration increases when a train passes by, its noise blocking Kenaoui's only access to what is happenning. He smashes an empty bottle against the wall in anger, and then goes off to buy a knife. This time, Kenaoui has a plan. His inability to posseess his object of desire leads to an urge to prevent anyone else from possessing her. He plans to murder Hanouma, but unwittingly kills her friend instead. Chahine here makes Kenouai's mental derangement more overt, explaining how the murder is a displacement for being with her. We hear him say, after he puts the woman's body on the train: 'I sent Hanouma's clothes on the train … no, I sent her on the train … We will get married … no, we have already married…' Later he spots Hanouma's cat and addresses it as Hanouma. In another allegory, the cat scratches him, so he hits it and stabs another picture of a woman on his wall.

The psychological repression and fantasy in *Cairo Station* link the film with Hitchcock's *Psycho* (1960), where violence is equated with sexual satisfaction. The anti-heroes of both films also face a similar fate. Kenaoui ends up in a mental institution, dragged away as the young woman who had met her lover but did not manage to say goodbye stands still on the train tracks, looking at the space left by his departed train. As Ibrahim Fawal notes, the audience's sympathy is divided between the frustrated young women and the unloved Kenaoui. His only chance of compassion had been through his relationship with the newspaper vendor 'Am Madbouli, who had taken Kenaoui in, given him a job and acted as his father figure. However the film emphasises Kenaoui's alienation by showing that this fatherly love is not enough. Moreover, it is this love that seals Kenaoui's fate. Madbouli manages to lure Kenaoui into wearing the strait jacket at the end of the film, convincing him that it is his wedding outfit.

Cairo Station is a unique film that successfully blends neo-realism and melodrama. It is a strong statement of protest against the harsh struggles people face and an empathetic representation of the struggle with the Self. Looking back at *Cairo Station* today, we not only see the development of Chahine's cinematic style, but also signs of his political commitment. His empathetic representation of the poor has continued throughout his career, sometimes presenting a story from the point of view of the marginalised (*The Land*) and sometimes weaving the narrative around a criticism of imperialism (*El Akhar* (*The Other*, 1999)).

The fleeting representation of the religious men on the train – who, upon seeing a group of dancing young men on one of the platforms, ask God to protect them from the devil – can be seen as a precursor to the accusations of blasphemy that were levelled at Chahine some forty years later, following the release of *The Emigrant*, by Islamic fundamentalists (the scene in *Destiny* refering to the incident portrays Islamic fundamentalists objecting to song and dance). *Cairo Station* thus also represents Chahine's life philosophy, where freedom lies at the heart of existence, despite censorship and criticism, whether by an audience shocked by *Cairo Station*'s audacity, or fundamentalists objecting to religious inspiration. *Cairo Station* confirms what Chahine was to write at the end of *Destiny*: 'Ideas have wings, no one can stop their flight.'

Lina Khatib

REFERENCES

Chmeit, Walid (2001) *Youssef Chahine: The Life of Cinema*. Beirut: Riad el-Rayyes Books.
Fawal, Ibrahim (2001) *Youssef Chahine*. London: British Film Institute.
Mulvey, Laura (1975) 'Visual Pleasure and Narrative Cinema', *Screen*, 16, 3, 6–18.
Stollery, Martin (2004) *Al-Muhajir/L'émigré*. Trowbridge: Flicks Books.

AL-MOMIA THE MUMMY

SHADI ABDEL-SALAM, EGYPT, 1969

Shadi Abdel-Salam's *Al-Momia* (*The Mummy* aka *The Night of Counting the Years*, 1969) attempts to 'bring back to life' the ancient past of Egypt through the cinematic medium, while exploring its significance in terms of a historical and national context. Completed after the Arab/Israeli war of 1967, at a time when questions of Arab nationalism were being addressed, consolidated and reformulated, the film explores nationalist considerations in the context of a more distant colonial encounter. During the nineteenth century Egypt's ancient past was 'rediscovered'. Antiquities were systematically unearthed and transported to the West for museum exhibition and scientific scrutiny. In both the examination of the mummies as bodies of physical evidence and the textual exploration of Egypt, the 'colonial imaginary' was scientifically supported by specifically political interests. Viewing the colonisation of Egypt's ancient past on the one hand, and its neglect on the part of contemporary Egyptians on the other, the film gives voice to those conventionally excluded from dominant Egyptological discourse.

The Mummy sets itself apart from the popular productions of previous decades, often characterised in terms of social realism, comedy, musical or melodrama. Few Egyptian films have taken on ancient Egypt as their subject, while others, such as Youssef Chahine's *Sir'a fil Wadi* (*Struggle in the Valley* aka *The Blazing Sun*, 1954) and Hussein Kamal's *Thowthara Fok Al Neel* (*Adrift on the Nile*, 1971) have used it as a backdrop to the narrative, with ancient monuments typically functioning as silent reminders of Egypt's colossal past. A committed nationalist and liberal of the Nasserist era, Shadi Abdel-Salam (1930–86) worked as a set and costume designer with Egyptian directors such as Youssef Chahine, Salah Abu Sayf and Henri Barakat. He also worked with Joseph Mankeiwicz on *Cleopatra* (1963), Jerzy Kawalerowicz on the Polish film *Faraon* (*Pharaoh*, 1966) and Roberto Rossellini on *La Lota dell'uomo per la sua sopravivvivenza* (*Mankind's Fight for Survival*, 1967). In 1968 he became head of the Unit for Experimental Cinema, in which directors were given more freedom to express themselves and for which he directed two documentaries: *Afaq* (*Horizons*, 1972) about the arts in modern Egypt and *Guyush-ash-Shams* (*The Armies of the Sun*, 1975) on the 1973 war with Israel.

Given his background in architecture, his experience in costume and set design, and his knowledge of history and philosophy, Abdel-Salam manifested his desire to rekindle the splendour of ancient Egypt, rejecting both socialist Pan-Arabism and Islamic fundamentalism – the two solutions offered for the salvation of Egypt. During the 1920s, a school of thought referred to as 'Pharonicism' was formed, which asserted that Egyptians were the direct descendants of their pharonic ancestors and therefore inherited the same characteristics and abilities. *The Book of the Dead* and its depiction of the resurrection of Osiris were referenced as a call for the 'reawakening' of Egypt. Abdel-Salam's work reveals a rigorous attempt to draw on and understand ancient Egypt and its significance within contemporary Egyptian society. His other films, including the short fiction film based on an ancient papyrus, *Shakawi al-Falah al-Fasih* (*The Complaints of the Eloquent Peasant*, 1970) and his unfinished project, *Akhenaton*, about the ancient king who sought to unify Egypt, highlight his conviction that this rich past is one that remains relevant to Egyptians today. He also directed three short non-fiction films on the subject of ancient Egypt: *Tut-Ankh-Amon's Chair* (1983), *The Pyramids and its Antecedents* (1984) and *Ramses II* (1986).

Internationally recognised for its distinct style, form and subject matter, *The Mummy* displays a meticulously constructed narrative in which each shot is carefully composed. Rather than resorting to the more familiar fantastical and epic portrayal of the mummy as a menacing figure of the living dead (typical of Universal and Hammer Horror productions), Abdel-Salam maintains a visual style that is explicitly non-realist in its depiction of the mythological and timeless aspect of ancient Egypt. At the same time, it displays elements of a 'neo-realist' style, primarily in its depiction of the significance of ancient Egypt to those who live amongst its ruins. The story is based on the account of the discovery of a cache of royal mummies in Deir el-Bahri. Apparently, during the twenty-first dynasty, a group of priests placed the mummies in a cliff tomb (rather than pyramid) in order to avoid the thieving of tomb robbers. The Abd-el-Rasul tribe, known for trading in antiquities, discovered the tomb by chance and, ensuring its whereabouts were kept secret, continued to draw on the treasures and sell them on the black market for a number of years. Realising that the tombs were known of and could be accessed, foreign members of the Antiquities Society scouted the area until a member of the tribe led them to their location.

By setting the film in 1881, a year before Egypt was colonised by Britain, Abdel-Salam converges Egypt's ancient past with its colonial history, played out in the arena of scientific knowledge, Western superiority and identification with Egypt's ancient civilisation. The sudden explosion of primary materials and research inaugurated by Napoleon's Egyptian campaign at the turn of the eighteenth century, and built on by subsequent Western science, fundamentally altered the perception of ancient Egypt. The influence of Egypt on architecture, literature and popular culture brought about what has been referred to by several scholars as 'Egyptomania'. The discovery of the Rosetta Stone in 1799 and its subsequent translation by Jean-François Champollion was seen as a breakthrough in Egyptology, enabling the mysterious hieroglyphic text to be deciphered. In 1858, August Mariette founded the Antiquities Organisation in Cairo, which was to ensure the preservation and management of the ancient Egyptian artefacts discovered. His role legitimised the continued presence in Egypt of foreign scientists and explorers, and necessitated that Egyptians remain ignorant and detached from the legacies of their past. His successor, Gaston Maspero, was head of the Egyptian Antiquities Service between 1881 and 1886 and again between 1899 and 1914.

Given Abdel-Salam's desire to renationalise Egypt's past, the figure of Emil-Brugsch Bey, who 'refound' the tomb, is replaced by the young Ahmad Kamal, the first Egyptian graduate of the School of Languages, who was struggling to enter the discipline of Egyptology. *The Mummy* tells the story of Wanis, the youngest son of Selim, chief of the Horabat tribe. After the death of his father, Wanis and his brother are told of the whereabouts of a tomb hidden in the mountains, which members of the tribe had been robbing and living off for generations. Wanis's brother is outraged and refuses to continue the trade. As a result, he is disowned by his mother and later murdered for disobeying the tribe elders. Carrying the burden of the secret, Wanis is left to grapple with the choice of continuing to trade illegally or to tell Ahmad Kamal and the Effendi's from Cairo the whereabouts of the tomb.

Wanis struggles to come to terms with how he is to relate to his personal past, his loyalty to the tribe, and his relationship with his pharaonic ancestors, in light of his recent discovery. Casting aside the two antique dealers, Ayyub and Murad, and his family, as represented by his uncles and the younger generation of cousins, Wanis finally decides to betray the tribe's secret to the Effendi's, rather than live off the dead without concern. State ownership of Egypt's national heritage is brought about at the expense of the Horabat tribe's future.

The story focuses on questions of death, memory, knowledge, trade and progress, capturing a vision of an Egypt fragmented by geography and class. Abdel-Salam highlights continuity in ancient traditions and customs, and also looks at contemporaneous national concerns. In the funeral scene at the beginning of the film, we are presented with the re-enactment of ancient customs. A high-angle shot shows the figures moving slowly amongst the mountains and the vast desert landscape. Such scenes bear similarities with Italian neo-realism. Long takes are dominated by the desert, sky and the Nile, and the overhead shots place the camera at the height of the vast ancient monuments. This serves as a constant reminder of the temporal distance between contemporary Egypt and its past, and the perspective that such a vast history offers. Many scenes feature character's looking to and away from the camera, Janus-like, as though looking both to the past and future. While Egyptians are characterised according to where they come from (Wanis and the Horabat tribe, dressed in black, from the mountains; the Stranger, in white, from the Valley or Nile Delta; the Effendis and mountain guards, with red fez and uniform, from Cairo), there are stark visual similarities between Ahmad Kamal, Wanis and the Stranger. Kamal and Wanis are often paired as brothers with Kamal's glasses – his only distinguishing feature – symbolising the scientific knowledge he possesses.

The film reflects the process of 'discovery', with the opening sequence working as a framing story, introducing the key themes of the narrative, as well as triggering the search for the hidden tombs undertaken by Ahmad Kamal. The camera pans from right to left, over a papyrus depicting a funeral procession, with the voice of Maspero reading from the *Book of the Dead*. In many ways, the film acts as a visualisation of what such a text could signify. The following shot depicts members of the Antiquities Society sitting around a table in the Cairo museum, as Maspero continues to read: '*Oh grant unto me my mouth that I may speak therewith; and that I may follow my heart when it passeth through the fire and darkness.*' The scene provides a ritualistic opening to their discussion, with their faces lit against a dark background. Here, the theme of language and identity is introduced. By virtue of its being read, the papyrus brings into play the 'living dead'. Ahmad Kamal reads, '*May my name be given unto me in the great Double House, and may I remember my name on the night of counting the years.*' Inasmuch as the value of the name in the context of ancient Egypt ensures the preservation of the identity of the 'deceased', the ability to speak and understand ancient Egyptian, and the scientific desire to know and preserve Egypt's ancient past, becomes politically loaded.

The metaphorical and political significance of the mummy is highlighted by the historical roots of the West's interaction with powdered mummies as medicine, as noted by Saima Ikram and Aidan Dodson in *The Mummy in Ancient Egypt: Equipping the Dead for Eternity*. The consumption of the mummy continually crosses boundaries and collapses distinctions between what could be referred to as 'inside' and 'outside'. The unification of speech and eating locates itself within or through the mouth, or more specifically the tongue, thus combining the commercial value of the mummy and its textual significance, based on the ability to read and understand hieroglyphics. Abdel-Salam's film makes it apparent that this is true for all those that engage with the mummy. He explains that, for the Upper Egyptians, what might seem to be a trade in useless antiquities is, in effect, tantamount to selling a piece of their own body. Here language is key since it is the spoken *articulation* of ancient Egyptian, or Arabic, that becomes central in the film in relation to the incorporation or *consumption* of the dead. The deliberate use of classical Arabic, instead of the spoken Egyptian vernacular adopted in popular film productions serves as the linguistic equivalent of what Viola Shafik calls 'monumentalism', while it draws attention to the questions of language and the unification of Egyptian – and Arab – identity.

The relationship between speech and language is manifest in the film explicitly in the dialogue, with references to tongues and flesh-eating throughout, and metaphorically in the animation of the ancient monuments and text. In its attempt to reconcile the characters with the surroundings, the film depicts Wanis and the inhabitants of the mountain as figures that have emerged out of the stone monuments and come to life. His position in the stairwell leading into the family house affirms what Elliott Colla calls the 'mummification' of Wanis. Throughout the film, he bridges the decaying traditions upheld by his tribe with modernity, as embodied by the nation-state. As such, Wanis is physically and metaphorically 'unhinged' or 'undead'. This is further compounded by exterior shots, where the sharp diagonals of the sand dunes that cut across the frame symbolise the shafts leading in and out of the ancient tombs and which Wanis appears to sink into or is climbing out of. The diagonals also reflect the passageways that meander towards the family house, or the path between the stone buildings that leads Wanis out of the labyrinth, where Murad's hiding place is located.

Throughout the film, the almost identical black costumes of the actors make them look two-dimensional as they stand against the stone backgrounds or on the sand dunes, their outline cutting into the blue sky. When Wanis chases Zeyna, both appear to be walking into and emerging from the walls. In the following scene, in Murad's hiding place, a woman asks: 'Am in not better looking than stone?' For a moment, she could be a painting on the wall, before the tableau finally comes to life, with her movement across the frame.

The two encounters between Wanis and the Stranger articulate the multiple timeframes in which the living and the dead co-exist, specifically in relation to the stone monuments and statues that surround them. Both sequences are marked by two faceless Osiris statues and the off-screen sound of the horn of the river steamer, El-Mansheya, on which Ahmad Kamal arrives. In the first instance, it is the statues – faceless and fragmented – that dominate. The precarious state of the monuments suggests that the nameless presence of ancient Egypt is one which nevertheless persists. Wanis asks: 'What fate can you read in a hand of stone?' To which the Stranger replies: 'The fate of all those castles and all those images … Men going to nowhere … And ships sailing to nowhere … And columns holding no roof.' As the Stranger speaks these words, his body moves in and out of shot, his voice gradually becoming more distant amongst the fragments. If these are traces of the past, then it is a question of how they are to be understood by those who walk amongst them, which determines the nature of their persitance – and of whether they are to be accommodated, used or neglected by the present.

In the second encounter, the hieroglyphic engravings dominate the shot. Upon seeing Wanis, the Stranger – limping and battered – backs away until he is leaning against a stone wall, behind a row of columns, unable to move any further. Wanis, eager not to scare him, kneels beside a column. The unknown fate mentioned in their previous meeting is now unravelling. Wanis, having destroyed his ties with his past, is brought literally to his knees. The Stranger tells him what he has discovered while working for the Effendis: 'They say they seek people upon whose ruins we live today. They call them ancestors, and can read their writings and their names on the stone. They care for them and preserve…' Wanis interrupts violently: 'Enough! They are dead! Dead! No one can recall their parents or their children.' As he leans his head against a wall, he continues: 'Tell me no more! You make the stone images seem alive to me.' The scene ends with the Stranger disappearing and Wanis left looking up at a high wall covered in hieroglyphic engravings so vast that the frame cannot contain it. The following shot depicts Wanis from the point of view of the wall, dividing the frame into half-body and half-text.

It is knowledge that brings the stone images to life and questions the characters' capacity to trade. With the names of the ancients unknown, the illegal trade in their bodies by figures such as Ayyub and Murad is made easier; knowledge of the ancients' history shifts legitimacy to the archaeologists. Boats, with their association with trade on the one hand and death on the other, carry the meaning of those who board them, and where they have come from, while those who live in the mountains are shrouded in secret. The association between death and the trade in ancient artefacts is highlighted by the significance of boats (believed in ancient Egypt to carry the soul of the dead). The first boat depicted in the film is that which identifies those who kill Wanis's brother (and throw his dead body into the Nile) and carries on it the ominous sign of two blue handprints, traditionally known in Egyptian Islamic culture as the 'hand of Fatima' or *hamsa* and believed to ward off the evil eye. Popular representations also conflate the *hamsa* with the ancient Egyptian symbol of the eye of Horus. Ayyub, on a larger ship, pays a bag of coins for the eye of Horus's necklace, for which Wanis is later beaten unconscious. The largest ship, the Effendi's river steamer, El-Mansheya (referred to as the Iron Ship and 'floating city'), is symbolic of Cairo, civilisation, modernity and economic 'advancement' or progress. Abdel-Salam has commented that the film is a depiction of two Egypts that collide: the old and the new. The first, marked by the traditions and customs of ancient Egypt, is overtaken by the dominating and consuming presence of urbanisation and progress. In the closing sequence, which mirrors the opening funeral procession, the mummies are moved from their tomb in the mountains to El-Mansheya and are thereafter transported to Cairo.

The relationship between progress, civilisation and mummies is thus established within the cinematic medium, which, in its own association with death, frames the narrative through the two funeral processions. Bearing in mind the emphasis on text and knowledge, or language, the cinematic aspect of the film is central to the construction of the way in which ancient Egypt is animated by Abdel-Salam. Such an investment in cinema is also one that carries with it a colonial past and is marked by the period in which the film is set. André Bazin's reference to the 'mummy complex' of cinema draws attention to the way in which the cinematic body in its potentially eternal representation is preserved as living dead. Here, one might note that the only evidence the archaeologists have of the existence of the tomb is the photograph presented by Maspero of an ancient papyrus. At the turn of the nineteenth century, photography and the presence of mummies (particularly in early cinema) coincided with Egyptomania. The capacity of cinema to manipulate space and time was materialised by the depiction of animated mummies and magical amulets and thus consolidated cinema's affinity with death. Through the cinematic medium, the temporal aspect of colonialism emerges in conjunction with the more apparent spatial formation of what Ella Shohat and Robert Stam call the 'imperial imaginary'.

It is not so much their presence but rather the context in which the mummies are re-presented that distinguishes how they are brought to life. The fate of ancient Egypt is one that remains at the mercy of those who control it. The colonial links with the cinematic medium extend back into a culture of exhibition in science, where mummies were dissected and animated as part of the colonial enterprise to accommodate the figure and claim it as part of the West's own history. The scene in which Wanis's uncle, having entered the tomb where the mummies are hidden, cuts the bandages and brutally pulls away the shiny necklace, presents a stark contrast with the more sensational (and supposedly scientific) public unwrappings undertaken by Western Egyptologists, including Maspero, who unwrapped one of the Deir el-Bahri mummies. This scene might further be compared with Ahmad Kamal's arrival at the tomb. He immediately puts on his glasses to read the inscription at the foot of a mummy-case. Here, the story of how the mummies had initially been placed in the cave tomb is explained. The 'presence' of ancient Egypt carries weight in both the surroundings in which the narrative takes place, as well as the temporal positioning of Egypt's ancient past. The film's alternative title, *The Night of Counting the Years*, mentioned at the start of the film, is enacted in the final sequence, where Ahmad Kamal literally calls out the names of the mummies and the dynasties in which they reigned as they are hauled out of the tomb.

There are two timeframes with which to examine the film: the colonial era, during which the British and French were organising themselves around a systematic unearthing of ancient Egyptian artefacts and transportation of these findings to Britain and France; and 'contemporary' Egypt, which had obtained independence from the British and was consolidating its own national identity after the catastrophic events of 1967. In *The Mummy*, both of these eras are linked to Egypt's ancient past. It is in this imaginary and necessarily cinematic configuration of ancient Egypt, supported by the material and concrete presence of monuments and tombs, that the anxiety of colonisation and the ambiguity of national identity are negotiated. In *Toward the African Revolution*, Franz Fanon refers to the way in which the process of colonisation does not lead to the dissolution of culture, but rather brings about a form of cultural stasis or 'cultural mummification'. Ultimately, this 'mummification of individual thinking' turns against those who were once full of potential, and renders them petrified, feeble and ineffectual.

The Mummy immediately reckons with such complexities in its exploration of literal and metaphorical significance of mummies and their impact on questions of identity. The tone of grim despair throughout the film suggests that any desire to reclaim this past for Egypt in terms of knowledge and preservation, would always be mediated through its colonial encounter.

The film does indeed rearrange time and it ultimately attempts to unify Egypt's past in the same way as mummies from five separate dynasties were brought together, and make them present. Time here is depicted in terms of its historical and fictional relevance and its importance to national memory. Ultimately, this is Abdel-Salam's acknowledgment of the fate of ancient Egypt, in his desire to reclaim or remember the past and incorporate it into the national agenda. The passage at the end of the film reads: '*Arise … thou shall not perish. Thou has been called by name. Thou has been resurrected.*' By establishing a relationship between body and text, the mummies exist as evidence of a past, which is passed on through language and from one generation to the next. However, this is not without its complications, given the recontextualisation of mummies and ancient Egypt in museums. As the ancient past is unearthed, and brought to life in the present, the mummies are, in what the original title of the film, 'Reburied', reflects.

Iman Hamam

REFERENCES

Bazin, André (1984) *What is Cinema?* vol. 1, trans. Hugh Gray. Berkeley: University of California Press.

Colla, Elliott (2000) 'Shadi Abd el Salam's *al-Mumiya*: Ambivalence and the Egyptian Nation State', in Ahmida Ali Abdullatif (ed.) *Beyond Colonialism and Nationalism in the Maghreb: History, Culture and Politics*. New York: Palgrave.

Fanon, Frantz (1970) *Toward the African Revolution*, trans. Haakon Chevalier. London: Pelican.

Ikram, Saima and Aidan Dodson (1998) *The Mummy in Ancient Egypt: Equipping the Dead for Eternity*. Cairo: American University in Cairo Press.

Shafik, Viola (1998) *Arab Cinema: History and Cultural Identity*. Cairo: American University in Cairo Press.

Shohat, Ella and Robert Stam (1995) *Unthinking Eurocentrism: Multiculturalism and the Media*. London and New York: Routledge.

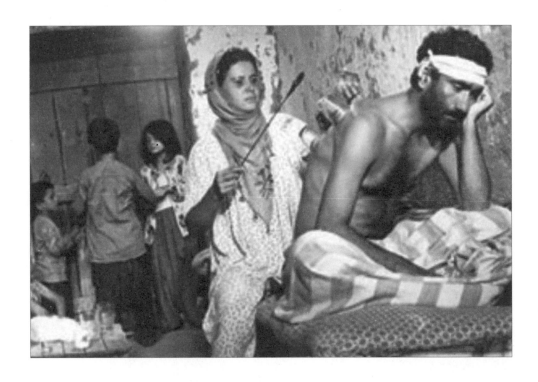

UMUT HOPE

YILMAZ GÜNEY, TURKEY, 1970

Umut (*Hope*, 1970) heralded the beginning of the New Turkish Cinema. It is often regarded as the first truly realist Turkish film and the country's finest film up to that date. Atilla Dorsay, one of Turkey's most prominent film critics, refers to the period between 1970 and 1980 as the 'Years of Hope'. Indeed, there has been a tendency to analyse Turkish cinema in two parts: those years before *Hope* and the years since. The story of a phaeton driver (a trade which became obsolete with the arrival of the taxi system), *Hope* is a realistic portrayal of Turkey in a period of rapid transition to capitalism. With this film, Yılmaz Güney brought a new dimension to the ideological analysis of the liminality of the common man in a period when the commercial film industry, Yeşilçam, failed to meet the needs of a changing society, and while filmmakers were busy polemicising about 'national cinema', 'nationalist cinema', 'popular cinema', 'religious cinema' and 'revolutionary cinema', sexploitation films entered through the back door, further alienating the audience.

In his short life (c.1939–84), a large part of which was spent in prison, Güney's name appeared on the credits of more than one hundred films, as actor, scriptwriter, producer and director. Many of these disappeared into the vaults of censorship boards or were left to disintegrate in miserable conditions. His reputation in the West is built around two important films that he scripted while in prison: *Sürü* (*The Herd*, 1979), directed by Zeki Ökten, and *Yol* (*The Way*, 1982), directed by Şerif Gören. Both were filmmakers influenced by the 'new cinema' and were ready for radical change, despite several productive years spent within the confines of Yeşilçam. *The Way* shared the Palme d'Or with Costa Gavras's *Missing*, at the 1982 Cannes Film Festival.

Yılmaz Güney entered Yeşilçam as a worker on the set and an extra, but gradually gained attention as a screenwriter and actor. He was attracted to the oppressed man, whose daily struggle for survival forced him into dead-end situations. He was always on the run and would often resort to violence, but would always lose. Güney broke the prevalent 'good-looking hero' image with his dark skin, large nose and thin physique. He was crowned the *çirkin kıral* (ugly king) of Yeşilçam. The films, often carrying episodes from Güney's own life, were denigrated as 'commercial trash' by the intelligentsia, but were very popular in the provinces. Their earnest sincerity, warmth and humanism set them apart from other action films; Güney's humanist focus on the plight of the common man struggling to survive in an unjust world was the underlining factor behind their success.

In the 1960s when Turkish society embarked on rapid economic change, Güney began to expose the conflicts and dilemmas of his country, with remarkable films such as *İnce Cumali* (1967) and *Seyyit Han* (1968), where he drew attention to the self-destructive mentality of the feudalist system. The social realism movement of the 1960s, led by Metin Erksan, Halit Refiğ, Ertem Göreç, Duygu Sağıroğlu and Lütfi Ö. Akad, had already produced noteworthy films pointing at the inequalities of the system. Although the number of films was insignificant and a breakaway from the commercial cinema was never really established, the movement eased the way for Güney's films, introducing the notion that cinema was not only a vehicle for entertainment but that it could communicate individual or social messages.

During the first period of his career, Güney was very much a product of audience demands. From 1970, however, he began to push audiences into thinking about the aims and reasons of the struggles of his characters, through realistic films depicting real people with real problems. The fights between macho gangsters or lumpen heroes gave way to social issues such as oppression, poverty and inequality, and acquired a class-conscious narrative. But the characters always remained loners; tragic heroes who tried to find solutions to their problems, not by collective action but by individual struggle, and faced with reality, they were destroyed. The message of Güney was to fight alienation; the individual had to gain political consciousness and unite with other less advantaged citizens. While systematically referring to fate and destiny in his films, he knew well that the reason behind poverty and desperation was not destiny.

With *Hope*, Güney defied the established nomenclature of the dominant Yeşilçam – the studio and star system, box-office-driven narratives and clichéd plotlines – by focusing on an anti-hero leading an un-heroic life, within a real environment and featuring non-professional actors. With the story of a poor phaeton driver suspended between the traditional ways of life and the rapidly changing modern urban society, unable to take on the system single-handedly, Güney entered into dialogue with his audience. Obviously, he was aware of the risk of alienating them altogether. The fact that *Hope* led to a positive synthesis makes it an important work in his filmography. Filmmaker Erden Kıral (director of *Hakkaride Bir Mevsim* (*A Season in Hakkari*, 1983)), who (along with Ali Özgentürk (director of *Hazal*, 1979)) apprenticed with

Güney and showed marked influences of the master in his earlier work, declared in a recent interview: 'With *Hope*, we stepped down the phaeton and onto the street!'

In an age of mechanisation and under threat from the taxi system, Cabbar tries to earn a living for his wife, his ageing mother and his five children, with two weary horses that pull a shabby phaeton. He is a family man with a gentle disposition, but he owes money to everyone. His only hope is the lottery tickets he buys regularly, although he never wins. When he loses his horse and the phaeton, in desperation he agrees to go on a treasure hunt masterminded by the local *hodja* ('man of religion'), reputed to have psychic powers. Critics have divided the film into two distinct parts: the story of the lottery ticket and the treasure hunt.

The narrative unfolds at daybreak, as the streets are washed in an area where new apartment buildings have been built. The clock at the train station shows 4:30am; Cabbar is dozing in his phaeton. There follows a montage of images showing morning life at the station, heralding the new day and with it the hope of earning money: the legs of a sleeping taxi-driver protrude from the window of his car, workers eat their breakfast, a newspaper is delivered by a motorcycle, phaeton drivers and food vendors position themselves in front of the exit, the kebab stall prepares for customers.

Filmmaker and critic Engin Ayça asserts that not only is the film divided into two parts, a prologue, interlude and epilogue are also present and integral to the structure. The prologue highlights the documentary approach of the film; the way the camera records, with meticulous detail, the dynamics of the station. It also establishes the main themes of the film. The futility of seeking solutions to poverty and oppression in sources outside oneself is introduced as Cabbar attempts to find out if he has won the lottery. His ticket is a symbol that reflects his hope of improving his present condition. This theme is further developed in the second half of the film with the treasure hunt motif. Another theme, that the Cabbars of this world are to remain hopeless and alone, is evinced when he is shown to be the only driver without a customer. The third theme is introduced through the large family that come out last. They have moved to the city to benefit from the new economy. They do not want to pay Cabbar the charge he has quoted out of fear of being cheated by what they perceive to be a corrupt city man. Alienation fed by the urban environment and lack of trust among those who should be supporting each other is stressed in another scene, when the illiterate Cabbar asks someone to check the lottery winners' list in the newspaper, but then buys the paper in order to check again.

Following this charged prologue, Cabbar returns home to his family, only to be faced with the worry of his escalating financial problems. The family live in desperate conditions, with a yard they share with their neighbours; the children are dressed in rags, and they envy other children who are able to rent a bicycle. Poverty has led to degredation and the loss of moral values, as Cabbar's son waits for another child to fall so that he can grab his bicycle.

Cabbar once worked in the cotton fields, but escaped serfdom by becoming a phaeton driver and moving one step up the social hierarchy. Even in his worst moments, he will not go back to the cotton fields as his wife suggests. On the other hand, he is devoid of other initiatives to solve his problems, except for buying a lottery ticket. Organising conscious resistance amongst his class does not occur to him. He does not take responsibility for his poverty. Like Ousmane Sembene's hero in *Borom Sarret* (*The Man and His Cart*, 1963) who also suffers the loss of his livelihood – his cart – Cabbar has not found his self-identity in the new economy and, as such, is unable to understand the role of his own actions because he sees himself as powerless to influence events. For a moment, he wavers between his friend, porter Hasan's suggestion of a treasure hunt, and joining the other drivers for a demonstration. However, he lacks the socio-political consciousness to see that his reality is no different to that of other drivers. He is only interested in saving himself. He joins the demonstration carrying the national flag, but under the pretext that he cannot participate since he has neither a horse nor a phaeton, he turns to Hasan to ask if they could manage the treasure hunt with 340 liras. While the drivers try to find a solution to their problem by taking collective action, he runs after empty dreams and finds himself alone again, as he was in the prologue.

The theme of alienation is stressed further when the artisans and small businesses turn their backs on Cabbar because he owes them all money, although the arrival of the taxi system would put an end to their jobs as well. Cabbar's children fight over a slice of watermelon in the garbage; his elder son is beaten by his master; his daughter, who fails her English exam, is asked 'in English' by the teacher why she did not study; Cabbar's last customer in the evening is a drunk prostitute, thrown out of a cabaret called 'Numune Pavyon', the neon sign of which has already lost several letters.

The death of Cabbar's horse is important in the dramatic structure of the film, in preparation for the episode at the police station. A bourgeois' car hits and kills the horse while Cabbar is buying cigarettes, but at the police station the man blames Cabbar for leaving his phaeton unattended and causing the accident. His only concern is finding matching paint to repair the scratch to his vehicle. Cabbar keeps repeating that his horse has died, with no discernable reaction. The class differences are palpable when the accused (the bourgeois driver) magnanimously 'forgives' the victim (proletariat Cabbar), and there is no doubt as to which side the police are on. Cabbar puts his dead horse on a cart and follows it – at a respectful distance – to an empty field outside the city. The simple man of Anatolia is caught between the arid land and boundless horizon, neither of which offer respite.

The death of the horse ends the first part. The next series of episodes that Ayça calls 'an interlude' demand active participation. Those Cabbar owes sell his phaeton and divide the money. He asks for a loan from his old masters, who refuse. Again it shows Cabbar's lack of insight, demonstrating that the episode at the police station taught him nothing. Interestingly, former bosses, whether they have now moved to the city and appropriated bourgeois lifestyles – as identified here with alcohol, well-kept modern women and swimming pools – or continue to live in the farms, have the same attitude of indifference to the misery of the less fortunate.

Cabbar's wife, who is portrayed as a demanding shrew (although her motive is survival) beats their children for renting a bicycle with the money she gave them to buy salt. Cabbar arrives home and displays a macho stance, previously bruised by his bosses, beating his wife for scolding the children. (Güney was often accused of a paternalistic machismo towards women in his films. However those who knew him claim that violence in his films is the violence of society, of which he was a part.)

The gun, integral to the 'ugly king' films as a symbol of hope for the oppressed to rise up and seek justice, serves a different purpose in *Hope*. Cabbar is a fallen hero who has no choice but to sell his gun. When a pickpocket tries to rob him of the money he received for the gun at a flea market, Cabbar vents the anger he could not demonstrate against his rich bosses on the man. Ironically, the fight between the two poor and oppressed individuals occurs in the neighbourhood of the petit bourgeoisie.

Cabbar finally gives up hope of winning the lottery and, with the initiative of Hasan, attempts a robbery in a rich neighbourhood. The victim is a black American whistling 'Yankee Doodle Dandy'. Güney may have included this scene in order to link American imperialism to Cabbar's situation. Cabbar is not able to fight the American the way he fought with the pickpocket; his values of right and wrong have yet to leave him.

The second part commences with the visit to the *hodja*, reputed to have supernatural powers, and is a contrast to the first part in rhythm as well as atmosphere. Where action and daylight were dominant, silence and – for the most part – darkness prevails; the stillness prefigures some impending tragedy. Cabbar, once more, has chosen a fruitless alternative and is again alone in his endeavour. He yearns to have money and to live like a normal human being, but his desperation for both impede his actions.

Nebihat Yağız ties the treasure hunt to the Ottoman mentality of 'here today, gone tomorrow', which stems from hundreds of years of wars, exile and chaos, which created a system that relied on itself; valuable goods were not invested in order to improve business, but were buried underground. As Hasan says, 'under this earth is full of gold and silver'.

The *hodja* seeks the help of Cabbar's children to locate the treasure, by searching for images in the water, but they see nothing. The younger daughter plays the game in order not to be punished and starts listing the objects on the wall, which leads Cabbar to the contention that the treasure must be under the yard. (Apparently, Güney's father once dug for treasure in their yard; Cabbar's house in the film is the house Güney grew up in.) Cabbar's digging is rewarded with a bad cold, which his wife tries to cure with hot suction cups, while scolding him for making her suffer for sixteen years. He promises her good clothes, meat and *baklava* (a Turkish sweet). The night before his departure for the treasure hunt, Cabbar's wife approaches him in a more human manner for the first time in the film, initiating their lovemaking.

Cabbar, Hassan and the *hodja* begin their journey along the Ceyhan River, observing the poor children bathing in dirty waters. A scene that evokes the traditional shadow play, *karagöz*, accentuating the dark silhouettes of men and donkeys between the black earth and a sky with black clouds, serves as a premonition for the ill-fated expedition. When they find the tree that Cabbar's daughter was supposed to have seen in the water, they become increasingly frustrated looking for the 101 white stones as prophesied by the *hodja*. With the stones placed in a circle around the desiccated tree and the 101 *suras* of the Koran written on them, and on the finger of Hasan, they pray. In another scene, again evoking the traditional shadow play, *karagöz*, the trio perform their daily prayer, *namaz*, the shadows of their hands forming mystical images.

They dig for one month under the scorching sun, but do not find the treasure. Cabbar begins to lose his mind, repeating incessantly that he left only 40 liras for his family. The bareness of the landscape seperates the characters from the world. In a powerful epilogue, Cabbar begins to whirl beside the brook, with his eyes blindfolded twice. Twigs of the dried out tree are caught by the wind and drift away, leaving the fate of Cabbar open-ended.

This last scene invites interpretations on several levels. When the trio arrive at what might be the scene of the hunt, Cabbar lifts his head up and sees the branches of the tree turning, and he turns with them. The scene foreshadows the ending, when Cabbar whirls like a dervish. Yağız connects the ending of the film with the *tasavvuf* (Sufi philosophy), pointing also to the thick lines on the tent the trio set up as symbols of the steps that rise to the centre, towards God. The Turks, who practiced shamanism before converting to Islam, believed that the sky had steps and God was sitting at the top. According to this belief, only the person who has reached a certain state could don the turban, with new pieces added as he ascended. The fact that Cabbar is blindfolded twice may suggest *tasavvufi* enlightenment, according to Yağız. She also draws attention to Turkey's Ottoman past when fatalism, predestination and hence surrender on the part of the Ottomans were the prevalent worldview. Although the concept of *kader* (fate) does not come from Islam, it was appropriated by the people of the steppes and deserts in their helplessness against the forces of nature, and became sacred within the feudal system that encouraged mysticism, to pacify the masses and to reduce them to being spectators of their own lives.

The character of the *hodja* as a man of religion is open to discussion. Neither Cabbar nor Hasan are fervent devotees. Cabbar sets his hopes on the so-called supernatural power of the *hodja* when all else fails and Hasan is a lumpen character whose only allegiance is to alcohol (he is seen drunk in a bar and later, when the *hodja* sends him to the village for provisions, he buys a bottle for the journey). The fact that Cabbar's daughter lies to the *hodja*, who wants her to locate the treasure by visualising its image in the water, is interpreted by some critics as the rising consciousness of the masses against religious oppression. However, the *hodja* is not a corrupt man who hopes to win money by fooling Hassan and Cabbar. He also partakes in the treasure hunt, spending his days with them in miserable circumstances. The *hodja* carries the remnants of the feudal system in a period when Turkey is in a transition; his attitude is not necessarily the feudal attitude of a religious man but rather the attitude of one who has become depraved in the race towards capitalism. He is the product of his society and believes in what he does. Intentionally or not, he delays the awakening of Cabbar and, as a result, is a necessary parasite for the dominant class.

Hope was a new beginning for Turkish cinema, but also unique for its period. It does not share many elements with the revolutionary cinema of the West or the Third Cinema movement in South America, although comparisons have been made, for instance, to Brazilian Glauber Rocha and the 'cinema of agitation'. One may speak of magic realism in Güney's preoccupation with images of borders and centres, which draw attention to the dominant disposition of the centre. He works to destabilise the embedding of images within the borders of the screen by casting understated fantasy opposite perceptions of reality moulded by the Yeşilçam film industry, of which he was a part, and the Hollywood mode of filmmaking that that industry emulated. *Hope* most closely resembles neo-realism. The first part shares certain similarities with Vittorio De Sica's *Ladri di biciciclette* (*Bicycle Thieves*, 1948): the loss of the object that is the livelihood of the protagonist is at the centre of the narrative in both films, the bicycle in de Sica's film and the horse in *Hope*; the victim turns into perpetrator in conflict with his true ideals – Antonio becomes a thief in desperation and Cabbar tries to rob a man but is too ashamed; both protagonists consult someone with reputed psychic powers – a fortune-teller in *Bicycle Thieves* and the *hodja* in *Hope* – both of whom represent the new commodified spirituality; both men are disillusioned by condescending policemen, who do not serve the poor; both men are somewhat naïve and less able than their wives to deal with the practicalities of daily life and finally both men are driven by motives of self-interest for personal benefit and often oblivious to others (although compared to De Sica's sentimental approach, Güney is critical of his character, as evidenced in scenes such as the humiliation of Cabbar when he asks for a loan from his old bosses). The second part of the film has been compared to John Huston's *The Treasure of the Sierra Madre* (1948). Despite certain surface similarities, *Hope* is different in what it attempts to convey and how it conveys it. Güney countered the accustomed clichés and superficiality of Turkish cinema to show what ordinary citizens did not see: the tragedy of day-to-day existence. He claimed that people did not know the meaning of hope: 'They are in a constant state of waiting … I wanted to show false hope … The man whose feet are on the ground does not build his hope on false dreams. When society reaches a certain level, people do not have imaginary hopes. *Hope* is the symbol of corrupt order.'

If the film found a solution, it would no longer be a film, according to Güney: 'This is not how I perceive revolutionary cinema. The revolutionary cinema does not show the way, but makes people think.' Cesare Zavattini, considered the father of Italian neo-realism, also stated that he prefers to leave the solution up to the audience, that the characters and situations in films for which he wrote the script remain unresolved from a practical point of view simply because 'this is reality', although each moment of the film is, in itself, a continuous answer to some question. It is not the concern of an artist to propose solutions, as it is enough to make an audience feel the need, the urgency for themselves. If the films offer solutions, these are only sentimental ones, Zavattini claims, resulting from the superficial way in which problems have been confronted.

With *Hope*, Güney shows the enigmatic coexistence of the traditional and the modern, feudal practices and bourgeois styles, dogmas and dialogue, socio-political awareness and lack of it, the way his earlier films married individual bravura and socialist values in a discourse that combined Western dramaturgy with documentary realism. *Hope* is a tragedy condemning established traditions and moral values that turn a blind-eye to human pain, a theme central to all Güney's films. Cabbar's wife suggests that he change the phaeton, but what would happen if he did? In a society at the threshold of industrialisation, to fight with motorised vehicles would only make those dependent on small capital gain poorer. Phaeton driver Cabbar, porter Hasan and even the *hodja*, reputed to have a 'powerful breath' that links him to the supernatural, cannot see this. In drawing attention to the marginal, or the 'other', the film challenges the hegemonic forces, but the most modern theme of the film is the idea that man is alienated from others in a segmented society where everyone focuses on their individual needs.

Films like *Hope* were rare in 1970s Turkey, although Güney continued with *Acı* (*Pain*), *Ağıt* (*Elegy*), *Baba* (*Father*) and *Umutsuzlar* (*Hopeless Ones*) all of which were made in 1971. Lütfi Ö. Akad also continued the trend, with the trilogy *Gelin* (*The Bride*, 1973), *Düğün* (*The Wedding*, 1973) and *Diyet* (*Blood Money*, 1974). Güney also made a few films in the style of his old studio productions.

Hope was chosen as the Best Film at the Altın Koza (Golden Cocoon) Film Festival in Adana (Güney's hometown) and was subsequently banned for propagating class differences (displaying the threadbare clothes of the phaeton driver as a symbol of poverty, giving the impression that the rich owner of the car would not be tried for hitting the horse, showing discrimination for the poor when Cabbar searches for a job) in a country where, officially, there are no classes; for alluding to American imperialism (military bases in Adana in the south of Turkey); for degrading religion (the morning prayer is done while the sun is rising); and for provoking workers to resist authority. The film was later smuggled out of the country in order to be shown at the Cannes Film Festival. It took twenty years for the veil of censorship to be lifted over *Hope*. Unfortunately, Yilmaz Güney did not live to see it.

Gönül Dönmez-Colin

REFERENCES

Yağız, Nebihat (1998) 'Zihniyet ve Toplumsallık İlişkilerinin Türk Sinemasındaki Yansımaları', unpublished MA thesis, Dokuz Eylül University, Izmir. On line; available at http://www. sinemasal.gen.tr/umutfilmi (accessed 30 June 2005).

Coş, Nezih, Engin Ayça and Abdullah Anlar (1974) 'Umut filmi üstüne tartışma', *Yedinci Sanat*, 15. On line; available at http://www.iletisim.bahcesehir.edu.tr/arsiv/sorgu_goster. php?tip=10 (accessed 12 June 2005).

GELİN THE BRIDE

LÜTFİ Ö. AKAD, TURKEY, 1973

In the history of Turkish cinema, there are few films that stand out for both narrative style and content. These films are remarkable because they touch not only universal problems but are themselves documents of their period. *Gelin* (*The Bride*, 1973) is one of these films, as it reveals the difficult phases of the transformation of Turkish-Anatolian culture into contemporary Turkey. The first in a trilogy with *Düğün* (*The Wedding*, 1973) and *Diyet* (*Blood Money*, 1974), *The Bride* focuses on the problems of urbanisation in the process of migration of the rural people to the large metropolis. The trilogy is among the most significant works of Lütfi Ö. Akad, produced during what is considered to be his mature period, and which was also a period of transformation for the Turkish film industry. Akad stopped making feature films after the trilogy.

The peak period of commercial Turkish cinema was throughout the 1960s until the early 1970s, with a cinematic production line turning out formulaic, stereotypical films. Producers who were not prepared to take risks refused to stray from familiar subject matter, simplistic storylines and unchallenging narrative structures to maximise the box-office figures. This tried-and-tested format was strategic in the rise of audience numbers and resulted in the financial viability of establishing new cinemas countrywide. During this bright period cinema became Turkey's primary family entertainment catering to both men and women of all ages and across every socio-economic group. However, it was to be relatively short-lived and was eventually superseded by television. The economic difficulties of the late 1970s and early 1980s which overtook the nation were concurrent with the advent of domestic television, a combination which was to become one of the prime factors in the decline of the Turkish film industry. In addition to this social collision was the artistic choice of the industry's established filmmakers. Instead of raising the aesthetic and visual quality of film, they continued to churn out the same tired formulae but now for the guaranteed financial success offered by the newly-developed and hungry medium of video production in the 1980s. The introduction and subsequent appetite for videos saw production costs slashed and quality sacrificed which ultimately led to the demise of the Turkish film industry.

Akad was a director who, whilst wishing to appear intellectually independent of the traditional industry structure, was nonetheless professionally dependent on the demand for the accepted indigenous style. He had proved his worth and reputation in Turkish cinema by audience-pleasing productions that were under budget, thus satisfying the producers as well as the public. Despite these confines, Akad's films are markedly distinguishable for their socio-economic settings and the depth of narrative, and this is in marked contrast to the bulk of films being made at this time. *The Bride* is evidence of his independent stance within the established industry.

The film occupies a significant place in the history of Turkish cinema for several distinct reasons. Although it can be said to follow a linear narrative with the subject matter moulded to fit the genre of melodrama, it is Akad's masterful cinematic language which lifts the film above the profit-assured raw melodramas of the era. The narrative is invested with power through his skilful use of appropriate cinematic space and setting, which is achieved by maximising the internal locations afforded by the family's shop and the home with its inner courtyard, and not straying further than the immediate neighbourhood. His decision successfully creates a subtle metaphor for the family's self-imposed isolation. In its entirety, the film only once moves into the wider city, when the bride goes to a hospital.

Akad achieves his unusual narrative depth by keeping the camera at a distance from his subjects to afford viewers a more objective look, revealing the tensions and differences between them. In his book published in 2004, Akad writes: 'Instead of close shots of actors, I was looking for a full, medium shot to reflect their presence as if they were closer to us. By doing this my plan was to make the audience feel the vibration of both the drama and the dramatic tension between characters.' He follows his urge to tell the story with a strong use of image and without reliance on dialogue, introducing the spoken word only when absolutely necessary. He crystallises this approach saying that 'the spoken word must occur as it does in life – used only when it is inevitable'.

Akad's observation of society and his analytical insight into its changing dynamics is harmonised with his plain, simple and unembellished style. Throughout the trilogy he displays a subtlety and depth, and demonstrates that cinema can be much more than simple family entertainment; it can be vehicle for raising important questions affecting contemporary social reality. Aware of *The Bride*'s critical content as discursive subject, Akad interlinks the general problems of migration with the traditional family structure in Turkey. By introducing social concerns into the already complex contrasting economic arrangements of the urban and the rural, Akad's film encourages and deserves reading on both metaphorical and literal levels.

The plot centres on a rural family who have migrated to Istanbul. The protagonist, Meryem (played by Hülya Koçyiğit, one of the popular stars of the period), her husband, Veli and their son, Osman, move in with Veli's family, who own a small shop on the outskirts of the city. Breaking all economic links with their hometown is one result of the family's decision to integrate into city life. Istanbul seems to offer endless opportunities for financial success, but the social construction and liberal conventions of the city necessitates adapting to a new lifestyle. Throughout the film, Akad exposes the process of rapid urbanisation, increasing economic problems and the political conflicts of the day, while addressing the perpetual unfairness and inequality in the issues of the female gender.

Although Veli's family relocated to Istanbul some years earlier, senior members maintain the traditional rural codes of domestic hierarchy, where everyone works for the good of all. By founding the business on this work ethic, the family hope to accumulate success, wealth, respect and a good name in the adopted city. This system, which functions unquestioningly in rural society, raises important moral questions when transferred to the city environment.

Ambition blinds the family from seeing how their own ties are loosening, which they ignore in the drive to attain financial success. Meryem continues to maintain the honesty and dignity of their former lives, yet at the same time she cannot help but become aware of the opportunities offered by city life, and the new set of stratagems required for living there. The turning point for her is triggered by her young son's ill health. This neatly functions as a device to illustrate the conflict between different family members, providing the constructive function of the narration.

A doctor in Istanbul informs Meryem that Osman requires a life-saving operation. Older family members reject this expensive modern treatment, instead suggesting superstition-based cures. That the father-in-law uses medical ointment to cure the pain in his kneecaps underlines their mixed values. Throughout the film, Meryem's constant pleas for hospital treatment and operation are rejected or delayed with financial excuses. However, the need for the medical intervention is urgent; the boy has only three months to live. Meryem is finally provoked into unsanctioned action, which serves to break the fragile domestic balance and sharpens the conflict between the bride and her in-laws. She decides to sell her golden bracelets and necklace, the dowry she has brought to the marriage, to raise money for Osman's treatment. But just when Meryem has the opportunity to save her son, the family announces it will open a new, bigger extension to the business in the city centre and she is pressured to hand over the money for family interests in accordance with the conventions of family ties and traditional obligations. The conservatively religious father-in-law ensures the anxious mother she will be given the money for the operation, but keeps withholding his promise.

Meryem becomes more silent and withdrawn, furious, worried and desperate during this period, marked in the narrative by Ramadan and the two religious festivities, *bayram*, which follow. The second festival has its origin in the Koranic parable about a prophet who attempts to sacrifice his son to prove his faith in God. God, however, sends a ram for him to sacrifice instead of the boy. Thus, the sacrificing of a ram has become a symbol of this event, which Akad juxtaposes with the boy's critical condition at the film's climax.

Akad's decision to place a bride at the centre of the narrative works on various levels. The position of the bride is a metaphor for the difficulties of adapting to the societal transition from the country to the city. Akad sharply illustrates how the change of environment and exposure to city life erodes the traditional rural network of extended family. This cultural transformation situates Meryem in a spatial liminality because of the traditional social role designated to her as a woman.

Staying with the theme of change, the gender role of the bride of the title can also be interpreted as an *in-between* position. The bride is no longer under her family roof, yet neither is she under the roof of complete strangers. Therefore, she must comply with a new set of domestic rules, which differ from the values of her own family. Meryem married her husband of her own free will, but little did she expect her husband to obey his family's rules. Couples become vulnerable to the societal oppression of their own families, from both the bride's side as well as the husband's. Brides remain without a voice, tradition dictating that they have no voice in decisions made for them, decisions that must be respected and obeyed. They are expected to sacrifice themselves for the good of the whole family without question. Furthermore, they are entrusted with the *namus* (honour) of the family name. Independent activities outside the home are viewed as threatening, with particular emphasis placed on the potential opportunities for sexual infidelity. Ironically, the most vocal contributors to this oppression can be immediate female family members and older married women who, despite their mature age, retain the status quo and stay within the limitation of the *gelin*, according to the traditions.

This vulnerability, characteristic of rural life, becomes more apparent in the urban environment of the film. During transition, such a position, combined with the harsh necessities of economic survival, could have a strong impact on a country bride. The dilemmas facing

Meryem become apparent when the problem caused by Osman's health affects the couple's personal life. Here Akad shows the subtle change of status for not only the bride but also her husband. The reasoning given for the conditions is plausible in the rural milieu, but not convincing in the urban environment, demonstrated by the clash between the modern scientific health facilities available in Istanbul and the prayer-based traditional treatment practiced in the villages.

Meryem's precarious position in this migrant family is further magnified by the fact that she is neither in her homeland nor fully ensconced in the *new country*. There is a clear implication that 'Istanbul begins outside of the walls of this house, inside these walls is Yozgat'. Yozgat is the area they originate from and, the new Istanbul location notwithstanding, is jealously preserved as an unassailable cultural extension, within which the conformities of their rural roots are vigorously upheld. However, nothing can isolate a house from its environment, and before long, the dynamics of Istanbul inevitably penetrate the walls of Yozgat.

In her quest for Osman's recovery, Meryem becomes familiar with the surrounding area where she lives and experiences, for the first time, a world beyond Yozgat. She is the first woman in the family to glimpse the other side of the cultural frontier; her female relations remain secure in tradition, obedient to the men without question. Tirelessly, Meryem undertakes her duties both inside the house and outside (in the family shop) while caring for Osman. This she does without help, as the family members stubbornly refuse to accept the child critically ill and ignore her pleas. Once again, Meryem is stuck in limbo; caught both inside and outside Yozgat, between the restricted Istanbul she inhabits and the unimaginable Istanbul, which begins outside the walls.

In Istanbul, Meryem finds her orientation through a woman, Güler, from the same rural area. She is a relatively independent woman, a factory worker who has acquired economic consciousness, in contrast to the housewife bound to a traditional family. Güler has her worker's insurance, in direct contrast to Meryem, who works all hours for the common interest of the family but has nothing of her own and is unable to demand any rights. Akad contrasts the exploitation of Meryem's position as unpaid domestic labourer to the benefits of Güler's factory job as part of a collective workforce that offers the possibility of protected employee's rights. The film draws attention to how migration from rural to urban areas creates the need for a new organisation of space in the economic dimension.

In the rural agricultural environment, the mode of production differs greatly from that found in developed industrial settings. In the rural instance, people own the agricultural implements; the only alternative available for those not possessing tools is to work for someone else as seasonal hired workers. In both cases, the production and everyday living are based on the equal physical input of all family members. The lack of means of production combined with such varying regional factors as poor soil and job losses due to mechanisation are noteworthy causes of migration.

In the city, should the capital accumulated from the sale of land prove insufficient for establishing industrial production, trade presents the next best viable option for the immigrant. For those unfortunate enough not to possess capital, as in the case of Güler and, eventually, Meryem and Veli, selling their labour becomes the first available option. Lesser options are found in the category of non-productive, low-status jobs for which no qualifications are necessary; peddling is one example, but such casual work does not constitute a stable living.

The family's introduction to urban life is through a small local shop selling household goods, food and cigarettes. It is located in the *gecekondu* area, the makeshift migrant slums which were formed on the outskirts of the city, creating a quasi-rural Istanbul. As it is seen in the film, Istanbul is a distant city, known to them by a tantalising horizon of tall buildings that epitomise success. By setting up a successful business, a supermarket in the shadow of high apartment buildings inhabited by high-income people, they expect to be accepted in the city, as they once were in their hometown. They aspire to become a part of Istanbul and recognised, despite the difference in the mode of production between the rural and urban market places.

The family plan is to expand their small shop, which partly functions on the labour of the women. As the expansion demands more capital, the quality of life inside the home becomes poorer with no amelioration to the situation of women who are running both the household and the new supermarket. While at home, the family consume only the traditional soup and pasta; the various kinds of food and the range of products on display in the supermarket reveal another life style. The tension mounts when Meryem, torn by anxieties for the health of her son, observes the ruthless struggle of the family to improve their lot. The domestic exploitation of women by the family becomes apparent only to Meryem while other female members see no alternative to the traditional role of women in the family structure. Akad also demonstrates how the rural mode of production is strongly interwoven with both cultural and religious traditions.

On the first day of the *bayram*, the ram, which little Osman has fed daily while still waiting for his operation, is to be sacrificed. Not able to face the slaughter of his favourite animal, the boy runs off, becomes breathless and dies from his heart problem. At his funeral, Meryem releases the ram in front of everyone with a gesture of angry defiance, implying that God has already taken her son as the sacrifice. Meryem's torment is unbearable; she sets fire to the small family shop, which is described by the father-in-law in theological terms as 'the gate of God'. With the loss of the old shop comes the loss of the family's carefully nurtured identity, which is now left to face the wild rules of trading in the city. They will keep living in the city but at the expense of their identity.

During the fire, the father-in-law tries to rescue goods from the shop, putting himself in danger, while Meryem flees to the home of Güler and her husband, subsequently finding a job in the factory. The family remain indifferent to Meryem's suffering over Osman's death and decree it is Veli's duty to kill his wife to clean the honour of the family. They have heard that Meryem is working in a factory. From their blinkered approach, her job is a disgrace and they brand her a fallen woman.

In the final scene, in front of the factory gate, Meryem sees Veli waiting for her. Face to face with Meryem, who is prepared to be killed by her husband, Veli asks if there is a job in the factory for himself. Finally, Meryem becomes a wife rather than a bride and Veli releases himself from the position of the unwaged worker exploited by his family.

Akad's film allows audiences into the closed world of the migrant and offers a wider understanding of the reality of migration during the 1970s in Turkey. He lays out the subject matter as a social phenomenon. His characters, as misplaced people, conform realistically to their cultural background in the way they perceive and position their social identity in the alien environment. Furthermore, he signals the transition as an agonising process and demonstrates how the inevitable result for individuals caught in this situation is moral loss at the expense of material gain.

Akad grounds this transition by comparing the class-based society, as the place of the organised workforce for the owners of the means of production, with the land-based society, where the production depends on shared work only maintainable if restrictive values and traditions are accompanied. Initially the range of business possibilities, which is perceived as opportunity offered by the city, seems to be promising for building a prosperous future. However, success in the city demands different strategies and presents problems beyond the limitations of the agrarian life style. The traditional relations within agrarian society, and particularly, the dependence on nature, have to be abandoned in the face of different moral values and a different social organisation needed for survival in the competitive urban environment. It is during this transition that the double standards arise from the dilemma created by fidelity to the ideals of decency, honour and integrity which become undermined with the need for ruthless competition in the marketplace. Hence, the conflict between essential social values and material gain become more evident in the transition from rural to urban life.

Akad chooses to visualise the subject matter through an objective approach by keeping the characters equidistant throughout the film, imbuing each character with her or his own plausible existence. He clearly demonstrates their particular social manner as the result of their personalities formed from existing social conditions and the role models they follow. An example is the older brother who has a shrewd side similar to his father's in comparison to Veli's own relatively lowly character. The two daughters-in-law, the brides, also display differences in their acceptance of the impositions visited upon them by their men folk. The older bride unquestioningly follows the example of her mother-in-law and avoids defying tradition for fear of her personal safety, whereas Meryem actively questions the situation she finds herself in. Although Akad's approach to his characters is neutral and unbiased it is the women who come to the fore in this powerful observation of society.

In the trilogy, *The Bride* is inseparable from *The Wedding* and *Blood Money* in the portrayal of women who are defenceless in every aspect of the rural-to-urban migration experience. These women all emerge empowered as a direct result of sacrificing themselves for the family. The older sister in *The Wedding* abandons her personal life to rescue her sister and family, while in *Blood Money* a single mother and a factory worker shows that solidarity is a necessity for all people in the joint struggle of the transition to the new mode of production.

In the process of cultural transformation, as in the film, women are more subjugated to both economic and established traditional coercion. Their liminality between their *selves* and the patriarchy becomes more evident when it clashes with a new, more complex lifestyle, such as the urbanisation of society. In *The Bride* women's economic independence, as well as solidarity between women, at least for deciding their own destiny, is demonstrated as one of the vital issues in the fight against the subordination of women in every phase of life. The character of the bride, Meryem, is transformed by circumstances beyond her control. As a woman trained to respect men and older members of the family as tradition dictates, she withdraws into silence. This period of silence gives her a chance to observe how the self-esteem of the family becomes corrupted when they forego essential social and humanistic values for their ambition. A good example is the hypocrisy they display by illegally selling alcohol while staunchly defending religious values. Meryem also comprehends that while women are used for common interests of the family they are allowed no voice even in basic decisions about themselves. From the point of view of Meryem's gender position, her central question is how one adapts to the new, unfamiliar and demanding conditions of the city while maintaining dignity. Faced with the impossibility of a situation which allows neither going back nor continuing to live with double standards, Meryem recognises that she has power of choice as to how she will take control over her own life and future. This silent observation, made amid all the opportunities offered by the loud city, makes her decide that she has no option but to adopt a radical stance. This stance takes its power from offering solutions to others who find themselves caught in the same deadlock of rural/urban conflict, an example being her repressed husband.

As with the other two films in the trilogy, in *The Bride* Lütfi Ö. Akad gives the central role to the woman – the most vulnerable gender in any social transformation. Thus in *The Bride* Meryem is revealed as the hero in both meanings of the word; she is the hero of the film and a hero as a woman who surmounts difficulties with a raw courage which leads to the liberation of others.

Ayla Kanbur

REFERENCE

Akad, Ö. Lütfi (2004) *Işıkla Karanlık Arasında*. Istanbul: Isbank Culture Publications.

TABIAT-E BIJAN STILL LIFE

SOHRAB SHAHID SALESS, IRAN, 1974

Tabiat-e Bijan (*Still Life*, 1974) is one of the most important films in the history of Iranian cinema. Its outstanding style, groundbreaking form and unsentimental and uncompromising vision having initiated a poetic cinema that was also highly political. This is the second film of the legendary Iranian filmmaker, Sohrab Shahid Saless (1944–98), and the last film that he made in Iran before he emigrated to Germany in 1975.

Despite the unprecedented success of *Still Life* as well as Saless's first film, *Yek Ettefaghe Sadeh* (*A Simple Event*, 1973), both inside and outside of Iran (wining many prestigious awards from several international film festivals), the Shah's censors were not happy with him. It was already obvious to them that Saless was critical of the system and was moving against the ideal direction of the regime. The images of extreme poverty, the forgotten poor in rural areas and a sense of despair of life in Iran under the Shah was against the idea of progress, modernity and hope that was propagated by the Shah's 'White Revolution' and his 'Gate to the Great Civilisation' motto. When Saless began his third feature, *Gharantineh* (*Quarantine*, 1975), which was about the unwanted children in an orphanage in the poor regions of south Tehran, the production was stopped by the censors (more accurately SAVAK, the Shah's secret police force) after three days of shooting. Despairing of the impossibility of making another feature-length film and unwilling to compromise with the system, Saless decided to leave Iran for Germany for good. He was fluent in several languages (including French, German, Czech and English) and had a good understanding of European culture having lived in Austria, France and Czechoslovakia for few years in his youth. He would always say that the world was his home and that art knew no borders. Interestingly, the world considered him only as an Iranian filmmaker in exile. When he passed away after living for twenty-five years in Germany and making more than eighteen films, the Western press ran the news of his death with headlines that read 'an Iranian director died...'.

Iranian cinema to this day regrets his loss and the kind of films that he could have made at home. Although Saless's third film, *In Der Fremde, Dar Ghorbat* (*Far from Home*, 1975) (a co-production of Iran and Germany) and the two that followed it, *Reifezeit* (*Time of Maturity/*

Bolough, 1976) and *Tagebuch Eines Liebebdeb* (*Diary of a Lover/Khaterate Yek Ashegh*, 1977) were shown in Tehran during the International Film Festival, Iranian audiences in general were deprived of seeing his German films in Iran.

Several film critics have called Saless the pioneer of the Iranian New Wave (*Moj-e No*) or the so-called 'progressive cinema', the kind of cinema that was thought-provoking, artistic and political and was often referred to as different, intellectual or committed, opposite to the commercial cinema which was referred to as *Film Farsi* (a derogatory term). The non-dramatic and minimal plot structure of *Still Life* and *A Simple Event* liberated Iranian cinema from the confines of literature and dramatic screenwriting. It also appealed to many directors who had no interest in dramatic filmmaking or lacked the skills in dramatic screenwriting. The film's interest in poor and deprived people, shot in the rural areas of Iran, encouraged others to pay attention to the rich resources of Iran for cinema, particularly after the Islamic Revolution of 1979.

It is important to note that the late 1960s and the 1970s, when Saless started his career, marked an active political period in Iran. Arts, poetry, theatre and cinema also flourished during this period despite the dominant political oppression. Oil income developed the middle class and increased the Western-educated technocrats as Iran moved fast through a modernisation process that angered many traditionalists, including the clergy. The close ties with the West, in particular America, was top of the Shah's agenda, and the market was flooded with Western art, pop music, television series and Hollywood movies as well as films from Europe, India and other parts of the world. Many international art festivals were established during this period that exposed the public to the latest and most modern productions of the Western art world. In particular, Shiraz Art Festival each year invited the most famous writers, musicians, performers and artists such as Jerzy Grotowsky, Karlheinz Stockhausen, Peter Brook, Morris Bejar and Shuji Terayama. There were several film festivals – including the Tehran International Film Festival, the Asian Youth Film Festival, the Youth Film Festival, the Free Cinema Festival, and the Children and Young Adult Film Festival – that screened the latest films and introduced audiences to a variety of art films. Also, several books on Western literature, art and cinema were translated into Persian, encouraging the public's knowledge and enthusiasm about cinema.

Many European and American film production companies had their offices in Tehran (including Twentieth Century Fox, Metro Goldwyn Mayer, Warner Bros.) and a number of foreign film agencies invested in some co-productions, including *Deserto dei Tarttari II* (*The*

Desert of Tatars/Sahra-ye tatar-ha, 1976) directed by Valerio Zurlini, co-produced by Italy, France, West Germany and Iran; *Carevan-ha* (*Caravans*, 1978) directed by James Fargo, co-produced by USA and Iran; *Il Fiore delle mille e una notte* (*Arabian Nights*, 1974) directed by Pier Paolo Pasolini, co-produced by Italy and France; *Le Vent des Amoureux* (*The Lover's Wind/Bad-e Saba*, 1978) directed by Albert Lamorisse, co-produced by France and Iran; and Claude Lelouch's *Iran* (1972), also co-produced by France and Iran.

A group of filmmakers who were educated in Europe or the US as well as those who had come to cinema from other disciplines made groundbreaking films in this period. The feminist radical poet Forugh Farrokhzad directed her award-winning short documentary, *Khaneh Siah Ast* (*The House is Black*, 1962), produced by a major writer/filmmaker, Ebrahim Golestan. Golestan himself also made several poetic documentaries and features, including *Khesh o Ayeneh* (*The Brick and the Mirror*, 1965) which was a complete departure from the contemporaneous domestic commercial narrative cinema. Parviz Kimiavi (considered as 'the Iranian Jean-Luc Godard'), returned to Iran from France to make *Mogul-ha* (*The Mongols*, 1973), Dariush Mehrjui – who was educated in the US – made *Gav* (*The Cow*, 1969), Bahram Bayzai made *Ragbar* (*Downpour*, 1971), and several other filmmakers including Mohammad Reza Aslani, Kamran Shirdel, Arbi Ovanesian, Amir Naderi, Farrokh Ghaffari, Nasser Taghva'i, Abbas Kiarostami, Jalal Moghaddam, Fereydun Rahnama, Hajir Dariush and Bahman Farmanara made their exceptional innovative films. It was in this cultural climate of the early 1970s that Saless started to make movies in Iran when he was twenty years old and although the films of the so-called New Wave filmmakers offered different possibilities of film style, the cinema of Saless remained the most influential and poetic.

A Simple Event established Saless as a director with a remarkable vision and personal style. It was shot in fifteen days and with the budget of a short film. The enormous success of the film paved the way for his second film, *Still Life*. Saless received more funding for this film and hired Houshang Baharlou, the most prestigious cinematographer in Iran at that time, who is responsible for the low-light images which give the film a rich painterly quality. The shoot took eleven days and Saless shot most of his scenes only once. He continued with his use of non-professional actors, real locations, minimal crew and minimal plot. As in the previous film, he tried to avoid performance in favour of capturing the truth: he would not rehearse his actors; his aim was to arrive at a documentary style. According to Morteza Momayez, who worked as art director on the film, Saless's style of shooting was very simple. His method of directing was mechanical; the emphasis was on the look of the scene.

The beautiful and meditative long takes of the film hypnotised audiences at the second Tehran International Film Festival and disarmed those who had some reservation about him as a great director. Such focus and attention on the trivial details of the uneventful life of an old couple in rural Iran were unprecedented in Iranian cinema. It was a risk that only the decisive camera of Saless could afford. The long takes of the old man in his room eating or smoking, and the long takes of his old wife serving tea and food, weaving rugs and walking slowly across the room could have bored audiences, but the orchestration of the simple movements of the actors, the pauses in dialogue and the editing, together with the exceptional general look of the film, created a poetic rhythm. Amir Naderi, one of the most important directors of contemporary Iranian cinema with films like *Davandeh* (*The Runner*, 1985) and *Ab, Bad, Khaak* (*Water, Wind, Dust*, 1989), has called Saless the master of rhythm. The rhythmic sequence of shots of sand storm and the lost child who is in search of water in Naderi's *Water, Wind, Dust* are almost a tribute to the earlier master.

Naderi has also admired the musical arrangement of Saless's shots and the quiet poetic moments that are visually striking – the kind of cinema that he himself has gradually been moving towards in his own work. Similarly, Abbas Kiarostami, who has shown admiration for Saless's work generally and *A Simple Event* in particular, respects films that are either minimalist or independent of a narrative structure – the kind of films that are meditative and poetic. In most of his films, Kiarostami focuses on small moments and turns them into extraordinary scenes. For example, in *Nema-ye Nazdik* (*Close-Up*, 1990), the driver waiting outside the house kicks an empty canister down the street to kill time and we follow the movement. Also, in *Five, Dedicated to Ozu* (2003) Kiarostami strips his film of narrative elements to provide a space for the audience to contemplate. He plants his camera on the shore of Caspian Sea (except for the second episode that is shot in Spain) to frame five simple views of the sea. The first one shows a piece of wood rolled back and forth by the waves, the second one looks at people walking across the screen ignoring the sea, the third one is filled with rushing ducks across the screen, the fourth view looks at a group of dogs sitting by the sea, and the last one reveals a night view of the water lit by the moonlight as we hear sounds of frogs and insects. Here, the pacing of actors and animal movements, light and colour, as well as sound and occasional music invite us to listen and meditate. Kiarostami had displayed his interest in the cinema of observation with his first feature film, *Gozaresh* (*Report*, 1977). But with *Five*, he shows that he has moved towards a more minimalist and abstract cinema. It is interesting to note that Saless also believed that his cinema was just a report of reality with no judgement and no analysis.

Still Life portrays the mundane monotonous life of an old switchman, Mohammad Sardari (Zardouz Bonyadi), who lives with his wife (played by Zahra Yazdani) in a remote northern part of Iran. All his life the old man repeats a simple job: lowering the fence on the road whenever a train approaches. His wife weaves rugs, cooks food and serves tea. Their visitors include two businessmen who come to buy the old woman's rugs, followed by two inspectors from the Railroad Office, and later on their son, a soldier (played by Habibolah Safarian) who spends one night with them. One day, the old man's routine comes to an abrupt end when he is given his retirement decree. Unable to accept it he goes into town to see his boss, but returns disappointed. A younger man arrives to replace him. The old man has to leave the home he spent the greatest part of his life in, with no idea of where to go.

Again, like *A Simple Event*, Saless sets his film near a railroad – the lines that connect one to the city. Where the old man lives is desolate and forgotten; the barren landscape and the bare trees add to the bleak atmosphere of film. (Momayez, as art director, had to burn the dry grass of the landscape to create the cracks on the walls of the old man's room to give them a more deserted-looking appearance.) The life of the old man is summarised in the routine of his job (blocking the road) and his daily habits of eating, sleeping and smoking. Yet when the fragile safety of his job is broken and taken away from him, he is left with nothing. The only time that the old man looks at himself and probably reflects on his life is when he is forced to retire. At the end of the film, during the last action of moving out, he takes a long look at himself in a small mirror hanging on the wall (in an extreme close-up) before removing it and revealing the ruined wall underneath. This powerful ending suggests his death-like exit since we see his face and then the image disappears.

Although *Still Life* had a simple look, it was more profound, subtle and sophisticated and visually more striking than *A Simple Event*. In this later film, Saless pays more attention to composition and the use of colour. The repetition of daily rituals like stopping traffic at the railroad crossing, rolling cigarettes, eating and drinking tea, threading needles and even walking across the room, captured in real time, are all more accentuated. To avoid dramatisation and the interpretation of action, Saless tries not to manipulate reality, like neorealist filmmaker Roberto Rossellini, who once said: 'reality is there … why multiply it'? In fact, the documentary look and realism of Saless founded a mode of film production that after the Revolution was called 'Iranian neo-realism'.

Saless had a great concern for the 'insignificant' moments on the screen. Although he admired Buñuel, he opposed the employment of symbols in his films and was uncompromising in his opposition to fooling the audience. He resisted sentimental moments and refused to use music or editing to entice his audience. Long scenes of walking, doing nothing, looking, the repetition of ordinary actions and embracing dead moments are some of Saless's typical shots – shots that are normally thrown away by other filmmakers. Similar to Alexandr Sokurov's extremely slow rhythm in *Mat i syn* (*Mother and Son*, 1997), Saless watches his characters' joyless, robotic life with such clinical scrutiny that, according to Olof Muller, he seems to be punishing his audience.

This was the first time an old couple was used as main characters in Iranian cinema. In an industry where young people populate the screens, Saless chooses to focus on the unwanted, undesirable or, according to some, 'unattractive' old people who live a dull life. Their jobs are unimportant and both their lives and deaths are inconsequential. Like Chekhov, his favourite writer, Saless looks at a slice of life of these people and challenges his viewers to witness and confront emptiness, isolation, a bare reality stripped of the common masks of narrative cinema. There is no cutaway to save the viewers from the imprisoned actors in their closed detached environment. Like the characters, the audience is trapped in the world of the film.

Old women in Iranian cinema have a longer history of appearing on screen than old men. They usually play the grandmother character that is a part of an extended family, as well as a source of wisdom, traditional values and stable identity. They have also been portrayed as a burden on the younger generation. For example, the dependent old and mute mother in Bayza'i's *Downpour* keeps her young daughter from marrying the man she loves, and the almost-dead old woman in *Dastforoush* (*The Peddler*, 1987), by Mohsen Makhmalbaf, is completely dependent on her grandson and drives him crazy.

Old men have generally had a positive image in Iranian films. They are portrayed as harmless, sweet, wise and occasionally crazy. For example, Asid Ali Mirza in Parviz Kimiavi's *Pe Mesle Pelican* (*P for Pelican*, 1970) is an old man who lives in the ruins of Tabas. He appears both wise and insane. The same character reappears in *The Mongols*. In the films of Saless, the old men represent the aged spirit of the artist or nation, a generation robbed of its childhood and that had to face reality at an early age. This is also expressed in Saless's poetry (that rhymes with the final scene of *Still Life*);

> Suddenly I was old.
> I looked in the mirror,
> The mirror had grown old too.

Then I remembered my childhood.

Back then I was old and aged.

The mirror laughed out of happiness.

Interestingly, in the later films of Saless, such as *Der Weidenbaum* (*The Weeping Willow*, 1983) and *Rosen Für Afrika* (*Roses for Africa*, 1991), the old men stand for the shadows of the past or as father figures.

Still Life has moments of irony and humour, despite its serious tone. In the sparse dialogue exchanged between the old couple, at the beginning of the film the old woman asks her husband for money to buy a new veil (*chador*), which is not an expensive luxury item. But the old man wonders why she needs one. He responds: 'Why? You want to go to a wedding?' Three times during three different scenes, the old woman reminds her husband to ask for sugar and tea from the man who usually brings them food from the city. Each time the old man says that he has forgotten to ask him. Consequently, every time we see the old man meeting the man from the city, we expect him to remember his wife's request but he forgets again and instead asks about the weather and the tracks. Also, the scene of the old man winding his clock seems to be ridiculous in a place where time does not mean anything. At the beginning of the film, after we see the old man blocking and unblocking the crossroad in the deserted area, we see a cattle of sheep crossing the railroad. The juxtaposition of the shots implies that he did it for them. It takes a very long time, almost two-thirds into the film, before we see a car approaching. Within the sad ending of the final sequence of the film, there are also moments of childish humour. When the young substitute comes to claim his office and house, the old man ignores him stubbornly by locking his office and later his house too, knowing that it is a desperate and useless attempt to save his job.

A significant aspect of *Still Life* is the use of setting and landscape. The deserted switchman's room next to the railroad and the impoverished architecture and desolate appearance of the house, its humble interior as well as the bare trees around it, all echo the isolation of the old man and his relationship to the rest of the world – off-screen society that is signaled only via the sound of the trains.

The similar use of location as foreground is noticeable in later masterworks of Iranian cinema, especially in the films of Kiarostami, Bayza'i, Naderi and some others. The beautiful forests and remote towns of northern Iran close to the Caspian Sea are used in many films as an important part of the drama. The war-stricken desert town of Bashu, the main character of

Bayza'i's *Bashu Gharibey Kuchak* (*Bashu, the Little Stranger*, 1985) is compared to the unfamiliar dormant and mysterious nature of a village in the north, to show the difference between the world of the boy and other characters. In Kiarostami's *Khaneh-ye Dust Kojast?* (*Where is the Friend's House?*, 1986), the maze-like pathways and narrow alleys of the remote northern rural areas are used to measure and reveal the dedication and commitment of the young boy to his friend. The landscapes of desolate desert scenes and the carcasses of animals in Naderi's *Water, Wind, Dust* show the loveless, cruel world of the boy and his desperate struggle to survive. And the images of the vanishing older parts of Tehran appear in films such as Majid Majidi's *Bachehaye Aseman* (*The Children of Heaven*, 1998) to portray the values and lost loving world of childhood. The locations of these films define and reflect the main characters' sense of the loss or threat of identity.

Many filmmakers followed in the footsteps of Saless, especially after the Revolution. They have made films that blur the line between documentary and narrative cinema, set in the rural areas of Iran, focusing on the deprived poor and old people and their daily routines, which were eventually broken by single incidents. Kiarostami's humorous and profound *Where is the Friend's House?*, Naderi's metaphoric saga, *Water, Wind, Dust*, Abolfazl Jalili's visual anthropology *Raghse Khak* (*Dances of Dust*, 1998) and Babak Payami's *Yek Rooz Bishtar* (*One More Day*, 2000) all display Saless's marked influence in this respect.

Critics have compared Saless to Robert Bresson for the economy of his language and the suppression of acting. When Bresson focuses on a still shot on his hero's face in the opening scene of *Pickpocket* (1959), a blink of his eye turns into a revealing action. Similarly, when Saless focuses on his old woman character in *Still Life* as she is trying to thread her needle to fix her son's jacket, nothing happens for a long time. But when finally she succeeds, this simple action turns into a significant moment. This scene that takes approximately five minutes is intercut with the shot of her son laying down on the bed and then with shots of the old man entering the room, exchanging a couple of lines with his wife, and then rolling his cigarette in silence. When she manages to pass the thread through the needle the old man also completes the rolling of his cigarettes and lights it. That is the only sound we hear throughout the scene. Mohsen Makhmalbaf has quoted the famous long scene of the threading of the needle by the old woman in *Still Life* in his own film, *Naseredin Shah Actor e Cinema* (*Once Upon a Time, Cinema* 1992). In this film the king character invites the public of Tehran to watch the screening of *Dokhta-e Lor* (*Lor Girl*, 1932), the first Iranian talkie, made by Ardeshir Irani and Abdolhossein Sepanta in Bombay, India. We only see parts of *A Lor Girl* created by Makhmalbaf as the king's dream.

The real movie on the screen which has put all the wives of the king to sleep and made the public angry is the scene of the old woman threading the needle in *Still Life*. After watching the old woman having difficulty doing the job for a while, the frustrated king orders his jester to help her. Thanks to the magic of cinema and special effects, the jester enters the screen, gets the needle from the old woman and walks outside the frame where he can stand on the side of the screen. The audience applauds. But we see that he too has a hard time threading the needle. It is interesting to note that when *Still Life* was screened at the Tehran International Film Festival as well as its subsequent public screening in Tehran in 1974, the audience also applauded at the end of the threading scene when the old woman finally manages to pass the thread through the needle.

Makhmalbaf has publicly stated that all Iranian filmmakers, including himself who, after the Revolution, are enjoying their success at international film festivals, owe this to Saless since it was he who had 'corrected' their views of cinema. Makhmalbaf believes that Saless brought cinema closer to the reality of people's lives in Iran. That is why he has called Saless the father of realism in Iranian cinema. Indeed he was so eager to have a retrospective of Saless's films at the Locarno International Film Festival in 1988 that he had planned to invite Saless to Locarno to pay homage to him. Sadly, a few days before he launched his plan, Saless died in Chicago.

Mehrnaz Saeed-Vafa

REFERENCE

Muller, Olof (2004) 'Olof's World: Sohrab Shahid Saless', *Film Comment*, 40, 4, 12–13.

TRAVERSÉES CROSSING OVER

MAHMOUD BEN MAHMOUD, TUNISIA/BELGIUM, 1982

Born in Tunis in 1947, Mahmoud Ben Mahmoud belongs to the generation that has dominated Maghrebi cinema. A group of – largely male – filmmakers, they have shared many of the same experiences, including a childhood under colonialism, followed by the heady excitement of independence. Like most of his contemporaries, Ben Mahmoud studied abroad for several years in the 1960s; a time of change in student politics and a golden age of European filmmaking. He spent three years (1967–70) at the Belgian film school, INSAS (Institut National des Arts du Spectacle et Techniques de Diffusion), followed by a further three years at the Free University of Brussels (where he took diplomas in art history and archaeology, and in journalism and social communication). While completing his studies, he collaborated on the scripts of the first feature films of two fellow INSAS graduates, Jean-Jacques Andrien's *Le Fils d'Amr est mort* (*Amr's Son is Dead*, 1972) and Lebanese documentarist Borhan Alawiya's *Kafr Kassem* (1974). He later worked on the scripts of Alawiya's *L'Émir* (*The Emir*, 1975) and Philippe Lejuste's *L'Odeur angulaire* (*The Angular Scent*, 1975), just as Lejuste was to contribute to the scripting of his first feature. Ben Mahmoud is now a permanent resident of Belgium.

As might be expected, the image of Europe that emerges from the films of Ben Mahmoud's generation is a complex one. One of the few direct representations of emigrant life is the Tunisian film *Les Ambassadeurs* (*The Ambassadors*, 1975), made by the Paris Film School graduate, Naceur Ktari. It deals with the problems faced by challenging racism and is a forceful and committed study of the lives of emigrant workers in France. Equally impressive is Algerian Ahmed Rachedi's *Ali au pays des mirages* (*Ali in Wonderland*, 1979), in which the protagonist works as a crane operator. From high up on his perch, he is philosophical about the world, but when he tries to intervene on the ground the results are disastrous. Aside of these films, Europe is largely depicted as an unattainable Other. Ben Mahmoud's fellow INSAS graduate, the Moroccan Ahmed el-Maânouni, set the pattern with his first feature, *O les jours* (*The Days, The Days*, 1978), at the centre of which is a young peasant who wishes to emigrate. But al-Maânouni's perceptive and realistic look at everyday life in a Moroccan village reveals that Europe can ultimately be no more than a dream. *Le Grand voyage* (*The Big Trip*, 1981), the first film of another Moroccan director, Mohamed Abderrahman Tazi, also offers precise insights into contemporary Moroccan society. It utilises the classic motif of the journey; in this case the trip is that undertaken by a lorry-driver, Omar, who travels from the south of the country to Casablanca. Along the way, Omar is cheated and robbed. He decides to emigrate, but realises too late – when he is already at sea – that he has been cheated and will never see land again. Tazi's third feature, *A la recherche du mari de ma femme* (*Looking For My Wife's Husband*, 1993), is a rare Maghrebi comedy, which enjoyed great popularity in Morocco. However, the mood of the film darkens towards the end, with the polygamous husband last seen trying desperately to reach Belgium as an illegal immigrant. Perhaps the most poignant of Moroccan film narratives is Jillali Ferhati's *Chevaux de fortune* (*Make-Believe Horses*, 1995), in which the two protagonists struggle throughout the film to find a way of emigrating, only to die attempting the narrow crossing from Tangier in a seaside pedal boat. Ferhati creates a suffocating world, reminiscent in some ways of French 1930s poetic realism: the enigmatic blind man, rain-swept darkened streets, characters whose dreams are blocked, escape which is in sight but always just beyond reach. The ending, inevitably, is death.

Two Tunisian films offer further perceptive insights into the notion of emigration. Perhaps the most pessimistic view of exile is to be found in Taïeb Louhichi's *L'Ombre de la terre* (*The Shadow of the Earth*, 1982), the tale of an isolated rural family community – a patriarchal father with his sons and nephews and their families – whose life is slowly torn apart by natural forces and the impact of the modern world. As natural disasters increase pressure on the group, the young men leave for exile or are conscripted. The film is an elegy for the passing of a traditional way of life, but the emigration of the young is seen to offer no solution. The film ends with the frozen image of the coffin in which the body of a young man who has chosen emigration is returned to his family. Amongst these films, Ben Mahmoud's *Traversées* (*Crossing Over*, 1982) is arguably the most sophisticated and universally relevant Maghrebi parable about emigration, exile, borders and bureaucracy.

For this first feature – mostly shot in English, the only language shared by the diverse range of characters – Ben Mahmoud surrounded himself with a crew that included three major Tunisian film directors. Selma Baccar, one of the film's executive producers, was the first woman to direct a Tunisian feature, *Fatma 75* (1978). Moufida Tlatli, the film's editor, later directed the most celebrated of all films made by a Maghrebi woman, *Les Silences du palais* (*Silences of the Palace*, 1994). The lead actor, Fadhel Jaziri, who also worked on the script, is the co-director of two of the most striking experimental features in Tunisian film history, *La Noce* (*The Wedding*,

1978) and *Arab* (1988); both with Fadhel Jaïbi, his collaborator in the New Theatre of Tunis Collective, which they set up together in 1976.

Crossing Over was based, it seems, on the director's personal experience, when he was sent back from Dover (UK) to Ostend (Belgium) (although he was later allowed ashore to renew his expired visa). His two protagonists are not so lucky; they are permanently trapped on a similar cross-channel ferry. The film begins on 31 December 1980 and plots the parallel fates of the two travellers; Bogdan, a working-class Slav economic migrant and Youssef, an Arab middle-class intellectual trying to reach London. Both are refused permission to land at Dover because the authorities claim they lack the necessary documents. They are sent back to Ostend, but by the time they reach there, it is 1 January 1981, a new year has begun, and their visas have expired. Unable to disembark, they are trapped in a bureaucratic purgatory worthy of Kafka.

The film opens in documentary style, as the ferry arrives from Ostend: footage of queues, passports being stamped, arrivals and departures. Everything is detailed, from the time and date that the events take place to the locations – the ferry and the customs area at Dover. When we first see the pair, who have not passed through customs, they are framed by a mob of British policemen, incongruously gathered – we later discover – for a group photograph. The different temperament and attitude of the two unnamed protagonists is already apparent. Bogdan, en route – he claims – to Canada, always endeavours to make contact, constantly trying to explain, begging a cigarette, shouting at those around him. Youssef, by contrast, maintains a haughty silence. Though the film was not intended (Ben Mahmoud tells us) as a denunciation of European peoples or institutions, the British customs officers are shown as brutal and unsympathetic. At the interrogation, Youssef is humiliated, verbally abused and made to strip. To show this humiliation without any compromise was important to Ben Mahmoud, since he admitted that he has experienced various humiliations because of his Arab identity.

But Youssef does not help himself by the answers he gives when questioned. Asked what he was doing in Germany, he replies he was just passing through, on his way to somewhere else, and adding that he cannot remember where that was. Why has he come to the UK? To enjoy himself, for fun, to continue with his research. Asked to be more specific, he becomes sarcastic, defining his research interests as scientific: 'occult sciences, sorcery, the black mass, vampirism and psychoanalysis'. It is as if he is trying to ensure that his application for entry into the country will be questioned. Bogdan claims – more plausibly – that he is avoiding military service at home, visiting an aunt who will give him money in London and will then be on his way to Canada, where he claims to have a girlfriend. The interrogators explain that, of course, they do not want to be nasty, but both applications for entry are turned down. We never learn of Youssef's true motives for travelling. He is certainly not an economic migrant and there is no evidence that he is a political refugee fleeing a physical threat in an unnamed Arab country. The film is intended to be less about socially-motivated emigration than about migration in general.

The interrogation is intense and often aggressive, but we learn very little about the two protagonists, not even their precise nationality. They are just a man from somewhere in Eastern Europe and an Arab from an unnamed Muslim state. There are later hints that Bogdan is Polish, as there are several references to political developments in Poland (a magazine cover reveals that Lech Waleska is *Time* magazine's man of the year and a news report on Poland is the last broadcast Bogdan listens too). But nothing is certain and we have no way of judging Bogdan's various stories: that he has an aunt in London and a girlfriend in Canada, for example, or just how he made his escape from Eastern Europe. He may be a communist or a political dissident. From Youssef's interrogation, we learn even less about him (he is never named in the film). He seems to have travelled widely in Europe – he arrives from Belgium and the police question him about visits to Germany and Czechoslovakia – but we never learn his motive for so many journeys. He has money and good clothes, but no apparent occupation and we hear nothing about his family background. This refusal to give basic knowledge about the characters is the film's first step away from its documentary beginning and towards a more oblique ending.

After the interrogation, the pair are sent back to spend the night on the ferry, prior to deportation. Because it is New Year, the atmosphere is very different. Everyone is in a party mood, including the two policemen sent to ensure their deportation, who accept the offer of a drink even though they are on duty. Bogdan, as always, is the more outgoing, savouring the food and drink he is offered and joining in the dancing. Youssef, by contrast, remains aloof. He ignores Bogdan's question about the languages he speaks (English, Italian, Russian, Chinese?) and complains at being ordered to enjoy himself. Neither here nor at any other point in the film does anyone refer directly to Youssef as an Arab or address him in his own language. He himself uses only English and French.

At dawn, a new voyage begins and during it Youssef mellows for the first time, offering Bogdan money. But they are isolated on board as they return to Ostend and their experience at customs, which mirrors that of Dover, is filmed like a mime show, accompanied by Francesco Accolia's expressive music. Bogdan takes on the active role, trying to integrate by working as a dishwasher on the ferry, earning a bottle of vodka which he shares with Youssef. At this point, he is keen not to let himself go, to retain his appearance and self-respect. He tells his story to two black travellers also temporarily trapped on board, talking about his escape to Vienna in a refrigerator lorry at the cost of a month's wages, but no one is really interested in him or in the photographs he shows of his personal life. These images are also kept from the audience.

Then, in Ostend, Youssef discovers a possible way of escape – the quay side is not guarded. They go ashore 'for a breath of fresh air' and find a bar where they have what starts as a 'normal' evening: a few drinks and a game of bar billiards. But their encounter with Vera, another transient, who sings a sad gypsy song, leads to a violent confrontation with a gang of local youths. The pair, acting in coordination for once, manage to save Vera from her assailants and make their escape. But Youssef, who is scared and does not want to live the life of a fugitive, realises that their dream of escape is over and the repeated musical motif heralds his sad return to the ferry. Bogdan stays behind to go in pursuit of the girl, but finds only her belongings on the pavement – the gang have clearly caught up with her. There is nothing for him to do but look out over the harbour. Throughout the film – from the time he was first stopped – he has challenged the police to arrest him. Now the Belgian police oblige by taking him into custody for a beating and then returning him to the ferry. Here, for the first time, the pair are openly confronted by bystanders as a threat: 'You've no place here. Arabs and communists are the nightmare of people here.'

The boat sets off again for England, with Bogdan tending the wounds he has received at the hands of the Belgian police, whom he refers to as fascists. Unable to accept his loss of freedom he breaks down, desperate to escape this nightmare while also vowing to take revenge. Youssef remains silent and aloof. For him there are no explanations to be made, no accounts to be settled. He has, he admits, no idea how they can get out of their predicament, but claims that, as far as he is concerned, the problem has been put behind him. Certainly, real solidarity with his fellow victim is not an option. Instead of helping Bogdan, he turns on him and accuses him of missing his chance in life, the possibility of helping in the overthrow of Communism. By abandoning everything, Youssef argues, Bogdan lost his chance of becoming a martyr, his chance of power. Though he does not seem to realise it, Youssef's words apply as much to himself as to Bogdan: 'You need roots, somewhere you can call home. It's not a country, it's an idea, an identity, a cause, a territory. It all comes back to territory. There are no countries, there is no land, either promised or to be conquered or recovered, there are only floating masses like this damn boat.' And, addressing Bogdan by name for the only time in the film, he proclaims that they do not belong to the same world.

Now, as they approach the English coast again, the sea is blood red. When the boat docks, Bogdan resumes his work in the kitchen, but the action is suddenly and unexpectedly cut off by a freeze-frame and a cut to a confused scene on the deck where Youssef is being questioned. Someone nearby mentions a murder. We return to Bogdan's preparation for his act of vengeance – the killing of a policeman guarding the quay side – which is intercut with the simultaneous (and unconnected) actions of the crew: eating, going ashore for a drink and so on. In what is initially a confusing shift for the audience, synchronisation with the image is lost, as we hear – in voice-over – a police inspector's questions and the crew's answers about the events of that evening. This is followed by the killing and Bogdan's scream of rage fuses with the sound of a foghorn. Clearly, Ben Mahmoud's aim is to indicate the futility of Bogdan's action – an absurd act of existential violence like the murder of the Arab in Albert Camus' novel *L'Etranger* (*The Outsider*). However, it is questionable whether we need to see the build-up to the act in this complex way, as its futility is already clearly indicated (Bogdan makes no attempt to run away or to save himself).

The stylistic shift does serve to mark a transition in the film's focus, however. Now we are concerned solely with Youssef. Initially, nothing seems to have changed. He is typically non-committal when questioned about a shirt he had given to Bogdan, merely 'supposing' that the signs on it are Arabic. He also scornfully rejects the advice of the Purser to contact people in Belgium or contact his ambassador. This only reminds him of the humiliations he has endured (particularly the initial strip search). He has now withdrawn completely into himself: 'I'm dead now and you can do nothing.' Instead of taking practical steps, he composes – in one of the film's most remarkable sequences – a letter 'To Our Ambassador Abroad' (again, nationality is not specified):

'We have left the earth and got on board. Behind us, they've smashed the deck. Or better, they've smashed the earth. And now little boat, pay attention. The ocean is beside you. It's true it doesn't always roar. Its sheet sometimes spreads, like silk and gold. A dream of happiness. But hours will come when you will see that nothing is more terrible than infinity. Poor bird who felt free and who hits against the bars of your cage. Woe to you who are seized by the ache of the land of the earth. As if there were more freedom there! There is no more land'.

It is a striking moment, since it is the first time in the film we have heard him speak Arabic (though only in voice-over). The imagery is equally distinctive, with shots of the ferry, the crew and Youssef writing. It is accompanied by the chanting, in Algerian dialect, of a verse from the Koran, mixed with modern American rock music.

In a sequence reminiscent of Bogdan preparing himself for the killing of the policeman, Youssef exercises on deck, cleans his teeth and showers. The next morning, the sound of the foghorn as the ferry leaves marks the entry into yet another new world. But Youssef does not kill. Instead he picks up one of the new passengers and makes love to her. The lovemaking in one of the ship's storerooms begins naturalistically, though they do not exchange names. But Youssef's second speech in Arabic (heard over a close-up of his face) – 'Down here I've loved only three things: perfume, women and prayer' – leads to a sequence of scenes of the couple on the deck. There, as they are increasingly shrouded in mist, the initial banalities of a couple who have just made love become a final incantation by the woman, which echoes and answers (in English) Youssef's letter to the imaginary ambassador:

'Your lifeline, it's as if it were a line of flight, an escape route. I see a journey, a long, long journey. There are still seas and oceans that you have to cross. The land is behind us now, we're surrounded by the sea. Its roar may be stilled, its surface shimmer silk and gold, a dream of happiness. But there will be times to remember that there is nothing more terrible than the infinite'.

As Christian Bosséno notes, at this stage of the film the woman is a symbolic place, a mystical being who liberates the character from exterior and objective necessities, a place of rest.

Crossing Over is a remarkably assured first feature, with confident direction of the actors, impressive camera work and a frequently striking and subtle use of soundtrack. Most critics commended its exploration of exile and loss, and its probing questioning of language and identity. Its view of human existence is extremely pessimistic; the outside world is hostile and no solidarity or real sharing is possible between the two men. While Youssef is not a typically downtrodden migrant, his example gives no real hope of an affirmed and assertable Arab identity. Bogdan's resorting to violence is answered not by positive commitment but by a retreat into a private world, as the film completes its shift from documentary realism to myth and legend. In making this shift, the film is typical of much of the best Tunisian filmmaking of the 1980s; a time in which the previous decade's social and political concerns were replaced by a variety of explorations of personal and interior, often autobiographical, worlds.

Following *Crossing Over*, Ben Mahmoud has gone on to make two further features, the dark melodrama *Chichkhan* (*Poussière de diamants*, 1992), co-written and co-directed with Fadhel Jaïbi, and *Les Siestes grenadine* (*The Pomegranate Siesta*, 1999), a study of lives and relationships spanning the Sahara. He has also directed a considerable number of video documentaries, including one on the Tunisian film pioneer Albert Samama Chikli, and a trio produced by Hassan Daldoul (on a Tsarist immigrée, the role of Italians in Tunisia and Islamic music), described by Hédi Khelil as works of far-reaching importance for future generations. But *Crossing Over* remains Ben Mahmoud's best-known film and is highly regarded by Tunisian filmmakers and critics alike as one of the most significant Maghrebi, and indeed Arab, films. The producer Hassan Daldoul has described *Crossing Over* as one of the founding films of Tunisian cinema, and as one of the half dozen or so Tunisian films he would most want his own children to see. Filmmaker and critic Ferid Boughedir is one of many who noted its combination of technical mastery and visual beauty, and Tahar Chikhaoui describes Ben Mahmoud as one of the great Arab filmmakers of the 1980s, while for Hassouna Mansouri, *Crossing Over* is the crucial work which first stimulated her to write her book on African film identity. With its mixture of precisely observed images of reality and sensitively achieved formal abstraction, *Crossing Over* is still, 25 years after its making, one of the most striking and original of all Tunisian feature films.

Roy Armes

REFERENCES

Bosséno, Christian (1983a) 'Le Cinéma tunisien', *La Revue du Cinéma*, 383, 49–62.

_____ (ed.) (1983b) 'Cinémas de l'émigration 3', *CinémAction*, 24, 60–80.

Chikhaoui, Tahar (1998) 'Le Cinéma tunisien de la maladroite euphorie au juste désarroi', in Abdelmajid Cherfi *et al.* (eds) *Aspects de la civilisation tunisienne*. Tunis: Faculté de Lettres de Manouba, 5–33.

Khelil, Hédi (2002) *Le Parcours et la trace: Témoignages et documents sur le cinéma tunisien*. Tunis: MediaCom.

Mansouri, Hassouna (2000) *De l'identité, ou Pour une certaine tendance du cinéma africain*. Tunis: Éditions Sahar.

DAVANDEH THE RUNNER

AMIR NADERI, IRAN, 1984

Among the masterpieces of Iranian cinema, few have achieved the status of Amir Naderi's *Davandeh* (*The Runner*, 1984) as a landmark event that has defined much that happened after its release. Although it exists halfway through Naderi's career, *The Runner* marked the height of a global audience's awareness of developments in Iranian cinema. Much has happened since the mid-1980s when the film took the Festival of 3 Continents by storm. Today, the names of Abbas Kiarostami, Mohsen Makhmalbaf, Jafar Panahi and Bahman Qobadi have overshadowed Naderi, who has long since moved to New York, although he continues a productive cinematic career (with considerable global success). Whether or not he can even be considered an 'Iranian filmmaker' today is subject to debate.

Naderi's most celebrated film, *The Runner* is in many ways autobiographical and it is this factor that became a critical component of what has now flourished in Iranian cinema at large. When Naderi was six years old, he says that he was accidentally stranded on a ship and taken to a foreign land, although to this day he does not know where. The story of this mysterious voyage, indelibly carved in Naderi's childhood memories, is very simple. His aunt and uncle adopted him following the death of his mother. Each day, he would take lunch to his uncle, who was a painter on a ship in Abadan. Young Amir was assigned to bring lunch to this uncle every day. Afterwards, Amir would roam through the ship and play on its various decks. One day he made his way to the engine room, where he fell asleep on some potato sacks. Soon after he fell asleep, the ship pulled anchor and left port, carrying six-year-old Amir to its next destination. He woke up frightened and was soon discovered by the crew. He was kept on board for about ten days during which time he remembers only the sea. At their next destination, Amir remembered seeing a traffic cop with white gloves, controlling traffic on some street off the sea front, where the ship had come ashore. The ship then returned to Abadan and Amir returned to his aunt, now obviously terrified as to what could have become of him. Amir's Aunt later told him that for six months he was not able to speak a word after that incident, and the first thing that he said after he started talking again was that he wanted to leave on a ship for some faraway land.

What happened to Amir Naderi during this strange, ambiguous, outlandish journey? He speaks of it in realistic terms, like another biographical detail of his life. But did it really happen, or did he dream it? (All indications suggest that it did really happen.) He also tells of how, when he was eleven years old, he tried to run away to Kuwait. However, he did not make it beyond a couple of islands off the coast of Abadan. That there has always been a restless disposition about Naderi, and his desire to be somewhere else, is evident in almost all his films. But the story that he narrates about his accidental journey on board a cargo ship is saturated with images of a lonely child, a solitary *mosafer* (sojourner), lost on an unknown ship, leaving a familiar island for an unknown destination, of which Naderi only has a memory, seen through the small window of a cabin where he was stranded. That small window is transformed into the lens of his camera; his cinema is like watching the world from a child's point of view.

The abandoned ship in *The Runner*, on which Amiru lives, is the miasmatic memory of a ship on which Amir Naderi has always dreamt of living, departing for other destinations. In some sense, he still lives on that ship. His small apartment in downtown Manhattan has a remarkable similarity to a cabin aboard an abandoned ship. Central to this ship, the abode of both Amir and Amiru, is the solitary disposition of its whereabouts, a space removed from society, suspended in midair between his dreams and his visions as a filmmaker.

A poor orphaned boy growing up at the seashore of a nameless land, Amiru is fascinated with every moving object – huge ships, small boats, speeding cars, lazy bicycles, noisy motorcycles, rambunctious trucks, slumbering trains, flying airplanes – anything and everything that moves by itself and can carry him away from where he is. He is terrified when he sees a man with one leg, or an ageing woman, or a crippled man. They are people who cannot run away. In the absence of any access to a moving vehicle that can carry him away from where he is, he runs. He runs until he can barely breathe. After drinking a glass of iced water out of the bucket that Amiru carries around in order to make a living, a man attempts to escape on his bicycle without paying. Amiru runs after him, both to get his money and for the challenge of trying to catch him. When another man steals a piece of his ice, Amiru runs after him wrestling the ice off him. He runs back, triumphant that he has retrieved the ice from the much larger man and succeeded in returning it to the bucket before it has melted.

Running has become essential to Amiru. What is he running from? What is he running to? Nothing and everything. Running is his state of being. He becomes mesmerised by moving objects. Anything that moves can carry him away from where he is. Because he cannot gain access to these objects, he runs. He runs because of the indeterminacy of not being where he is not. There is a scene early in the film: Amiru and his friends are collecting empty bottles that foreigners have thrown into the sea, when they are suddenly attacked by a shark. A fisherman alerts the kids and they run out of the sea. Amiru is frightened out of his wits, not by the possibility that he could have been killed, but by the terror that the shark could have eaten his limbs, his claim to mobility, to running away. It is wrong to read Amiru as someone simply running away from poverty. Amiru is poor, but his life is not desolate or joyless; he has the company of a band of young, equally poor boys, with whom he plays soccer, rides bikes, chases after running trains and shares joyous songs on top of speeding wagons. His relationship with his friends is not free of quarrels. Poverty reigns supreme. But there is a serenity about Amiru, a gentility about his manners, a solidity to his friendship. While trying to run away (from nothing and everything), Amiru lives a rich and fulfilling life – rich in dimensions of his solitude that he explores, fulfilling in the company of friends he keeps. There is a scene where Amiru is washing his shirt in the abandoned ship (his home), where Naderi leads his camera to come close (ever so gently) to a diverted gaze on the face of this poor, orphaned, solitary soul. That diverted gaze on the face of Amiru is the look of humanity at a loss, facing an abyss beyond recognition. At that moment, *The Runner* is no longer the story of a lonely boy and Amiru is no longer a poor orphan. Naderi pictures humanity at a loss.

Naderi is capable of the cruellest insights. It is as if he has seen something terrorising, a nightmare perhaps, a metaphysical cruelty beyond human measure. He has seen the absurdity at the root of a solitary being that for him is the state of humanity at large. He seems to have seen a disturbing nightmare, the solitary visage of a journey, and he has mastered a way to show and tell it – ever so softly, gently even, for the vision he wishes to reveal is no source of solace.

Amiru is illiterate. He collects pictures of airplanes and hangs them on the wall of his cabin/room on the ship. He goes to a magazine seller, and buys more magazines to look at their pictures. His illiteracy bothers him so he registers his name at a school. There his teacher begins to teach him the letters of the Persian alphabet. The result is not that Amiru now learns how to read and write; conversely, the characters of the Persian alphabet are taught how to un-learn themselves. The alphabet sequence of *The Runner* is a memorable example of literacy beyond words. Sounds of water, wind, fire and dust collect momentum to syncopate Amiru's recitations of the Persian alphabet.

Naderi himself is not a very literate person. He dropped out of school early in life and has since had no formal education. To him, the letters of alphabet are strange creatures, not just Persian (as we see them in *The Runner*), but also English (which appear in *Marathon* (2003)).

To him and to his visual disposition, letters of the alphabet are strange creatures. What are these things, he seems to ask? Who are they? And who, by the way, gave them this authority to sound, seem and suggest one thing or another? Amiru takes the letters of the Persian alphabet to the seaside, into the heart of rocks and waves, and starts memorising them – there for Naderi to teach them to behave. Amiru memorises them to the beat of the waves storming the sea rocks; he memorises them to the sound of wind, water, fire and dust (the theme that Naderi will pick up in his next film, *Ab, Bad, Khak* (*Water, Wind, Dust*, 1989)). In the alphabet sequence of *The Runner*, humanity is reduced to literacy, literacy to words, words to letters, letters to alphabets, alphabets to sounds, sounds to noises, and these noises given back to the earth. What Abbas Kiarostami would later do in his mature cinema by way of his ingenious fictive transparency of the real, Amir Naderi had already achieved in *The Runner* through his trademark visual realism.

In the final memorable sequence of *The Runner* Amiru and his buddies have made yet another wager as to who runs faster. A huge block of ice is placed near a roaring fire; the object of the wager is to be the first to get to that block of ice before it melts. What do people see when they see this block of ice near that fire? A universe. Those two items are insignia of a universe – ice the soul of salvation from the ungodly heat of summer, placed next to a fire whose raging flames exude an elemental violence at once life-affirming and deadly. The visual contrast of the block of ice and the raging fire command the camera's undivided attention. Again, collected here are fire, wind, water and earth, and racing towards them boys running from a fate they cannot articulate; a useless flight, and yet made meaningful temporarily, by virtue of the significance it has occasioned – and it will soon lose, as soon as the game is over.

In this elemental space, history no longer has much of a claim over reality; reality has become evidence *sui generis*. Naderi is a master of crafting these moments – where all signs of historicity vanish. These are metaphysical moments, where Naderi has brought the humanity at large for a quick look, a cursory visit. We are no longer in Iran, or Asia, or Africa, or Planet Earth, or anywhere in that vicinity. Here we have entered the miasmatic zone of what medieval Persian philosophers would call *sarmad* – 'the everlasting'. Time is suspended here, space morphed into a cinematic site of visual contemplation. There is no sign of society – solitude is writ large. We are inside Amir Naderi's creative intelligence. All signifiers have metamorphosed into their originary signs.

The marathon begins and Amiru and his friends race towards the melting ice. On the way, between the origin of that match and its destination, a brutal banality becomes evident. If you cannot get there, then you must also prevent others from succeeding. In that match, Naderi has discovered and displayed a barbarity of unsurpassed terror in the very heart of our innocence. Amiru and his friends sabotage each other's progress, blocking each other's way, as they run towards the fire. In no other Iranian film has a banality of such disturbing proportion been so vividly and honestly captured. The kids do everything to be the first to get to the ice, or at the very least prevent anyone else from getting there. Amiru gets there, against all odds, against all that was meant to prevent him. He gets to the ice by the fire, reaches for the barrel on which the piece of ice is (was) placed. He begins a triumphant, joyous, jubilant beat of victory on the barrel/drum. He is calling out, 'Barandeh shodom' – 'I won'. Beating on the drum, on the melted ice, rhythmically, splashing the water, he is ecstatic with joy. He picks up the last remaining piece of ice, lifts it above his head and begins a triumphant dance, dancing to the rhythm and tune of his own victory. He brings the piece of ice to his lips, drinking his victory, juice of his exultant defeat of the fire. Reality finally creeps in and Amiru comes to his senses. He turns around, looks at his fallen friends, his comrades-turned-rivals. They beg for a drop of water; they are passing out from thirst, at the vicinity of the brutal fire. Amiru holds out the piece of ice. It is no longer a trophy. The moment of myth has passed. The first boy immediately behind Amiru drinks from the ice, then passes it on. Boys unite in the last drop of life that the melting ice can give. Life is restored. Amiru is victorious.

At the moment of his triumph Amiru is the picture of solitude. No one is there to share his victory, his joy, his accomplishment. Naderi's is a cinema of solitude – solitude as the aesthetic articulation of social alienation and cultural anomie. And yet this sense of anomie is not ailing or fraught. It is predicated on an enabling solitude, pregnant with all of its own opposites. As an artistic space, Naderi's cinema is the site of a creative transformation of alienation and anomie, for cinema is where society comes together in solitude – we watch films in the company of strangers, in the social presence of all our singular solitudes. The result is a creative entry into the social function of solitude, constitutional to a creative space that is no longer culture-specific, that it smells and looks local, and yet it is global by virtue of the creative space it has cultivated in solitude, in a socially significant, communally enabling and emotively charged solitude.

The solitude definitive to Amiru's character extends beyond *The Runner* and runs through the rest of Naderi's cinema. He undertook his haphazard apprenticeship in cinema in the 1950s and 1960s, first in southern Iran and then in Tehran, where he was exposed to the best of world cinema at the capital of a thriving cosmopolitan culture. Almost all of the eleven feature films that Naderi directed between 1970 and 1986 while he was in Iran deal with a solitary figure at the centre of their narrative. All such solitary characters, in one way or another, are narrative translations of his own life, orphaned at a very young age, and raised by a maternal aunt until he was old enough to leave home for good. Most of the menial work that Amiru does in *The Runner* to make a living – selling iced water, shining shoes, collecting bottles from the sea – are jobs that Naderi himself had as a boy. His first cinema-related job was as a still photographer on film sets of the most important filmmakers of his time. There he listened, watched and learned the minutest aspects of the craft of filmmaking. In the pictures he took, he looked for more than just a proper angle and a matching light on an actor or a scene. He framed the forms of reality the way he envisioned them in his own mind. Still photography, snapshots of what there was to see, and solitary visions of reality became definitive to his cinema.

A sense of overwhelming solitude was already evident in Naderi's earliest films. In *Tangna* (*Deadlock*, 1973) we meet Ali Khoshdast, a solitary soul roaming through the slums of Tehran, engaged in petty crimes, a victim of his own delusions, the very fabric of his being imbued with loneliness and a sense of anomie. Tehran as a cosmopolis emerges in its full urban landscape as the background to Ali Khoshdast's soaring solitude. The same Ali Khoshdast resurfaces in Naderi's next film, *Tangsir* (1973), where we follow the legendary life of Zar Mammad, a local hero who singlehandedly rebels against tyranny and kills the officials who have been torment-ing him. Zar Mammad is the split image of Ali Khoshdast, transformed into a more compelling political figure, both seen through the childhood memories of a solitary filmmaker. In *Saz Dahani* (*Harmonica*, 1974), it is as if we go back to the neighbourhood of Zar Mammad or Ali Khoshdast's childhood, where we witness the fixation of a young boy on a harmonica that a tyr-annous friend has somehow acquired and with it rules mercilessly over his covetous playmates. That *Harmonica* soon mutated into the political allegory of a monarchy is almost inciden-tal to Naderi's preoccupation with solitude. In *Entezar* (*Waiting*, 1975) Amir Naderi's solitary boy enters adolescence and we are witness to his inarticulate sexual fantasies, fixated on the extended hand of a young woman who offers him a bowl of iced water. In *Marsiyeh* (*Requiem*, 1978) it is as if this young man has grown up, committed a petty crime like Ali Khoshdast did, gone to prison and now comes out as Nasrollah, again a lonesome and solitary soul, roam-ing through the streets of Tehran trying to make a meagre living against the rambunctious and indifferent background of a cruel and calamitous urban landscape. Thus when we get to *The Runner*, the solitary figure of Amiru needs no introduction. We have known him as Ali Khoshdast, or as Zar Mammad, or as Nasrollah. Although the backdrop has changed with each film, he remains the same solitary figure preoccupied with life and the mysteries of growing up in the miasmatic company of a soulless society. In *Water, Wind, Dust* we see the same Amiru in the heart of a heartless desert, looking for the inhabitants of a long since forsaken village – just like Amir Naderi himself, lost in the wilderness of a mercilessly vast and boundless wonder.

Naderi brought his solitude with him when he moved to New York and began the second cycle of his cinematic career. In *Manhattan by Numbers* (1992) we meet George Murphy, a laid-off journalist with only 24 hours to come up with the back rent he owes his landlord or face eviction. Murphy's journey through Manhattan in search of someone to lend him the money is identical with the journey of all Naderi's other characters through the slums of Tehran, the land-scape of southern Iran or the desert of its heartland. The same is true of *A, B, C, ... Manhattan* (1997). This time the story of three solitary souls, three young women – Colleen, Kacey and Kate – with three autonomous but interrelated life stories, is at once simple and singular and yet full of the inner violence of a cosmopolis they share as their home. The failed marriage of Colleen, the bisexual wonderings of Kacey and the incestuous relationship of Kate with her brother are examples of what happens to these solitary souls when they dare the elements and find a partner in life. The same holds true for Gretchen in *Marathon*: a young woman obsessed with solving daily puzzles of newspapers, roaming through New York subway cars and stations and setting for herself one insane and obsessive goal after another, her only connection to the rest of the world being the answering machine of her home telephone on which her distant mother keeps leaving unreturned messages. The solitary disposition of Naderi's cinema finally comes to a crescendo in his most recent film, *Sound Barrier* (2005), at the centre of which is Jessie, a dumb, deaf and mute young boy in search of the mystery of his predicament in a audio-tape that his deceased mother has left with some talk-show radio station.

From the facts of his own life, Amir Naderi has cultivated a cinematic sense of solitude as the creative space where the society on whose sidelines he lives is seen more proportionately to both its cruel and caring compositions. In his small apartment in downtown Manhattan, which, as mentioned above, has an uncanny similarity to a cabin aboard an abandoned ship, dwells a filmmaker questioning the moral and normative whereabouts of an unruly universe he cannot but call home. A space at once removed from society and yet embraced by it, suspended in midair somewhere between his lifelong dreams and his recurring visions as a filmmaker, Naderi's cinema is solitary but not hermetic, wondering but not asocial, monadic but never nomadic. He is invested, morally and ethically, aesthetically and even politically, though in a *long durée* too long to cut, too short to remember. He knew Tehran like the palm of his hand, as he does New York, and yet he walks through their streets and alleys, parks and slums, as if every single scene he sees is a singular shot in a film that will make the world wonder at its own strangeness – all seen and suggested from the self-assured solace of a solitary but ultimately caring filmmaker.

Hamid Dabashi

LO SAM ZAYIN I DON'T GIVE A DAMN

SHMUEL IMBERMAN, ISRAEL, 1987

Lo Sam Zayin (*I Don't Give a Damn*, 1987) is an excellent example of Israeli war cinema where young men are instructed to commit their body to injury and death and in fact abandon it in the name of the belief in the, as it were, sacred idea of the nation-state. While there may be several more recent Israeli films, features as well as documentaries, that might represent Israeli national cinema differently and more forcefully, this film perfectly explores the national malaise of militarism.

In early Israeli war films, such as *Giv'a 24 Lo Ona* (*Hill 24 Doesn't Answer*, 1954) or *Amud Ha'esh* (*The Pillar of Fire*, 1959), wounds are seldom displayed on screen. When a combatant is killed or wounded, his disfigured body rarely appears in close-up. When the shelling begins in *The Pillar of Fire*, for example, we hear an explosion and then see a shaving kit landing on the rubble. A moment before, a young combatant was shaving outdoors, but when the shaving kit falls on the rubble it tells a story that we do not see – that the soldier's body was shattered by a direct hit. In such films, when soldiers are killed, their bodies either remain intact or are not shown. The slaughterhouse imagery, characteristic of the twentieth-century battlefields, has been sanitised. In later and more complex films, the camerawork itself camouflages the shattering of male bodies, caused by the impact of highspeed objects or the blast of an immense shockwave.

The post-1967 Six Day War film *Kol Mamzer Melekh* (*Every Bastard a King*, 1968) includes a striking sequence of desert combat between Egyptian and Israeli armoured divisions, where hundreds of tanks participate. Exemplary in the way it obliterates the combat wound, the film manifests a *tour de force* of machine/body/cinema-frame choreography that suspends all judgement, facilitates the instability of dimensions, and distances the spectator from the inevitable outcome of combat: bodies of young men wounded, mutilated and disfigured. The cinema falsifies the appearance of war by creating what Paul Virilio calls a *langue inconnue*, an unknown language in which 'traffic between persons (subjects) and bodies and machines becomes visible [in the wound] as a type of communication'. *Every Bastard a King* demonstrates this concept of 'wound as communication' when, after a combat sequence, two fatally injured soldiers of the two fighting sides fall on top of one another, their bodies intertwine and their unseen wounds communicate their death.

Such Israeli war films as *I Don't Give a Damn*, *Za'am Ve Te'ila* (*Rage and Glory*, 1985), *Be'tzilo Shel Helem Krav* (*Shell Shock*, 1988), *Resisism* (*Burning Memory*, 1989), *Ekhad Mi'shelanu* (*One of Us*, 1989), *Onat Ha'Duvdevanim* (*Time for Cherries*, 1991) and *Kippur* (2000) present more than a fleeting view of destroyed male bodies. These films sometimes employ a narrative trajectory in which a male figure forms a connection with the female figure by imitating and identifying with 'The Big Wound'. For Kaja Silverman, the battlefield wound reminds men of an imaginary site of castration, because men see the woman's body as wounded in the place where the penis is, so to speak, absent. Conversely, however, the combat wound in films – the bursting open of the male body – imitates the opening of the female body in childbirth. The birth of a child is associated with profuse bleeding, exposed flesh and a blood-covered mass that emerges from an opening in the female body; childbirth has imprinted upon male collective consciousness as the ultimate female experience. In pre-modern societies, women's lives too often ended in childbirth. The relationship between childbirth, danger and death is replicated in male experience when a male combatant, lying wounded on the battleground, covered with blood, sometimes eviscerated, moans in anguish like a woman in labour. The image of a male body injured by the explosion of a hand grenade, a shell, a bomb or a burst of machine-gun bullets resembles the image of a woman in childbirth. Like her body when a child is born, the massively wounded body of the combatant also articulates vulnerability and danger.

I Don't Give a Damn features a disabled war veteran in a wheelchair: an iconic image of a wounded male body, suffering what Silverman calls 'the anatomical lack' that marks women and threatens men. The film highlights this lack when the paraplegic veteran asks his girlfriend to acknowledge his wound. 'Say: You're a cripple, a poor thing, and I feel sorry for you.' She hesitates. He insists: 'Can't you say the word "cripple"?' She kneels by his wheelchair, reassuring him: 'I love you just like before.' 'I touched death', he says, 'I just barely escaped.' She responds, again reassuringly: 'I want you as you are.' He rejects reassurance. 'Do you know how it will be from here on out? Lift my legs a little. Move the right leg a little to the side. Now lie on top of me.' When she says 'it's possible' for them to marry and have children, he retorts, 'perhaps, but not with you … maybe with a woman who knows me as I am. Half dead.'

His insistence becomes hostile as the 'useless legs' motif intensifies: 'I can't stand to see your health. I can't stand to see your legs.' He starts yelling: 'Get out of my life, Nira!' And Nira whispers back: 'You're a cripple, Rafi … now I know you are a cripple', before yelling 'A cripple! A cripple! A cripple!' She stands alone in the physiotherapy hall, next to the rehabilitation instruments that will never restore Rafi to what he was. He dashes forward in his wheelchair, clashing with a drug cart, dashing all the bottles to the floor, until his chair crashes into other wheelchairs: 'Whores! They're all whores! Just fuck them and give them kids. All the rest is a big show-off. She'll talk to you about philosophy and about literature, but in her head she just wants you to fuck her three times a day. If you don't have a dick she won't look at you, maximum pity you.' He sums up his anger in a laconic new *cogito ergo sum*: 'If you fuck it means you exist!'

After ending his relationship with his girlfriend, Rafi returns to the group of disabled combatants where he reiterates his frustrated masculinity and reasserts his homoerotic bonding with the fellow combatants: cripples with various disabilities, amputations, and so on. Unlike them, Rafi suffers from erectile dysfunction; thus, his self-conceived masculinity becomes precarious. He is marked by two specific losses that link him to the 'female lack': he believes he can no longer penetrate a woman sexually, and he has an open wound in his abdomen. Thus, two recently acquired female attributes reconfigure his gender positioning without his being aware of it. He becomes positioned in the limbo between the two normative genders. When he rejects his girlfriend he might begin to disavow heterosexuality, but instead, as pointed out by Mihal Friedman, he regresses to the homoerotic group and embraces what can be termed a 'rejection heterosexuality': I want relationships neither with women nor with other men, only with myself. The melancholia caused by the shattering of his body, by his paraplegia and sexual dysfunction, translates into a discourse that vacillates between embracing and disavowing male subjectivity. Illicit female subjectivity will become his last resort. In *I Don't Give a Damn*, this paralysed veteran, haunted by memories of combat injury and death, rejects the metaphysics of the fallen asserted by George Mosse as a sacrificial death prefacing resurrection, and forcefully states his newly-found material nihilism: 'I fuck therefore I am.'

In a short prologue before they are inducted into military service, Rafi and his friends have a discussion. A girl says, 'I don't feel that the state has done much for me that I should serve' and one guy responds, 'I think that drafting women is a waste … stay at home … knit something!' Rafi's close friend agrees that women should not be drafted. This short exchange foreshadows what the film will problematise – the combatant's abhorrence of women's presence on the battlefield. But while Rafi now worries about the risk of committing evil in a battlefield situation where the victims might be civilians, he will soon change physically when he becomes himself the victim of absolute violence.

The action shifts to a hilly terrain, covered by yellow chrysanthemums the height of human beings, where a platoon prepares to storm Palestinian fighters who have holed up inside a small Sheik's tomb. Rafi is the first to storm the structure. The moment he rises up, a rifle barrel emerges from an opening in the building; a short burst hits Rafi in his stomach. His body stretches into an arc and he falls on his back. Soldiers storm in. A medivac helicopter makes a quick landing; Rafi, lying on his back, bleeding heavily from his stomach, his hands stained and his fatigues soaked in blood, is hauled into the chopper. In the next scene, he is lying unconscious in a hospital bed. From this point on, the narrative progresses in a series of flashbacks that alternate bet-ween Rafi's army life and his relationship with his girlfriend. She becomes the witness and, in part, the victim of the plight of Rafi. The film portrays her painful situation but, at the same time, it articulates the protagonist's masochism. Kaja Silverman claims that the war veteran experiences the anatomical lack that marks the female body and threatens the male body. But in war films like *I Don't Give a Damn*, instead of 'living with the lack', the veteran 'lives with the wound'. Veterans who have experienced combat live with the stigma of the wound that Mark Seltzer calls the tormenting 'fascination with torn and opened bodies and torn and opened persons'. This torment radically reshapes the veteran's male subjectivity whose rapprochement to female subjectivity derives from both his identification with the female in childbirth and from a deeply-seated anxiety of women's presence on the battlefield.

The role of the female in male post-traumatic subjectivity comes clearer when we examine the different ways in which a combatant perceives his options of violent death. The most common combat death is caused by the penetration of a pointed object – an arrow, a dagger, a lance, a spear, a sword, a javelin, a bullet or shrapnel – into the body. Klaus Theweleit believes that military pedagogy prepares men for violent death by inflicting torture on trainees; its objective is to cause an incessant throbbing pain in the bodies and minds of young recruits. Through endlessly repeated drills, exercises and harassment, men are forced into a bonding that blurs their individual borders and creates a shared envelope, the fighting unit. In training, the skin of each man becomes 'eroticised', so that the whole body surface becomes prepared, even longs, to accept penetration through the skin. Readiness to be penetrated through the skin, and the simultaneous urge to penetrate the enemy through the skin, makes the combatant powerful in battle.

I Don't Give a Damn also highlights the artificial limb, another kind of bodily mutilation and a link to the male soldier's fear of women on the battlefield. In the rehabilitation ward, Rafi takes pictures of his fellow disabled combatants wearing or holding and waving their prosthetic limbs. The amputated young men look happy with their artificial limbs; a hilarious moment that Rafi documents. They may be feeling relief that what happened to them was only the loss of an arm or a leg, not the removal of their head. Decapitation through the use of a flat sharp object, such as a slaughterer's knife, a wide sword, a sabre or an axe, is familiar from the legal system in states where executions are carried out in this way. This type of killing became infamous during the French Revolution when the guillotine decapitated thousands of people and pointed at the metaphysics of modernity: the creed of war for the nation-state.

The connection between decapitation and the constituting of the modern nation-state has submerged in historical memory. But this submerged memory resonates with pre-modern practices described in biblical stories: the decapitation of enemy warriors whose heads were exhibited in public. The now obsolete practice served, in pre-modern warfare, to restore the fertility of the royal female. African myths, as anthropologist Luc De Heusch observed, often convert a lower natural orifice into a higher orifice within the bodily context of bloodletting. Menstrual blood, which was believed to possess cosmic properties, was interchangeable with the bleeding necks of enemy warriors decapitated in battle. Head-hunting became a symbolic remedy for a royal female's menstrual bleeding that refused to stop. When menstrual bleeding continues for a longer time than the usual, conception cannot take place; consequently, dynastic continuity and the continuity of the kingdom are under threat. African myths suggest that the bleeding stump of a warrior's neck mirrored the menstrual bleeding of the royal female and could therefore serve as its symbolic replacement. The renewed fertility of the royal female guaranteed the continuation of the royal dynasty as well as the durability of the state. The purpose of war was to restore female fertility and to safeguard the state.

In the boot camp, Rafi and his fellow soldiers experience long hikes and marches, practice at firing ranges and endure assault courses. In letters to his girlfriend, he describes basic training: '...stretchers hike ... forty kilometres ... shoulder's torn up, you're busted ... dead tired, you lose control of your feet ... you're dying to sleep ... running and shooting, crawling and shooting ... falling asleep and shooting...' Theweleit explains that as the body becomes addicted to pain in such exercises, pain becomes pleasure. Estranged from pleasure, ruled by pain, for the combatant's body: 'What is nice is what hurts.' Harassment afflicts the body not in order to make it immune, or to teach it to endure pain, but to make the body vibrate as it suffers, mirroring the moment of orgasm.

The climax of the body's alienation from its natural needs takes place when Rafi first encounters the pained body of another soldier. Rafi's father, who, in the patriarchal order, represents the death principle as well as the demand to sacrifice the son, now leads the way to the war zone. When he drives Rafi to the paratroop base after a short term of leave, he is beaming with satisfaction: 'You grow up too fast, son … the army … and now a girlfriend … can't you wait a little…' The scene suddenly cuts to a chopper landing troops in the night and Rafi's voice is heard reading a letter to his girlfriend: 'I remember our first encounter … in combat … with blood…' It is raining heavily when Rafi's detachment advances cautiously in the dark towards a dilapidated building. Soldiers' boots sink in the mud when suddenly a landmine blows up. A close-up frame shows a charred-black, bleeding and mutilated leg. The wounded soldier writhes and screams in pain; his blood-covered body shakes in spasms as he is dragged in the mud by his rescuers. Rafi face turns pale. A friend hugs him. The scene cuts to a birthday party where everybody dances except for Rafi, who sits alone in an armchair. When his girlfriend invites him to the dance he mutters: 'Can't get it out of my mind … one moment he was a whole person … in just a second he became a meatball soaked in blood.' For the first time, Rafi becomes aware of the vulnerability of the body in combat, and also realises the intimate relationship between his corporality and the mortality of his body. As Gianni Vattimo explains, we see our limits in the fear of pain and death; human existence is only the 'temporal succession' of the generations, and the 'paying of the price'. What follows in the film is the story of Rafi's pain and his will to die. In the surgery ward, only half-conscious, we hear him say: 'I have nothing more to tell … the story's finished … I'm finished … everything's finished.'

Transferred to a rehabilitation ward, Rafi stays with other amputated and paraplegic soldiers who train themselves to live with their 'paying of the price'. Only Rafi remains sullen and depressed and behaves badly towards his family and his girlfriend, unwilling 'to pay the price'. One morning, Nira, wearing a clown's dress and make-up, arrives in the ward, offering pretzels and kisses to the soldiers and tries to cheer Rafi up but he refuses to cooperate, saying: 'I know what you feel … all the shit that you feel when you stand next to a rag.' As the nurse comes to change his bandage, Rafi forcefully grabs hold of Nira and pulls her close to his repulsive wound that drips pus and mucus: 'Watch! Pretty, isn't it? Pretty, huh?' Nira storms out of the room and into the restroom where she throws up. When she adds her vomit to the blood and pus in the wound she rounds off the abjection of the male body.

The process of abjection begun in military training converts the male body from subject to object. The lower half of Rafi's body has been permanently converted in this way, as we see when he plunges a syringe needle again and again into his own thigh and fails to feel it. Because penetration and the art of being penetrated through the skin are the undeclared objectives of military pedagogy, the whole body surface becomes erogenous and sexually excited during training, when men are denied opportunity for sexual fulfilment. The intimacy shared by men living together fans the sexual drive, but simultaneously prohibits its homosexual satisfaction because the dominant fiction of our culture is exclusively heterosexual. Deflected aggression sometimes targets the soldier's own body – as one trainee's suicide in *Massa Alunkot* (*Paratroopers*, 1977) and one soldier's broken leg in *One of Us* suggest. But most of the blocked sexual energy finds expression on the battlefield.

Male desire to die from 'a great wound' is evident in the sci-fi film, *Alien* (1979), when an astronaut is impregnated by an alien creature. Back on the spacecraft, the astronaut convulses violently before a creature bursts through his abdomen. In what clearly resembles childbirth, the monstrous offspring emerges through the astronaut's abdominal wall, tearing apart his muscles and skin. In utter disbelief the crew watches it scurry away to the far reaches of the ship. The shape of the newly-born offspring that grows inside the spaceship evokes internal organs and bone fragments. This image reverses the shattering of the male body on the battlefield; here, a shattered body is reconfigured as a monster. All attempts by male astronauts to exterminate the monster fail, bringing about their deaths. Only the female astronaut Ripley (Sigourney Weaver) is able to destroy the alien. The male astronauts' powerlessness underscores the empowerment of the female astronaut. While *Alien* allegorises the predicament of male subjectivity within a patriarchal order, it casts the female as a commanding mythic power to destroy the chthonic monster.

The fragmented human bones and internal organs the alien projects suggest another clue to the allegory. Anna Tsing has studied relations between a Muslim patriarchal community and a Meratus polytheist matriarchal community in Indonesia. From the practices of the local shaman of the matriarchal Meratus, Tsing learned that women were seen not as emasculated men, but rather as generic humans; the shaman was considered a superwoman, taking on a maternal identity and offering an image of the body as unbounded. The shaman – a subversive, feminine presence – evoked dangerous and powerful maternal connections from within the cracks of the patriarchal law. The Muslims believed that their polytheistic neighbours, especially the women, were granted supernatural powers because they did not guard their body boundaries: they wandered at night, removed their heads, dislodged their intestines and left their bodies like empty containers as they hovered over the roofs of houses. But they could not speak. Shamans, magician-healers, developed a technique of how to open the body boundaries of men in order to mimic the openness of the female body in childbirth. The shamans inserted splinters into men's skin and muscles, allowing the body 'to absorb the fullness of the whole world' and become like women. Unlike Muslims under patriarchal law, this polytheistic matriarchal community conceived the female not as a derivative gender, 'a male with a lack', but rather as a fully accomplished human being, whose bodily openness set an example for society as a whole, and for men in particular. Sealed and tightly closed, men lack an aperture through which to connect to the world. But in Western society, the combat wound in the bodies of young men becomes the gold standard protocol in order to 'recreate powerful maternal connections in the cracks of patriarchal law' and reconstitutes male subjectivity as female.

I Don't Give a Damn shows the results of this transformation. When another disabled veteran invites Rafi home to dinner, asking whether he likes grilled fish, Rafi becomes sarcastic: 'I don't believe it. You work, play basketball and cook, a perfect woman.' When Rafi, the now disabled veteran, quarrels with his best friend in the army, the friend yells at him: 'What's wrong with you? … you don't care. I want you to give a hand … say something … if I'm doing something wrong, tell me!' And then he says quietly, 'I love you Rafi…' before leaving. This love scene in which one man feels betrayed by the other, this suppressed unconsumated love between two male combatants, surfaces for a short moment when Rafi no longer aspires to realise his silenced love for his handsome friend, nor does the friend wish to reciprocate, and therefore he gives voice to this frustrated love that no longer threatens to unravel their heterosexuality. His friend is later killed in action. After his funeral, Rafi makes love for the first time since he was wounded. He does have an erection but does not feel anything. As he asks his ex-girlfriend to leave, she tells him she is getting married, but wanted to see if they could still make love. She asks: 'Why did you throw me out? What was it that I threatened? … Because I had to help you in bed? With sex?' She yells at him, 'Tell me what you want?' He replies flatly: 'I want to die.' At night he wheels himself through the cemetery, to his friend's grave, and for the first time he cries. Crying about his beloved one moves him from melancholia to mourning; no longer able to 'make love' to his combatant friend, Rafi need not suppress his homosexual love and can start his mourning.

The end of this process comes in a scene with his parents. To reject his mother's belief that he will walk again, Rafi throws himself from his wheelchair to the ground. Thus he renounces the social birth into verticality conferred by ancient Romans: in order for the infant to be bestowed with the gift of life, it had to be raised from the ground by the father of the family. When Rafi intentionally falls to the ground, he refutes his parents' ambition to see him 'stand on his feet'. He symbolically disengages himself from the 'Law of the Father', from the patriarchal order that sends young men to war and destroys their bodies. Now he can mourn his loss, and effect his own childbirth or re-birth from his own wound.

Yehuda Judd Ne'eman

REFERENCES

De Heusch, Luc (1982) *The Drunken King, or The Origin of the State.* Bloomington: Indiana University Press.

Friedman, Mihal Regine (1993) 'Between Silence and Abjection: The Film Medium and the Israeli War Widow', *Filmhistoria*, 3, 1/2, 1–18.

Mosse, George (1990) *Fallen Soldiers: Reshaping the Memory of the World Wars.* Oxford: Oxford University Press.

Seltzer, Mark (1997) 'Wound Culture: Trauma in the Pathological Public Sphere', *October*, 80, 3–26.

Silverman, Kaja (1992) *Male Subjectivity at the Margins.* New York and London: Routledge.

Theweleit, Klaus (1989) *Male Fantasies – Male Bodies: Psychoanalyzing the White Terror, vol 2.* Minneapolis: University of Minnesota Press.

Tsing Anna (1993) *In the Realm of the Diamond Queen.* Princeton: Princeton University Press.

Vattimo, Gianni (2004) *Nihilism and Emancipation: Ethics, Politics & Law.* New York: Columbia University Press.

Virilio, Paul (1989) *War and Cinema: The Logistics of Perception.* London: Verso.

NUJUM AL-NAHAR STARS IN BROAD DAYLIGHT

OUSSAMA MOHAMMAD, SYRIA, 1988

If films were attributed a life, *Nujum al-Nahar* (*Stars in Broad Daylight*, 1988) could be said to have had, so far, an eerily sad one. A jewel of contemporary Syrian cinema which has invariably earned critical acclaim, standing ovations and awards wherever it has screened, the film has never been shown to the Syrian public. There is no official memorandum prohibiting its exhibition, yet government bureaucracy has never granted a single public screening and is unlikely to do so in the near future. This is one of paradoxes of Syrian cinema, which *Stars in Broad Daylight* emblematises.

Another aspect of that paradox lies in the remarkable feat by Syrian filmmakers, with Oussama Mohammad at the helm, who have succeeded in carving an independent, critical and often subversive cinema under the sponsorship of a vigorous state, ruled by a single party that has been actively involved in suppressing dissent and coercing official dogma. Syrian cinema is almost exclusively produced by the state and yet it is the furthest removed from a cinema of propaganda, or a cinema that serves to anchor and disseminate tenets of the regime's hegemony. Quite the opposite, in fact. For the most part, Syrian cinema has been, and remains, fiercely independent. It represents one of the rare venues for artistic expression in contemporary Syria, where an intelligent and compelling critique of the state has forged a site for the manufacture of meaning and image.

Furthermore, resisting seductive and lucrative temptations of market paradigms borne in the increasingly ravenous appetite for world cinema or more specifically, Third World cinema, Syrian filmmakers have crafted a body of work that has not shied from being deeply embedded in its locality, spurning the ready-made formulas favoured by consumers of Third World cinema.

Film production, distribution, as well as import and export, fell under the complete control of the state in the 1960s. The National Film Organisation was instituted as an independent arm of the Ministry of Culture and Guidance, to oversee all aspects of the industry and screenings throughout the country. The state monitors the entire process, from approval of the script, issuing of permits for location shoots, through production and until a special committee views the final product before allowing its projection to the public. *Stars in Broad Daylight* passed 'all the tests', so to speak, except for the last.

The film has been widely discussed as the most scathing critique of the Syrian regime, as Lisa Wedeen has noted. The storyline is cast in the sort of limpid structural simplicity that allows the film to be attributed several central themes or drives: it has been read as an intimate study of family, patriarchy and violence in Baathist Syria, and as a detailed analysis of how arbitrary forms of violence in society unravel at the level of the cellular unit of the family. When asked to explain what his film was about in an interview with Elie Chalala, Oussama Mohammad replied: 'My film is about illusions in general, and in particular the illusion of belonging to a power or an authority.'

The motif of violence is precluded in the title, in colloquial Arabic, *nujum al-nahar* (stars in daylight). It is the abbreviated utterance of 'to show someone stars in broad day'; a threat of violence that would leave the victim 'seeing stars'. The study of the legitimisation of violence in the meshwork of social relations is certainly a central concern for the filmmaker. It is also one of the guiding motifs of his second feature, *Sunduq al-Dunia* (*Sacrifices*, 2003).

The film opens in a sleepy village in the Syrian countryside, its dwellers busy with preparations for a double wedding celebration. We learn soon enough that none of the betrothed couples are marrying out of love. Rather, two peasant families with humble means want to render the cultivation of their plots more profitable. The focus is on one of these two families, the Ghazi family. There is a grandfather, nominally the patriarch, whose poor health has rendered him dependent on his children and grandchildren, and thus effectively marginalised. There is a father, who has toiled the land all his life and still does, in order to survive. And there are three sons. The eldest, Safi, works and lives in the city of Aleppo, a province removed from the native village. Khalil works and lives in nearby Lattakia, the capital of the province in which the native village falls. Kasser lives with the parents in the village, and toils the land. He is deaf in one ear due to a severe beating administered by his father when he was a child. Because of his partial deafness, he is treated like a village idiot. Sana, attractive and ambitious, also lives and works with her family in the village. In contrast to the 'village idiot', cousin Tawfiq is the village's self-appointed intellectual, who recites poetry and philosophises tirelessly to legitimise the social order.

The first wedding involves Sana and Maarouf, her cousin, who had migrated to Germany but decided to return to his homeland. Although he had worked as a physical education teacher in Germany, everyone in the village believes he has a doctorate in physical education, engineering or medicine, and refers to him as 'the doctor'. He is treated with obsequious deference by all, as all returning 'guest-workers' from Germany and the rest of Europe are treated in their native villages in the 'developing world'. 'Doctor' Maarouf has not exactly returned wealthy and offers no lucrative promises except in reclaiming his share of the plot of land and partaking in a business partnership with Khalil.

The second betrothal is between Kasser and Maarouf's sister, Mayada. She is in love with the driver of a bus that passes through the village, collecting travellers. She was not allowed to marry him because it would foil the land consolidation deal engineered by Khalil, whose ambitious business scheme is to use profits generated from land cultivation to buy a small microbus and operate it on the routes connecting the city of Lattakia with neighbouring villages.

In the middle of the celebratory feast, Kasser's bride suddenly rises from her seat, and runs into the night. At the edge of the field, her beloved microbus driver is waiting. The bus drives away as Khalil, who failed to catch up with her, watches on in dismay. To stall the scandal, Khalil turns off the electricity. The darkness of night envelops all. In solidarity with her brother, Sana locks herself into the house, refusing to go through with the wedding. A fight breaks out. Infuriated, humiliated and his machismo injured, Maarouf decides to go back to Germany, returning to his German wife Ulrica, who had spurned him because of his snoring. 'All Arabs snore', she had said to him, snidely. Re-enacting the scene to his cousin, Tawfiq (who has received an education and is therefore seen by the family as Maarouf's equal), he claims his response was one of anger: 'Damn your father and the father of your Great Rumenige!' Ulrica telephoned and confessed to him that she wanted him back. He sells his plot of land and goes back to her.

To deflect the impact of the 'shame' Sana has brought onto her family, Khalil takes her to live with his wife and children in Lattakia. She becomes his household's domestic servant. Eventually she is induced to find wage-earning work in a tobacco factory. As she begins to earn a living and a sense of empowerment, Sana is attracted to a fellow worker who is finishing his doctorate in Arabic literature at the local university. He is of equally humble means and hails from a nearby village. Their courtship is brutally ended when she takes her beau to her family home in the village so that he can ask for her hand in marriage, and her brother Khalil dismisses him with contempt. He enlists Kasser to follow his sister and her beau as they stroll through the market and administers a brutal beating.

Hurriedly, Khalil schemes to marry Sana off to yet another cousin, Abbas, who lives in Damascus and is clearly psychotic. On the way to the wedding celebration in the village, she gets off the bus and runs into the woods. Abbas catches up with her and rapes her. During the celebration (this time only restricted to close members of family), Sana runs away again. We watch her at the dinner table surrounded by her family, Abbas hovering around her. She is traumatised, her body frozen. As the two eldest brothers, Safi and Khalil, proceed to beat and humiliate Kasser, we find out that she has escaped again, into the night, and this time no one was able to catch up with her. Kasser takes the blame for no other reason than he is as powerless as she was. Humiliated, he packs his bags and moves to Damascus. He has a dream of opening a shop to sell birds and soda, so that customers 'can drink soda while listening to the singing of the birds', he tells a cousin and childhood friend in Damascus. In the last sequence of the film, we see him walking, intimidated – as a country boy would typically be in the big city – but resolute, seeking Abbas, the cousin from whom Sana escaped. At the dawn of this new day, pick-up trucks spraying insecticide blow thick white clouds in which his figure melts and disappears.

The film was deemed too subversive for public screening by the state censors. It was widely read as the most biting, lucid and poetic critique of the Baathist regime to date, partly because critics identified echoes of archetypes in the array of characters that make up the family. The levels of identification are multiple. On one level, the family's story is emblematic of the political, social and cultural climate, and the transformations brought forth by the rule of the Baath to rural families – the largest social group making up the nation during the Party's ascent to power – seen from the purview of the 'cellular' scale of a single family. The total failure of agricultural reform – that brought an overhaul of a feudal system of land ownership – touted by the regime as the vanguard engine for economic and social redress of historical injustice, resulted in massive migration to cities. Economic and social state-planned growth geared with excessive bias towards the capital and urban provincial centres absorbed unskilled and semi-skilled labour in droves. The social fabric of rural areas was disrupted abruptly; while older generations tilled the land, younger generations could only seek a future in urban economies performing low-wage labour. The social and cultural order of relations was reversed: empowered by a (slightly) improved degree of literacy and the status of salaried-labourer that would precede the expansion of urban values, sons subverted claims of patriarchal authority from their fathers. There is no instance in *Stars in Broad Daylight* when the father opposes the schemes of his two sons, Khalil and Safi, or intervenes to defend their unbridled abuse of their sister Sana or brother Kasser. The power subverted by subordinate agents from those in command echoes the coup that brought Hafez el-Assad to power in 1971 under the guise of a 'Corrective Movement', which was introduced to steer the nation onto the course of rectitude, progress and prosperity. Meanwhile, the sons balk at paying the grandfather dutiful respect, only for the sake of legitimising the tenets on which the tradition of patriarchal rule is founded. He is the living emblem of that system of values and rituals of deference are in effect intended to reinforce the sacral status of that 'tradition'. In other words, the abuse and injustice that patterned the social fabric throughout the history of the country, under a system of feudal relations of political control and economic production was not dismantled by the rise of the Baath, and certainly not by the 'Corrective Movement'. Rather, they were reinforced.

Baathism is an ideology that emerged in Syria and also acquired significant currency in Iraq. It is very much the fruit of the historic moment in which it was spawned; a transformative ideology that contains ingredients of socialism and nationalism insofar as the state is posited as the central force in steering economic growth and social justice, coupled with a utopian underpinning of the 'renaissance' of Arabs, to reclaim a lost glory. The Syrian state, particularly since the 1971 coup by the 'Corrective Movement', has been dedicated to enforcing state dogma in all spheres of civic life. This state dogma appears in *Stars in Broad Daylight* as cynical satire. In perhaps the most uproarious sequence of the film, Khalil's twin sons are coerced into to 'performing' for the audience of the double wedding celebration. Barely five or six years old, they stand, like trained monkeys, behind the microphone and recite a 'patriotic' poem:

'Papa got me a gift, a tank and rifle,

me and my brother are small children,

we learned how to join the army of liberation,

in the army of liberation, we learned how to protect our land.

Down with Israel!

Long live the Arab nation!'

Their father, watching, glows with self-righteous pride. Meanwhile, when Kasser asks his cousin, a soldier on leave in Damascus, what he plans to do when his military service is completed, the cousin replies that he wants to open a tank repair shop, because they are falling apart. And when he asks him what Israelis look like, he replies, 'they are human beings, like us'.

In parallel to satirising official ideology, none of the characters appear to be imbued with any of its values or tenets. Rather, the regime and its order has turned Khalil, Safi, 'Doctor' Maarouf, cousin Tawfiq, Kasser – despite his status as victim – and other secondary characters, into ruthless, selfish, greedy, violent monsters. Theirs is a 'dog eat dog' and 'everyone for himself' world, where goodness, the generous, the loving and the principled are punished, banished or crushed.

On another level of identification, these protagonists and their larger family can be interpreted as emblematising 'the nation'. Khalil, the patriarchal ruler who has trumped authority from all those in line of command, looks uncannily like Hafez el-Assad. The character is played by actor and celebrated filmmaker Abdellatif Abdul-Hamid, who bears a degree of physical resemblance to the army commander who presided over Syria at the time. His demeanour and body language are accentuated to suggest attributes associated to Assad as he marches through sequences dispatching orders with an authority that is never questioned. Khalil works as a telephone operator in Lattakia and monitors phone conversations – one of the ways in which he is able to secure control over people around him. This fact supports the analogy with the regime of Assad, which has relied significantly on monitoring the citizenry – their conversations, the conduct of their lives, their agency – to shape their destiny. There is a frightening moment in the film when Khalil, wearing sunglasses, is reflected in the glass of a car window; he looks exactly like Hafez el-Assad. His moral disposition reinforces the analogy further, in his unprincipled pursuit of power. He does not balk at manipulating the lives of all those around him and resorts to ruthless violence without hesitating. He is also in tacit alliance with his brother, Safi, potentially the only challenge to his authority, who is safely kept at bay but is reigned in when the enforcement of absolute power is necessary. Safi is present at all family occasions and whenever a beating needs to be administered, as was Hafez el-Assad's brother, Rifaat; kept far enough not to present danger but close enough to rally force when necessary.

If the brother Khalil is the absolute ruler, the ruled are Kasser, Sana and the members of the village. Kasser labours to satisfy his brother, to whom he feels he owes his place in the world: a home, work, a bride and dignity. He does not question his brother's authoritarianism until the threshold of violent abuse becomes intolerable. Only then is the arbitrary nature of Khalil's authority and administration of order and justice revealed to him, insigating him to break from the family. He finds refuge in the company of his cousin, the soldier living in Damascus. He has also broken ties with the village and his family. He tells Kasser that he would only go to visit 'if he died or if someone dies'. He is wise, lucid and bitter from the experience of serving at the front, the liminal point where the regime's dogma is confronted with the poignancy of lived reality; the experience of witnessing the state-enforced triumphalist mythologies unveiled.

Sana, too, is another example of the 'ruled'. Using her character, Mohammad writes women back into the narrative of the nation from a fully-fledged feminist purview. He departs from the flat, one-dimensional characterisation familiar to Arab cinema, where the system of abuse and subordination of women is denounced but where female characters are deprived a full-bodied agency, or complex subjectivity. Mohammad brings women back to the centre-stage. The land consolidation deal is predicated on the two brides giving up their respective dreams, the social order on denial of their agency, and economic prosperity on their giving up their labour (or wages) to their patriarch. These are the foundations on which the regime of absolute power is built and the actions of the two brides drive the narrative into controversy. They are not rescued by a 'good man'. Rather, they take their destiny in their own hands and take flight. They dare to fall in love and to dream. The first bride wants to travel and discover the expanse of the country. Sana wants to continue her education and earn a diploma. At the height of their courtship, as they stroll through a market, Sana's face lights up when her co-worker assures her that she could resume her schooling.

Mohammad's endorsement of the women's viewpoint aids in unmasking and deriding the hypocrisy of Baath ideology and its purported progressive commitment to gender equality. After Sana runs into the family home and refuses to go through with the marriage to her cousin she is hounded by a crowd of angry relatives, men and women, screaming their outrage at her injurious behaviour. She is accused of being obstreperous and of having 'given herself' to another man. In the midst of the *mêlée*, Kasser attempts to rescue his sister, pulling away a woman who is beating her. The woman screams hysterically. Suddenly, 'European-educated' Maarouf emerges, releasing the woman from Kasser's grip. Slapping him, he self-righteously scolds Kasser: 'Stop that you man. Are you aware that you are beating the half of society?' In another sequence, Khalil's family is having dinner in his small cluttered apartment in Lattakia with the pompous *literati*, cousin Tawfiq, as a guest. Sana, who has cooked dinner, is stuck in the kitchen. Tawfiq, who covets her secretly, finds an opportunity to lay claim on her after marriage with Maarouf has fallen through. He launches into a speech, spoken in the ornate syntax of official ideology, in which he declares his admiration for Sana, whom he hails a modern-day heroine who has dared to imagine a future for herself, in defiance with what society had designed for her. Sana is oblivious to his declarations. The next scene depicts Tawfiq asleep on his chair at the dinner table. Khalil and his wife tip-toeing nervously around him to go to bed, leaving Sana to clean up after them in silence. In the middle of the night, when all are asleep, Tawfiq goes to Sana's bed and grabs her breast. She awakens, startled and frightened. He locks her body onto the bed and, declaring his love for her by reciting a poem, tries to rape her. When her struggles to push him away fail, she grabs the alarm clock and bangs it on his head. It rings, forcing the much-respected intellectual to leave Sana alone. In another instance, after her other cousin, Abbas, rapes her in broad daylight, throwing her body in the mud, a cow breathes above her head as Abbas swears he loves her. Khalil often professes love to his sister Sana shortly before or after he has been unjust. Thus, the exercise of absolute power, subversion of agency and administration of violence are almost invariably cloaked by declarations of love.

At the double wedding celebration, Khalil makes a speech:

'I love you with all my heart. If something happened to any of you, I would wish it for myself. If you are happy, I will be happier than you. I swear, I would sacrifice one of my children for you, good people. I would sacrifice anything for the sake of my brothers. What is a man without his brothers? Damn the money!'

He cries as he tells the audience of his feelings. The gypsies hired for entertainment strike up the music, Khalil walks over to the grandfather, urging him, with cunning, to approve of his scheme: the land plots are not parcelled and sold away, and the sons of the country are repatriated to the homeland; what could be better? Love of family flows into love of the land, of the country, the nation, and all these loves are the guises for the unbridled ministration of violence.

The wedding celebration provides a fantastic opportunity for mocking patriotism. Four respective individuals, with their dreams and ambitions, are forced into giving them up for the expansion and consolidation of a family's property. Their subordination is celebrated as 'love of country' and 'love of family'. The most ridiculous speech is delivered by the cousin Tawfiq, in classical Arabic, again in the tone of official lore:

'You are my poetry and this occasion is my muse. We are happy three times over. Our son has returned from his absence to the homeland with the wish to give and to build. He drank from the fountain of goodness and came back. He came back to plant a tree in this land, under this sky. He was never seduced by cities, nor women. He said no to Paris, to London, to Berlin. What is Berlin, compared to a fig tree?'

The 'educated' groom gives a speech in the same vein, but in the local vernacular: 'I am you and you are me', he tells the audience. 'Berlin is nothing compared to the village.' The satire reaches apotheosis when Maarouf is handed a loaf of bread. After his speech, he kisses the loaf and lifts it above his head, then hands it to Sana, who holds it, hesitantly kisses it and passes it to Kasser.

Kasser smiles, raises it to his forehead, and then, with two hands, tears a piece off to eat. The music stops. The audience is petrified. Khalil hurries to Kasser, snatches the remainder of the loaf off him and whispers in his ear: 'This is the loaf of bread of the homeland, you jackass!' To him, it was merely a loaf of bread. In order to move beyond this small 'glitch', Khalil urges the famous entertainer, Fouad Ghazi (also a relative of the family) to begin his performance. The camera travels slowly, from the spectacle of the balladeer to the vehicles and buses stationed at the edge of the celebration area. Khalil, hiding behind the bus, eats the very same loaf that symbolised, only minutes earlier, the nation.

If the film displays a love for country and family, at no point do any of the protagonists profess love for their leader. The portrait of Hafez el-Assad fails to appear in any of the scenes, particularly those filmed in the cityscapes of Lattakia and Damascus. Instead, both cities show posters, banners and billboards for rising star Fouad Ghazi. Mohammad's intention is multifold. On the one hand, because of its recurrence, the striking presence of the portrait is an obvious substitute for presence of the purportedly adulated leader. Lisa Wedeen argues that the title of the film, *Stars in Broad Daylight*, is actually a pun that refers to a colloquial expression in Arabic, but also, more literally, to Syria's contemporary political celebrities. On the other hand, the rise of star-entertainers in the public sphere shows the title to have been prophetic. Ten years after the film was released, the urban landscape of Syria has become populated with billboards featuring superstars of the entertainment industry.

Ultimately, the protagonists who break free from the ruthless social order that oppresses them disappear into the fog of night, or the fog of pesticide. Their destiny is not concluded, it is left open for speculation. It is not clear if they escape or fall prey to a similarly patterned social order. This open-ended plotline creates the impression of a cinematic fable, a modern fable without a moral to its story. It is furthermore reinforced by the tightly-knit and explicit coherence of the filmmaker's cinematographic vocabulary, an admirably individualistic language that steers clear of either the fantastical or the self-consciously realistic. The opening sequence of *Stars in Broad Daylight* recurs in Mohammad's second feature film, *Sacrifices*, an unveiled homage to Andreï Tarkovsky, the master of Soviet cinema in which Mohammad was schooled. A close-up pan of a slowly-moving wooden door gives the film the cadence of book pages turning; the cinematographic equivalent, as it were, of the traditional opening sentence of a fable, 'once upon a time, in a remote village…'. Furthermore as Sana contemplates her first attempt at an escape, the sequence that depicts her seated on the bus, anxious and fidgety, is intercut with the image of her as a young child. Similarly, when Kasser steps out onto the streets of Damascus, scenes of him as a boy, adults dripping liquid in his ear as he writhes in pain, are shown. The moment he lost his hearing is let go as he breaks free.

It is arguably Oussama Mohammad's eye for striking imagery that distinguishes his work. The framing of every shot, the movement of his camera, his skill for visual composition all display a supreme talent. Scenes are almost invariably filmed through a bias; the camera follows characters from within a window or door frame, or films their reflection in a mirror or a puddle of water. This frame within the frame reminds the spectator of the director's self-conscious subjective sensibility. The use of mirrors is particularly powerful, as it re-composes a character from a skewed perspective, as if to reveal another ordering, often in relation to the psychological state of the characters in the scene. The double wedding sequence is particularly breathtaking with the use of a television monitor – of the live video-recording of the celebration – to reveal how the characters shape the footage of their own events. Filming from within frames, filming the reflection of illusions and staging archetypal characters allow Mohammad to say what cannot be said and to visualise what cannot be visualised. To paraphrase Lisa Wedeen's concluding note on the film, it is extraordinary because it uses the symbols and language of the regime in order to subvert the regime's system of signification and succeeds in what cultural critics have failed to do, namely, to represent what it must not show.

Frozen into single shots, the visual composition of every frame is attractive, seductive, perfectly calibrated. Mohammad cannot be described as an *aesthete*; rather he is a *plastician*. In the play of light and dark, characters seem carved; every image is three-dimensional, at times even tactile. With compositions set in mud-brick houses, chicken coops and poor peasants in the Syrian province of Lattakia, casting characters with large noses, short gaits and plaid suits, embattled with blind violence, love and pursuit of absolute power, Oussama Mohammad, a secular humanist filmmaker, achieves a feat that postmodernity has long since denied to artistic practice: the ability to induce the spectator towards a transcendence, a dizzying upward lift.

Rasha Salti

REFERENCES

Chalala, Elie (1997) 'Interview with Oussama Mohammad', trans. Gabriel Kartouch, *Al-Jadid*, 3, 14, 1.

Wedeen, Lisa (1999) *Ambiguities of Domination: Politics, Rhetoric and Symbols in Contemporary Syria*. Chicago: University of Chicago Press.

DOCHARKHEH SAVAR THE CYCLIST

MOHSEN MAKHMALBAF, IRAN, 1988

Docharkheh Savar (aka *Bicycleran*) (*The Cyclist*, 1988) is the first important Iranian film to focus on the plight of Afghan refugees in Iran. It is also representative of a period in the career of Mohsen Makhmalbaf, one of the most prominent filmmakers of Iran, who once was an ardent supporter of the Islamic Revolution. Along with *Dastforoush* (*The Peddler*, 1987) and *Arusi-ye Khuban* (*Marriage of the Blessed*, 1989), *The Cyclist* belongs to what Makhmalbaf calls his 'second period' when, having gradually become disillusioned with the regime that failed to bring justice to human misery, he moved from religious dogma to contemporary social issues. All three films expose urban squalor, social avarice, cruelty and crime. *The Cyclist* is challenging to review, because it gives clues to the evolvement of Makhmalbaf's career and stance as he attempts to reconcile religious faith with a pluralistic point of view. His uncertainties in both areas reflect the predicament of the Iranian people in trying to remain faithful to traditional values in the face of modernity.

Makhmalbaf was over twenty when he first set foot inside a cinema. As a child, he refused to talk to his mother when he found out that she had gone to the movies. As his mother, who was divorced from his father, had to work for a living, he received his religious education from his grandmother and aunt, and political education from his stepfather, a devout follower of Ayatollah Khomeini. By the time he reached puberty, he was already deeply involved in politics, forming a religious activist group to fight the regime of the Shah. At the age of seventeen, he was arrested by SAVAK, the secret police of the Shah, for disarming a policeman and as a result spent several years in prison. He was released, like many other political prisoners, before the end of the 1979 Revolution. 'I got fed up with leftist ideology when I was in prison', he reminisces in Houshang Golmakani's portrait film. 'People were becoming Marxist by reading Gorky's *Mother*, or religious by one religious book. When I turn to dust one day, what does it matter whether I am a socialist or a capitalist? I have always been a guerrilla, but after the years in prison, I chose the road to culture.' He set up the Islamic Propagation Organisation to present Islamic ideology through artistic media and challenging artists whose ideas and modes of expression were not harmonious with those of the organisation.

During the decade following the Islamic Revolution, now referred to as the First Republic, 'radicals' and 'militants' supported by Ayatollah Khomeini won the struggle to control the post-revolutionary state, excluding the 'liberals' and 'moderates' from power and establishing the *feqh*-based Islam that was to suppress reformist and modernist views. The newly created Ministry of Culture and Islamic Guidance (MCIG) was given the directive to Islamise art and cultural activities. Mohsen Makhmalbaf, along with other Islamic intellectuals and artists disillusioned with the policies of the Islamic Republic, gradually began to voice objections to the regime. He argued that art can free an artist from the clutches of oppression and it cannot be contained within the straitjacket of ideology.

Makhmalbaf earned recognition as a talented filmmaker with his fourth film, *Baycott* (*Boycott*, 1985), made during his revolutionary period. The protagonist of the film is a young member of a leftist group arrested by SAVAK, and sentenced to death. Thinking about his past relations with the other members of the group, he begins to doubt the validity of the ideas for which he is giving his life, while his comrades in prison try to make a hero out of him. In this film, one can sense a tolerant attitude towards a worldview; a deviation from young Makhmalbaf's previous stance as a devout Islamist revolutionary.

The Peddler, three episodes on birth, life and death, resonates a strong sense of alienation, which is also at the core of *Marriage of the Blessed*, a film about the mental anguish of an Islamic combatant suffering from shellshock. After this film Makhmalbaf announced that he was giving up filmmaking for a while, in order to re-examine his past work. He advocated a relativistic approach to cinema, regretting the absolutist view which, he said, had marred his earlier work.

The Cyclist is based on a real incident Makhmalbaf witnessed as a ten-year-old, when a Pakistani refugee cycled non-stop for ten days to raise money for flood victims in Pakistan. In that incident, Makhmalbaf explains, people were first sceptical about the man's honesty; children would sneak up on him to see if he went to sleep at night. But people soon became genuinely interested. Even Queen Farah Diba went to the marathon and offered a present. By the fifth day, it was like a bazaar. As the cyclist faded, the bazaar grew. On the seventh day he collapsed, but the bazaar was still there. The man repeated the stunt in another neighbourhood. Makhmalbaf affirms that sometimes the cyclist is not a person in a specific place but a class, society or even a nation. Initially he wrote the story with the cyclist finishing the endurance ride but not being able to walk anymore, and dying a few steps further from the 'bazaar'. But 'circumstantial advice' prevented this ending. Why should it be pessimistic, he was asked. It was suggested that he should take a trip to Pakistan. As a compromise, Makhmalbaf shot part of *The Cyclist* in Pakistan and left the ending open to interpretation.

Like *The Peddler*, *The Cyclist* is the story of the 'other' pushed to the margins of society. Nasim is an Afghan refugee, a *muhacir*, who needs money for his sick wife's hospital bills. Digging fails to bring in enough, but he is unwilling to be involved with the black market. His alienation is augmented by the avarice, cruelty and self-serving motives of others; ordinary swindlers as well as corrupt politicians. Nasim does not seem to have a previous existence. In the temporal and spatial movement between homeland and the new country, what Laura Marks calls 'cultural knowledge', is lost. As a refugee, Nasim is deprived of his local vernacular, which would aid him to convey his culture, feelings and thoughts. (It is significant to remember that Makhmalbaf was also cut from his familiar surroundings while shooting the film, in a country other than his own and where a different language is spoken.)

Nasim is silent most of the time, just like his country, which does not have a voice (the same motive later surfaced in *Baran* (*Rain*, 2001) by Majid Majidi, where the protagonist, an Afghan girl, is silent throughout the film.) His identity is reduced to the Afghan money in his pocket, which is of no value. He carries these few bills like 'the key to the house', which many refugees or exiles keep for generations, when the house or the lock may no longer exist. Patricia Seed has argued that these keys remind those in exile of a homeland they can dream of, but never return to.

Nasim's muteness is not a withholding of sounds or words, but is caused by the fracturing of both time and narratives. This has led to a linguistic retreat into himself; a symbol of entrapment but also a form of death. It is as if he lost the capacity to speak when he lost his home. On the other hand, his silence is the only voice of sanity amidst the mayhem that faces him. His silence questions the values of the real world. Language as truth is always on the move and words are incapable of describing the ever-changing world.

A window opens from darkness to light. A man jumps in from the fog and dust, undresses beside his motorcycle and closes the window. Next we see him as a motorcycle daredevil circling while Nasim and his son, Djomel, watch. Nasim turns his eyes away from the spectacle and in his mind's eye sees his wife lying in a hospital bed; in deep humiliation he is collecting coins thrown at his feet. These opening scenes (before the credits) function metonymically for the rest of the film.

Nasim's most vital link to his homeland is his wife, who he must keep alive at all costs. At the hospital, he is obliged to sign and pay in advance in case his wife dies. Afghan money is not acceptable. Next he and Djomel walk hurriedly, but determinedly, among the crowds and the dense traffic of auto rickshaws and phaetons, to the rhythm of the theme song. A jump cut to Djomel watching *They Shoot the Horses, Don't They?* (1969) on television, dubbed in Farsi, foreshadows the film's plot and its theme of human fortitude. Nasim is introduced to a smuggler who wants to know if he is courageous. His friend says 'courageous but not dishonest'. The answer is, 'nobody is born a thief, but becomes so afterwards'.

Nasim is not the kind of man who gets involved in illegal deals; however, when he has a nightmare about his son falling into the well as he turns the wheel, he decides to accept the job. But now the smuggler is gone. Desperate Nasim visits his wife lying in an oxygen tent in the hospital. As he watches the horsemen playing *bouzkachi* outside, he notices a man lie under the bus. Soon he is pulled out and beaten, but some coins are thrown at him. The camera focuses on Nasim's eyes alternating between the cruelty to animals displayed by the *bouzkachi* players and cruelty to men. He then decides to lie under the truck while his son watches on anxiously. When the boy yells, Nasim is grabbed by the crowd. He runs with his son and people chase after them. Having failed in this last attempt to earn a few coins, he has no choice but accept the endurance ride on the bicycle.

As the promoter announces that Nasim rode with closed eyes in India, the arena slowly turns into a carnival, and Makhmalbaf's lenses are very sharp in picking the details to give the audience a slice of life with all its cruelties and foibles. Comedy and tragedy are hand in hand in what looks like perfect mayhem. The body of a man who committed suicide is carried away as a woman throws dirty water on the crowd without looking. The fortune-teller, a young woman abandoned by her husband, arrives with her daughter to make a few pennies herself. Mafia-type politicians with their big American cars are placing bets. Some of the spectators jump on the bicycle to take souvenir photos. Journalists looking for a sensational story try to interview Nasim. The disabled and the lepers are brought to the scene, but an old woman among them dies as the sick are encouraged to sing 'We are very happy, full of hope'. Someone tries to get rid of the Afghans with the promise of a job to reduce the numbers cheering Nasim. More and more are lured away each day, but none are paid. Naïve Nasim is given sedatives and he falls, and someone discreetly replaces him. The supposedly blind accordionist with the black shades witnesses the incident, but the promoter threatens to expose him if he opens his mouth. But there is no worry. The accordionist has also made a bet! Nasim observes the crowd but he is not part of it, except when they drag away his son. Disturbed by the incident and unable to vocalise his agony, he gets hold of a stick and starts waving it at the crowd until they release the boy. The businessmen, politicians, the embassy, along with the doctor of the ambulance, are all involved in a wager that has no regard for the welfare of a human being.

The film is shot in the same simple style as *The Peddler*, *The Marriage of the Blessed* and *The Actor*. The visual and narrative quality is eclectic and at times unpredictable, even hallucinatory, but through the harsh realities of post-revolutionary Iran, it succeeds in transcending national borders to reflect a true picture of a society more concerned with personal gains than the wellbeing of others.

The editing and framing is also eclectic. Various camera angles are employed, with the central image often obstructed by objects of buildings. Combined with the overall sense of chaos that the film emanates, this gives Makhmalbaf's style a certain freshness. The film also possesses a sense of magic particular to Makhmalbaf, but whose range, from burlesque to supernatural, is sometimes reminiscent of Fellini and, in particular, *La Strada* (1954). The world Makhmalbaf presents is subjective, often grotesque, and tinged with irony and pathos, but always filtered through his humanistic concerns. Reality and surreality (Nasim's wife sees him riding in the clouds when she hears that he will do the endurance ride) or reality and dreams (Nasim repeatedly has nightmares about his son falling into the well he used to dig) merge in 'amalgamation', or the fusion of realism and fantasy, and affinities with magical realism are countless. Nasim is a hybrid: an Afghan in a foreign land and a family man of gentle disposition who is advertised as having superhuman powers. 'His name is Nasim – the breeze, but he is now like a tempest. In India, he stopped the train with a gaze. In Pakistan, he lifted two bulls with one finger', the promoter claims. Makhmalbaf employs the polar opposites of life and death. For his wife to live, Nasim must ride to death, so he cycles until he collapses. Time is cyclical (symbolised by Nasim – just like the motorcycle daredevil of the opening scene – riding in circles, to his death) and not linear. What happens once is ordained to happen again and the repetitious theme song reinforces it. Nasim never realises his dream (making enough money to cure his wife).

Another complex theme of magical realism, the carnavalesque, serves as a tool for irony and paradox in the film. Carnivals are supposed to be a cultural manifestation to celebrate relations between human beings. In the arena where Nasim performs the endurance ride, all elements of a carnival are present – the music, the children in uniform who throw flowers at Nasim, the fortune-teller and the madman. But the blind accordionist is an impostor who expects to benefit from the betting game; the flowers only distract Nasim and the fortune-teller runs away with the promoter and the money.

Post-revolutionary Iranian cinema has often been compared to Italian neo-realism. *The Cyclist's* attention to the less fortunate and the marginal reflects the politics of neo-realism and its aim of developing the cinema as a tool for representing and analysing the experiences of ordinary people. Evidence of omnipresent poverty and the wounds of socio-political instability are skilfully integrated into the *mise-en-scène*. Makhmalbaf's use of actual locations and several non-professional actors (in minor roles), naturalistic lighting, acting, filming and editing, and his preoccupation with ordinary events, follow the basic principles of neo-realism that aim at presenting a more realistic image of the world. The closely-knit father and son relationship, their walk through the city looking for a way to provide for the wife/mother, the crowds chasing Nasim when he lies under the truck (when Antonio steals a bicycle) and the fortune-teller are all reminiscent of Vittorio De Sica's *Ladri di biciclette* (*Bicycle Thieves*, 1948). The level of desperation that forces Nasim to lie under the wheel of a truck recalls De Sica's *Umberto D* (1951), where a desperately poor man throws himself in front of a train to escape his economic and moral impasse (saved only by his concern for the welfare of his dog). But neo-realism is also about the attitude and message of the films.

The Cyclist goes beyond a committed recording of the mundane reality of poverty and deprivation to deliver a profound commentary on the nature of the human condition. Makhmalbaf turns human tragedy into a carnival and often resorts to burlesque to criticise a society that has become corrupt at every level; in pouring rain, men line up with plastic bags over their heads; conspirators who place nails on Nasim's path to deflate his tires fall into their own trap; his friend steals the ambulance in order to find another bicycle to replace the broken one and grabs the first cyclist that comes along; the explosives that are meant for Nasim scare away the politicians and their cohorts.

Several critics have read Nasim's cycling as a reference to the struggles of Mojahedin in Afghanistan against their occupiers. Having defeated the communists and the Red Army, they were not able to evade another war. Nasim's determined quest is a celebration of the triumph of the human spirit. But, in the end, he realises that against the men of power who use him for their own interests, his pursuits are futile. The last frame, showing Nasim still cycling even though the event has been cancelled, freezes as the credits appear. Such an ending is as uncertain as the destiny of the Afghan people.

During an interview conducted in Locarno in 1996, Mohsen Makhmalbaf was clear in expressing his political stance:

In the history of Iran, we have had two important persons who somehow created two different ways of looking at things. One of them was a prime-minister called Amir Kabir who lived about a hundred years ago. He was a revolutionary in the sense that he opened universities and schools and brought the question of education and science to Iran. Another one, who also lived around the same period, was Mirza Reza Kermani who tried to kill Nasraddin Shah because he thought that by eliminating someone, you could change things. I believe we still have this second approach in Iran today. Many opposition movements that try to get rid of the government seem to think that by changing the government or by killing people, they can bring change. I feel much closer to Amir Kabir who tried to change the minds of the people. I believe in change through changing thought patterns. I believe cinema can change people's way of thinking.

He has referred to his career in cinema as encompassing four periods. The first concerned political and ideological problems, along with issues of life and death, but saw the director less interested in the medium. In the second period, his films were governed by his id; the mind and the social and political background overriding the individual. Art was a tool to express social and political commitments. In the third period, he followed the 'logic of the heart' and not the 'logic of reason', adhering to the principle he calls 'relativity', as opposed to 'dogmatism'. In the fourth period, he is drawn to poetry and pure cinema, which does not mean that his work is devoid of political, social and philosophical tendencies.

Numerous films, both successful (including *Rain* and *Delbaran* (2001) by Abdolfazl Jalili) and unsuccessful, have been made about the plight of Afghani refugees in Iran since *The Cyclist*. Due to its geographical position, Iran has always been subject to a flood of refugees, particularly from Afghanistan. During the Soviet occupation and the Taliban rule, more than two-and-a-half million refugees arrived. Makhmalbaf continued his commitment to the plight of the Afghan people with *Kandahar* (2001). In fact, the protagonist of that film, the Canadian journalist Nelofar Pazira whose family emigrated from Afghanistan in 1989, chose to approach Makhmalbaf with her story after watching *The Cyclist*.

Unlike Majidi's *Rain*, which recounts a love story and through this exposes the plight of the refugees (albeit with postcard imagery of the landscape), *The Cyclist* deals with inhuman circumstances of the refugees, although love for a woman is the driving force behind the actions of the protagonist. To find the money for his sick wife's treatment, Nasim becomes part of a wager and accepts to cycle non-stop for seven days. This love, even though it palpates through the narrative, is, on the surface, subsidiary to the main theme of the film: man's cruelty to fellow man, which is rendered through the sufferings of the main protagonist. The wife is hardly seen (which is in accordance with other post-revolution films). Her physical presence is marginal although she is the dynamic force behind the narrative. She is the pillar of the family and valuable to her husband and son. In doing so, Makhmalbaf cleverly handles the strict codes of censorship of the time, which became more relaxed in the 1990s. Whereas *Rain* became an international success, *The Cyclist* has remained within the art-house circuit.

Gönül Dönmez-Colin

REFERENCES

Golmakani, Houshang (1995) *Stardust-Stricken, Mohsen Makhmalbaf: A Portrait* (video). Farabi Cinema Foundation.

Marks, Laura (2000) *The Skin of Film: Intercultural Cinema, Embodiment, and the Senses.* Durham: Duke University Press.

Seed, Patricia (1999) 'The Key to the House', in Hamid Naficy (ed.) *Home, Exile, Homeland.* New York and London: Routledge, 85–94.

BAB AL-SAMA MAFTOUH A DOOR TO THE SKY

FARIDA BENLYAZID, MOROCCO/TUNISIA/FRANCE, 1988

Bab al-sama Maftouh (*A Door to the Sky*, 1988) is the debut feature of Farida Benlyazid (who also wrote and produced it) and as such is impressive for its literary allusions and cinematic language. It is also the film of a Moroccan director with a spiritual agenda, who uses her camera to tell the story of an enlightened woman's journey to faith and beyond.

As its title implies, *A Door to the Sky* opens new worlds for its protagonist, Nadia, who crosses several thresholds throughout the film before finding her calling: between France and Morocco; outside and inside; solitude and sisterhood; atheism and belief; aimlessness and spirituality. Nadia returns from Paris, where she has been living with French press photographer Jean-Philippe, to Fez, where her father lies dying. Nadia's mother, a French painter, died when she was a child. In contrast to her two siblings – Leyla, who lives in an affluent, modern suburb of Fez with her Moroccan husband and children, and Driss, who lives in France with his French wife and children, and has 'chosen to be French' – Nadia has hitherto refused to choose one identity over the other: she 'wants it all', as she says at the beginning of the film.

Her father's death precipitates a form of depression that isolates Nadia. However, the voice of Kirana chanting a Koranic litany at the funeral elicits buried emotions imaged through Nadia's childhood flashbacks. Kirana, a devout Muslim woman of great wisdom and tolerance, gently coaxes Nadia out of her melancholy and mourning, and initiates her into a woman-centred interpretation of Islam. Nadia, under Kirana's guidance, discovers her Moroccan Muslim cultural and spiritual heritage, and distances herself from the French elements of her identity (she breaks up with Jean-Philippe). She then decides to turn the family house into a *zawyia*, a shelter and spiritual centre for women, but soon finds herself on the verge of bankruptcy. The spirit of Ba Sissi, a family friend who died a long time ago, comes to Nadia in a vision and advises her to unearth a treasure buried under the palm tree in the garden. She also discovers that she is gifted with the healing powers of a *sherifa*, a descendent of the Prophet who possessed special powers. Nadia's *zawyia* is successful, until the women start resenting the presence in their midst of newly arrived, jeans-clad, smoking and drinking Bahyia, and refuse to let in Abdelkrim, a sick young man whom Nadia is trying to heal. In the end, Nadia's open spirit cannot flourish there: she and Abdelkrim leave both the *zawyia* and the city of Fez.

Benlyazid came to cinema through writing. Born in Tangiers, she left Morocco for Paris in 1971 to study French literature at the University of Paris VIII and then, in 1974, filmmaking at Institut des Hautes Études Cinématographiques. Since then, she has led a multifaceted career in both countries, initially as a scriptwriter, then a producer, director of documentaries and films for TV, assistant director and production manager. A sought-after scriptwriter, she is the author of several film plays, most notably for two Moroccan filmmakers: her husband, Jillali Ferhati (*Jarha Fi Lhaite* (*A Hole in the Wall*, 1979) and *Poupées de roseau* (*Reed Dolls*, 1981)), and Mohamed Abderrahman Tazi, for whom she co-wrote the scenario of *Badis* (1989) and *À la Recherche du Mari de ma Femme* (*Looking for My Wife's Husband*, 1993).

A fiercely independent filmmaker, Benlyazid created her own production company, Tingitania (from the ancient name of Tangiers: Tingis), in order to make the films she wanted, without having 'to worry about the market'.

A Door to the Sky was the third film to be made in the 1980s by a female Maghrebi director trained in France, after *Al-jamr* (*La braise/The Embers*, 1982) by Moroccan Farida Bourquia and *La Trace* (*The Trace*, 1988) by Tunisian Neja Ben Mabrouk. It could be seen as a precursor to the work of Tunisian filmmaker Moufida Tlatli, the film's editor, in its cinematic treatment of the Maghrebi female subject. As Touria Khannous points out, in their sensitive portrait of the interior spaces of cloistered women in the Maghreb, Benlyazid and Tlatli offer portraits of Maghrebi women that are distinct from cinematic colonial and Maghrebi patriarchal representations. Benlyazid thus joins the rank of female filmmakers from other Islamic cultures, whom Gönül Dönmez-Colin calls 'image constructors'; boldly presenting women seeing rather than being seen. Her approach to her projects is reminiscent of that of Agnès Varda, who controls most aspects of her filmmaking through what she calls *cinécriture*; an organic process of filmmaking that involves the director in all stages of the film, from script to shooting and post-production. In a Varda-like fashion, Benlyazid also constructed her film in a highly intertextual mode, with references to both French and Moroccan culture. Her film is the work of a literary *auteur* keenly aware of the cross-fertilisation of texts and the reverberations of their voices across the territory and history of the Mediterranean.

A Door to the Sky has been ascribed several readings, ranging from the identity crisis of a Moroccan generation divided over its double allegiance to French and Moroccan culture, to an exploration on how to reconcile a feminist agenda with Islamic values. It has been read as paving the way for a Maghrebi form of feminism, as distinct from white, Western, bourgeois models of feminism, rooted in a female (re)interpretation of Islamic values of faith and solidarity. Ella Shohat sees in it an alternative to both Western feminism and Islamic fundamentalism. However, Sumi Colligan cautions that this proposed model might only apply to well-off educated women, and is oblivious to class issues. Meanwhile, Benlyazid rejects the gender segregation that she sees in both the Western feminists' project that creates a woman-only space away from the male world, and the Moroccan tradition in which women are confined to a woman-only space within the house and the *hammam*.

What makes Benlyazid's voice unique in *A Door to the Sky* lies in her cinematic exploration and representation of a spiritual path, 'the way Islam really is', as she stated to Lynn Teo Simarksi; somewhere between what Touria Khannous calls the 'purely Eurocentric terms' of feminists in the North, and the patriarchal interpretation of Islam leading to Islamic fundamentalism in the South. Benlyazid also reminds us that women have a history of occupying important social positions in Islam.

These thoughtful readings of *A Door to the Sky* mostly rest on an interpretation of its main narrative. And yet, one might gather other clues from intertextual clues disseminated throughout the filmic narrative, a process that Benlyazid uses in her next film, *Kaïd Ensa* (*Wiles of Women*, 1999), based on the traditional folk tale, 'Laïlla Aïcha, the merchant's daughter', of Andalusia. Similarly, *A Door to the Sky*'s multi-layered fabric produces a complex multiplicity of meanings. These transcend a mere 'native feminist' affirmation into a form of what Evelyne Accad calls 'femi-humanism', while imaging an exemplary individual woman's journey from the narrow spaces of humankind to the vast, spiritual expanse of 'the sky' of its title.

Let us start with a look at the narrative of Nadia's initiation into the Muslim faith. The narrative follows the traditional structure of a Sufi tale, with its archetypal characters: Kirana the master and Nadia the eager disciple embark on a spiritual quest. However, the film also subverts elements of the tale: the characters are female; the voyage of initiation takes place within the walls of the Moroccan *zawyia* instead of far away Orient; a female *zawyia* is created in an appropriated male space: Nadia's father's house, a male space, morphs into a female shelter. Furthermore, the concept of *zawyia* as a religious centre founded by a known spiritual figure or saint, for religious education and social and political consciousness, shifts, in Nadia's words, to 'a shelter open to destitute women, to the most miserable women'. Nadia, who reminds her female lawyer that Muslim women have a history of disposing of their own wealth and creating such spaces for women, actually snatches the family house away from her unwilling siblings, especially her brother, in order to create her *zawyia*. She thus asserts the right and possibility for women to take their lives and destinies into their own hands, instead of leaving them up to their husbands, brothers, fathers or patriarchal law, while following the teachings of the Prophet. The *zawyia*'s communal narrative, by turning a domestic space into a religious one, points to a new liberation narrative for Muslim women: they can free themselves not by exiting the house – the womanly space – but by appropriating and reinvesting that very space. Nadia's departure in the end would then suggest that she has transcended the stage of the *zawyia*, as an initial step in the apprenticeship of independence and spirituality, rather than its end.

The Sufi-inspired tale is also studded with intertextual, intercultural references that resonate on different levels. For instance, the character of Abdelkrim may add a political dimension to the narrative, since his name echoes that of the hero of the Moroccan resistance against the French, Mohamed Ben Abdelkrim (1883–1962). In keeping with his namesake, our Abdelkrim is a resister too: he resists the traditional male role ascribed to him by Moroccan patriarchal society and allows Nadia to be the leader in their couple, the caretaker and provider. Furthermore, just as Kirana cured Nadia, Nadia has healed Abdelkrim. In the process, she has developed her own brand of 'femi-humanist' healing: at first, it means sheltering and soothing the pain of a community of battered women away from the violent, patriarchal world, and building a sisterhood within the protective walls of the *zawyia*. However, once the members of the *zawyia* have reconstructed their whole selves, her next step is to open the doors of the shelter to other victims of patriarchal violence and order, be they female or male, believers or non-believers. In the end, it means letting in others from the outside world. Nadia's story would then caution against subscribing to any dogma, whether feminist, religious or anything else, which excludes others. In the end, Nadia the resister (together with Abdelkrim) fashions her own independence, outside the prejudices of religious or ideological institutions. In this, Nadia may be reaffirming old Sufi missions that precede her own, as several intertextual references infer either directly, in Nadia or Kirina's mouths, or obliquely, in Benlyazid's subtle aural and visual clues.

Nadia, who belongs to the highly educated bourgeoisie of Fez, is well read in at least two cultures. In her talks with Kirana, both women discuss the Koran, of course, but also several Sufi thinkers: Al Hallaj, the Persian Sufi master and wandering dervish, so famously misunderstood when he said 'I am the Truth' to describe a state of perfect unity with God, which he attained in a trance; famous Persian Islamic jurist, theologian, thinker and teacher Al-Ghazali, who, after a severe spiritual crisis, became a Sufi and is largely responsible for bringing Islamic recognition to Sufism; and Ibn Arabi, whose quote from his essay 'The One Alone' adorns one of the walls of Nadia's bedroom in its French translation – highlighting the cross-cultural relevance of Sufism that can be expressed in Farsi, Arabic, French, and so on. Ibn Arabi came to Fez, where he attained his second 'abode of light', which he described as suddenly seeing a white light more visible than what was in front of him during his prayer. Nadia – and the viewer – are given the opportunity to see such a light twice in *A Door to the Sky*. The first time, Nadia is staring at her mother's portrait of Ba Sissi: the close-up freezes on the painting until its colours fade to a luminous white, and lead Nadia to a vivid reminiscence of her mother's close friend, and her own childhood's 'master of magic'. The second time, during the Night of Miracles that celebrates the birth of the Prophet, she loses consciousness and has a vision during which she finds herself in the garden in the middle of the night, when a glaring white light from above shines down upon her (unlike the previous sequence, where the viewer shares Nadia's point of view, here she is seen from a high angle): Ba Sissi then appears to her off screen to reveal the secret of the buried treasure. It is through her filmic visual rendition of the white light that Benlyazid suggests that Nadia, like Ibn Arabi, attains her 'abode of light', her moment of revelation – and in the same city, no less. Finally, quoting Sufi thinkers might be an oblique reminder of the tradition and practice of a moderate Sunni Islam in the Maghrebi *zawyiat*, for the latter have typically integrated local rituals of magic and faith-healing, while also, as Alexander Knysh reminds us, often welcoming reformist Islamic movements and secular political groups of Marxist and liberal tendencies.

The bi-cultural Nadia also reads anti-establishment authors such as the 'doomed poet', Rimbaud, Marx (who regards religion as 'the opium of the people'), the American Marxist revolutionary Angela Davis, and remembers so fondly Jean-Luc Godard's film *Sauve qui peut (la vie)* (*Slow Motion*, 1980). Her references to engaged, 'intellectual' people, in the French sense of the term, attest to the inherent political nature of art, writing and even the sciences: after all, was French chemist Lavoisier (whose famous maxim 'Nothing is created, nothing is lost' Nadia keeps quoting) not executed at the guillotine in 1794?

These conscious narrative references reveal a rich subtext that complicates the picture. Nadia has a political consciousness that transcends geopolitical borders. But beyond it, it is the development of her spiritual consciousness that Benlyazid seems interested in projecting onto the screen, which justifies the other aural and visual intertexts through which the director shows an innovative way of filming a human spiritual exemplar growing and flourishing out of the particular regional context of Morocco.

The musical pieces and chants on the soundtrack reflect the multicultural mosaic of Morocco and trans-Mediterranean Nadia. We hear Arabic, Muslim litanies either from Sufi masters or from the Koran – such as the one chanted by Kirana; Berber songs – Benlyazid herself is of Berber descent; Andalusian music – a hint at the history of Fez; an excerpt of Bach's *St Mathew's Passion* – a European spiritual voice. The latter is heard twice in the film, each time announcing the presence of Nadia's mother. Most significantly, its first occurrence coincides with the preamble of the film (before the credits), during which Nadia's ailing father remembers returning home to his pregnant wife after a trip. As he enters the luxuriant patio, she is listening to the Aria No. 70, 'Sehet Jesus, hat die Hand', the last aria before Jesus's question to God, 'Father, why have you forsaken me?' and his death, in the *Passion*. The music bathes the entire scene, over the Arabic words of her husband's mother, who is trying to teach her the Muslim credo, 'Allah is the only God, and Mohamed is His prophet'.

The preamble aurally juxtaposes both religious systems and cultures, assigning the Bach piece to the side of Nadia's French mother, and the spoken words of the Koran to her father's side. In the fashion of programmatic music, it also foreshadows the imminence of her father's death, and of Nadia's subsequent feeling of utter abandonment. Finally, the *Passion* shares some of its themes, such as human solitude, doubt and faith, with *A Door to the Sky*.

Benlyazid links the character of Nadia's mother to another European intertext: that of Orientalist paintings. Nadia's mother was a painter and Nadia often finds refuge in her studio. As she looks at the paintings on the wall, we recognise allusions to Delacroix. These 'unfinished' paintings – as stipulated by the credits at the end – remind us, on the one hand, of Delacroix's 1832 sketch book from his trip to Morocco, covered with jotted-down drawings and watercolours as glimpses of potential works, and on the other, of the life of the mother/painter cut short. Here again, values are subverted: Delacroix is famous for his *Femmes d'Alger dans leur appartement* (*Algiers Women in their Apartment*, 1834), his fantasy of a Maghrebi harem, painted after he had caught a glimpse of Algiers. In *A Door to the Sky*, however, the woman artist painted one man – her friend 'with whom she used to talk for long hours'. Beyond a gender reversal between painter and subject, this intertext reasserts the role of woman as 'image constructor': the painter here does not capture the object of her gaze and fantasy, as did Delacroix and other Orientalists. Her portrait of Ba Sissi results from sitting together with her subject, not object, for long hours, talking; from contemplation and sharing rather than voyeuristic peeping.

In the end, the busy texture of the narrative alludes to the making of a different film, a film in which old meta-narratives – the history of colonisation and the European Orientalists, the

Christian myth of death and solitude, the history of women's positions as objects of the male gaze rather than subjects gazing and creating, the history of Islam and Sufism in the Maghreb region – are deconstructed and reinterpreted by one woman inside a house, hinting perhaps at a new cinematic representation and value of space.

This – often literally – labyrinthine film not only opens doors, but explores the spaces beyond them. It starts with a focus on two distinct spaces: the city of Fez and, within its old walls, the *zawyia*, and leads to the possibility of yet another space outside them both. However, that ultimate space – sacred, mysterious and inviting – is only suggested at the end of the film.

The choice of Fez as location for this film reverberates with significant connotations: cinematic, religious and political (feminist). Fez is a landmark in the history of cinema in Morocco, since this is where the first films were shown in the country: the Lumière brothers projected them in the Royal Palace of Fez as early as 1897. The famous city of mosques and traditional Muslim learning centre is also, as the credits immediately signal, where the woman to whom the film is dedicated, Fatima al-Fihriya, founded its first university, the Al Qaraouine Mosque, in the tenth century. Hence, the film takes us to a city whose women are agents of Islam, or as Viola Shafik points out, a regional brand of Islamic religiosity – as opposed to the universalistic approach of fundamentalism. Fittingly enough, the very first shot of the preamble is a slow vertical pan of Al Qaraouine Mosque's minaret, from the sky down to its street door that Nadia's father can push to enter. In this emblematic scene, the tower connotes the feminine, Fatima al-Fihriya, and the masculine, Nadia's father.

Fez is not only a religious city but also the native land of Moroccan feminism: two of its daughters (in the wake of Fatima al-Fihriya?) are famous for their resistance to patriarchal and/or colonial powers: journalist Malika Al Fassi, who founded a women's association within the Moroccan Nationalist Movement that demanded and obtained that Al Qaraouine University open a women section in 1949; and feminist Fatima Mernissi.

The dual geography of Fez is equally significant, mirroring Nadia's dual cultural allegiance: the old city at the core, with its old universities, mosques and tiny, busy streets, is the centre of the narrative, since it is where the family house/*zawyia* is located; the modern European city on its periphery shows sprawling affluent suburbs spreading away from the *medinah*. This is where Leyla, Nadia's sister, lives with her family. The Fez Nadia inhabits is the old vertical city that opens doors to old narratives of Fez that may be new to Nadia and the viewer.

Space in this film is represented along two axes: a vertical one, Fez, along the first shot of the film, and a horizontal one: the house, with its traditional architecture along a central, open patio. The image of the house as womanly space is frequent in Maghrebi cinema, but the uniqueness of this film derives from the fluid visual representation of passage from one room to the next; of liminal spaces that Nadia crosses, or where she lingers. It suggests that the house is not strictly partitioned, that doors will open for Nadia, seen against a wall, a window, next to a door, looking through a door, a window, a *musharabieh*, passing from one room to the next, from one space to the next. Similarly, thresholds are highlighted throughout the film by numerous shots of windows, doorways, glass surfaces reflecting the outside landscape.

The outside spaces that are shot in or from the house (low-angle shots towards the sky, shots filtered by the light let in through a window), suggest both a clear border between the inner sanctum of the house and its exterior. We also see the blue gate open to let in women, an openness to the outer world – albeit a selective one. This is not the case when Jean-Philippe flies to Fez to visit Nadia. The aural and visual montage and shots of this sequence show how impassable the divide has grown between Nadia's receding French identity and her Moroccan one. They meet in the lobby of a modern hotel. The camera is behind Jean-Philippe, who is seated, reading a newspaper. Nadia enters through glass doors, clad in white from head to toe, accompanied by syrupy muzak. She takes him to the café outside the hotel. A medium close-up of Nadia against the backdrop of Fez cuts to a counter medium shot of Jean-Philippe against the cold, modern design of the hotel. Their dialogue mixes with the sounds of the city, dominated by the calls to prayer, emanating from the various mosques. The camera then cuts to Jean-Philippe's bedroom: the latter is shot from the balcony, through closed windows that reflect the cityscape. The rumours of Fez and the muezzins' calls outside mute the couple's dialogue. Finally, Nadia walks towards the camera, slides the glass door open and pauses, in the same interstitial space she has occupied, symbolically, since the beginning of the film. Jean-Philippe claims he wants to understand her, while she accuses him of being a tourist. She walks out of his room – his Western space – onto the balcony. The camera rotates and shoots her from behind, in medium shot. He joins her at the threshold of the bedroom and the balcony. Both are framed side by side, against the backdrop of the old city: she faces the camera; his back is turned to it. 'Listen to the timelessness of Islam' she tells him, pointing to the muezzins' calls.

In this short sequence, each character is framed with a signifying backdrop: she belongs to Fez; he belongs to the modern Western hotel. The soundtrack also emphasises, through the loud muezzin calls almost drowning their dialogue, their complete breakdown in communication. Neither belongs to the other's landscape or soundscape. Although the liminal spaces (windowpanes) here are transparent it is as if an iron curtain of separation – a heavy *hejab*

– had been drawn between both worlds. This scene is the site of one of the most disturbing value reversals of the entire film. Nadia's ease with the West is forever a thing of the past. The West does not hear her.

As this sequence shows, the city's sonic landscape resounds with the calls to prayer emanating from the many mosques of Fez. Religion definitely has a voice – or voices – in this film. It is, after all, the voice of Kirana chanting the sacred text that attracts Nadia like a magnet. The voices and the space of the old city seem to come together in the telling of the narrative. Hence, perhaps, the significance of the last sequence of the film, in exact counterpoint to the preamble described earlier. In the very last shot, the camera frames Nadia and Abdelkrim, dressed in white, seated in an embrace. They are outside the city, in the countryside, in the sun. Prior to this, we have seen them hike through an olive grove, do their ablutions, pray, then resume their journey, to the sound of one male voice off-screen. It is the voice of a man intoning a litany in Arabic praising Allah, the Creator. The voice recites as the camera pans vertically in the opposite direction to the preamble: up from the loving couple to an intensely blue, cloudless sky. The sacred litany goes on, as the entire credits roll, then fade and leave an empty sky-blue screen before it turns blank. The images have vanished, but not the litany. The film thus becomes part of a larger narrative: just as the preamble had alluded to a 'pre-history' to Nadia's story, the lingering voice is now suggesting the existence of an immense narrative beyond Nadia's, somewhere in the blue expanse.

In the end, Benlyazid has helped her characters push many doors open since Nadia's father first pushed the door home at the beginning of the film: the door to women's communication and solidarity; the door to femi-humanism; and finally, the literal door to the sky, and to the miracle of film as creation which, to paraphrase Ibn Arabi, is a mirror in which we might see ourselves.

Florence Martin

REFERENCES

Accad, Evelyn (1992) *Sexuality and War: Literary Masks of the Middle East*. New York: New York University Press.

Colligan, Sumi (2000) '"To develop our listening capacity to be sure that we hear everything": Sorting out Voices on Women's Rights in Morocco', *Journal of International Women's Studies*,

1, 1. On-line; available at http://bridgew.us/SoAS/jiws/vol1/sumi.htm (accessed 13 March 2007).

Dönmez-Colin, Gönül (2004) *Women, Islam and Cinema*. London: Reaktion Books.

Khannous, Touria (2001) 'Strategies of representation and postcolonial identity in North African Women's cinema', *Journal X: A Journal of Culture and Criticism*, 1, 6, 49–61.

Knysh, Alexander (2000) *Islamic Mysticism: A Short History*. Leiden: Brill.

Shafik, Viola (1998) *Arab Cinema: History and Cultural Identity*. Cairo: American University in Cairo Press.

Shohat, Ella (1997) 'Framing Post-Third-Worldist Culture: Gender and Nation in Middle Eastern North African Film and Video'. On-line; available at http://152.1.96.5/jouvert/v1i1/shohat.htm (accessed 11 January 2005).

Simarksi, Lynn Teo T. (1992) 'North African Film through North African Eyes', ARAMCO World, 1–2. On-line; available at http://www.sas.upenn.edu/African_Studies/Audio_Visual/North_African_10051.html (accessed 11 January 2005).

YOUCEF OU LA LÉGENDE DU SEPTIÈME DORMANT

13

YOUSSEF OR THE LEGEND OF THE SEVENTH SLEEPER

MOHAMED CHOUIKH, ALGERIA/FRANCE, 1993

Youcef ou la Légende du septième dormant (*Youssef or the Legend of the Seventh Sleeper*, 1993) was the third film by Mohamed Chouikh, who had played a key role as an actor in the early years of Algerian cinema. Born in 1943 at Mostaganem, Chouikh wrote his first play at sixteen and, as a teenager, worked extensively in amateur theatre in his native city. He was nineteen at the time of the Algerian liberation in 1962, and the following year began his career as a professional actor, joining the company that was to become the Algerian National Theatre. Like so many young Algerians, Chouikh had developed a passion for the cinema, revelling in the American, Hindu and Egyptian films that filled Algerian screens at that time. In addition to his stage work, Chouikh began his practical work in Algerian filmmaking in a very different atmosphere from that of his childhood, passing swiftly, as he has put it, from a system of colonial oppression to an East European-style state structure, in which mere slogans served as expressions of culture.

Chouikh became involved in the first significant Algerian production, Ahmed Rachedi's *L'Aube des damnés* (*Dawn of the Dead*), in 1965, and also starred in several of the key pioneering Algerian films of the late 1960s, including Mohamed Lakhdar Hamina's *Le Vent des Aurès* (*The Wind from the Aurès*, 1966) and Tewfik Fares's *Les Hors-la-loi* (*The Outlaws*, 1968). Chouikh continued his acting career into the 1970s and early 1980s, appearing in the French director Michel Drach's *Élise ou la vraie vie* (*Élise or Real Life*, 1970), Sid Ali Mazif's *Les Nomades* (*The Nomads*, 1975), Amar Laskri's *El Moufid* (1978) and the television serial, *Barbelés* (*Barbed Wire*, 1981), directed by Ahmed Rachedi. In 1971 he also wrote the commentary for Annie Tresgot's *Les Passagers* (*The Passengers*, 1971) and subsequently wrote and directed two 16mm feature-length films for RTA (Radio-Télévision Algérienne): *L'Embouchure* (*The River Mouth*, 1972–74) and *Les Paumés* (*The Wrecks*, 1974). He gained further production experience by acting as assistant director on Mohamed Lakhdar Hamina's *Vent de sable* (*Sand Storm*) in 1982.

He has subsequently written and directed four features, three of which were for the successive Algerian state-controlled production organisations: *La Rupture* (*Breakdown*, 1982) for ONCIC (Office National du Commerce et de l'Industrie Cinématographiques); *La Citadelle* (*The Citadel*, 1988) for CAAIC (Centre Algérien pour l'Art et Industrie Cinématographiques);

and *Youssef or the Legend of the Seventh Sleeper* which was a CAAIC-ENPA (Entreprise Nationale de Productions Audiovisuelles) co-production. Chouikh's fourth feature, *L'Arche du désert* (*Desert Ark*, 1997) was independently produced. This context is important because, as he has observed in interview with Camille Taboulay, until the mid-1990s making a film outside the state structures was a counter-revolutionary act, which just did not happen. It was impossible to get permission to shoot or even film stock outside of the state sector. Though there was a certain security (in that filmmakers were paid by the month, whether they were actually producing or not), the position was far from ideal. As Chouikh noted, working for the Algerian state production organisation meant doing all the pre-production work yourself and then handing the project over to a bureaucracy which paid a low salary but had the power of life or death over the film's production.

Since *Youssef...* presents an image of Algeria's post-independence seen through the eyes of the traditional Arab figure of the holy fool, a little knowledge of that history is required for a full understanding of the film and its importance for Algeria.

In the years that separate independence in 1962 and the shooting of *Youssef...*, Algerian society had transformed. The population had doubled and the country had moved from a rural to an urban economy, with huge migrations of (especially young) people to the cities and to Europe, which created huge social and cultural upheaval. From Ahmed Ben Bella's instalation as head of state, the army had ruled Algeria through the single permitted political party, the FLN (National Liberation Front). But as Benjamin Stora points out, by the time the film was conceived, the FLN had already lost the historical legitimacy it claimed from the war of independence and had long been discredited by such factors as bureaucracy, corruption and careerism. Faced with growing national crisis, the FLN hesitated between liberalisation and repression, and the people came gradually to see that the glorious myth of a people totally united behind 'its' army and the claims of the FLN as sole founder and guarantor of the country were both mere myths. Yet this was the story that Algerian cinema had told over and over again since the first Algerian features in 1965.

October 1988 saw riots in Algiers and the sudden surge of popular support for Islamic fundamentalism. The latter's political arm, the FIS (Islamic Salvation Front), swept the FLN away at the 1990 elections (obtaining 54 per cent of the votes against 18 per cent for the FLN), forcing the army to take direct control once more. As state support for film production was eroded in the 1990s, films co-produced with French companies began to reflect this national turmoil. Malik Lakhdar Hamina's impressive debut feature *Automne: octobre à Alger* (*Autumn:*

October in Algiers, 1992) and, later, Merzak Allouache's brilliant tragicomedy *Bab el Oued City* (1994) are among the most striking of these films. But the most comprehensive reflection of the national confusion is Chouikh's *Youssef...*, written in 1988 and shot somehow within the state system in 1992–93.

Denise Brahimi has drawn attention to Chouikh's unusual position within Algerian film-making, particularly in the constant use he makes of non-realistic images, symbols, parables and allegories. This is certainly true of *Youssef...* which begins in a deliberately confused manner, with the apparent escape of Youssef from French imprisonment. He 'sees' images of betrayal, capture, torture and rape, but the escape rings false – something is wrong. It is only later that we discover that Youssef is in fact a wounded former combatant who has been held in an asylum in the south of Algeria for thirty years, prior to the end of the war in 1962 (though, for those familiar with Arab legends, this is implied by the title which refers to the popular legend of seven men who slept for three centuries and woke to find the world a very different place). Having lost his memory because of his wounds, Youssef thinks he is still in the 1960s and in an Algeria still colonised by the French. Here he represents a classic figure in Arab literature, the holy fool who says and does apparently crazy things, but in fact states the obvious truths that the authorities would like to gloss over; similar to the small boy in the Western fairytale of the emperor's new clothes. As the film unfolds, it is the state of Algeria that is mad, not the protagonist. Chouikh's often grotesque images and situations increasingly make this clear.

Outside the prison, nothing makes sense to Youssef. He seeks refuge as a guerrilla fighter in one of the first houses he comes to, but is called an impostor and a thief, and is shot at by villagers. He struggles through the desert, eventually collapsing. He hallucinates that a woman comes to his rescue, but he is in fact found and rescued by male *tuaregs*. He enters an isolated village, where he is given bread and dates. But he immediately he stumbles on a disquieting scene of a woman disowned and taunted as impure, and confronted with her child, who has been burnt alive. Youssef assumes this is the work of racist colonialists, but in fact it is the woman's own pitiless, tradition-based family who are to blame. Youssef sets off again, returning to his old haunts in search of his comrades in arms. He 'sees' them cut down in battle. Exhausted, he falls asleep in their secluded hideaway, only to awaken to find six skeletons, as well as the bones of his faithful old dog. He buries them and prays over their graves, promising to fight on until independence is secured. He tries to call headquarters on the old radio to announce their deaths, but of course, there is no reply. Descending into the village, he finds incomprehensible scenes: his old chief Athmane is now living like a coloniser in a villa built by the French, while the ordinary people are queuing for bread. He makes another desperate appeal to headquarters denouncing his chief and lamenting the fate of the colonised.

Returning to the villa, he confronts Athmane who protests at his stupidity. Athmane is now the FLN. How can he be a traitor when he has only one villa, while others have factories in their wives' names? Chased off by Athmane's dog, Youssef tries to book a room in the male *hammam*, but his old coins are no longer valid currency. This is one of the many symbolic details in the film; the pre-independence coins are now useless, just as the values of the period are now of no concern. Youssef sets off to seek the families of his dead companions, as the chanting crowds that appear in this section of the film march past him, this time to rally to Athmane. Youssef finds his dead friend Ali's nephew, who now has to disguise himself as a woman, because he lives in fear of the father of the beautiful girl he loves and was caught with. The father turns out to be Athmane, who has threatened to cut his throat. Youssef is persuaded to disguise himself as a woman too and they go off together. When a man tries to pick him up, Youssef takes off his black robe, pulls out his gun, scaring off the man, who flees after pleading that he is a husband and a father. Youssef's own scenes are farcical, but Ali's nephew is treated by Youssef and the film's narrative with respect. He is a figure to whom the film returns regularly, while most of those whom Youssef meets (such as the fundamentalists) are seen only once. As Tahar Chikhaoui has noted, there is an immediate rapport between Ali's nephew and Youssef, who accepts the thwarted nephew's decision to live as a woman. To take a transvestite, who seems at home in his role, as a symbol for Algerian youth crippled by thirty years of FLN rule and a society based on the total segregation of the sexes is one of Chouikh's most daring symbols.

Returning to his old hideaway, Youssef again tries to use his antique radio: 'If anyone hears me, things are bad in this region.' Encountering a band of smugglers, he asks them to send the message to the high command that he – Youssef the Patriot – is still alive, the sole survivor: 'Long live the front, long live the people.' Then he sets off once more on his travels. He eventually falls asleep, only to be woken by what he thinks is the noise and shadow of a French military helicopter. He is terrified, until he realises it is only a windmill. He then goes to the house of Si Larbi (his old companion who is now dead), but is met only by his brother. When he describes himself as a combatant, he is mistaken for an Islamic militant and is invited to the meeting a group of militants are holding. After calling for a minute of silence for the martyrs, he meets the all-male group for whom he is living proof of existence of prisons and of society's ills; the young have no work, cannot marry and are lost. One militant denounces the liberation of women as the root of all their current problems:

'The worst thing in our society is women. Instead of bringing up children and giving them our moral values, they flout them in every sphere. They always find somewhere to live; they have priority when it comes to work. You find them everywhere. They claim to participate in the development of the country in the same way as men! How do they help that? Tell me! They are responsible for the moral degradation of society. Licentiousness and light morals are the cause of the rottenness of society.'

Youssef, of course, opposes such a view – these are attitudes he fought against in the liberation struggle. Accused of being a provocateur and spy, he replies that he is a combatant in the national army, which makes the militants even angrier and they chase him off. Continuing his search, he finds a group of disillusioned young people sat by the sea drinking alcohol and being serenaded by a young singer, Baaziz, with his song, 'Bye Bye My Country'. Whereas youths of Youssef's generation were committed to creating a better Algeria, these young men simply dream of emigrating. For them, abroad is the only place where a better world can be found. When one of them says he wants to go to hell, he is mocked by the others. Where does he think he is? He is in hell already. Continuing his travels, Youssef happens upon a villa where workers are being harangued. He is told by a woman of his own generation that if the colonisers were bad, this lot (the new Algerian owner who has property both here and in France) are worse. Youssef tries to carry out the justified execution of such a traitor, but of course, his old gun jams and he is again chased away.

This time, when Youssef goes back to his old base, he is followed. It is at this point that the narrative turns, as Youssef discovers what has happened to him. When he tries to use his radio, he hears himself described as a dangerous mad man who has escaped from an asylum. This is news he rejects, but it is supported by the man who has been trailing him – an old friend, who calls him Youyou. The man has been sent to find him. He is accompanied by doctors and an ambulance, friends and former combatants who fought with him. Youssef still refuses to believe the truth, even when the x-ray of his head wound is produced as evidence. He thinks these are all lies to lure him back. When told that independence has come to the villages, everywhere, he argues on the basis of what he has seen; do they think he is mad? Even Fatima, the nurse from the group who treated him when he was wounded, is unable to convince him. As he explains, he could not imagine independence would turn out like this; a country rife with oppression, suffering, poverty, cowardice, injustice and humiliation.

To try to convince him, his friends show him film of the national liberation, in a grotto illuminated only by the light from the projector. This complex, multi-layered scene brings together various images from earlier in the film and explicitly raises questions about the notion of seeing and believing; of cinema and truth. In interviews, Chouikh, who has shown Youssef afraid of his own shadow during his initial escape and of the windmill when he was sleeping in a field, explicitly relates the new shadow play to Plato's cave. He argues that by putting Youssef on the screen, he has been able to draw attention to Algerian cinema's role as a very partial and biased witness to the truth of post-independence society. Ironically, the scenes chosen to convince Youssef are from the fictional feature *La battaglia di Algeri* (*The Battle of Algiers*, 1966) which has a French-language commentary and was directed by an Italian, Gillo Pontecorvo. Chouikh's view of Algerian cinema's portrayal of post-independence society is bleak, seeing it as a reflection of the subjective reality of the state authorities who commissioned the films, and hence little more than an instrument of propaganda.

Youssef wants to see old friends, but many are dead, some are now businessmen, others perhaps in prison (though officially there are not supposed to be political prisoners any more). The words – socialism, capitalism, communism, liberalism – have all lost their meaning and there is no longer politics. Only money. Youssef also demands to see Aïcha, the girl he imagined being raped by the French in his 'prison'. Before she arrives, he learns other truths about independent Algeria. The men may have some sort of freedom, but not the women. Fatima, his ex-battlefield nurse, who now has to be veiled, tells of being married, beaten by her husband, and divorced. Aïcha, when she arrives, also fails to convince him as to where he is. But both are treated sympathetically by Youssef. Chouikh films women with a tenderness rare in Arab cinema. Like Ali's nephew, they appear almost as facets of Youssef's personality. But instead of personally debating the role of women, Youssef finds himself embroiled in an argument about party membership. When he is told about the advantages of his FLN party membership, he is driven to extreme anger. Did he make the revolution in order to get the authority to import a cow or a car? The party official is unfazed: since he originally trained as an architect, how would he like the monopoly for building martyr's monuments? Youssef then begins to ask himself, is it the world that is mad, or is it him?

At this point Chouikh has a narrative problem: how to find a way of welcoming Youssef back to conscious awareness of contemporary Algeria. The solution is one of the finest twists of the film's storyline. Since Youssef is a distinguished ex-fighter who has missed independence, then the party (the FLN) will organise an independence ceremony just for him: 'an independence day for a comrade who arrived late'. He is hailed as a pure spirit, a man who has not been corrupted, the people's only hope. He is taken away by helicopter, but when he lands he is swamped by petitions from poor people who desperately seek his help. He places a wreath on the monument to the martyrs of the liberation struggle, surrounded by veiled women. He is summoned to the platform by the party elite, but at the last moment he hesitates, unsure of what is in store for him, suspecting a trap despite the welcoming arms outstretched towards him. Instinctively, as an old combatant, he pulls out his gun, only to be shot down, anonymously from a balcony. He dies, less an individual character than the embodiment of a truth which cannot be allowed, mourned not only by the two women in his life, now united in grief, but also by an anonymous child (Algeria's future?). In keeping with the confused situation in Algeria at the time the film was shot, the ending is deliberately ambiguous. We are not shown who kills Youssef, and Chouikh claims that he does not know either. Interviewed by Camille Taboulay in 1997, Chouikh stood by the comment he had made when the film was released, that on the day that he came to know what was happening in Algeria, he would add an explanatory subtitle.

Youssef offers remarkable insight into the complex and contradictory situation in Algeria at the beginning of the 1990s. Though the script was originally written in 1988 and submitted to the authorities in 1990, there are chilling parallels with the assassination of the Algerian President, Mohamed Boudiaf, on 29 June 1992 (while the film was being shot). At the age of 35, Boudiaf had been one of the leading figures in the Algerian Revolution, participating fully in the eight years of struggle for independence. He was arrested and imprisoned along with Ahmed Ben Bella when the latter's plane was intercepted by the French air force. But from 1962 he opposed both Ben Bella (the first Algerian post-independence president) and Houari Boumediene (who led the 1965 military coup). Imprisoned, exiled and written out of the official history of the Algerian liberation, he was eventually allowed to live in southern Algeria (where the fictitious Youssef was hospitalised). But in the perplexing situation of Algeria, when he was unknown to the mass of the people, Boudiaf was suddenly hailed by the FLN as a potential saviour – a man untouched by corruption and the ideal person to solve the problems posed by Islamic fundamentalism. Boudiaf was summoned back after 28 years of political exile in January 1992, following the initial triumph at the polls by the Islamic fundamentalists, to head up the Republic on behalf of a new 'pure' FLN. But just a few months later, at his second official function, he was assasinated at a meeting in Annaba. The official account of his assassination (murder by a single officer in the presidential guard) is generally distrusted.

Youssef or the Legend of the Seventh Sleeper is hardly a seamless work, veering from black farce to tender emotional scenes and episodes of real horror. Chouikh denies any desire to bring solutions or make definitive judgements, but what emerges with total clarity is the failure of the FLN over thirty years; what Chouikh has described as its thirty-year coma during which everyone tried to give the FLN intensive care and vainly prescribed ideological remedies. Chouikh's chosen device is to view events through the eyes of a man who assumes – because of his amnesia – that the country is still colonised. Youssef finds nothing in his perceptions to alter his initial (mis)understanding. The title indicates that this is not intended as a realistic account of Algeria in the 1990s but as a fable that uses all the resources of narrative to communicate its meaning. As such it stands aside from the mainstream of official Algerian filmmaking, which is generally crippled by its lack of originality in form and its conformity of message. Mohamed Chouikh, here and in his other works of the past decade and a half, thus shows himself to be a major figure in Maghrebi filmmaking.

Roy Armes

REFERENCES

Brahimi, Denise (2004) 'Images, symboles et paraboles dans le cinéma de Mohamed Chouikh', in Michel Serceau (ed.) *Cinémas du Maghreb*. Paris: Corlet/Télérama/CinémAction, 154–9.

Chikhaoui, Tahar (1994) 'La Réalité de la fable', *Cinécrits*, 5, 4–5.

Camille Taboulay (1997) *Le Cinéma métaphorique de Mohamed Chouikh, suivi de L'Arche du désert (Scénario & dialogues)*. Paris: K Films Éditions.

Stora, Benjamin (1994) *Histoire de l'Algérie depuis l'indépendance* Paris: Éditions La Découverte.

MOUFIDA TLATLI, TUNISIA/FRANCE, 1994

Samt al-qusur (*Silences of the Palace*, 1994) by female director Moufida Tlatli is one of the most acknowledged and highly praised fiction films from the Arab world. It circulated in numerous international film festivals, going on to receive the Jury's Special Mention at the Cannes Film Festival, the International Film Critics' Award at the Toronto Film Festival and the Best First Feature at the Chicago Film Festival. It was not only considered a successful art-movie, but also a politically critical feminist film. However, it can be argued that the emphatic reception of the film and its categorisation as an art-movie, particularly in the West, is more due to a Western predisposition to the issue of women and Islam than to the film itself. Indeed, upon a closer reading, the work may be regarded as a successful reinterpretation of the rules of classical women's film, namely melodrama redesigned for the international art film and festival circuit. Something that seems even more true because of the fact that *Silences of the Palace* was only distributed in its original homeland, but did not – like other Arab productions of its kind and unlike Egyptian popular feature films – find an inter-regional Arab distributor who would distribute it in the rest of the Arab world.

The film represents the coming-of-age story of adolescent Alia as performed by two actresses, Hind Sabri as young girl and Ghalia Lacroix as grown-up woman. It is also the story of female seclusion and thwarted liberation. It unfolds at a decisive historical moment, in the early 1950s, on the eve of national Tunisian independence from the French protectorate. Young Alia is the daughter of maid Khadija, who has been sold at the age of ten and brought up in the palace of two affluent *beys*, members of the traditional ruling elite and sympathetic to the French occupier.

The status of the maids is comparable with that of slaves in their economic and emotional, even sexual, dependence on their masters (even though slavery had been officially abolished more than a century before). However, there is something exceptional about Alia. Even though she is her mother's illegitimate daughter, one of their masters, Sid Ali, whose wife did not conceive any children, treats her and her mother with affection and tenderness. However, he does not break the class barrier by giving his (suspected) daughter any legal status, nor does he protect Alia from the sudden sexual interest of his brother, which results in his raping her mother. This violent act brings about her death, as she undergoes a secret abortion. It will also cause Alia to leave the golden cage of her childhood with Lutfy, a nationalist-oriented school teacher, who has been working and hiding in the palace, only to dwell in a new cage because of her morally questionable position as a singer and Lutfy's mistress.

The story stretches over a decade, opening with with Alia's visit to the palace following the death of Sid Ali. During the visit, she meets the family of the *beys* and her mother's colleagues. This enables her story to be retold through several extended flashbacks, starting with Alia's birth, on the same night as Sara's, the daughter of Sid Ali's brother, Sid Bashir. The two grow up as friends, but with a marked distinction between them. Alia's place is the kitchen and the realm of the servants, most of them women who never leave the palace. Education also seperates Sarah and Alia. While Sarah receives, among other classes, regular lute lessons, Alia is condemned to silent observation. However, her mother is aware of her growing interest in music and saves money to offer her daughter a lute upon which she progresses rapidly. As Alia grows up, she also draws the attention of Sid Bashir, who demands services from her. Desperately, the mother tries to protect her daughter by meeting the *bey* himself and is finally raped by him in her own room, an incident watched in horrorific silence by Alia.

The servants have managed to hide the young nationalist Lutfy, who works as a teacher for the *bey*'s children. He also begins instructing Alia, who feels increasingly attracted to him. At the same time, the palace prepares for Sarah's engagement party at which Alia is asked to sing to the guests. Only her mother is opposed to it, for the sake of her daughter's safety. However, the night turns out to be the dramatic climax of the film's events. For, while Alia prepares to sing, her mother prepares to abort the child resulting from the *bey*'s recent rape. While the abortion turns into a bloody agony, terminating the mother's life, the daughter uses her presence among some of the country's most influential personalities to sing the forbidden Tunisian national anthem, thereby heavily offending the guests. In this decisive night, she leaves the palace with Lutfy without returning for a decade.

The opening scenes of the film do not only lead Alia back to the palace, thus giving space to the different extended flashbacks, but introduces us also to Alia's present-time condition. In the first shots, we see her singing at a wedding party. Struck by a strong migraine she is collected by Lutfy, her lover. On this occasion, we learn that she is pregnant but he urges her to abort the child as she did several times before, for he is evidently unwilling to marry her. At the end of the film, that initial conflict is taken up again; we hear her arguing in an inner monologue with herself, uttering her intent not to abort the child this time as she feels that it has already taken roots in her.

The film's modernist and feminist orientation in dealing overtly with the issue of female oppression was certainly responsible for its positive reception, along with its impressive *mise-en-scène* and the fact that it was made by a woman. However, it offers numerous readings. I myself have elsewhere categorised the film as part of Arab *cinéma d'auteur* that showed the tendency to feminise Arab cinema; to break and deconstruct the metaphorical link created by anti-colonial cinema between women's liberation and the liberation of the nation. Indeed, the film supersedes the regular modernist stance of feminism that developed in Arab post-colonial societies. An indicator for this is Lutfy's ambiguous role in the film. His particular character stands for the enlightened nationalist movement that liberates the heroine from her traditional confinement, but does not transcend those traditions that consider Alia a social outcast. Instead, he upholds the same old moral values.

This view is in line with other opinions proposing that *Silences of the Palace* alludes to what Ella Shohat has described as the 'gendered limitations of Third World nationalisms'. Shohat has also described the film as 'Post-Third Worldist', for breaking some of the fault lines of religion, gender and nation. She thinks that contrary to so-called Third Worldist works the film does not picture the moment of the birth of the nation as actively administered by women, as was the case in numerous anti-colonial films. Instead, it shows women restricted to servitude and the domestic space. They experience the moment of national struggle only through the mediation of others, namely radio and male household members. Thus, for Shohat, the social positioning of the heroines turns into a critique of failed revolutionary hopes as seen in the post-colonial era.

The film and its women do engender a strong moment of female resistance through the motif of the loyal female community, which contradicts Western concepts of the domestic space as the location of social isolation. Here home is also the place of female oppression and seclusion. However, the female servants form a strong community, sharing their joy and their pain. According to Shohat, these women become a non-patriarchal family within a patriarchal context. The kitchen is the place where the largest part of female servants' interaction takes place. Other less joyful occasions, such as the abortion, is also shared and prepared by them. These depictions are in line with current post-colonial feminist theory that has shown that in traditional society, the extended household entertained means to protect women, unlike the nuclear family where women have to face male physical dominance or even violence in isolation.

The critical preoccupation with the social position of women, but also gender relations in general, form one of the main threads of Tunisian cinema since the 1970s, ranging from modernist anti-colonial films such as *Sejnane* (1974) and *Aziza* (1980) to the very recent *al-Sitar al-ahmar* (*The Red Curtain*, 2002) by Raja Amari. This special orientation led also to a strong presence of women directors in what Tunisian critics call their *cinéma du femme*. The latter has become the source of pride for Tunisian cineastes, forming in their eyes one of their cinema's main trademarks; particularly Ferid Boughedir, a film historian and filmmaker who has become one of the spokesmen of this idea, insisting that women's issues are at the heart of almost every Tunisian film.

To Boughedir, the emergence of 'women's cinema' and the proportionally high participation of women in national filmmaking have been facilitated by Tunisian jurisdiction which is considered to be the most liberal in all Arab Muslim countries in terms of gender equality. However, comparing the proportion of Tunisian female directors to other Arab countries with a similarly limited cinematic output, it turns out that Boughedir's account is only partially true. Five female Tunisian filmmakers have succeeded in directing full-length fiction films, in contrast to Tunisia's two closest neighbours; Morocco has seen two and Algeria three. However, Lebanon has produced six female directors. This certainly means that the discourse on Tunisian cinema's 'feminist' outlook has to be qualified as a positive, though somewhat limited, claim. It is also originated in post-colonial modernist developmental thinking, which often confounds idealism with reality, and should, as such, be related to so-called Third Worldist ideology that has dominated the post-independence film, as well as the *cinéphile* movement in Tunisia.

The French-inspired *ciné-club* movement crystallised through the Tunisian Film Club Association (Fédération tunisienne des Ciné-clubs/FTCC). To the first Tunisian filmmakers it offered a platform for political and cultural discussion. The prevalent ideological orientation of the FTCC owes much to the exceptional personality of Tahar Cheriaa, who was later nominated director of the Film Service in the Ministry of Culture. He encouraged the creation of the Association of Tunisian Amateurs (Fédération tunisienne des cinéastes amateurs/FTCA), the Pan-African Film Maker Association (Fédération Panafricaine des Cinéastes/FEPACI), and the Pan-African and Pan-Arab Festival, known as the Carthage Film Festival (Journées Cinématographiques de Carthage/JCC). This would play a pivotal role in supporting new films from Africa and the Arab world, by offering them an alternative outlet to Western-dominated film festivals.

Moufida Tlatli herself was not a child of the FTCC. She studied cinema in France and began directing at a late stage in her career. But being of the same age as Boughedir and Nouri Bouzid, another prominent filmmaker – all were born in the mid-1940s – she worked for many years as an editor on some of the most sophisticated works of North African 'New Arab Cinema', including Algerian Merzak Allouache's *Umar qatlatu al-rujla* (*Omar Gatlato*, 1976), Mahmoud Ben Mahmoud's *Ubur* (*Crossing Over*, 1982) and Férid Boughedir's *Halfaouine* (1989).

Tunisia's limited production rate does not often exceed two films a year. It also struggles to enter the larger Arab market due to Egypt's traditionally strong position. However, this does not mean that its cinema has escaped signs of commercialisation, despite the constant attempts of Tunisian filmmakers, most notably Boughedir, to set their country's filmmaking apart from the Egyptian film industry and its mainstream productions. Boughedir admits that the foreign (European) subsidies which have helped to support a constant flow of Tunisian films create a product that is designed primarily for art film festivals and *cinéphile* markets in the West. This may be one reason why there have been attempts to capitalise on, if not commercialise, Tunisian feminism, and Moufida Tlatli is the best example of this.

Silences of the Palace was produced by the Tunisian production company Cinétéléfilm & Magfilm. Its owner, Ahmad Attia, has produced most of the award-winning Tunisian films, namely those by Boughedir and Bouzid. He also set up his own production company in France in order to administer the appropriation of subsidies. As a result, the credits of *Silences of the Palace* read like a Who's Who of European institutions and television channels: the French Ministry of Foreign Affairs, French Ministry of Culture and Francophonia, French CNC (Centre Nationale de Cinématographie), French Agency for Cultural and Technical Cooperation, Canal Horizon, the Dutch Hubert Bals Foundation and Britain's Channel Four.

It is hard to assess to what extent European financing influences the content of these films. However, there is no doubt that there must be a correlation between market and product, or supply and demand, particularly as the Arab films in question are not just funded by cultural foundations, but are co-produced with European television channels, who have clear marketing strategies, even if they are public-owned. There is little doubt that stories on female oppression and liberation are likely to arouse European interest, as it is one of the crucial topics related to dominant (and in parts still Orientalist) discourses on the Muslim world, which are in turn rooted in early colonialist critiques of Muslim society.

Oppression visualised in seclusion and the veiling of Muslim women had become, according to cultural critic Leila Ahmed, a 'centrepiece of Western narrative of Islam in the nineteenth century' and was modelled into a kind of 'colonial feminism'. The veil behind which women were 'buried alive' was denounced as a visible sign of backwardness and uncivilised behaviour. Missionaries and anthropologists described Muslim marriage as based on sensuality and not on love, rendering woman into a 'prisoner and slave rather than companion and helpmate'.

The problem of these Orientalist perceptions is their persistence and their uninformed conflation between social tradition and the teachings of Islam on the one hand and of past and present on the other. As a critic for the British national newspaper the *Guardian* commented: 'Though clearly a political statement, Tlatli's subtle film never loses its capacity to tell its quietly moving story in a way which illustrates, with seemingly great accuracy, the world that even now traps so many Arab women.' The student newspaper for Canada's Simon Fraser University was more blunt: 'The palace itself, which can also be seen as the oppressive traditions of Islam, is a prison for these women.'

Doubtless, these recurrent conflations have informed Western perception of women in the Muslim world until today; they have also shaped modernist secular Arab self-criticism and representation. To what extent these self-representations sell to Western audiences and producers becomes clear when comparing Tunisian and Egyptian productions. Despite a history of more than seventy years of local filmmaking, Egypt has been rarely able to attract the interest or confidence of European producers or funding bodies, not least because of its industry's outspoken popular and so-called trivial orientation, which stands in contrast to the committed topics and polished film language of co-produced art-cinema. Those few films that do succeed, like Youssef Chahine's later films or *al-Abwab al-mughlaqa* (*Closed Doors*, 1998) by Atef Hatata, dwell on issues of interest to the West, such as religious intolerance and Islam.

No wonder, therefore, that Tunisian filmmakers also do not escape a certain thematic channelling. Like *Silences of the Palace*, Tlatli's following, far less successful film, *Musim al-rijal* (*The Season of Men*, 2000) was also a European co-production, in this case between Muhammad Tlatli/Maghreb Films Carthage and the French Margaret Menegoz/Losange Films. It is set in present time in the southern provinces, on the island of Djerba that is pictured to be dominated by a 'traditional' surrounding. As with her first film, it dwells on gender inequality produced by tradition and on women's loyalty in countering it.

This is not the first Tunisian 'feminist' film to be set in the south. The same applies to one of the earliest Tunisian films made by a woman, namely Néjia Ben Mabrouk's *Sama* (*The Trace*, 1982–87), but this work rather displays the mechanisms of oppression at a moment of change between tradition and modernity, depicting a mother/daughter relationship as an ambivalent motor of preservation and change at the same time (for it is the mother who supports her daughter's education by any means but reinforces at the same time all the gendered oppressive sexual and social taboos in the latter's psyche) without dwelling too much on the persistence of traditions but rather on the moment of resistance.

In contrast with the ideological and psychological sophistication of Ben Mabrouk, Tlatli's accounts of oppression are more concerned with the schematised and rhetorical aspects of gender inequality and the victimisation of women. True that mother and daughter relationships in *Silences of the Palace* shows a similar ambivalence, as it pictures both struggling to come to terms with the gap between morality and the conditions inflicted upon them, yet they are much more portrayed as victims of society who have great difficulties in escaping their tragic fate and not as active agents. This particular difference can be seen as part of the (melodramatic) mainstreaming policy of the film, and certainly contributes to its strong emotional impact but also to the antagonisation of women and oppressive tradition.

Tlatli's subtle return to melodramatic mainstreaming surely astonishes. Arab, but also European critics of the post-colonial era, have been quite harsh in their dismissal of Egyptian cinema and particularly of one of its early and most popular genres, the melodrama, which they have considered to be the embodiment of the escapism of the colonial era. French critic Claude Michel Cluny, for instance, linked that genre to commerciality, schematised repetition and a lack of authenticity very much contrary to Egyptian cinematic realism that seemed to stand for original authenticity. Arab critics, among others the Egyptian Samir Farid, have also ventured to advance this view, by interpreting non-realist pre-independence cinema as a sign of misguided consciousness because of its preference for splendid upper-class settings, those 'feudal palaces' which were later in more realist accounts replaced by 'the apartments of employees and the alleys of Cairo'.

Contemporary Western film theory agrees that melodrama refuses to understand social change in other than private contexts and emotional terms and this is exactly what the genre was blamed for by 'revolutionary' *cinéastes* and Third Cinema supporters, as it does not depict class difference and social misery as bluntly as realism. However, by antagonising so-called escapist melodrama and committed social and political realism critics did not perceive the actual correlation between both genres. For what unites both, according to Christine Gledhill, apart from their common genesis during Europe's nineteenth-century industrial revolution, is the characters' dependency on 'a non-psychological conception of the *dramatis personae*, who figure less as autonomous individuals than to transmit the action and link the various locales within a total constellation'. In other words, both genres are strongly interested in relating a character to his or her social environment rather than displaying any individual or psychological peculiarity, something that in the case of realist films invites allegorical readings of film characters and their actions. Thus, similar to realism, melodrama offers a vessel for expressing general social concerns, representing just a different strategy for dealing with the same ideological tensions. Doubtless, *Silences of the Palace* does at instances invite the above-mentioned allegorical reading, for example when Lutfy compares Alia and her shy compartment when she avoids his touches with his homeland, saying that she also does not know where she is heading.

Unaware of these findings, the post-colonial criticism also exercised by Tunisian critics that labelled Egyptian cinema as escapist, contrary to their own domestic production, has helped to cement the schism between popular cinema and so-called New Arab Cinema or art film. Moreover, it obliterated the factual popular elements in some New Arab films. This applies also to *Silences of the Palace*, particularly because of its resorting to popular genre elements in plot-construction, setting, iconographic motifs and in its use of music.

First of all, the action is set in a splendid upper-class setting, in a feudal palace where it deals, just like innumerable early Egyptian melodramas, with insurmountable class obstacles, a topic that has been repeated over and over in early Egyptian melodrama, for example *Fatima* (1947) starring the so-called Star of the Orient, the singer Um Kulthum as a young woman from a lower-class background who has been duped by a young rich *pasha* into a secret relationship. Indeed, *Silences of the Palace* leisurely displays the beauty of the *beys'* traditional palace; its splendid furnishing and the sensuality of different fabrics displayed in setting and closing. No wonder, in a pivotal scene, Alia – upset after having discovered her mother performing a belly dance in the presence of the *beys* – clandestinely enters the bedroom of the *bey's* wife, dressing up in one of her exquisite traditional garments, indulging in the beautiful surrounding that contrast with the sober furnishing of the maids' rooms and the kitchen, thus uniting desire and resistance with morality and social status.

Like a typical melodrama, the film also reproduces the usual spatial configurations of the genre; to be more precise, it focuses on the home and the closed realm of the family, in contrast to action-oriented genres which are not only male-dominated but mostly set outdoors, in the streets or the landscape. Accordingly the palace forms Alia's whole world. The camera never leaves it except for the opening scenes and it hosts all its dramatic events including one of melodrama's most recurrent motifs: sexual exploitation. This theme, described by Thomas Elsaesser as 'the metaphorical interpretation of class conflict as sexual exploitation and rape', has been common to films since the 1910s, both Western and non-Western.

Film theory has also identified certain formal strategies – such as emotional twists, the implementation of symbolically-charged objects, the exaggerated gesture – and proposed to consider them in a psychological way. They are seen by Geoffrey Nowell-Smith as an utterance of un-discharged emotion which cannot be accommodated within the action, subordinated as it is to the demands of family/lineage/inheritance that is traditionally expressed in the music and in certain elements of the *mise-en-scene*. Therefore, melodrama is closely linked to music. This inherent affinity is already indicated by the genesis of the term 'melodrama': the Greek *melos* signifies song and *drama* plot. Combined cinematically both elements melt into an emotionally effective mixture.

Moreover, the dramatic discontinuity of action is expressed in emotional twists and a sudden drop in viewers' expectations due to unforeseeable turning points, underlined by strong gestures and emotional music. According to Laura Mulvey, they reflect the 'arbitrary nature of class justice'. Using this idea, we may assume that social fears and sexual desire are the two major generators of melodramatic action. In other words, music, body performance and objects in melodrama represent the location to which the emotion is displaced, an emotion created through unfulfilled desire. This desire, however, is not only sexual but clearly also of social origins.

Yet *Silences of the Palace* lacks the melodramatic gesture, generally expressed in a more declamatory style of acting. The same applies to the emotional currents within the narrative, which are underscored by sweeping music. Instead, Tlatli's *mise-en-scène* relies entirely on a more realistic acting style with some of the most pivotal dramatic scenes, such as the rape of the mother, played out with no musical accompaniment. It is not that these scenes lack any emotional impact, as when Alia is seen to cry out in response to what she saw being inflicted on her mother, but here her voice is muted. Soon after, she falls ill and remains in bed for a long time, not wanting – or able – to talk to anyone. It is only when her mother offers her a lute that her condition improves.

The lute represents an emotionally-charged object and symbolises the heroine's ability to express herself. In an earlier scene, Alia sits in her hiding place – a storeroom – trying to play on an old damaged lute. The instrument represents her desire to scale the social ladder, as seen in her requests to Sara for her lute, even though the latter's mother has forbidden her to lend it to Alia.

The film also uses music as an emotional vessel. Not only does it begin with Alia singing one of Umm Kulthum's famous songs, 'Amal hayati' ('The Hope of my Life'): 'My dearest, never ending love, the most beautiful unforgettable song my heart ever heard. Take all my life but never end this day.' These lines prompt the emotional trajectory of the film. Diegetically, the music plays an important role in key scenes; one of these moments takes place in the film's finale. Alia's singing in the salon, before her masters' guests, shifts from entertaining songs towards the forbidden national Tunisian anthem and is played in parallel to the screaming and eventual death of her mother. However, this tragic climax does not bring about the emotional resolution so typical of melodrama. Instead the action continues further with the framing present-time story in which the heroine realises to what extent she has repeated her mother's tragedy in her own life and decides therefore to keep her baby. Her now having the sufficient courage to take her own future in her hands provides the film's ending with a slightly optimistic tone even though the closure still keeps questions open regarding the prospects of her later success.

Once again we find the general politics of the film materialising, revealing the injustice and tragedy inflicted on its innocent female victims, but also offering some hope in the form of resistance. The film does depart from classical melodramatic patterns, particularly in the use of an open end, realistic performances and a more controlled approach to heightened emotions. However, it does rely on some of the most basic characteristics of melodrama, such as narrative subject matter, specific motifs and the use of music. The resulting amalgamation of realist and melodramatic tendencies confer on the film a more committed and less 'mainstream' outlook, which has been of benefit within the European art-film circuit, without depriving it completely of its popular appeal.

Viola Shafik

REFERENCES

Ahmed, Leila (1992) *Women and Gender in Islam*. New Haven, CT: Yale University Press.
Cluny, Claude Michel (1978) *Dictionnaire des nouveaux cinémas arabes*. Paris: Sindbad.
Elsaesser, Thomas (1985 [1972]) 'Tales of Sound and Fury: Observations on Family Melodrama', in Bill Nichols (ed.) *Movies and Methods, vol. II*. Berkeley: University of California Press, 165–89.
Farid, Samir (1973) 'Nahw manhaj li-kitabatin 'ilmiyya li-tarikhunna al-sinima'i', *al-Tali'a*, 3. 149–57.

Gledhill, Christine (1991) 'Signs of Melodrama', in Christine Gledhill (ed.) *Stardom*: *Industry of Desire*. London: Routledge, 207–29.

Morris, Aaron (1996) '*The Silences of the Palace* – the Ridge', *The Peak*, Simon Fraser University's Student Newspaper, 94, 5; On-line; available at http://www.peak.sfu.ca/the-peak/96-3/issue5/silence.html (accessed 17 March 2007).

Mulvey, Laura (1989) *Visual and Other Pleasures*. Bloomington: Indiana University Press.

Nowell-Smith, Geoffrey (1985 [1977]) 'Minelli and Melodrama', in Bill Nichols (ed.) *Movies and Methods, vol. II*. Berkeley: University of California Press, 190–4.

Shafik, Viola (1998) *Arab Cinema, History and Cultural Identity*. Cairo: American University of Cairo Press.

Shohat, Ella (1999) 'Post-Third Worldist Culture: Gender, Nation and Diaspora in Middle Eastern Film/Video', *al-Raida* (*Arab Women and Cinema*), 16, 86–7, 23–33.

KAN YA MA KAN BEIRUT ONCE UPON A TIME, BEIRUT

JOCELYN SAAB, LEBANON/FRANCE, 1994

Kan ya Ma Kan Beirut (*Once Upon a Time, Beirut*, 1994) was one of the first feature films to be made and released by a Lebanese filmmaker following the end of the Lebanese Civil War. The war, which began in 1975, lasted for fifteen years and left the Lebanese film industry almost completely paralysed, yet despite the lack of funding and state support, some Lebanese directors continued making films. It is therefore more accurate to describe filmmaking in Lebanon not as an industry in the traditional sense but as a collection of isolated productions by individual filmmakers. Although the output of Lebanese cinema is small compared to more established industries like Egypt's, individual filmmakers have produced notable films that are slowly establishing a position for Lebanese cinema in the international arena.

Lebanese filmmakers come from a variety of backgrounds and this aspect lends their films a distinct flavour. Jocelyn Saab, the director of *Once Upon a Time, Beirut*, made the leap from journalism to documentary, and eventually to directing feature films, albeit sporadically (she has made one feature film every decade, although she continues to direct documentaries). She is one of a number of female Lebanese filmmakers (others include Randa Chahal and Heiny Srour) who have had an impact on cinema in Lebanon and the Arab world. Her third film (*Dunia*, 2004) caused a great deal of controversy in Egypt due to its focus on the practice of female circumcision in the country. *Once Upon a Time, Beirut* is her second feature film (after *Gazl el Banat* (*A Suspended Life*, 1984)) and Saab's journalistic roots shine through in the film, with its focus on the search for 'truth' and its attention to media representations of Beirut.

In all her feature films, Saab presents a strong female point of view, placing women and women's issues at the heart of the stories. It is therefore not surprising that *Once Upon a Time, Beirut* presents its story through the eyes of women; two young Lebanese girls embarking on a journey to Beirut shortly after the end of the war. Like *El-Aasar* (*The Tornado*, Samir Habchi, 1992) before it, and *Ana El Awan* (*A Time Has Come*, Jean-Claude Codsi, 1994), *Beirut Phantoms* (Ghassan Salhab, 1999) and *Terra Incognita* (Ghassan Salhab, 2002) after it, *Once Upon a Time, Beirut* is one of several Lebanese productions tackling the subject of return to

Lebanon and its (re)discovery. It was released at a time when many Lebanese who had been exiled from their country because of the conflict began returning. Yasmine and Leila are such 'exiles', who have 'come back' to Lebanon in order to discover the 'true' identity of Beirut and its past. Their arrival 'home' reveals how their only experience of the city had been second-hand. As they are driven into Beirut for the first time, Yasmine declares it is her twentieth birthday; she is too young to remember the city before the war.

Once Upon a Time, Beirut can be read like the other Lebanese 'exile' films, as a way of coming to terms with the complexity of belonging following displacement; where the place of return is no longer recognisable and/or has become mythical. Thus, one of Leila's first comments as she is driven – blindfolded by choice – to Beirut is, 'I want to see the secret of this mysterious place.' We do not know whether Leila or Yasmine had ever lived in Lebanon before their 'return'. However, their urge to discover is similar to that of an amnesiac who is relearning their past as if for the first time. This focus on the subject of memory is invoked in a quote from *Hiroshima mon amour* (1959) that appears with the opening credits:

> Like you, I have forgotten … Like you, I wanted my memory to be inconsolable, a memory of shadow and stone. I struggle for myself, everyday, with all my might, against the horror of no longer understanding the reason for remembering. Like you, I have forgotten. Why deny the obvious need to remember? Listen to me, listen to me once more, it will start again.

But the film can also be read in a different way – as a comment on the representation of identity. It is almost entirely composed of a collage of clips from British, American, Egyptian, Lebanese, French and other films and newsreels. Those clips are intercut with the representation of the two girls as they view, comment on and sometimes 'participate' in the clips through simulated film texture. Over 104 minutes, the girls jump across time, from 1914 to the 1950s and the 1960s, back to the early twentieth century and again to the 1970s and the 1980s. This is done through the editing of clips of films from those eras, with each section preceded by a silent-movie-style title card. The story of Beirut's past does not progress chronologically; the clips are woven together thematically, although they are interspersed with a critical political subtext that emerges throughout. Saab uses the merger of factual newsreel footage and fiction, and Western and Arabic representations, to comment on the many media constructions of the Beiruti (and Lebanese) identity. Her deliberate composition of a fractured sense of time, where history is not reconstructed chronologically, but almost haphazardly, acts as a hint at the complex identity of Beirut and the intersection of representations across time and space.

The story revolves around two main themes. The first is the representation of Beirut as a fantasy and a commodity that is subjected to foreign possession and manipulation, and the positioning of Beirut as a playground for foreign activities. The second is the relationship between Beirut as a city and history, from colonialism to present-day conflict. What links both themes is an Orientalist imagining of Beirut, which can be found in both the Western and the Arabic clips compiled. Beirut emerges in the cinematic imagination as exotic and alluring. To Leila and Yasmine, who have come to Beirut to discover its 'truth', the Orientalist fantasy they encounter is one that is too familiar and unsatisfying. Shortly after the girls embark on their cinematic adventure, Leila addresses Monsieur Farouk, a Beiruti cinephile whose basement they raid in search of footage of Beirut, by saying:

> 'We haven't found anything else, Mr Farouk. Yasmine tends to fib, but for once, she is telling the truth. We found nothing else, except some clichés as: Beirut, the pearl of the Middle East, hidden in the blue casket of the Mediterranean. Lebanon, the Switzerland of the Orient. A haven of peace in the heart of a tumultuous region. Beirut, a cosmopolitan city where East meets West. That's all we've managed to come up with, on our city, Mr Farouk. A head-spinning series of clichés.'

Saab aims to deconstruct the clichés by emphasising their constructed nature. After the girls enter Monsieur Farouk's basement, they find themselves surrounded by parallel rows of film reels stacked on shelves. They start selecting which ones to view and saying the titles aloud: *A Day of Honey, Yours Until Death, Love of My Heart, With the Tears from Your Eyes, A Heart of Gold, When the Body Gives Up, On Cellophane Paper, A Bedouin in Paris, Flashman à Beyrouth, Kill My Wife and You'll Have my Blessing, Les Milles et Une Nuits, The Widow and the Devil…* The list of titles called out by the girls is only a fraction of the films used by Saab to weave the story of Beirut together. Despite its narrative-invoking title, *Once Upon a Time, Beirut* does not have a classical narrative structure, an identifiable plot or a climax. It instead takes the viewer on a journey of fragmented representations.

The theme of the construction of Beirut as fantasy is the first myth that the girls encounter in their cinematic adventure. The first clip the girls see is from *Les Milles et Une Nuits*, a French film about the famous Eastern legend of the same name. The clip shows a king – who, due to his boredom and tyranny, had been killing one virgin every morning after spending the night with her – praising the exceptional beauty of Shehrezade, his latest conquest. Shehrezade was one of the virgins destined for death, but each night she forced the king to spare her life until the next day by narrating stories with unfinished endings that kept the king longing to find out what happened next. Through Shehrezade's cunning trick to create another cliffhanger every night, by the end of one hundred and one nights, the king decided to spare Shehrezade's life forever. As Shehrezade survived because of her stories, so does Beirut in the film. We rarely see Beirut in the present. Instead, we are presented with a seemingly endless stream of narratives about the city. The non-chronological presentation of those narratives recreates Shehrezade's trick, leaving the viewer wondering what historical era we will encounter next, which face of Beirut we will see, what characters we will meet. Saab delicately hints at the imminent destruction of Beirut through Shehrezade's reply to the king's comment on her beauty: 'The beauty of a woman is short lived. It's the beauty of love that survives.' Beirut as woman may have lost its external beauty, but its internal allure remains, drawing exiles back and seducing them to discover its past.

The first title card appears on the screen after the Shehrezade sequence, and declares: '1914. Leila and Yasmine play a trick on Mr Farouk.' We are then presented with footage of early twentieth-century Beirut, with its markets, marina and local inhabitants. Black-and-white shots of Yasmine and Leila, dressed in the period's attire, are intercut with old footage, but behind them we can see war-destroyed buildings, similar to the buildings framing the streets that the girls were driven through when they first entered Beirut. Yasmine and Leila's immersion in clips serves to link the past with the present, but also graphically hints at the girls' budding involvement in Beirut's history. This continues after the second title card announces: 'The 1950s. Leila and Yasmine meet two handsome young men.' We are shown a set of wide-angle and tracking shots of Beirut city centre in the 1950s. The city appears as a wealthy place, with rows of banks, people shopping for luxurious fabrics and jewellery, and holidaymakers on speedboats in the glistening sea. The position of Beirut as a commodity is hinted at in the sequence by the accompanying non-diegetic French song, 'Souvenir Souvenir'. As Leila and Yasmine, having entered the sequence and now sitting with two young men on the beach, comment that 'Beirut was wonderful then', we are taken into the world of an Egyptian film set in Beirut, back when Beirut briefly replaced Cairo as the centre for Arab filmmaking. The clip depicts the famous singer Farid al-Atrash as a romantic lead, meeting his stylish lover Hanan in a café by the sea.

The theme of Beirut as a playground for passion continues after the third title card announces: 'The 1960s. Our two heroines become besotted with a gangster.' Clips from the Egyptian/Lebanese film *A Bedouin in Paris*, starring 1960s Egyptian heartthrob Rushdie Abaza, follow. Abaza's character, the rich and indulgent Nabil Radwan, is shown holidaying in Beirut in the summer and seducing a number of bikini-clad women. The clip is interrupted by another depicting a man dressed in a beret and a red cap singing by the pool in Arabic about his conquest of French, German, Italian and Spanish women. Although the song sequence depicting the singing man, who calls himself Romeo, is sarcastic, the film nevertheless exposes the embrace by the Arab cinema industries at the time of the Orientalist fantasies of the seductive Arab male and the depiction of the Arab world as Bedouin, and therefore exotic themes that had been made popular in Hollywood in the 1920s with productions like *The Sheik* (1921).

The film then moves back to *A Bedouin in Paris*, with a scene depicting the Lebanese singer Samira Toufic, who is famous for her Bedouin persona that she played numerous times in films like *The Bedouin Lover* (1963), *A Bedouin in Rome* (1965) and *The Conquerors* (1966). In *A Bedouin in Paris*, she plays a Bedouin singer who has to pretend to be a French-educated blond aristocrat called Violette in order to attract Nabil. Saab shows us Violette seducing Nabil in a Beirut nightclub then cuts to the finale, when Nabil agrees to meet Violette in the Lebanese mountains but is faced with the Bedouin instead who throws her blonde wig at him in anger. Beirut is not only a playground for passion; it is also one for hidden multiple identities.

Hidden identities are also found in the spy films sampled in *Once Upon a Time, Beirut*. Saab alternates between clips of Lebanese folklore songs and clips from spy films to hint at the innocence of Beirut and its ambivalence towards the foreign activities taking place on its soil. A panning shot of pine trees in the Lebanese mountains highlighted by the song 'Lubnan ma ajmalak!' ('Lebanon, How Beautiful You Are!') by one of Lebanon's singing icons, Sabah, is followed by a title card declaring: 'The 1960s. Leila and Yasmine "star" in some big budget foreign films.' We then jump to a scene from *Where the Spies Are* (1965), starring David Niven, where his character the secret service agent Dr Jason Love escapes death by missing his flight to Beirut, as the airplane he is supposed to be on explodes in mid-air. This is followed by a scene at Beirut International Airport where the villain is asking a Lebanese policeman about Love. In a prophetic way, the policeman replies: 'Beirut is a very small place ... Sit down on the riverbank and wait. Sooner or later you will see your enemy's body go by. Your friend's too of course.' A taxi ride by Love follows, where a conversation between him and the driver verifies that there are 'a lot of foreigners here ... French, German, British...'.

Next, we are presented with a French action film where a group of Frenchmen in Beirut discuss their plans to blow up the city using a radioactive bomb in order to protect their petrol stocks there and to get their hands on Beirut's treasures: 'The Middle East contains all the treasures of the world. Gold, diamonds, oil. Huge fortunes shared by the powerful financial companies are placed in the safes of Beirut's banks', one of them declares. The scene is cut to panning shots of a destroyed Beirut, the camera revealing masses of rubble as it moves along the bombed buildings. Beirut becomes a shadow of its former self, almost unrecognisable and empty of people. The scenes from spy films are interrupted twice by songs sung by Lebanon's greatest singer, Fairuz. The first is superimposed on the French spy film: 'Nassam alayna al-hawa', a traditional song about the breezy Lebanese landscape. The second song is from a film that Fairuz acted in, *Bint al-Haris* (*The Guard's Daughter*, 1968). Fairuz's character Nejma is seen in a classroom teaching the students a children's song ('Tik tik tik yam Sleiman'), as they sing along and repeat her gestures innocently. To emphasise this theme of innocence, Saab depicts Leila and Yasmine commenting on the films: 'All those spies and no one seems to suspect a thing.'

Beirut is presented as an exotic commodity manipulated by others, often imagined as an irresistible, attractive woman. Later in the film, Saab shows a video clip of coquettish Lebanese singer, Houeida. The song, 'Lamma bimshi 'ar-rasif' ('When I Walk on the Pavement'), was popular in the 1980s and is used by Saab as yet another comment on the status of Beirut as a desirable female. As the singer walks down a street in her colourful dress, she is surrounded by a group of men who follow her every move: '[*Singer*:] When I walk on the pavement, whether they [the men] are fat or thin, they all follow me. And I feel very shy when [all the men] stare at me; [*Chorus sung by men*:] Oh how pretty this beautiful woman is! Every time she passes by she makes us all dizzy.' The scene is then cut to Leila and Yasmine as they ride in the back of a truck in Beirut and ask the Lebanese-Armenian driver, 'Has Beirut always been like that?' He replies in his thick Armenian accent, 'That's Beirut. The Saudis come shopping in Lebanon. They want to buy everything. They buy a plot of land, a house, a mountain, hotels, sea, they want to buy everything. Lebanon, you know, manufactures everything. We even make local Madonnas and Lebanese Michael Jacksons.'

Beirut is not only a place of romance and greed; it is also a political playing field. The film particularly focuses on Lebanon's colonial past, under the French mandate, and uses this political subtext to comment on Lebanon's current lack of actual independence (despite its official one). France is first introduced as culturally imperialist, with a French song accompanying a montage following sequences from *A Bedouin in Paris*: 'To the children of the nation, the day of glory has arrived. Tyranny against us, the bloody scaffold has been raised.' As this plays, we see footage of French soldiers riding on camels in Beirut, the election of Miss Europe in Lebanon, a fashion show by the French designer Carven at Lebanon's Jeita Grotto, a performance by Maurice Bejar at the Roman ruins of Baalbeck during its annual festival, European artists painting Lebanon's scenery, and finally the image of a French woman wearing the traditional Arab headdress, the *kaffiyya*. While this can be seen as a celebration of Lebanon's cosmopolitanism, Saab hints at the sinister undertones of this seemingly innocent foreign presence in the next sequence which follows the fifth title card: 'Leila and Yasmine cross the burning desert of the Lebanese cedars.' The sequence, from a black-and-white French film, depicts an Orientalist view of the region as a land incapable of ruling itself and therefore in need of Western (French) interference. The film depicts a Frenchman who has been chosen to serve in Beirut to calm inter-tribal fighting between Bedouins. It is interrupted by a French newsreel showing French officials arriving in cars in the region, met by local people dancing in the streets. The voice-over announces: 'The Druze are celebrating the visit of our high commissioner to Syria. We are home in these far-flung lands. In virtue of a moral right that dates from the Crusades. Consecrated by a Society of Nations mandate. The wild warriors on all sides who have always fought each other are now reconciled and live under our flag and protection.'

A sixth title card reads: '1940s. Leila and Yasmine witness some historical events.' Another French newsreel comments on the strategic position of Beirut as a gateway to the Middle East, as we see scenes of the opening of Beirut International Airport. A second newsreel declares that 'the Lebanese have elected their first parliament as they celebrate their independence'. As a massive crowd of people celebrating the independence gathers in the streets of Beirut, Leila and Yasmine enter the clip and look out of a window overlooking the crowd, waving a Lebanese flag. 'The independence!', says one sarcastically. 'Patience', the other replies, 'We'll end up by taking it one day.' Saab is thus not afraid to confront sensitive issues in the Lebanese context. This also extends to the criticism of religious conflict in the country, symbolised by a scene from a French film depicting a Lebanese Maronite priest condemning a father for letting his daughter run away to marry a Muslim man, even though the man had been described earlier as respectful of Christians. Leila, a Muslim and Yasmine, a Christian, comment: 'History doesn't repeat itself, it stutters.'

The comment on French influence is also hinted at in the language used by Yasmine and Leila. Although the girls speak some Arabic at the beginning of the film, they mostly use

French to communicate with each other and with Monsieur Farouk. In the middle of the film, Yasmine comments on how her and Leila's parents used to play loud music to avoid listening to the girls' Francophonie. Saab uses a figure from Lebanese folklore to comment on this linguistic use, the character Chouchou. Chouchou is an old-fashioned traditional Lebanese man with long, unkempt hair and a heavy moustache who appeared in several plays, films and television shows in the 1960s and 1970s, played by the actor Hassan Ala' Ed-Din. Chouchou's work usually revolved around social criticism and is generally associated with an 'authentic' image of Beirut's past. After Hassan Ala' Ed-Din died, his son Khodr revived the character briefly in the early 1990s, appearing in a play and in *Once Upon a Time, Beirut*. Speaking in Chouchou's heavy Beiruti accent, the new Chouchou, played by Khodr, enters Monsieur Farouk's basement and, after promising Leila and Yasmine that he will show them Beirut without any lies or illusions, makes fun of how they speak French and not Arabic. Later in the film, after the girls ask Monsieur Farouk for a factual history lesson, we see Chouchou riding a donkey on the beach, facing Leila and Yasmine. Chouchou recites historical events that they repeat after him: 'Nationalisation of oil. Mossadegh 1951 [1951 Agreement]. Nasser 56 [they repeat this one in French]. Nationalisation of the Suez Canal [again they repeat this in French]'. After he asks them about the significance of 14th July, Yasmine answers, 'A national holiday! The storming of Bastille!' Chouchou is disappointed at her lack of historical awareness, pointing out that he was referring to the death of King Faisal of Iraq in 1958. He tells Yasmine: 'What's the matter with you? I speak to you about the Orient and you reply about the West!' French language and history become a sign of the detachment of the war generation from Arab history.

The detachment from history is coupled with a detachment from memories of peace by the war generation, to the extent that the imagination of Beirut as peaceful becomes almost impossible. Another title card appears: 'And there are more surprises in store for our heroines'. A short silent black-and-white film follows, its original title cards telling the story of a depressed princess called Daoulah (meaning 'State'), who was about to be forced by her father to marry a tyrant, but who escapes to be with her lover, Prince Salam (meaning 'Peace'). A dwarf helps her escape, and to reward him she grants him a kiss, which turns him into a handsome man. Daoulah and Salam discover that the dwarf is actually the prince of Beirut who had been under an evil spell. The final title card from the silent film announces: 'In Beirut, Prince Peace and Princess State lived happily ever after'. Leila comments to Yasmine: 'Princess STATE Daoulah and Prince PEACE Salam; Beirut, State of Peace, d'you see?' Yasmine giggles and replies 'they will laugh when we tell them Beirut is in fact, a legend of peace'.

As the film approaches its end, it tackles yet another conflict in the Middle East that has been manipulated by the media. We hear a French song sung by a young man playing a guitar outside a Lebanese house. He sings: 'It's 1967, girls. The war started and you know nothing about it … The Palestinians have been chased and are walking in the desert. It's 1967, the beginning of our Vietnam. Rock and roll and Beirut is on fire. It will last so long that you'll almost have time to be 20 years old.' As the song plays, we see black-and-white footage of Palestinian refugees arriving in Lebanon, carrying their food and few belongings on their heads and their children in their arms. The song continues: 'Israel is in our sky. There are sparks. Everything will go up in smoke. The war will not stop now…' as we see an image of an injured person carried on a stretcher. This is followed by an audio announcement of an imminent Israeli attack on a village in the south of Lebanon in 1975, then by a scene of a meeting condemning Zionist attacks as well as the silence of Arab nations, calling it a conspiracy against the South. This is shortly followed by scenes from the American film *The Little Drummer Girl* (1984) which depicts a misguided American woman taught how to assemble a gun in ten seconds and how to plant car bombs by the PLO.

The film thus brings together a multitude of complex, sometimes contradictory, overlapping themes. It has therefore been interpreted in several ways. According to Mark Westmoreland, the film is a comment on the nonsensical nature of war. Ella Shohat and Robert Stam point out that it depicts a voyage that links the imagining of old Beirut with the longing for the future one. For Kiki Kennedy-Day, the film is a nostalgic look on pre-war Beirut. The film focuses on too many themes to have a central one. From colonialism to religious conflict to international espionage, alongside the Arab/Israeli conflict and Beirut nightclubs and Lebanese folklore, one cannot establish any causal relations between the themes, or any direct relation between the themes and the occurrence of war. What the viewer does take from the film, however, is a sense of chaos and instability, a journey through illusions all claiming to hold the truth about Beirut's past. At the same time, Saab warns against the reduction of history to a singular issue, and the understanding of the war as a simple conflict. In its final moments, the film presents a quick clip of a Lebanese Christian man talking to the French press. The man's statement is both ironic and 'true'; he says: 'It's not a religious war. The Muslims are our brothers.' The film ends with its own self-reflexive take on the construction of truth, with a clip from a French film depicting a group of Islamic sheikhs at a *madrassa*, all preaching to their own circle of students about the nature of truth. Each sheikh describes truth differently: it is a 'shortest road', 'round', 'obscure', 'celestial', 'dripping', 'suspended', 'sovereign', 'invisible', 'straight', 'radiant' and 'very far away'. The final scene is of a student, fed up with the many confusing versions he has heard, who concludes: 'Truth is a monkey, it pulls all sorts of faces.'

Once Upon a Time, Beirut is a unique film, taking the artifice of media representations of history and identity to the extreme. While several of its nuances may not be noticeable to a non-Lebanese audience, its stance towards the politics of belonging are universal, and its peeling away of layers of familiar representations of Lebanon is a fresh means of resistance to the dominant images of the country that have persevered throughout the twentieth century and beyond.

Lina Khatib

REFERENCES

Kennedy-Day, Kiki (2001) 'Cinema in Lebanon, Syria, Iraq and Kuwait', in Oliver Leaman (ed.) *The Companion Encyclopedia of Middle Eastern and North African Film*. London: Routledge, 364–406.

Shohat, Ella and Robert Stam (1995) 'Festivals: The Carthage Film Festival', *Cineaste*, 21, 1–2, 96.

Westmoreland, Mark (2002) 'Cinematic Dreaming: On Phantom Poetics and the Longing for a Lebanese National Cinema', *Text, Practice, Performance*, 4, 33–50.

SEGELL IKHTIFA CHRONICLE OF A DISAPPEARANCE

ELIA SULEIMAN, PALESTINE, 1996

'...I'm encircled by giant buildings and *kibbutzes*. As if that was not enough, my collar is choking me. An odd bond unites me to those people, like an arranged marriage, with this lake as a wedding ring. Not long ago, those hills were deserted, at night, when I gazed at the hills from the monastery, I contemplated a particular spot, the darkest on the hills. Fear would grab me, a fear with a religious feeling, as if this black spot were the source of my faith ... Then, they settled on those hills, and illuminated the whole place; that was the end for me, I began losing faith ... I feared nothing any longer, now my world is small ... they have expanded their world, and mine has shrunk. There is no longer a spot of darkness over there.'

– Russian-Orthodox priest speaking by Lake Galilee, *Chronicle of a Disappearance*

Elia Suleiman's *Segell Ikhtifa* (*Chronicle of a Disappearance*, 1996) looks at the background of the Al Aqsa Intifada and is discussed here, not only because of its innovative aesthetics, but due to its prophetic and disturbing political analysis of the Zionist enterprise, embedded within its unique cinematic style.

From its inception, the Zionist project has set itself no clear territorial boundaries. Thus while historical Palestine is a definable territory that of Zionism is not. Subsequent Israeli governments, both left and right, have continued this ideological policy of territorial ambiguity conquering and occupying new territories, disrespecting the legal status of internationally recognised borders and making territorial claims for Palestinian lands.

Examining Palestinian existence against the backdrop of Zionist colonisation presents us with an ongoing process of the loss of land on the one hand, and the purchase on reality on the other. The two processes are locked together in a cruel dynamic of interchangeability; the *ingathering of the exiles* to Israel, mirrored by the parallel process of the *Nakba* (meaning 'catastrophe' – the name given by the Palestinians to the loss in 1948 of most of Palestine to the emergent Israeli state), and the spreading waves of Palestinians refugees – millions since 1948 – all over the Middle East, and later, further afield. In this process, in which one side's gain is the other side's loss – as is evident from the priest's speech in the film – both dynamics are locked together; Zionism has gained a territory, while the Palestinians have lost most of theirs, including its very heart – the whole of the coastal plain, with cities such as Jaffa, Haifa and Acre, much of Jerusalem, and after 1967, the rest of the country. The flashpoints of this struggle became the hundreds of roadblocks and checkpoints; the forced separation of conflicting entities, of identities in conflict. In this way, the two nations are now mortally locked in a struggle around boundaries, in which the subtext is the struggle of identity.

Much of Palestinian film deals with the liminality of *loss* and *disappearance* – of country, of the people, of the self. In no other Palestinian film, however, are these processes of loss and disappearance more beautifully captured than in *Chronicle of a Disappearance*. Using a diary format, the film tells the story of a visit to Palestine by a film director (played by Suleiman himself).

Even given the liminality of film *per se* as a medium, Suleiman's film is an extremely liminal affair. It travels along and above boundaries of generic identity, never to settle on either side during this cinematic journey. Its fields of cinematic reference – and reverence – are complex, from Jacques Tati's *Mon oncle* (1958) to Nanni Moretti's *Caro Diario* (*Dear Diary*, 1994). The silent skills of Tati are here perfected by the Keaton-esque Suleiman, who is not heard once throughout the film. Instead of the moving and humorous voice-over of Moretti, Suleiman restricts himself to laconic inter-titles, at once offering us 'information', but also reflecting or commenting on the incredulity of such a practice. Like Tati he constructs the physical domain in which to express, and like Moretti he never misses an opportunity to use reality as a backdrop, speaking its own absurdities. Side by side, we find scenes that can only be termed as documentary, together with docudrama, fiction and scenes straight out of the Theatre of the Absurd. This veritable hybridity, reminiscent of Jean-Luc Godard at his best, is merely the formal envelope of the film; its structure, subjects, topics and techniques all deal with, and are expressed through, liminal means. It starts with the pre-titles sequence. The camera travels over some dark and rocky terrain, completing a half-circle, revealing, through a gradual tracking shot, the face of an old man: Suleiman's father. Only gradually do we realise that this is a double journey, not only over a human face, but also, by proxy, a poetic journey over the countryside of Palestine. This journey around physiognomy is but one example of the film dealing with liminal experiences – the outward appearance, the outer skin, the unspeaking. Throughout the film Suleiman makes us aware of the closure of his father's universe – both his parents are seen but seldom heard – his father talks mainly to his dog, and to his canaries, in both cases through a border; the canaries are caged, the dog locked inside a fenced pen. When the father is seen on one occasion hand-wrestling with a line of younger men, the scene is shot through the window of a bar, while we usually gaze at his parents through doorways, most of their bodies obscured by the various structures of the space termed 'home'. The preoccupation with the skin of things is clear in the kitchen scene, in which both parents are preparing an enormous pile of little fish for dinner, by scraping their skin, or in the priest's speech where the tourist excreta has become the skin of lake water. In another scene, the women who came to visit Suleiman's mother are all discussing at great length the finer points of peeling garlic, and the best time to get rid of its skins.

If the Jewish-Israeli society is for Suleiman a distant and bizarre manic order, a physical and aesthetic manifestation of hysteria, then the Palestinian society appears moribund, trapped in its past and its social tradition, crystallised in a web of inertia. While the Israelis are seen to evaporate though absurd hyperactivity, Palestinians are shown as static, almost to the point of disappearance. In most of the shots in the director's home, there is little movement; the film starts with the face of the sleeping father, and ends with a shot of both parents sleeping in front of the television.

This inertia is expressed by linking various scenes through the main character, Elia Suleiman, a film director, coming back from 'his forced exile, to make a film about the peace'. In a scene reminiscent of Beckett and Ionesco's silent speech-makers, Suleiman is invited to speak of his work, and 'of his use of the cinematic language', to a crowd in an East Jerusalem cultural centre. Try as he might, battling with the microphone, he fails to utter a single word, defeated by out-of-date technology. Through the speechless Suleiman, his father, cousin and friends, a certain feature of Palestinian reality – a reality of being throttled, of being silenced – is being spoken here by passages of expressive silence.

Here is a richly reflexive, even Brechtian, cinema at its most poignant. The film is sub-divided by titles into parts – the first part being a 'Personal Diary – Nazareth', with the second one called 'Political Diary – Jerusalem'. Suleiman is equally-distanced from both environments, but in different ways. Nazareth, his Nazareth, is seen as home, hive, tribe, total stasis. His parents and tourist shop-owning cousin representing the various aspects of death and decomposition, are intimately and lovingly portrayed. In his Nazareth, there is no space occupied by the Israeli Jew, by soldiers of the Israeli Defence Force, by Hebrew. The only evidence is in the tourist shop where the postcard rack is loaded with two kinds of postcards – Christian-ritualistic, and Zionist-stereotypical. Apart from this incursion, his Nazareth is Arab and Christian. Being the largest centre of Palestinian life within Israel, Nazareth is not just home but a tangible piece of the lost past, a frame grabbed out of time. Suleiman is shooting his film during the first phase of the painful conflict in Nazareth between Christians and Muslims – a conflict so bitter that at times it seems to obscure the bigger conflict with Zionism. Indeed, this fraternal inner conflict is seen in many scenes, by showing couples of Arab men in bitter and meaningless conflict – father and son, two friends, men at a restaurant; in all cases we are mystified by their aggression, but are also aware of its utter irrelevance. This inner conflict within Palestinian society, reflected elsewhere – Bethlehem, Jerusalem – is an integral part of Suleiman's critique of his own milieu, no matter how close to it as he might be.

Suleiman's cinematic Jerusalem, on the other hand, expresses a world of difference. It is the locus of the Israeli/Palestinian conflict, the place where it is kept alive. In Jerusalem, Suleiman moves precariously and furtively; apart from his rented rooms, he scans the city like a ghost, avoiding its public sphere and thoroughfares, meeting few people, if any. He calls this part 'Political Diary' because in Jerusalem he finds it increasingly difficult to act as the *person*, to act *personally*, the way he did in Nazareth. If the Israelis, and the Israeli army, are missing from Nazareth, Jerusalem is a space reverberating with the occupation and its iniquities. His picture of the holy city is a Jerusalem-of-the-Absurd, in which Israeli police vans scour the night with flashing lights and blaring sirens, searching aimlessly, leaving their searing mark on the dark expanses which are broken, never to return to peaceful silence again. In an iconic scene, a police van careers wildly into an alleyway, emptying its cargo of robotic police clones who line up meticulously along a wall and urinate in unison, again leaving their mark on Arab Jerusalem. The event is over before we have fully captured the image and the crazed crew is on its way, reporting on the radio, 'mission accomplished'. The phased-out Suleiman, a silent witness to this absurd scene, notices that the police clones have left behind them a military-type communicator, which will end up as one of the main symbols of the film – a small object, hiding behind it the huge and invisible machinery of oppression and control. Suleiman picks it up, not sure what he might do with it, or indeed what it may do to him. Later on in the film the communicator will be used in a way which it was not intended for: A'dan, a young Palestinian woman who Suleiman meets at the Arab estate agent in East Jerusalem, uses it in an unforgettable scene, to give the radio command in Hebrew: 'All units, vacate Jerusalem immediately! Jerusalem is no longer *united*. Jerusalem is *not* united!' Having done this, she then softly sings to the units, presumably now leaving Jerusalem, the Israeli national anthem 'Hatikva'. Thus, through a montage sequence of unique power, inter-cutting the singing A'dan, the police vans careening through empty streets, and an Arab dance troupe in a funerary dance, the sequence inverts the meanings, both of the communicator and the anthem – what has been a tool of oppression now becomes a vehicle of liberation, and the anthem of the oppressor (itself speaking of liberation and homecoming) is used by the oppressed. This filmic device offers great power, derived from the very act of transgressing, of breaking boundary lines, of stepping into Hebrew, into the national anthem of Israel, of Zion. This cinematic transgressive device is similar to the ones discussed by Yosefa Loshitzky in her book on identity in Israeli cinema, where she identifies forms of transgression, especially sexual transgression, as typifying its recent output. Such subversive and deconstructive use of objects, of speech, of iconic music, of iconic symbols such as the Israeli flag, is strewn throughout the film as pointers, as signposts, as devices of liminality. A grenade and a gun, both on A'dan's desk, turn out to be cigarette lighters; a mannequin in ethnic attire, in the same room, ends up being arrested in A'dan's place, after the police agents have mislaid the real woman. They seem not to notice the difference. Reality is seen here not as the order of things, but the device undermining reason and logic. In a country where reason is no longer viable, Suleiman uses it as an ironic and deconstructive tool.

Suleiman's is no easy message. It mourns the impossibility of the reversal of events, while brimming with contempt for the naked power and brutality of the occupation. Despite their humour, the scenes in *Chronicle of a Disappearance* described above display clear traits of melancholia. One such example is the beginning of the second part of the film, 'Political Diary – Jerusalem'. It starts with a very long tracking shot from a car, travelling down from the Mount of Olives towards Jerusalem's walls, and specifically, the Gate of Mercy. During this moving shot, the opening lines of the Palestinian song 'Why Do We Fight' can be heard: 'Why do we fight? We used to be friends once...' This revealing choice of music is of great interest. The film was shot during Prime Minister Benjamin Netanyahu's derailing of the peace process, a time when all hope was lost. The song mourns that other time, in which 'we were friends', knowing it is now unlikely to return.

In Freud's key work on mourning and melancholia he wrote of 'the economics of pain' when designating mourning as a reaction 'to a loss of a loved person, or to the loss of some abstraction which has taken the place of one, such as one's country, liberty, an ideal, and so on'. In analysing the causes and course of the mourning process, he outlined the self-denial which is socially normalised into it, and sanctioned by society, contrasting it with the same manifestation in the melancholic, where this denial has become pathological, fixated and damaging to the self, instead of being an agent of healing, as in the case of the 'mourning work'. The link made here by Freud between the self, a loved person and 'one's country' and 'liberty' is of special interest to us when examining films that also juxtapose such entities in their narrative structure. But Freud distinguishes between mourning – a normal process that duly ends – and melancholia – a pathology that may destroy the subject. Indeed, this essay is thought by Peter Gay, Freud's biographer, to have marked Freud's transition towards allotting part of the self a special, censorious role, later to be called the *superego*, and marks an important stage in the development of his model of the mind. The ability to rally against *oneself*, to criticise oneself almost to death (and sometimes practically to death), as is the case with melancholia, had given Freud a new direction to his thinking. That same self-destructive mode is obviously of great interest to Suleiman in his film – there are many scenes in which two Palestinians are fighting each other for no apparent reason. This process of criticising, or fighting oneself, is a debilitating and paralysing one, as is often the case in the film. In the end, one has to disappear, as happens in pathological cases of melancholia leading to suicide.

One of the most interesting differences Freud notes between the mourning process and the pathological loops of melancholy, is the fact that the latter may well be triggered by a loss of what he calls an 'ideal kind': 'One can recognise that there is a loss of a more ideal kind. The object has not actually died, but has been lost as an object of love.' Hence, the loss that may trigger the melancholia is not necessarily a death, or total loss, but a loss akin to the one representated in this film. The loss of one's country, real as it is, is different from death. After all, the country is still there, and thus the loss continues, gets fixated, cannot be mourned and done with, as in the case of death. The loss of one's country never ends. It is even more pronounced when the loss is experienced *in situ*, while living in the lost country.

Although personalisation of Palestinian losses does not absolve Israel of political responsibility, understanding them in terms of melancholy provides new insight into the state of stasis, where resistance is temporarily disabled, delaying the process of mourning and healing. The healing process seems to be bound up with storytelling – it has been so ever since Freud developed the 'talking cure'. Here the therapeutic process is centred around telling one's own story, or, if we wish, a structured *return of the (political) repressed*. Going back to the roots of it all, to the moments of crisis and trauma, actively working out the details and the 'deeds done,' seems to provide a close approximation of the psychoanalytical process. But here, more is at stake. The dispossession brought about by occupation is even deeper and more painful than 'just' losing home and country. The ultimate loss is that of losing your story, your identity, losing the right to tell your own story, your own history. That loss is different from physical loss

– Freud distinguishes between mourning and melancholia in an additional way – mourning is a process that is wholly conscious, while the loss in melancholia is mainly unconscious. If the loss of the land is a conscious loss, the loss of identity is not – it operates in the twilight zone, hence its greater destructive power. People affected by deep melancholia lose their voice – they are no longer able to speak for themselves as their main argument is *against* themselves. This tendency of melancholia and its intrinsic connection to narcissism are two qualities much in evidence in *Chronicle of a Disappearance*, a film steeped in melancholia, also built around the self-image of the director. This observation may well relate to the Lacanian nature of the self-image in this film, something that is well beyond the scope of this chapter; suffice to say that the film clearly serves Suleiman as some kind of pictorial, emotional and conceptual mirror, and through him, the Palestinian people. The Elia Suleiman of the film is an iconic – and laconic – Palestinian clown; there to be affected by whatever is happening, as both a messenger on our behalf, and scapegoat. Thus, by looking at his unchanging countenance, we see ourselves. This was always true of film clowns, from Charlie Chaplin to Roberto Benigni. After all, Lacan tells us that in the mirror everything looks much clearer – the baby sees the mirror image as perfect and coordinated, as having some logic of its own, lacking in him, the source of the image.

If we accept Freud's notions about melancholia as having some value when related to the complex and multifaceted processes involved in the Palestinian loss since the *Naqba*, and specifically in relation to Suleiman's film, then the very *liminality* of the 'genre' of *exilic* cinema becomes an expression of the conditions of the nation and the individual alike. Hamid Naficy's assumptions on the nature of such cinema are a further development of the liminal natures of cinemas once called 'independent' or 'Third Cinema' – forms of cinematic creativity bound up with extremes of *loss* or *lack*, through the processes which range from cultural imperialism, to the complexities of globalisation. The methods which are then carved out by filmmakers from this new reality are contradictory – the onset of the power which robbed them of identity – Globalism, Imperialism, Zionism – has also meant some new forms of expression and dis-semination have become available. Naficy points this out, reminding us of the complex nature of exilic cinema – he defines the two modes powering the exilic production as 'dependence' and 'autonomy'. Hence, the very nature of this cinema, its existential drive, is deeply liminal and contradictory. All this has been clearly identified in Suleiman's film. The silencing and 'depend-ence' are powering both active resistance and fatalistic silence, with A'dan and Elia Suleiman being their respective engines in the film. Both are telling the story of silence in their different ways – Elia Suleiman (the main character) by perfecting his silence, then disappearing, while

A'dan perfects her *voice* – she transmits it further than it could ever reach, by using the army communicator, and also by using the enemy discourse with all its reverberations – talking and singing the Israeli national anthem in Hebrew.

So, Elia Suleiman, and the filmmakers in Palestine, must fight for the right to – at least – have their own voice, tell their own story and history, in their own way. Conceptually and ideologically, they operate on the interstitial space between cultures: the Israeli and Palestinian, the Palestinian in Israel and the Palestinian in the occupied territories, the Palestinian in Palestine and the Palestinian in the Diaspora, Palestine and the Arab world, and Western versus Oriental discourse. Suleiman himself is an example of this interstitial existence – he divides his time between New York and Palestine, and his film is a co-production: Europe/Palestine is given as its place of origin, in terms of production partners. This interstitial mode of production, as termed by Hamid Naficy, is forced and justified by the normative state of Palestinians in Israel, living on the seams of Israeli society. They are always situated between two other points; by the virtue of power relations, Israeli and Hebrew points on the virtual map of Palestine. The names of their habitations are missing from road signs, as is their language, an official language of Israel, noticeable by its absence. Some of their habitations are not even midway between Israeli/Hebrew name places, because no road leads to them, and they are not connected to the electricity grid. They are called 'unrecognised settlements' and receive no assistance from any government agency – they simply do not exist, however large and populous they may be. But of course, the Palestinians see this relationship in reverse – all the Jewish settlements are either built on the remains of Arab settlements, or lie between such remains, however difficult to discern. The Hebrew place names are but a smoke screen – in most cases, they hide behind them the Arab former name, like some hidden crime from a dark past. All existence in Palestine/Israel is double existence. So there are two virtual countries within the same space, two parallel universes disregarding and disparaging each other, and yet totally bound to each other. The deeper irony is that the victorious newcomers are also refugees, claiming this as the justification for that which cannot be justified.

Not only are there two parallel universes superimposed on this landscape, but Palestinians are also situated on another interstice: that of the space between the Jewish distant past in Palestine, and the current control of it by Israel. The normal use of language in Israel, as well as its dominant ideology, connects both instances into a continuum, despite the two thousand years between them, filled as it were, by non-existent people whose non-existent settlements have filled the non-existent gap.

It is against this background that the film operates; a doubled-up reality whereby the Palestinian is there and not there, is present and absent, all at the same time. Towards the middle of the film, the weight of the scenes, autonomous in a true Brechtian fashion, begin adding up to a critical mass. We start reading the absent *other* into the collapse of realities; the absent other of Zionism, Elia Suleiman, coming from exile in New York, to a double exile at home in Nazareth, and ending up in a worse exile: that of life in Jerusalem, under control of the occupying power. Instead of finding an old and cherished self, Suleiman is gradually and painfully disappearing, a metaphor for the disappearance of Palestine, and of the Palestinians. This disappearing act is everywhere. It is in the slow frailty of his parents, who, in the last scene, fall asleep in front of the television, while the Israeli TV channel is broadcasting the closing item of the day – the national anthem – with the Israeli flag waving. It is there in the Jericho scene, in which Elia Suleiman sits alone in a Palestinian café on a fine evening, in 'liberated' Jericho, with a flag of Palestine beside him, in a further attempt to find the missing Palestine; the café lights, which were put on to mark the passage of day into night, fail badly, and keep arcing away as he looks at the darkening town, causing him to appear then disappear. In a similar scene, at the rooms he rented in Jerusalem, the lights also falter, blinking with a will and rhythm of their own. So obvious is Suleiman's absence, that when an Israeli SWAT team is searching his Jerusalem flat, they do not seem to notice him, though he does all he can to be noticed. At the end of the film, the exiled director chooses to disappear altogether, with a proverbial suitcase, reminding us of the famous poem by Mahmoud Darwish, in which 'My home is a suitcase/and my suitcase is my home' ('Mount Carmel is in Us'). Suleiman's alter-ego in the film, the young A'dan, is staying on to fight, representing, like his parents, *zumud*, adherence to the land, resistance and survival. If the struggle of the old generation is by powerful passivity, A'dan chooses the active road. To fight an enemy like hers, one must adopt some of its tactics, some of its methods, use some of its machinery. Hence, she operates through the ether, using the found communicator for her messages to the enemy, delivered in Hebrew, using the military nonsense-codes so beloved of the IDF. As an ultimate weapon, she uses the Hebrew national anthem, speaking of the hope in every Jew for a return to Jerusalem. It is then read in its original sense, as an anthem of the oppressed who have lost Jerusalem, who have lost the land, who have disappeared. Liminality is fought with liminality. Those without means, deprived of everything, have to use the power of their oppressors in order to survive, in order not to disappear.

How can one make a film about people and places that are disappearing, about the fragility of this subconscious process? Memory is not enough. It proves nothing. The foundation of *homeland* must be fortified by one's own story and storytelling. Yosefa Loshitzky quotes the poet Mahmoud Darwish again: 'Whoever writes the story [of the place] first – owns the place.' Hence, the identity and the narrative must be regained, the *community* must be *imagined* anew, in order to exist in the future. The place of home is now taken by narrative icons of the lost *heimat*, recreated for and by the film, such as the stories told by the priest or the writer Mohammad Ali Taha. Palestinian cinema therefore exists on a series of exilic interstices: between fact and fiction, narrative and narration, the story and its telling, and *documentary* and *fiction*. Facts are not enough, this film seems to tell us. In order to have some space to live in, to bring an end to personal and political melancholia, one must employ fiction and imagination, one must tell stories, even stories of disappearance.

Haim Bresheeth

REFERENCES

Freud, Sigmund (1991 [1917]) 'Mourning and Melancholia', in *On Metapsychology*. Penguin Freud Library, Vol. 11. London: Penguin Books.

Loshitzky, Yosefa (2001) *Identity Politics on the Israeli Screen*. Austin: University of Texas Press.

Naficy, Hamid (ed.) (1999) *Home, Exile, Homeland: Film, Media, and the Politics of Place*. London: Routledge.

EŞKIYA THE BANDIT

YAVUZ TURGUL, TURKEY/FRANCE/BULGARIA, 1996

In 1996, when the long awaited *Eşkıya* (*The Bandit*) was released, it attracted a large female audience, specifically housewives that for years had been absent from cinemas. They came in groups to see the film. Consuming the food they brought from their homes, and reacting noisily to what was happening on screen, they behaved as they would when they watched television in their own homes. It was its ability to draw a wide and varied audience, after so many years during which cinema had lost these groups, that guaranteed *The Bandit*'s success. The film was also able to attract international audiences; it not only entertained the Turkish diaspora in Europe and America, but also struck a chord in even the remotest or the most indifferent viewer. Does that mean that film critics and reviewers were able to provide audiences with the appropriate tools that would help them come to grips with the film?

Reviews of *The Bandit* show a tendency to represent the film not as a work of fiction, but as a mirror, reflecting the often harsh realities of Turkey. This is symptomatic in the sense that Western critics expect Turkish films to be topical, and either authentic (if they are exotic enough) or pretentious (if they are modernist in their own way). Even if they deploy the modalities of the fantastic they are expected to convey the actual state of things going on in their country. For instance, Stephen Knitzer, who appears to have lived in Turkey for some time, wrote in the *New York Times* that *The Bandit* concerned a scandal that intimated at the degree of real political corruption.

What these and other reviews apparently lack is the ability to see the film in its own right and link it to the general framework of cinematic experiences. Instead of appropriating the film into the already existing patterns of perception of Western viewers, the aim here is to offer a set of clues to read the film primarily in cinematic terms, beginning by situating these terms within the contexts of Turkish film history and culture. Furthermore, in the mid-1990s, *The Bandit* was significant in pointing to the ways by which filmmakers had to struggle with the hardships of the industry. In other words, it played a crucial role in the course of Turkish cinema's endeavours to cope with its unending crisis, namely the lack of a proper industry and regular audiences.

The director of the film, Yavuz Turgul, began his film career writing screenplays for the director and producer Ertem Eğilmez, who contributed to the formation of Yeşilçam, the popular cinema of the 1960s and 1970s with a studio system akin to that of Hollywood. Eğilmez, who came from a left-wing tradition, was anti-intellectual and anti-elitist, and strove to make popular films, particularly melodramas, favouring the American way of storytelling. A rumour exists that he had a bestselling American screenwriting book translated into Turkish and he made his films 'by the book'. He is known as the 'unforgettable director of love films', a name which Turgul would later use as the title of one of his films about Yeşilçam, *Aşk Filmlerinin Unutulmaz Yönetmeni* (*The Unforgettable Director of Love Films*, 1990). Ironically, just before his death, Eğilmez made a final film, *Arabesk* (1988), which highlighted and mocked the clichés of Yeşilçam, thus disowning his heritage, which he helped to create.

Turgul's first film, *Fahriye Abla* (*Sister Fahriye*, 1984) was an adaptation of a famous poem of the same title about a girl who, having failed to continue a healthy relationship with her boyfriend, decides to become a factory worker. Turgul's later films present a more consistent oeuvre. The central theme of all the films he has made so far is the conflicts, dilemmas and hesitations of a main protagonist who fails to adapt to the changing rules and values of the society. In *Muhsin Bey* (*Mister Muhsin*, 1987), Muhsin (Şener Şen) is a music agent who, understanding that his musical taste and understanding of how the industry operates is no longer profitable, undertakes the difficult, if not impossible, task of producing an album for a young would-be singer. Turgul went on to make films focusing on cultural conflict, particularly the tension between vanishing traditions and the corrupting power of a peculiar kind of modernisation.

The protagonist of *The Unforgettable Director of Love Films*, Haşmet Asilkan (again played by Şener Şen), who has a reputation as the director of love films, tries to give a twist to his career by making a social film. However, everything goes wrong: he cannot raise the money he needs, the rushes turn out blurry because his cameraman cannot focus due to an eye disease, and the story just does not work. Neither Muhsin nor Haşmet can cope with the changing conditions of the culture industry. *Gölge Oyunu* (*Shadow Play*, 1992) has a more philosophical inclination. The film tells the story of two stand-up comedians (played by Şener Şen and Şevket Altuğ) who, despite great effort, cannot make their audiences laugh. They find a deaf-mute girl (Larissa Litichevskaya) in the street and begin to look after her. The girl, just like the visitor (played by Terence Stamp) in Pasolini's *Theorama* (*Theorem*, 1968), changes the lives of the people around her, giving death as a gift to an old lady suffering from insomnia, initiating one of the comedians into manhood, and so on. Unlike Turgul's previous films, the film explores the realities of fiction.

The success of *The Bandit* enabled the Turkish film industry to win back audiences it lost two decades earlier, both to television and Hollywood. It beat *Braveheart* to become the most successful film in Turkey in the year of its release. This is particularly significant when one recalls the drastic fall in the number of movie theatres in the mid-1980s. The attention *The Bandit* received heralded the growing interest in indigenous film. However, it is not simply an indigenous film; its success internationally – outside of the Turkish diaspora – is significant. In London, for instance, the film was first shown at a movie theatre located in a prominent Turkish neighbourhood, and then exhibited in two cinemas in the city centre. This encouraged the producers and the Ministry of Culture to apply to the Academy Awards for the Best Foreign Film category, an attempt which stirred heated discussions. But the film was not even nominated for an Academy Award, which came as no surprise, for it did not look like a foreign (that is, exotic) film, an observation that invites a closer look into its cultural identity and cinematic style.

The Bandit tells the story of Baran (Şener Şen again), who is released from prison after 35 years. Returning to his native village, he finds out that it has been flooded due to the construction of the controversial Ilısu Dam on the River Tigris, which destroyed many Kurdish villages and historical towns. He meets an old woman from the village, a half-crazy loner who apparently possesses supernatural powers. In order to protect him from dangers that await him, the woman gives Baran an amulet – an indication that his ordeal is not over. Baran learns that it was his close friend, Berfo (Kamuran Usluer), who turned him in 35 years ago and stole his beloved Keje (Şermin Hürmeriç). To take revenge, Baran heads for Istanbul. On the train he meets Cumali (Uğur Yücel), a young drug dealer who is trying to make his way in the big city. They subsequently establish a rapport resembling a father/son relationship. In Istanbul, Baran finds out that Berfo, now using the name Mahmut Şahoğlu, has become a successful businessman. Baran finally meets Keje, who has refused to speak since she married Berfo, and they decide to leave Istanbul together. Cumali's girlfriend begs him to save her jailed brother, who has been receiving death threats. To his disappointment, her brother turns out to be her secret lover. Cumali catches them in bed and murders both. Cumali's boss, Demircan, discovers that Cumali has been stealing money from him and decides to punish him. However, Baran learns that Cumali is in trouble and with the consent of Keje, he makes a deal with Berfo. Keje will stay with Berfo on the condition that Berfo pay the money to save Cumali from his crime boss, Demircan. Berfo does not keep his word and Demircan has Cumali killed. Baran takes revenge, killing Demircan and his men and then finally Berfo. The police begin to chase him. He hides on the roofs just as he hid in the mountains 35 years ago. Baran loses the amulet that the old woman of the village gave to him. He is shot and falls from the top of a building. The old woman feels his death and looks to the mountains in sorrow.

The Bandit is noteworthy for its stylistic and narrative elements, which combine the tradition of Turkish cinema with the contemporaneity of modern Hollywood. It is important to understand that the film cultivates the heritage of Turkish popular cinema and silently seeks new directions in storytelling, attempting to explore the cinematic means to be able to make sense of a world in transition. Does *The Bandit* accomplish these tasks?

The film clearly utilises the star system, employing familiar faces from cinema and television. Şener Şen, Uğur Yücel, Kayhan Yıldızoğlu, Kamuran Usluer, to name only a few, come from cinema. The media celebrities Mithat Bereket and Gülgün Feyman are known for their news programmes on television, and finally two pop stars, Özkan Uğur and Yeşim Salkım, also appear in a number of dramatic scenes. The leading actor is Şener Şen, one of the most popular actors of Turkish cinema. Except *Sister Fahriye*, Şen has played the lead in all of Turgul's films, and looking at the roles he has played one can see a number of patterns emerging. One of them depicts a man whose moral and aesthetic values are out of place. He tries hard to adapt to the changing society, but having failed to convince even his wife, he ends up a loner. Şen lacks the charm of a typical star; physically he represents the ordinary man (husband, father, teacher, peasant, and so on), and character-wise he can be mistaken for a little man. However, as the narrative unfolds we understand that this is his ordeal and he is going to take the challenge to overcome his weaknesses and fight the corrupting power of, for example, the money coming from an unacceptable source, or sex made possible through power games. Şen is perfectly capable of adjusting his acting to the needs of his roles. Comedies can become particularly demanding in this respect: effeminate gesticulations of the body in a frenzy, thus pointing to a sort of hysteria, and rich mimicry accompanied by his varying voice in a wide range, which can at times reach a very high pitch. Although *The Bandit* may display traces of these, the role of Baran must have forced Şen in an opposite direction. Though he is a 'loser' in some respects, a different set of signifiers are required interpreting Baran's character. Şen has established a certain 'trademark' with the Turkish public regarding the way he uses his body in his films, which is a form of burlesque; this 'trademark' is often the underlying factor of his success with his audiences. The character of Baran, however, does not lend itself to burlesque. In *The Bandit*, through careful manipulation of his body, Şen is able to convey Baran's inner turmoil as he tries to adjust himself to his new environment. His performance from this point of view is particularly remarkable in the scenes of his arrival in Istanbul.

The Bandit opens with scenes from the southeast of Turkey and very quickly moves to Istanbul. The topographical picture it offers is a fluid one. Originally Turgul had the idea of making a film on the roofs of Istanbul. When Baran returns to his home village he finds out that it is under water due to a dam being built. Baran and Cumali meet on the roof of their hotel. Cumali hides his gun on the roof and from there Baran has a birds-view of Istanbul. The body of the bandit is aware of the fact that the setting, the conditions of the body's configuration, have changed – from the mountains to the jungle of the city. Every day Baran leaves his shabby hotel and dives into the crowd, desperately seeking Keje, the long-lost lover. He carries with him binoculars, just as he did 35 years ago. Just as he scanned the landscape when he was on the mountains, he now scans the cityscape. The initial clumsiness of the body in this strange environment does not prevent us from noticing how determined it is in the way it moves – movement at the service of a strong will, which enabled him to survive the harsh conditions of 35 years of life in prison.

The film carefully utilises the melodramatic heritage of Turkish popular cinema which, like many other national cinemas, foregrounds frustration and deprivation in earthly love to lead to paternal love and sacrifice, with clear references to divine love. This is achieved through a play on passion and desire. Cumali is in trouble. Baran is desperately seeking Keje. Both, in their own way, are betrayed, forsaken and helpless. They each desire something: for Cumali it is success; for Baran, Keje. And they are aware of the impossibility of their desire. Cumali tells Baran the story of his name: his father was a great fan of Yılmaz Güney and therefore he was named after one of Güney's greatest characters. Cumali concludes his story by remarking that had his father not died, he would have been Baran's age. Baran replies that if he had married he would most probably have had a son Cumali's age. Out of this frustration and deprivation they establish a father/son relationship, a bond stronger than his desire for Keje. This is how melodrama operates on the emotional structure: sexual desire is subsumed in favour of something more spiritual in nature.

Having paid homage to Yeşilçam with its melodramatic style, *The Bandit* moves on to search for more contemporary forms of expression. It took ten years for Yavuz Turgul, who also penned the screenplay, to problematise the antagonism between Baran and Berfo. In many instances, the melodramatic conventions require the clash of the good and the bad, represented by the main characters who are presented as enemies. As Thomas Elsaesser observes, there are no characters in a typical melodrama; they must be understood rather as types which lack psychological depth and gain meaning only by reference to other types, thus forming a complicated system of signification. *The Bandit* establishes the good/bad opposition (and then expands to good/evil) and through identification with Baran it appears to side with the good. However, this is precisely the point where *The Bandit* produces its difference not only in terms of tradition in general but also in generic terms. Baran finally tracks down Berfo and in a highly-charged exchange, Berfo challenges Baran by admitting that he betrayed him, his best friend, by turning him in. He took his best friend's lover from him, and he is prepared to burn in hell for what he did. However, he never regretted it because he was a man in love. We cannot see any traces of regret; on the contrary, he is proud to have done what he did in order to win Keje, and belittles Baran for being so simplistic. Here we witness a twist in the conventions of melodrama, which resembles Lars von Trier's playfulness with the genre in *Dancer in the Dark* (2000). Just like Bill (David Morse, an actor with an innocent face), who steals Selma's (Björk) money to meet his wife's unending demands and in order to get killed to end his pain, Berfo is not a typical 'bad guy'. Rather, he is more complicated than Baran, who simply assumes the role of Cumali's father, gives up on Keje and is determined to act accordingly. Here Baran represents the heritage of melodrama, operating on binary codes, whereas Berfo represents a break with those codes, moving from the stereotype to a real character, full of desire, neither good nor bad. Thus *The Bandit* fosters a paradigmatic shift in the melodrama by inserting a 'proper character' and also by presenting via that character an alternative formation of desire which is cut off from its metaphysical possibilities.

There is also a spiritual edge. When Baran gives up on Keje in order to save Cumali's life, he is not simply trading in his beloved for a miserable tramp. Berfo has married Keje through coercion, but Keje has refused to speak a word since. Did she give him her body? Although Berfo implies that they did not sleep once, it would not make any difference because this is a body deprived of her voice. Here the film appeals to Turkish popular cinema's usage of a body/soul opposition. The body can be visually represented, whereas it is mostly through the voice that the soul is made present in cinematic terms. What Berfo won turned out to be a waste, a body without a soul. Keje speaks only when she meets Baran. Keje is in the garden of roses when Baran appears before her. The time splits into two, the present and the future, a time out of time. On one level, it is the Garden of Eden. They have finally reunited although they will soon separate for good. True to the tradition of Turkish melodrama, death is made bearable only by implying that the lovers will re-unite in the hereafter.

Turgul was reproached by some critics for ignoring the Kurdish problem. The film starts in the southeast of Turkey. The characters are Kurdish, but one cannot find any overt references to ethnic issues. This problem, however, should be examined on another level, a metaphorical one. The representations of topography give us a clue to read the film from this point of view. The way in which the terms cityscape/landscape and roof/mountain are used suggests that Istanbul is no different from the southeast and Baran eventually has to become an urban bandit. It would be misleading to illustrate oppression as confined to an underdeveloped region – it has diffused throughout the whole country.

In terms of cultural identity *The Bandit* was Turkish, then international, and finally it looked like a Hollywood film. Many Turkish critics praised the film for its technical achievement. It was one of the first films shot with sound in fifty years. Just before the opening, two significant commercial marks are given: first, the train of the early Dolby logo appears and points to a more or less technological advancement; second, a caption announces that it was a Eurimages film with French and Bulgarian partners, suggesting that we, the spectators, would see a film which conforms to international standards. Indeed, the print displayed technical perfection. In addition to lab processes, sound mix, lighting, the use of filters and camera movements, the editing also impressed the critics who declared that *The Bandit* was no less than a Hollywood film. In fact, it makes several explicit references to American cinema. The scene when Cumali discovers his girlfriend and her secret lover in bed and murders both of them is shot with a style that reminds one of Quentin Tarantino, and in the finale, as Baran is trying to escape from the police, suddenly a helicopter appears in the sky, an archetypal image which one can find in almost every chase sequence of Hollywood.

The Bandit came out at a time when Turkish cinema was in decline and hopes for a vibrant home industry were diminishing. Today, looking at filmmakers' endeavours in developing original styles and new ways of storytelling to appeal to wider audiences, one can appreciate that the film has served as a great source of encouragement. Having survived the economic crises of February 2000 and the 9/11 attacks, and despite more than a hundred national and international television channels that recycle films and other forms of fiction on a daily basis, the film industry is able to produce comedies like *Neredesin Firuze?* (*Firuze, Where Are You?*, Ezel Akay, 2004), *G.O.R.A* (Ömer Faruk Sorak, 2004), *Hırsız Var!* (*Thief!*, Oğuzhan Tercan, 2005); try its hand at a new genre, horror, in *Okul* (*The School*, Yağmur and Durul Taylan, 2003), *Büyü* (*The Spell*, Orhan Oğuz, 2004); or look into human dramas in *Bulutları Beklerken* (*Waiting for the Clouds*, Yeşim Ustaoğlu, 2005) and *Meleğin Düşüşü* (*The Fall of Angel*, Semih Kaplanoğlu,

2005). After the success of *The Bandit*, Yavuz Turgul waited for another eight years to produce his latest film *Gönül Yarası* (*Lovelorn*), which was released towards the end of 2004. Şener Şen plays the role of an idealist teacher who can even dare to lose his wife and two children for his students. Although one can find traces of the character of Baran in this later character, Turgul tends towards increasingly minimalist expression with elements of musicality. However, these characters still retain the values of an extinct world.

The unprecedented success of *The Bandit* lies in its special quality as a popular film which is also complex and sophisticated in form, blending the traditional and the modern. Thus it offers possibilities in melodrama as a modality, in the usage of music as an entertainment value (which Yeşilçam exploited heavily some three decades ago), in the revival of a star system and, most important of all, in challenging Hollywood, not only in enticing audiences back to Turkish films but also in offering an alternative imagery, and the possibility of diverse pleasures.

Nezih Erdoğan

REFERENCES

Elsaesser, Thomas (1985 [1972]) 'Tales of Sound and Fury: Observations on Family Melodrama', in Bill Nichols (ed.) *Movies and Methods, vol. II*. Berkeley: University of California Press, 165–89.

Knitzer, Stephen (1997) 'In a scandal torn land, the screen is a mirror', *New York Times*, 25 May, 9.

BEYROUTH AL GHARBIYYA WEST BEIRUT

ZIAD DOUEIRI, LEBANON/FRANCE/BELGIUM/NORWAY, 1998

The opening shot of *Beyrouth Al Gharbiyya* (*West Beirut*, 1998) is of a military jet captured on 8mm film by kids in their school playground, as they joke and fool around. The teenagers, clad in their 1970s shirts and bell-bottoms, seem to think it is all a game. 'It's been hit, it's a MIG 21', says one of the school children. Tarek smacks him on the neck knocking off his nerdy glasses: 'Look at the tail dimwit, it's a Hawker Hunter.'

The teenagers' fascination with the developing conflict and the absurd humour they build around it set the tone for the rest of the film. This is not just a cinematic device to lighten-up the weighty subject of the Lebanese Civil War (1975–90), rather it reflects the experiences of many of Lebanon's war generation. Indeed, the film is partly autobiographical. It is *West Beirut*'s ability to mirror the war, not through a chronological account or political blame games but through its contradictions and feelings, that sets it apart. This intimate story of friendship between three people, Tarek, Omar and Mai, ordinary teenagers living in extraordinary circumstances, gives us glimpses of bigger events that are not only shaping them, but also their country and region.

Tarek's father is, at first, in denial about the possibility of a civil war. His mother had to pick him up from school that day, as children were sent home early after fighting broke out. Back at home, Tarek's parents are affectionate and flirtatious with each other, enjoying a bottle of red wine over dinner. The father reminisces about the revolutionary past, which the day's events brought back to him. He speculates that Israel is trouble-making, with the Lebanese having nothing to do with what is going on. There is the sound of explosions and Tarek goes to the balcony to watch. His father reassures himself, believing that they are flares, while the sky lights-up.

The next day, Tarek is woken up by the mosque's call to prayer and the shouts of a fat neighbour hurling abuse from her balcony, complaining about the crowing of another neighbour's cock. Indeed, the morning acoustics of the neighbourhood are one of the few things that remain constant throughout the war, which has brought new sounds to Beirut – children imitating the shattering sound of bombs from balcony to balcony, the sound of actual bombs and gunfire, and new cries from street peddlers. This time their carts offer glass panes to replace shattered windows, and packs of cigarettes to calm the nerves.

Tarek's parents, still in denial, get him ready to go to school, while he protests that 'the Bastille is closed'. His dad buys a newspaper en route and sees that 31 Palestinians were killed the day before by Lebanese militias, with PLO leader Yasser Arafat calling for international support. Their car is suddenly surrounded by militiamen. Tarek sarcastically claims that he will be late for school. A militiaman in a *kaffiyeh* tells them that only Christians can cross. His father protests, saying that he is from Beirut. The militiaman's response is that there is only one God but there are now two Beiruts, east and west. The mother poignantly asks which part they are in while Tarek mockingly recites his French poetry lesson pointing out that his dad is driving in the wrong direction with his school the other way.

This scene exemplifies the film's director, Ziad Doueiri's, use of personal stories to capture darkly iconic moments in Lebanon's history. This is also evident in his narration of the genesis of the Lebanese Civil War. At the start of the film, Tarek is expelled from his classroom after he provocatively defies the school's requirement that the students sing the French national anthem (it is a French Lycée) and sings the Lebanese anthem instead through a loud speaker, egging on his classmates from a balcony. Although this is not the engagement of serious anti-colonialist revolutionary politics – just a kid playing around at school – it captures the position of Lebanon at the cross-roads: over twenty years after its independence from the French mandate, Lebanon remained strongly francophone, while also trying to assert an independent cultural identity as a unified nation-state. While expelled, Tarek watches the street from the balcony and notices balaclava-clad militiamen hiding, preparing for an ambush. As a bus approaches them, they shoot at it, massacring the Palestinian refugees inside. And so the Lebanese war, with its regional and international dimensions, begins.

Doueiri develops the neighbourhood characters, employing them to show how quickly Beirut and its inhabitants start to change. The loud-mouthed, fat neighbour, with permanently dishevelled hair and wearing a nightgown, comes across as quite mad, but might also be saner than most. She despairs when she finds people are chain smoking in the shelter, exclaiming 'bombs outside and smoke inside!', then goes running after the militiamen in their vans, hurling abuse, while everyone else remains passive towards them. Her abuse ('you are more unpleasant than a clot in my blood') is more comical than offensive. She presents a gentler, if desperate, side when trying to seduce her impassive husband. Throughout the film, we only see the back of her husband's head, as he sits in his flannel vest watching television. He never utters a word or moves from his seat, not even to go to the shelter. He maintains his wall of silence as his wife ties to arouse his passions. It is a tragicomic illustration of a dysfunctional relationship made worse by war; he shuts out reality by staring blankly at a television, while she longs for affection before they have to rush to the shelter. In particular, her behaviour is also a reminder of a spirit of the time, when living for the moment and enjoying life while you still can became a common psychological motif in Lebanon.

Tarek introduces Mai, who had just moved to Beirut, to the characters living in the neighbourhood. He points out the local dirty old man, Khristo, who fancies young boys; the baker who is fatherly towards Tarek, providing him with free falafel sandwiches; and the local militiaman, with the *nom de guerre* Abu Hanash. Each one of them is different in his outlook and a potential threat, yet Tarek seems equally friendly with all. They greet each other with rhyming slang that became common parlance during the war years.

Abu Hanash exemplifies a plausible trajectory for the progression of an ordinary local boy into bearing arms and then becoming a thug. He starts under the excuse of protecting his neighbourhood before eventually terrorising it. He and Tarek seem friendly in the beginning, speaking in militia-style rhyme. When Abu Hanash cleans his weapon and Tarek asks him how his Kalashnikov is, Abu Hanash answers that now he handles RPGs (Rocket Propelled Grenades).

Yet the neighbourhood harmony soon starts to unravel. The first signs are when Tarek overhears local men playing backgammon complain that Christians never wanted to live with the Muslims anyway. The friendly baker warns him that he should not give way to national schisms, if anyone asks him whether he is Muslim or Christian, he should say he is Lebanese. Later in the film, there is an ugly confrontation between the baker and Abu Hanash as provisions run low and long queues form for bread at his bakery. The baker improvises a rationing system to be fair to everyone. But Abu Hanash takes advantage of the power of his gun. He jumps the queue demanding stacks of bread and is turned down. He beats up the old baker in response and spoils the flour bags for all.

In the film, Abu Hanash is not the only type empowered by the war. The school nerd that Tarek used to tease is now aggressively assertive, seemingly fortified by his prejudices. On spotting Mai's cross pendant, he childishly taunts Tarek that he is 'having it away' with a nun. Mai's cross, obstinately hanging around her neck, acts as a magnet for tensions throughout the film, and eventually a symbol for reconciliation.

The friendship between Omar and Tarek is at the heart of the film. We share in their joking, smoking, talking about girls, and their love of disco music and filming with their 8mm camera. One scene sees the boys walking down the street to the sound of disco music. The shot opens with their bell-bottomed footsteps, reminiscent of John Travolta walking down the streets of New York in *Saturday Night Fever* (1977).

It is the passion for filming that eventually takes Tarek and Omar, with Mai in tow, on adventures around Beirut. Omar's initial encounters with Mai did not go well. He was worried about the reaction of his father, who has turned religiously conservative, to her cross. He is concerned by Mai and Tarek's insouciance about how Mai's pendant might act as provocation and place them in danger, as Beirut seems to have reached new levels of communal division, suspicion of the other and intolerance.

Omar confides in Tarek that his household is not what it used to be. His father is insisting that they should learn the Koran now that school is closed, wake up early for prayer and fast during Ramadan. His mother wears the *hejab* and music is now considered a work of the devil – with certain random exceptions made for Um Kalthoum's music. Omar does not know a word of the Koran and Tarek, in an attempt to lighten him up, jokes about disco and Arabic music and asks him to repeat the opening verses of the Koran after him: 'In the name of God the all-beneficent, the all-merciful. Praise be to God, lord of all the worlds...' A reminder, perhaps, that religion does not need to be an ideological tool or a threat. However, the film is never as prescriptive as this reading of the scene, nor does it allow itself to become tragic without counter-weighing this with a good dose of humour.

The brothel in the notorious Olive neighbourhood of Beirut becomes an unexpected magnet for Tarek, Omar and Mai. Tarek and Omar had joined a street demonstration protesting the assassination of Kamal Jumblat, the leader of the Lebanese Socialist Party and a national figure. They joined in for the fun of it, only to ask, at one point, who Kamal Jumblat was. The demonstrators come under fire and in the melée Tarek and Omar are separated, with Tarek hiding in the back of a stationary car.

The car starts-off and Tarek soon finds himself locked in a garage at an unknown location. He gets out of the car and walks into the adjacent house, only to find himself surrounded by young girls dancing, accompanied by a group of militiamen. Um Walid, the brothel's matron, is horrified to see him there. But Tarek cannot believe his luck in coming face to face with the legendary Madame. She was notorious for running her 'love house' in the middle of what became known as the 'green line', separating East and West Beirut. She eventually manages to bundle him off with her driver back home. As they drive through no man's land, with snipers waiting to shoot at anything that moves, the driver explains that the secret to safe passage is to hang a bra on the car antenna. It is a code that allows militiamen from both sides of the conflict to visit the brothel.

This pragmatic arrangement between the militiamen is rumoured to have truly existed in wartime Beirut. For Tarek, as well as in Beirut's mythical history, the Olive district brothel comes to symbolise, at one level, a space where common humanity is recognised and where warring factions can unite. The brothel is also important in the film, featuring as a major part of a coming-of-age story, with Tarek, Omar and Mai curious about the world they inhabit and, while naïve to its ways, slowly discovering their sexuality.

Tarek takes Omar and Mai to the brothel, using Mai's bra for safe passage. But they discover on this second visit that even the idealised brothel is not immune to conflict. For them, the brothel is an island that exists in the hottest spot of the war while simultaneously remaining outside of the conflict. It represents the last possibility for hope, an illustration that the Lebanese are capable of unity and tolerance. Um Walid is complaining that a militiaman picked a fight because the girl he wanted to be with had gone before him with a militiaman from another faction. She claims that in her house Beirut is one, but it no longer appears that anyone is exempt from the conflict.

Tarek and Omar's adolescent understanding of the world contrasts with its dangerous realities. Yet Omar seems to be developing better streetwise instincts. His premonition that Mai's display of the cross spells trouble proves to be right. The three of them cycle into the 'green zone' not realising what a wasteland it had become, hoping to find the shop that normally develops their 8mm films. Instead, they are intercepted by a wolf-like militiaman who is off his head on drugs. While Tarek clumsily tries to save the situation by dropping Abu Hanash's name, Omar immediately hides Mai's cross under her collar and tries to calm the militiaman with cigarette offerings before they all run for their lives.

Mai seems torn between wanting to safeguard the freedom to be who she is and not wanting to be a source of conflict. In a gesture of both reproach and reconciliation she takes off her cross after the incident with the militiaman and hands it to Omar. He eventually shows her how he can wear it round his neck together with a Koran pendant, joking that this way he can go everywhere; they were thus able to create in the microcosm of their friendship what the country is unable to achieve.

Tarek is about to be jolted back to reality by events closer home. For the first time, we see him in tears as he confides in Omar. Money has run out at home and he is afraid to ask for pocket money. He is worried that he might lose his parents and be left alone with no one.

What seemed to be an exhilarating holiday from school is turning into a nightmare. He is left to reminisce about the good old days with their headmistress, Mme Vieillard.

Tarek's mother has been struggling to maintain the façade of normal family life, but falters through worrying over their family. A lawyer by profession, she is attractive and affectionate. Tarek's parents are obviously in love and he enjoys watching them flirt and be playful together. His father is not able to work because of the war, and the mother becomes the sole breadwinner, although the courthouse is open less frequently. Nights of shelling and running to the shelter are taking their toll on her, abd she also worries every time Tarek is out of the house. She wants to leave the country and live somewhere else.

The father has been trying to stay calm and positive throughout, saying there were other times when people thought that Lebanon had broken into a civil war and it had not, and that this time it would be the same. His relationship with Tarek is warm; they shave together (unnecessarily, in the case of Tarek), spar playfully, and Tarek is always encouraged to complete his homework now that he no longer has school. He is firmly against the idea of leaving, saying that 'they will stay like everyone else'. He does not want them to start their lives all over again from scratch, taking lowly jobs because they do not have the right foreign qualifications. 'Leave to where? The Swiss call us Refugees de Luxe, in London dogs sniff us at the airport.' He would rather live poorly than in exile and, to him, humiliated. Tarek's mother encourages his father to play the *oud*, whispering that she loves him as he plays; she seems reconciled to the idea of staying. As he plays, an eerie sound takes over, with newsreel footage of the horrors of the Lebanese war through the years, filling the screen. Tarek's father continues to play the *oud*, but his wife is no longer by his side and Tarek listens from behind a door, sobbing. The final scene is footage of Tarek with his mother by the sea. We are never shown the death of the mother or the events surrounding it. The viewer is nonetheless left with the strong sense that she is now gone, her fate embodying the tragedy of thousands of Lebanese during the Civil War.

West Beirut combines humour, good characterisation, a script that captures the language of the time, convincing acting, a fast pace and a strong visual narrative that is well complemented by the soundtrack. While much has been made of the fact that Doueiri has been Quentin Tarantino's cameraman, the strongest cinematic influence on *West Beirut* was John Boorman's *Hope and Glory* (1987), which was also partly auto-biographical and set around the life of a child growing up during wartime (Britain during World War Two).

The actors playing the three main characters had no acting experience prior to participating in the film; they thus bring with them a naturalness and spontaneity. The character of Tarek is played by Doueiri's brother and his own father appears in a minor role as the taxi driver working for the brothel. Doueiri also uses well-established actors from television sitcoms that Lebanese viewers would associate with the era in which the film is set. The use of grainy news footage of the Civil War, inserted at different points in the film, also works as an effective throwback to some of the darkest days of Lebanon's recent past. These elements have combined to make *West Beirut* popular with audiences, without being overtly commercial. Such considerations are particularly important from the point of view of achieving growth in the Arab film industry, and for *film d'auteur* to become culturally influential within the region.

Though *West Beirut* is not the first Arab film to focus on an intimate story, it stands out for its mood and accessibility to general audiences. At the time when *West Beirut* was made, Lebanese cinema was dominated by the documentary genre. There has been a proliferation of films from Lebanese directors since then, many taking intimate stories set during Lebanon's war of 1975–90 or its aftermath as their basis. This broad theme is often the only point these films have in common, as they differ in style to an extent that makes it difficult to group them together. Some of these films are: *Beirut Phantome* (1998), *Terra Incognita* (2002) and *Le Dernier Homme* (*The Last Man*, 2006) by Ghassan Salhab; *The Kite* (2003) by Randa Shahal Sabbag; *In the Battlefields* (2004) by Danielle Arbid; *A Perfect Day* (2005) by Khalil Joreige and Joanna Haji Thomas; *Zozo* (2005) by Joseph Fares; *Bosta* (2005) by Philippe Aractangi; and *Falafel* (2006) by Michel Kammoun.

It took Doueiri six years from the release of *West Beirut* to launch his second film, *Lila Says* (2004). Doueiri did not seek to build on his existing audience base and went in a different direction. He set his film in Marseille this time, with a young European girl as his main character, and used sexual fantasises to express her insecurities. Although *Lila Says* was generally well received, its setting and the basis of the story did not have the impact and appeal to Arab audiences that Doueiri achieved with *West Beirut*.

Are *West Beirut* and *Lila Says* 'Arab' films and is it useful to refer to Ziad Doueiri as an 'Arab' director? The diversity of approaches, mentioned in the case of Lebanese filmmakers, is even more marked when one compares film directors from across the Arab region to one another. This begs the question of whether they can justifiably be grouped under one umbrella. Labelling them as 'Arab' may be counterproductive when this is not the defining quality of their films, or when this is not necessarily how they choose to identify themselves.

However these films are grouped, whether as part of a curatorial or film-critical process, this categorisation can potentially restrict the many entry points to a film. The generality of a regional label may be less restrictive and leave the door open for more nuanced approaches; it is sometimes easier to find an overarching geographical theme as the initial point for engaging with further complexities.

The development of filmmaking in the Arab region and among its diaspora is an important aspect of carving out and enlarging the space in which the region projects its own images and cultures. Great damage has been done by surrendering the means of narration to third parties. The author Jacques Shaheen, in his book *Reel Bad Arabs: How Hollywood Vilifies a People*, documents 350 instances of films made since the 1970s that portray Arabs as 'insidious cultural others' (a documentary based on this book was released in 2006 bearing the same title). Grouping films as 'Arab' can help empower cultural representations from the region. More subtle approaches often do not achieve the same impact on the media and the audiences.

Filmmakers from the Arab region and its diaspora are often severely constrained by a shortage of funds and platforms for their works, and by rigid expectations on behalf of funders and others as to the subject matters that they are expected to tackle. Despite extraordinary hurdles facing them, they have nonetheless succeeded in producing award-winning and innovative films. *West Beirut* was given the Francois Chalais Award at the Cannes Film Festival, and won the International Critics' Award at the Toronto Film Festival in 1998, as well as other international awards. It was one of the first among other award-winning movies by Arab filmmakers, which include *Yadon ilaheyya* (*Divine Intervention*, 2002) by Elia Suleiman which won the International Critics' Prize at the Cannes Film Festival, *Milles Mois* (2003) by Fawzi Bensaidi which won Le Premier Regard at the Cannes Film Festival, *Paradise Now* (2005) by Hani Abu-Assad which was nominated for an Academy Award and won 17 prizes including the Golden Globes, and *Indigènes* (*Days of Glory*, 2006) by Rachid Bouchareb which was nominated for an Academy Award and won Best Actor and François Chalais Awards at Cannes.

West Beirut, through its international accessibility, has succeeded in giving voice to the region. It has also made a significant contribution to Arab filmmaking, and altered expectations among local audiences in relation to their national cinema.

Mona Deeley

REFERENCE

Shaheen, Jacques (2001) *Reel Bad Arabs: How Hollywood Vilifies a People*. New York: Olive Branch Press.

KIKAR HAHALOMOT CIRCLE OF DREAMS

BENI TORATI, ISRAEL, 2000

When *Kikar Hahalomot (Circle of Dreams)* was released in 2000, it took the public discourse about Mizrahim (Oriental Jews) in Israel into somewhat unfamiliar territory. The dialogue between Mizrahim and Ashkenazim (European Jews) was no longer in a predominately Ashkenazi public forum, but rather Mizrahim were telling their story independently from Ashkenazi existence, infrastructure and misconceptions. The film was written and directed by Beni Torati, a Persian Israeli, and Mizrahi actors played the majority of the roles. The Israeli-Turkish composer, Shem Tov Levy, wrote the original music. In a move that shocked some Ashkenazi and Mizrahi critics alike, the director cast Muhammad Bakri, a Palestinian actor, as his lead character, Avraham Mandaboon. This graphically demonstrated the inevitable cultural alliance between Mizrahi Jews and Palestinians.

Though the population of Israel is composed of immigrants from all over the world, it can be divided into two main categories: Ashkenazi Jews, people who came from Europe and America, and Mizrahim, people who came from Arab countries. (The word 'Sepharadic', indicating a specifically Spanish extraction, is an older word that is improperly used in place of the word Mizrahi, meaning 'Oriental'). To understand the role of the Israeli film industry in shaping public discourse about Mizrahim, it is important to first examine the social roots of East/West dynamics in Israeli society.

Israel suffers from the constant tension between Mizrahim and Ashkenazim. As critical researchers of Israeli society such as Shlomo Swirski and Ella Shohat have noted, this tension derives from the complexity in which Eurocentrism and Orientalism operate within the state of Israel, causing deliberate marginalisation of Mizrahi Jews in Israeli society. For Ashkenazi Jews, the experience of meeting Mizrahi Jews in the 1950s was as any Western coloniser meeting an Oriental native, and practicing the Jewish faith accorded Mizrahim no special status in the eyes of European Jews. Rather, the meeting of culturally distinct peoples organised and controlled by Western immigrants reinforced how white society already perceived its natural superiority.

The state of Israel is driven on the one hand by the Zionist ambition to create a Western state with Western national identity, and on the other, tension rooted in failing to recognise

Israel as a Middle Eastern country where almost fifty per cent of the Jewish population is of Arab origin. As Shohat claims, unlike other minority groups in the world, Mizrahi Jews and Palestinians together constitute a majority of the population in Israel. Despite the fact that Israel is not a Third World country, Shohat says, both Palestinians and Mizrahi Jews 'can be seen as Third World or at least as originating in the Third World'. David Ben-Gurion, the first Israeli Prime Minister, declared once that Israel was going to be the Switzerland of the Middle East, and to this day Western identity dictates Israel's public perception of what constitutes acceptable Israeli identity. The state of Israel, through its Ashkenazi leaders past and present, desires to Westernise Israel through every form of state domination, ignoring the Arab and Arab-Jewish cultural presence in the immediate geographic environment.

Zionist-European philosophy was founded on an Israeli-Jewish identity that ignored Oriental Jews as any sort of cultural entity. They were labourers and second-class citizens, never material for equality or partnerships. As Jewish Arabs, the Mizrahi represented the best of both worlds for the birthing – and still youthful – Israeli state. They belonged both because they were Jews and because they nullified the security threat of using Arabs they just displaced, or people sympathetic to them. This set a trap for myriad Mizrahi Jews aspiring to become Israeli without realising the inherent cultural bias of the identity. Israeli nationalism is strongly rooted in the aftermath of the slaughter of Eastern European Jewry during World War Two, and is behind the rationale of every move in attack or defense: never again. The homeland, though on sacred soil, is far from safe, and the sentiment is easily transferred to the Arab threat Israel faces inside and outside its borders.

Fear of the Arab threat, and disdain for that which is Arab, permeated the culture from its inception, and Mizrahi culture is rejected as an extension of the enemy's image. As those who should be feared, they cannot be incorporated into unified Jewish national identity. The victim image, a cornerstone of Israeli nationalism, justifies any Israeli action in the name of self-defense, and the German threat has been replaced by the Arab threat. Mizrahi Jews who pursue an 'Israeli' identity learn to despise themselves and instead are pressured to become Israelis or Ashkenazis, depending how you wish to decode the term. In *The Ashkenazi Revolution is Dead*, Sami Chetrit describes a conversation with Adaal, a Palestinian activist who was unaware of his cultural connection with Arab Jews until he was incarcerated with them.

I was the only Arab in the cell. Everybody else was Mizrahi. One of the prisoners said, be careful, they are going to kill you. I was afraid. I stayed up all night with my eyes open, and some time in the middle of the night, they started to sing Um Kulthum [perhaps the most famous female Egyptian vocalist]. They sang it so well; I was impressed. Then they moved to Palestinian songs and sang them with a flawless accent. I was impressed and confused at the same time … then I got the courage to tell one of them that one of the other prisoners said they were going to kill me. 'Are you kidding me?' he replied. 'We're your friends, we're your brothers.'

Ella Shohat was the first to recognise the myriad cultural similarites between Arabs and Jews. She deconstructed the commonly used divisions of Arabs and Jews and suggested looking beyond class-analysis into questions of race, colonialism and identity, thus locating the problem of Mizrahi Jews within Israel as already beginning with the ideology of Zionism. Shohat offered a new angle of looking at questions of First/Third World and East/West across the divisions of Arabs and Jews while analysing the oppression of Mizrahim in relation to the dispossession of Palestinians (although emphasising that these are linked yet different histories) and as part of the broader European attitude toward the East that the Ashkenazi Jews adopted.

Circle of Dreams offers one of the first film texts to support this theoretical approach. While many Jews in and outside Israel flinch at the term Arab-Jew, Shohat, Chetrit and other theorists of Israeli society believe that overcoming cultural oppression can be achieved through coalitions of global minorities. Through connecting to others who share the same culture, even if it means a coalition with the 'enemy', the cultural entities strengthen themselves. By casting the Palestinian actor Muhammad Bakri as his lead character, Totati thus empowers Mizrahi discourse through pointing to the alliance and connection between Mizrahim and Palestinians.

The film, which was released in English under its original title, *Desperado Square* (and changed to *Circle of Dreams* in Israel because the studio found the original title too depressing), tells the story of a Mizrahi/Israeli sub-culture in a small and neglected neighbourhood on the outskirts of Tel Aviv. The story takes place in the 1960s, before television dominated the public domain, when the local cinema was the cultural centre of the neighbourhood. Although the local cinema in this neglected neighbourhood screened westerns and martial arts movies, the most successful pictures were Indian dramas. The melodrama appealed to the need for emotional nourishment and escape in a culture constricted by money and what society allowed in small ethnic neighbourhoods. *Sangam* (1964), starring Raj Kapoor, one of the major actor/directors in Indian cinema, was the most popular of these dramas and a commercial success not only in

India but also Israel and Egypt. The attraction of Indian cinema can also be seen as what Ella Shohat and Robert Stam view as the forming of a coalition of global minorities through Third World cinema, especially in light of Western criticism of 'stupid and unsophisticated' plot lines. Torati changes this misconception by reconstructing the divisions of centre and periphery. As Chetrit notes, *Circle of Dreams* makes the Western/Ashkenazi hegemony the cultural periphery of the global minority/Mizrahi neighbourhood.

The film focuses on two central themes: love and reunion. The main plot line follows neighbourhood residents trying to resurrect the old cinema. They head the programme with *Sangam*, perceived as the finest Indian drama of all time. Viewers simultaneously follow the community's passion for Indian cinema and the unfulfilled love of the lead characters of *Circle of Dreams*, Avraham and Seniora. 'Sangam' in Hindi means 'confluence', literally 'flowing together'. The presentation of this movie within a movie creates nesting plot lines within the greater context of the Mizrahi pursuit of identity within the Ashkenazi world, a deep and subtle unrequited love. The romance of Avraham and Seniora parallels the unfulfilled love of the characters in *Sangam*. *Sangam* also serves as a distant memory of love, and the desire to resurrect that love motivates people to act while the passion to breathe new life into this warm memory moves the plot forward.

The film tells the story of the generation of Torati's parents. The director's love of cinema, the neighbourhood and the culture is evident in every scene. He also closes with a dedication to his 'parents' generation with love'. Despite the gloomy physical environment of unpaved streets, dirt and the feelings of desertion, the dominant mood in the movie is of love, celebration and joy. Viewers cannot help but fall in love with the people of this neglected and ugly place and identify with their romantic desire to revive the past, even if just for a short while.

The tempo of life in the film is slow, as in any Middle Eastern place that has not been violated by Western capitalism. People spend time together, hang out, sip tea, play backgammon and dance to Greek music in the local nightclub. A sense of community and bonding is developed between the neighbourhood's residents who care about each other's feelings, and know each other's deepest secrets and desires. In the end, the old movie theatre is revived due to joint efforts of all people in the neighbourhood, and the community's dream is fulfilled. When Aaron, the projectionist, tries to convince Avraham to hand him the only copy of *Sangam* he says: 'Come on, let's relive our old dreams … give me the movie.' However, it is not until Avraham, who appears throughout *Circle of Dreams* as a loner and an outsider, gives in to the community, that his own dream, of getting his love back, can come true.

The unique Mizrahi representation in *Circle of Dreams* lies in not only disconnecting Mizrahi-Israeli cultural life from the dominant Ashkenazi culture, but in the director's ability to magnify and highlight the margin. Torati has a long history of contributing to alternative discourse in Israeli media. He was one of the writers of the influential alternative newspaper *Hapatish* ('The Hammer'), which appeared in Tel Aviv in the 1980s and early 1990s. The newspaper took a refreshing, innovative perspective, and sharply criticised the mainstream from its inception. Among *Hapatish*'s most memorable columns is Torati's 'Bus #16', a column about Hatikva neighbourhood life. Through his column, Torati brought life at this neglected place into the centre of public interest, a method he later developed with *Circle of Dreams* as well as other movies he wrote and directed.

Torati is a master of centralising the outsiders and the neglected. His film *Yona Nam* (1987), which won the best short film award at the Jerusalem Film Festival, features an outsider kid who develops friendship with a cockroach, and his documentary *Gagot Shel Brazent* (*Homeless*, 1994) follows the harsh reality of the homeless in Israel.

As an outsider himself, Torati's approach to issues of representation are free of misconception and superiority typical of other Ashkenazi filmmakers in Israel. He even includes himself in a short cameo in the synagogue scene, as if to say 'I am here, too; this is where I belong, in this marginalised neighbourhood' rather than the mainstream normally inhabited by filmmakers. It is not coincidental that he chose to make this cameo in one of the most controversial scenes in the movie, when the Palestinian actor Muhammad Bakri worships as a Jew, complete with a *yarmulke* and prayer book.

In her political critique of the East/West discourse in Israeli, Ella Shohat confronted the dominant Zionist Eurocentric ideology with questions of racism and oppression and shows how colonisation of Mizrahi culture and identity is evident in different forms of public discourse. She notes that Mizrahi representation in Israeli films follows ideological and social treatment of Oriental Jews in Israeli society. Mizrahi actors are usually cast as criminals, prostitutes or lower working class, easily characterised as uneducated, sneaky and obedient. Although the Israeli cinema industry is small and undeveloped compared to Hollywood, or even Bollywood, it had a strong impact on Israeli society. The impact was especially strong in the 1950s and 1960s, when there was no television in the nascent Israeli state. The images of Mizrahi Jews put forth in the media and film thus reinforced their marginal place in Israeli society, and ignored the rich cultural life of Oriental Jews both domestically and in their Arab homeland. According to Shohat, in early films such as *Salah Shabati* (1964), *Fortuna* (1966) and *Aliza Mizrahi* (1967),

Ashkenazi directors and producers Westernised Mizrahim to help them move into 'civilisation', bringing to mind Kipling's reference to 'The White Man's Burden'. In *Don Quixote and Sa'adia Panza* (1956), one of the earliest efforts of the Israeli film industry, these ethnic/class relations are presented as natural. Ashkenazim play detectives and investigators, where Yemenite actors play the servants. These Ashkenazi heroes represent the Sabra, the first generation of Israeli-born European Jews. In Hebrew, a Sabra is a prickly pear cactus, transferring the connotations of resilience, hardiness and the occasional beauty of flowers and fruit protected by a defence of vicious spines.

Shohat points out that in a later movie, *Hassamba* (1971), based on a popular children's book series, the ethnic/class relations and the stereotyped casting is even more obvious. Young Sabra children are creative and courageous. They employ sophisticated technology against the underworld antagonist, an Oriental Jew who, despite being older and more experienced, uses primitive methods. Mizrahi Jews in literature, as well, are typically described as violent, primitive, ugly and inferior to Ashkenazi characters. The Yemenites, however, win the image of sweet, cute and happy to the point of being dumb. Menashe, the Yemenite kid in the book *Hassamba*, source novel of the film, is too stupid to take any initiative; he only follows the orders of the more intelligent Ashkenazi kids. Menashe is also so dark-skinned as to appear black next to Tamar, the pretty Sabra girl with the long black braided hair, which turns to blond in the picture.

Western domination is evident in the Israeli advertising industry as well. Mizrahi images in television commercials are either of a backward, uneducated person or absent altogether. Advertisers sell hope by juxtaposing a product with a desirable outcome; in Israeli advertising, the desirable outcome is almost exclusively represented by people with blond hair and pink skin. The doctors and lawyers we should believe, the babies who need protection, and the satisfied people who had their needs met by product X have a distinctly European look. The models of winning campaigns are, in fact, often hired from Europe. Mizrahi Jews are most often the dumb consumer who might be improved by switching detergents, and the authoritative Mizrahi in a commercial is usually trustworthy because he is an experienced mechanic or air conditioning maintenance worker. Even an ad for hummus, the consummate Middle Eastern food, features a little blond girl pronouncing the Arabic brand name, Ahla, meaning great or fantastic, with a distinctly Ashkenazi accent.

Circle of Dreams shatters these images and stereotypes by contributing to the new Mizrahi alternative discourse emerging in the last decade in Israeli media, literature and film. Torati joins other Mizrahi authors such as Sami Michael, Dudu Busi and Dorit Rabinian who tell Mizrahi stories from a Mizrahi point of view that does not refer to Ashkenazi existence or the Mizrahi/Ashkenazi conflict at all. Torati frees Mizrahi Jews from what Shohat calls 'the dialectics of dependency'. These relationships of dependency between Mizrahi and Ashkenazi Jews, says Shohat, are evident not only discursively but also in the deliberate marginalisation of Mizrahim, geographically and economically, in Israeli society.

In interview, Torati has discussed Mizrahi culture as the key concept in the ongoing conflict between Mizrahi and Ashkenazi Jews. He says there was no proper coverage of Mizrahi culture from the 1960s until the late 1980s. What did appear in the media about Mizrahim was stereotypical and disrespectful:

> If they wrote something about it in the mainstream media, it was written with ridicule. Music critics, for instance, wrote that Mizrahi music flourishes are whiny. It was a result of ignorance and disrespect. I always claimed that the war is first of all cultural. The oppression is cultural, we were born to a world were our cultural feathers were taken from us so we will forever slip. That is why I dedicated my film to my parents' generation.

In this film, as Chetrit notes in 'The Desperation and the Dream of Beni Torati', Torati not only fights the misconception of Mizrahi culture but also connects the local neighbourhood to the universal community. Chetrit views the power of *Circle of Dreams* through its intimacy, as it relates a specific Mizrahi tale in specific neighbourhoods in Israel to universal themes. Chetrit calls this genre 'the universal neighbourhood', and explains that in this time of Western global economy, the flipside of globalisation is a universal connection of local places. Thus people in other marginalised neighbourhoods of the world such as Egypt, Ireland and India can easily identify with what this specific southern Israeli neighbourhood represents.

In *Circle of Dreams* form and content are closely linked. Torati chooses the purest form of storytelling in the tradition of neo-realist Italian films. Although the main characters are famous actors, he uses many non-professional actors (some are his neighbourhood friends) in supporting roles, such as the three local 'clowns' whose parts create the comic relief between the dramatic parts of the story. Also, the documentary-like camera work successfully conveys the realistic atmosphere of the film, and lends an air of veracity to the tale and the characters on the screen. As Shohat and Stam claim in *Unthinking Eurocentrism*, many oppressed groups around the world use what they call 'progressive realism' as a means of hegemonic representation. Using realism or neo-realism in cinema allows the oppressed to counter the discourse of oppression created by colonialism with their version of reality.

Torati's simple rendition of reality and brilliant casting sweep the viewer into this emotional tale without overloading the text ideologically or politically. The narrative is subtle. As pointed out earlier, Shohat claims Mizrahi Jews and Palestinians are on the same side of the analytical map. When Avraham first appears in the movie, after a 30-year absence, he walks through the neighbourhood with a suitcase that marks him clearly as a refugee. Now the viewer is confused. Muhammad Bakri's presence on screen is strong and appealing, but at the same time it makes the audience uncomfortable. His appearance makes some people in the neighbourhood uncomfortable as well. His brother's two sons and their mother Seniora, his lost love, are not sure what to make of his return. Overall, Bakri's role throughout the film moves between creating uncertainty and discomfort to bringing people together and finding his former love.

His nephews clearly state their disapproval of his reappearance, and his first meeting with Seniora does not give him much hope for reconnection. For the first time, she confronts him for not telling his brother and her former husband Morris of their love before she was thrown, by society's rules, to this arranged marriage: 'Why didn't you speak to Morris?' she asks. 'He was so happy when he told me about his marriage to you that I couldn't tell him about us', he says. 'I wasn't courageous enough, I was wrong.' 'Now there is no one to talk to', she replies. 'What we had we can never have back.'

One again considers the perceptions of First and Third World cultures in Israel. That which is First World – good, modern, healthy – is the European import, and that which is Third World – coarse, primitive – is the native Arab culture, Jewish or not. The Arab Jew growing up Israeli learns to distance himself from the Arab as the European distances himself from the Arab, despite having a far stronger cultural connection with the Arab, even considering religion as a factor.

Avraham Mandaboon is asked to leave again when he joins the memorial service for his brother Morris at the local synagogue. At this point of the narrative, the movie subtly raises its political and social subtext. The appearance of this proud and strong Palestinian man in a synagogue with his head covered holding a Jewish prayer book and praying in an obviously Arab, and not Mizrahi, accent is shocking. In the Jewish tradition, the sons and the brothers of the deceased are required to say a mourner's prayer called *Kaddish*. When Avraham attempts to join his nephews in this prayer, one of them, Nissim, is outraged by the participation of his outcast uncle. He angrily asks Avraham to leave in front of the congregation. 'I will not say *Kaddish* with him,' he says, and Avraham walks out of the synagogue.

In actuality, this outcast man holds the community's only key to its warmly remembered past. His copy of *Sangam* is the artefact with the power to revive the old cinema, and the community it supported. When Avraham finally hands his copy of *Sangam* to the projectionist, he feels that this gesture supports the community but takes away his only real memory of his love for Seniora. As the projectionist puts it, '*Sangam* is not just a movie … it was their movie'. When the members of the neighbourhood gather for the celebratory screening of *Sangam*, Avraham and Seniora are the only ones left out.

With the melodramatic music of *Sangam* in the background, we see Avraham getting ready to leave the neighbourhood, and Seniora sitting alone outside her house. As Avraham walks out onto the streets, the large poster of Raj Kapoor and Vyjayanthimala on top of the newly revived movie theatre attracts him. The projectionist is not surprised to see him and welcomes him for a private screening with the Arabic phrase *tefadal*, which means 'please welcome'. The formal screening of *Sangam* is over, and Avraham sits alone in the empty theatre.

Only two people in the neighbourhood knew about his love for Seniora in the past, the projectionist and Israel that everyone refers to as 'the Indian' guy who, then as now, is watching the movie from the rooftop. A few minutes into Avraham's private screening of *Sangam*, Seniora shows up at the door of the theatre. Their renewed love, just like the revival of the theatre itself and the new joy found within the community, happens in part due to the magical tragic love of the characters in *Sangam*. And with *Sangam* playing for the second time in one day Avraham and Seniora find their way to each other's hearts again.

Circle of Dreams is part of the on-going new Mizrahi discourse created by a new generation of Mizrahi writers, poets and scholars. Unlike other more painful discussions about the heart of this social divide in Israeli society, Torati shows a different path to healing. The film offers a window to Mizrahi culture from within as a way to fight racism and white supremacy. Mizrahi Jews can relive their past and connect to each other guided by love and a true Mizrahi-centred reality instead of society's negative images of them. And only then, as the text of *Circle of Dreams* suggests, after healing within the community can one find true love.

Shoshana Madmoni-Gerber

REFERENCES

Chetrit, Sami (1999) *The Ashkenazi Revolution is Dead: Reflection on Israel from a Dark Angle.* Tel Aviv: Kedem.

_____ (2004a) *The Mizrahi Struggle in Israel: Between Oppression and Liberation, Identification and Alternative 1948-2000.* Tel Aviv: Am Oved.

_____ (2004b) 'The Desperation and the Dream of Beni Torati', On-line; available at http://www.kedma.co.il (accessed 4 July 2004).

Shohat, Ella (1988) 'Sepharadim in Israel: Zionism from the Stand Point of its Jewish Victims', *Social Text: Theory, Culture and Ideology*, 19/20, 1–35.

_____ (1989) *Israeli Cinema: East/West and the Politics of Representation.* Austin: University of Texas Press.

_____ (2001) *Forbidden Reminiscences.* Tel Aviv: Kedma.

Shohat, Ella and Robert Stam (1994) *Unthinking Eurocentrism: Multiculturalism and the Media.* London and New York: Routledge.

Swirski, Shlomo (1981) *Orientals and Ashkenazim in Israel: The Ethnic Divisions of Labour.* Tel Aviv: Segal.

Torati, Beni (2001) Personal interview with the author.

KIPPUR

AMOS GITAI, ISRAEL/FRANCE, 2000

Amos Gitai's film *Kippur* (2000) uses compelling formal configurations to articulate a strong notion of besiegement. In this, the film is emblematic of the contemporary Israeli cinematic figuration of war. This chapter locates *Kippur* within the cinematic trajectory of Israeli war films, with the extra-textual reality perceived as forging its embedded conception, as well as the trajectory of Gitai's own filmmaking.

The notion of Israel being under siege, as held by Israeli Jews, derives from historical experience, religious traditions and Israel's predominant state ideology. It encompasses Israelis' recent experiences of conventional war and acts of terror, as well as the sporadic condemnations of Israel by world organisations. This often evokes for Israeli Jews the long history of anti-Semitism that culminated in the Holocaust, a history constituting traumatic past experiences both for the individual and the collective. This is a history that has been memorised in relation to deeply ingrained biblical tenets linked with the Jews being a chosen people (*Am Nivchar*), alone among the nations (*Am Levadad Yshkon*), with no one but God almighty and their own resources to protect them in a hostile world seeking their destruction. The biblical tribe of Amalek, who sought to destroy the Jews, has become the symbolic (read: ahistorical) name given in Jewish religious circles, but also in secular discourse, to Israel's enemies, past, present and future. Amalek's ahistorical symbolisation already occurs in the Bible. Furthermore, as shown by Charles Liebman and Eliezer Don-Yehiya in their book *Civil Religion in Israel*, Israel's dominant state ideology since the late 1950s has used the collective remembrance of past atrocities inflicted upon the Jewish people to maintain the idea that the world is against Israel because it is a Jewish state.

This dominant notion is widespread in Israeli culture. It is embedded in educational textbooks, in secular national monuments and holidays and in the literature. The notion of siege, deeply resonating in the Israeli Jew's mind in times of socio-political or geo-political unrest, is functional in the cohesiveness of a society otherwise divided along class, ethnic, religious and ideological lines. As noted by Daniel Bar-Tal and Dikla Antebi, this notion influences the ways in which Israelis evaluate fundamental socio-political and geo-political concerns. This influence is often detrimental to Israeli society, particularly in its potential blocking of serious consideration of feasible solutions to its problems.

A look at some of the cardinal films produced in Israel on the subject of war (such as Thorold Dickenson's *Giv'a 24 Lo Ona* (*Hill 24 Doesn't Answer*, 1956), Gilberto Toffano's *Matzor* (*Siege*, 1969), Rennen Shor's *Bluz Lahofesh Hagadol* (*Summer Blues*, 1987), Raffi Bukai's *Avanti Popolo* (1986) and Eli Cohen's *Two Fingers from Sidon*, 1986)) shows the recurrence of compositions and figurations whose interrelations evoke notions of claustrophobia or agoraphobia, violence, threatening encirclement and suspicion. These often include shadowy patterns of lighting, visual and aural configurations composing closed and labyrinthine spatial formations, open threatened spaces where there is no refuge, unexpected abrupt editing patterns and camera movements creating violent surprises, temporal circular structures whose synchronic framework disjoints their diachrony, fatalistic or bounded story structures, recurrence of suspicious and violent interactions among characters, conspiratory modes of action and the thematic and formal isolation of threatened individuals or groups. These configurations, whose dominance varies in different periods, formally and thematically embed in these films the notion of Israel being a besieged nation. This notion, to a varying degree, semantically colours the films' conception of war as being irresolvable, dead-ended and threatening.

Articulation of the notion of siege in films on war produced up to 1977 underwent a radical change in films of the 1980s, producing a new perception that has remained dominant to this day. In post-1977 films, the traditional notion of siege becomes acute, while co-existing with a vague critique of Israel as responsible for its own besiegement. In these later films, war is presented as a constant threat, erupting out of nowhere and ending suddenly. It figures as an event whose different expressions – terror, mines, explosions, violent military encounters and death – sporadically invade the narrative trajectory, generating a disrupted plot. The plot, in turn, is made coherent by the films being framed by war (Yaky Yosha's *Ha-Ayit* (*The Vulture*, 1981) begins with the October war of 1973 and ends with preparations for another, unspecified war). War is posited as the sole origin of a society that is morally, emotionally, aesthetically and mentally corrupt. Society is represented as anxious and suspicious, its members being malicious and violent, or naïve and therefore lost, confused and in despair. This confusion, anxiety and despair are supported by disjointed story and plot lines, articulated within an enclosed narrative space.

Nevertheless, the films protest against their fabricated reality. This finds occasional explicit expression in what some characters say, which consists mainly of a vague desire for peace.

This protest and desire, however, are presented as imaginary, lacking resonance in the overall structure of the films (as some variation of Job's complaint to God). This lack of resonance derives primarily from the representation of war as the sole source of societal corruption, while the representation of the source – war itself – has no reason and repeatedly reappears. Any possible relevant protest and desire for peace in the films that could result from the structured reality and figuration of war, and be substantiated by it, is thus eliminated.

The delineated trajectory and its general characteristics recur with slight variations in most contemporary Israeli films whose thematic concern is war and its effects upon society. Hence, films like *Summer Blues*, which retrospectively deals with the War of Attrition (1967–70), *Avanti Popolo*, dealing with the Six Day War of June 1967, or even *Two Fingers From Sidon*, an Israel Defence Forces-subsidised film tackling the Lebanon War of 1982, all feature and even focus on characters who seek to evade the reality of war, either through political subversion (*Summer Blues*), solidarity with the enemy (*Avanti Popolo*) or passive resistance (*Two Fingers From Sidon*). However, the subversive characters' desire to evade the reality of periodical wars is undermined by their positioning in the narrative (and other formal and thematic strategies) leading either to their awareness that war is a natural and necessary evil (in *Summer Blues* and *Two Fingers From Sidon*) or to their death, in *Avanti Popolo*.

This perception is particularly evident in films addressing the 1973 Yom Kippur War (so-called because it began on Yom Kippur, the Jewish day of atonement and holiest day in the Jewish religious calendar), in which Egypt and Syria initiated a concerted attack from south and north leading to heavy casualties on the Israeli side. Although the 1973 war was eventually won by Israel, which re-established its pre-1973 ceasefire borders, the price paid in human lives was unprecedented for Israelis. It is significant that whereas the Six Day War victory quickly generated a series of films that focused thematically upon it, the Yom Kippur War was not addressed at all in the years immediately following it. This war, and the type of shock of recognition it generated (after the post-1967 euphoria), was one of the cardinal factors leading to the downfall of the Labour Alignment Party, and the rise to power of the right-wing Likud Party in the 1977 elections. In fact, the first explicit cinematic consideration of the Yom Kippur War was *The Vulture* in 1981. The year in which it was produced and the peculiar form in which the war is addressed attests to this shift in the cinematic perception of war, not only due to the specific war addressed but mostly to the changed political climate in Israel following the overturn in the 1977 elections. These elections brought the Likud right-wing party to power, after a 60-year-long hegemony of the Left. The reaction of Israeli filmmakers as well as that of various artists and intellectuals aligned with the Left was critical of the geo-political and socio-political reality that they feared the Likud would bring about, along with a deeply embedded anxiety regarding their own wellbeing and that of the State of Israel. Ironically, the fear of Israeli filmmakers for their wellbeing was misplaced, given that under the right-wing government the film industry received massive governmental support and suffered little censorship, following the establishment of the Committee for the Encouragement of Quality Films that funded the highly critical and politicised films produced during this period.

Notwithstanding this perplexing situation, we might term the cinematic perception that evolved after 1977 as evidencing a contradiction between explicit critiques of Israeli society, along with their aesthetic grounding within a cinematic reality of besiegement, making these vague critiques irrelevant to what the films perceive to be Israel's real situation.

Kippur follows this ongoing perception, making powerful use of formal and thematic configurations to articulate the notion of siege. The film, which follows a group of soldiers haphazardly formed into a rescue unit amidst the chaos of war, offers a vague protest against warmongers and the horrors of war, instead suggesting the option of sensual love. It opens with a long lovemaking scene between one of the leading characters and his girlfriend, followed by his departure to the front with a friend. On the way, they meet a militant officer who leads his troops enthusiastically into the middle of a heavy bombardment, in which all but he are killed. This is followed by the protagonists' rapid assignment to an airborne rescue unit and their various encounters with the wounded and dead soldiers they have to evacuate from the front. This they do until their own helicopter is hit and are themselves evacuated. The film ends with the hero's return from the hell of war to his lover's bed, to a lovemaking scene identical to one that opened the film.

An analysis of *Kippur*'s formal structure reveals its detailing the psychology of seige mentality. The recurring use of long and lingering shots of battlefields, in which we witness rescue attempts by the protagonists, evokes a strong sense of agoraphobia. A continuing visual motif is that of the rescue unit. Consisting of four defenceless reserve soldiers, they are seen slowly carrying wounded soldiers upon stretchers across the middle of an open, muddy and cold battlefield, bodies falling around them; casualties of the constant shelling and occasional bullets, whose source is unspecified. A particularly powerful scene, projecting this sense of agoraphobia, is composed of three lengthy shots in which the protagonists are seen extricating a wounded soldier from a tank and trying to bear him on a stretcher to the evacuation point. However, they are unable to advance in the heavy mud. Their tired, pathetic efforts to carry him end in his falling from the stretcher into the mud. The unit's doctor attempts to tie muddy bandages over his open wounds, but the soldier dies in their arms. Their frustrated attempts to resuscitate him, their refusal to leave him there despite the constant shelling, and their tired resignation after his death are seen in lengthy, impassive, slow-moving tracking shots. The repeated scenes showing the rescue attempts enhance the sense that their mission is a Sisyphean task. The feeling of claustrophobia is enhanced by the close-ups of the protagonists, crammed within the confined space of a helicopter, hovering above the battlefield, accompanied by the constant, monotonic and disturbing soundtrack of the helicopter's propeller blades. Almost every battlefield shot shows from afar, through a slow-moving camera, the small rescue unit advancing slowly, amidst tanks and helicopters that cross the frame in different directions, enhancing the overall sense of disorientation. This is particularly strong in a lengthy shot taken from inside the helicopter hovering over the muddy battlefield. The shot looks down from the helicopter at the ground without showing the horizon, constantly circling over the same field. Within this shot, among occasional views of tanks moving in different directions, the camera focuses upon the wet terrain crisscrossed by the caterpillar trails left by the tanks, and forming a disorderly web whose pattern is disrupted by the detritus of destroyed military vehicles.

This formal sense of entrapment finds emblematic representation in the function and character of the rescue unit's doctor (played by Uri Ran Kaluzner) whose tragic figure focuses the film's approach to war as senseless, yet irresolvable, carnage. Hence, at the centre of the rescue unit's continuous encounters with the graphically presented mutilated and burned bodies of soldiers, stands a podgy, bespectacled doctor, older than the others, whose physique and gentle manners contrast with the tiring and difficult job of carrying the wounded on stretchers and the horrific images of the mutilated bodies they encounter. Moreover, as the doctor's main function in the film is not to heal the wounded but rather to assess their condition in order to decide who gets evacuated and who stays behind in the battlefield, either because he is lightly wounded, beyond redemption or already dead, this slowly builds up in him and in those around him an acute sense of frustration, futility and helplessness. Moreover, the role of the doctor's life-story in the narrative explicitly references the larger Jewish-Israeli mentality of siege and entrapment. Hence, towards the film's end, in the emergency room to which the doctor is evacuated, along with the others, after their helicopter has been hit, he is seen whispering that he wants his mother beside him. However, as we know from the story he had earlier told one of the soldiers, his mother, who survived the Nazi death camps, had died in grief after he refused to join her and leave the Catholic family that had sheltered and raised him during World War Two. The doctor's guilt-ridden longing for his dead mother strongly projects the larger Jewish-Israeli mentality of being besieged and entrapped in a world seeking their destruction.

The film's dominant formal and thematic structure contradicts its occasionally explicit critique of Israelis as responsible for the war. This takes place with the initial insinuation that the militant officer encountered at the beginning of the film is responsible in his arrogance and warmongering for the subsequent death of his troops. However, the initial anger at his irresponsibility turns to sorrow and pity for a tragic figure, due to the circular, hallucinatory back-tracking shot of the disillusioned officer as he runs back and forth from one dead soldier to the next, along the labyrinthine trenches of the bunker, where his platoon was hit. Likewise, the film's bookending of the lovemaking scenes is transformed from a naïve, but viable, opposition to war along the lines of 'make love, not war', into a temporary, albeit brittle, refuge from the ongoing hell of war. This occurs not only because the war in the film is not over when the protagonist is finally released, but mostly because in his return to his loved one, his desire to hold and make love to his lover is now charged with the anxiety and fear of an experienced threat outside, rather than with the sensual, innocent atmosphere that had characterised the opening love scene.

Kippur is Gitai's most autobiographical film, based upon his experiences during the Yom Kippur War, in which he had been a member of a helicopter rescue unit that was shot down on the Golan Heights by a Syrian missile. Weinraub, the name of one of the characters, was Gitai's surname before his father Hebraised it to Gitai. Perhaps because of this personal experience, *Kippur* offers a powerful variation of the post-1977 Israeli films' siege-based critique of a society at war. Aesthetically, it continues Gitai's unique use of disquieting, recursive and slow, long shots, offering an expansive and tangible sense of location. However, it forgoes his earlier use of dialectically arranged layers of images and sounds that projected conflicting points of view upon a single location.

This was the case, for example, in his early documentary, *Bait* (*House*, 1980) In *House*, which can also mean 'home' and even 'homeland' for Israelis, Gitai inquires into the changing ownership of a ruined house in the midst of intense renovation. As it turns out, the house, recently purchased from an Oriental Jewish couple by an East European Jewish economics professor, was originally the property of an Arab Palestinian family that fled the country during the War of Independence in 1948, and the house was declared absentee-property by the government. The house's history, concisely encapsulating the main geo-political and socio-political conflicts and power relations generated by the Zionist project, is articulated through a series of interviews shot on location. These are carried out with an impassive camera that records the interviewees, the house and its surroundings in very lengthy, often recursive long shots. The camera, frequently leaving the interviewees and, wandering around on its own, comments, recontextualises and relativises the different perspectives of the current house owner, the Palestinian workers that are re-building the house and others, while clearly placing the camera on the side of the repressed Palestinian workers whose poor dwellings in a refugee camp are inserted into the film. This complex dialectical approach to location recurs in Gitai's *Wadi* (1981) and its sequel *Wadi, Ten Years Later* (1991), documenting the Rushmia Valley (Wadi) near Haifa, inhabited by Israeli Jews and Arabs in a fragile coexistence.

Gitai's split dialectical approach to location and narrative in his documentaries recurred in his fiction films, such as in his first feature *Esther* (1985). The film tells the tale of Esther, who saved the Jewish people from Haman, one of King Xerxes' trusted advisors, who persuaded the king to have all the Jews in Persia slaughtered. By risking her life, Esther persuades the king to reverse his decision, allowing the Jews to slaughter their enemies in the realm. Just as Xerxes reversed his verdict, Gitai reverses the traditional Jewish celebration of the tale's conclusion, lamenting instead its dire consequences for non-Jews. This dialectic in the presentation of the tale's narrative re-surfaces in the blending of the biblical tale with its performance among the ruined houses of the valley of Salib in Haifa, with the sporadic, anachronistic aural interference of ambulance sirens, along with the camera's intermittent shift to show the modern-day shabby surroundings. The location of the tale's performance in a valley inhabited by low-income Arabs and Oriental Jews, from which the first inter-ethnic riots broke out in 1959, is a powerful, demystifying and critical comment on Israeli reality.

The complex, politically subversive films of Gitai were distinctly different from, and even alien to, the 1980s Israeli critical political films. After *House*, commissioned by Israeli Television and then banned by it, Gitai left Israel for more than a decade, settling in France, where he produced several documentaries and features that gained him an international reputation. Upon his return to Israel in 1993, following the election of the Labour Party leader Yitzhak Rabin as Prime Minister and the re-awakened hope for peace with the Palestinians, his filmmaking slowly turned away from the dialectical and subversive images of his earlier productions. While still maintaining a critical position towards Israeli politics and society, and with some of the aesthetic tropes he evolved in his early filmmaking, such as the over-layering of sounds over lengthy recursive shots, the dialectic and split rendering of continuous space characterising his early films became transformed into complementary, concentric structures, rendering a homogenous space. This is already evident in the documentary film *Kippur War Memories* (1993), which formed the basis for *Kippur* and in the sequels to *House* and *Wadi*, respectively entitled *Bait be Yerushalayim* (*A House in Jerusalem*, 1998) and *Wadi Grand Canyon* (2001), which offer concentric rather than decentred histories. It is also evident in the feature films *Yom Yom* (*Day by Day*, 1998) and *Kadosh* (*Holy*, 1999) that preceded *Kippur*, as well as in the recent films *Eden* (2001), *Kedma* (2002), *Alila* (*Plot*, 2003) and his latest film to date, *Ha Aretz Hamuvtachat* (*The Promised Land* (2004). In all these films, as in *Kippur*, each a critically compelling account of key Israeli historical or social processes and events, the film's location encloses the various narrative threads rather than letting them spill over into different disjunctive and non-cohering perspectives. Hence, Gitai seems to have changed his subversive politics and his dialectic approach to a type of filmmaking that not only falls within the confines of Israeli national filmmaking and ethos, but often, as in *Kippur*, offers powerful emblematic projections of a widespread Israeli mentality.

Nitzan Ben-Shaul

REFERENCES

Bar-Tal, Daniel and Dikla Antebi (1992) 'Siege Mentality in Israel', *Journal of Intercultural Relations*, 16, 3, 251–75.

Liebman, Charles and Don Yehiya, Eliezer (1983) *Civil Religion in Israel*. Berkeley: University of California Press.

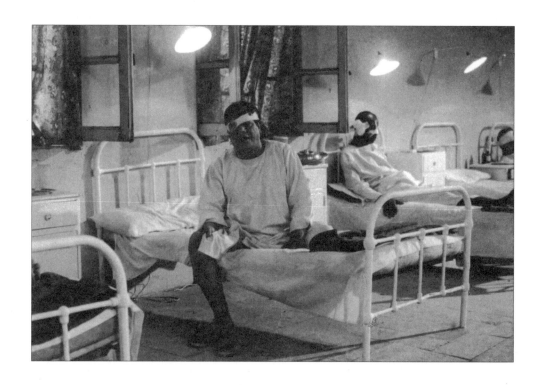

MUWATIN, MUKHBIR WA HARAMI CITIZEN, DETECTIVE AND THIEF

DAOUD ABD EL-SAYED, EGYPT, 2001

Muwatin, mukhbir wa harami (*Citizen, Detective and Thief*, 2001) is a highly satirical and fairly successful musical, written and directed by Daoud Abd El-Sayed. It represents a parody of a social success story by depicting a citizen's gradual decline into cultural and religious conservatism, becoming an acclaimed member of the new Islamic bourgeoisie. The question of class – an ever-present topic of popular Egyptian cinema – is depicted here as a clash between highbrow culture and kitsch, a central motif of the film on which El-Sayed, as director and author, elaborates on different levels, less evaluating but rather deconstructing it by means of presenting the much contested popular folk (*sha'bi*) singer Sha'ban Abd al-Rihim in the role of the citizen's opponent, the thief. This fact, and the special character of the film's music, is pivotal to the politics of the work, not only as a means to exploit the singer's popularity at the box office but also adding to the complexity and contradictory character of the film's meaning.

Citizen, Detective and Thief narrates the story of a well-cultured, rich and handsome bachelor who is about to finish his first novel. A *bon-vivant*, he inhabits a majestic old villa, attends parties, appreciates wine, good food and regularly seeks inspiration with beautiful female muses of his own social class. Yet this idyllic state is not to last, for step by step he gets drawn into a strange web of relationships, involving a cunning detective, a bold thief and a beautiful but depressive maid.

A small incident initiates the plot. One day a citizen, a writer, finds his car stolen. At the police station where he wants to report the theft he is given a warm welcome by a fairly impudent yet cheerful detective who seems to be very familiar with the writer's personal history, his friends and even the intimate details of his house. No wonder, as the detective admits that he had been in charge of observing the citizen on behalf of the state security during the latter's time as a student. The detective offers him his help because of their old 'friendship' and succeeds in locating the stolen car, but asks the novelist in turn for a favour, namely to help him obtain a job for his son. Before the citizen finds an opportunity to do so the detective visits his villa, thanks the gentleman feverously for his intervention and offers him in turn the services of the young and poor domestic worker Hayat (performed by the Tunisian actress Hind Sabri, known for her lead role in *Samt al-qusur* (*Silences of the Palace*, 1994)). Left with no other choice the writer takes in the girl, whose presence alters his life. He gets more and more used to her, to the point of physical attraction.

However, one day Hayat suddenly disappears, stealing some precious artefacts from his house, including the only copy of his recently completed novel. Again the detective is called in, who brings back the stolen goods, but without the novel. Because of this, the writer becomes increasingly desperate, particularly when he discovers that his manuscript has ended up in the hands of the thief al-Margushi, Hayat's boyfriend, who has been just released from prison. Visiting the thief in his little shack, he learns that the latter has read the manuscript, disliked it for having no educational value and starts offering the unnerved author some advice on how to improve it. Eventually, the writer succeeds in retrieving the manuscript and returns to his former peaceful life. He is soon disturbed again by the thief who wishes him to intervene on his community's behalf, for the police are about to remove their market to another, more remote, area. As a gift, he offers him a carved nude that he has covered with a dress and underwear because he considered the sculpture's nudity to be too offensive. Outraged by the thief's obvious uncultured mind, the citizen throws him out without listening to his pleas. Something he is soon to regret, for he becomes the victim of a series of thefts, to the point that he returns home one day to find the novel stolen once again.

The citizen turns to the detective, who tries to mediate between the two. However, it is too late; the thief burns the manuscript in their presence because of its immoral and blasphemous nature, literally for not containing 'a single word on God'. At this point, the writer loses his temper and pokes out the eye of his adversary. But his conscience makes him take care of al-Margushi, so much so that he befriends him. He is even won over by his ideas on life and literature. Finally, citizen, thief and detective end up as business partners, with the writer reworking his first book according to the thief's ideas, while the latter opens up a publishing house through which he edits and publishes the writer's subsequent work. There is also resolution on a sexual level, with the maid marrying the writer and the thief wedding the writer's former girlfriend. Later, their grown-up children fall in love and marry each other.

Citizen, Thief and Detective proceeds as an allegorical narration of recent social developments in Egypt, condensing more than two decades – from the mid-1970s to the present-day – into its story. By alluding indirectly to the crackdown on the leftist, anti-Zionist, student-movement during the first half of the 1970s, it also presents a quasi-political temporal framework, although this particular reference in relation to the main protagonist turns out to be misleading. The majority of the students at that time, even though secular-oriented, were by no means members of the bourgeoisie. They belonged to the middle and lower class, with a large proportion suffering severe deprivation in order to continue their studies.

On the narrative level *Citizen, Detective and Thief* presents a quite stringent account of the formation of what it perceives as the new bourgeoisie, focusing firstly on the citizen/novelist as the centrepiece of action, or its main narratological bearer. Reading his character allegorically, he seems to represent the creative individual; the modern 'citizen' firmly installed in his highbrow cultural environment, first victimised and then overrun in the course of the events by the tide of his lower-class acquaintances, or 'masses', who, in collaboration with the state, embodied by the detective, first take over his house and then his mind. This depiction is quite telling, if not contemptuous, favouring the modern, educated, male individual and placing him in opposition to the illiterate, conservative masses, even though – as we will see later – the film often distances itself on the stylistic level from his hero by mocking his development and by using the off-screen persona of the *sha'bi* singer to problematise the notion of lowbrow culture.

It is the thief's character who defies highbrow cultural aspiration and then defines the 'new' taste and cultural orientation of the 'citizen' by criticising, destroying and eventually re-editing his literary output. It is precisely this character's actions that offer more than anything else an allusion to the real-life mechanisms – namely to religious censorship of literature – that have lately been practiced by the Islamic al-Azhar Institution, as well as to so-called 'social' censorship regarding cinema that has developed gradually during the 1980s and continued throughout the 1990s. Thus it seems that the film wants to tackle the new conservatism that has seized Egyptian society since the 1980s and reversed many of those modernist achievements made in the past, particularly regarding female dress codes as well as the absorbtion of so-called Western culture. However, the film works that out in a strongly impressionist manner without describing all the factors which have contributed to this ideological shift.

In relation to cinema, the new morality reached its peak in 1983 with an outraged public debate sparked off by the prohibition of two mediocre productions in the same year, *Darb al-hawa* (*Alley of Love*) by Hussam al-Din Mustafa and *Khamsa bab* (*Gate Five*) by Nadir Galal. Most journalists and officials spoke in favour of the verdict and demanded more respect for traditions and good morals. In fact, since that time the press and the courts have increased their censorial roles, initiating furious media campaigns in combination with the suing of certain films and their makers. One of the most spectacular cases was initiated by Islamic fundamentalists against Youssef Chahine and his film, *al-Muhajir* (*The Emigrant*, 1994). It was accused of presenting one of the Koran's prophets, disregarding the official ban on these kinds of representations, despite the fact that the film had been passed by official censors. It is these events that form the silent background of the artist's anguish in *Citizen, Detective and Thief*, whose director clearly holds new bourgeois culture in Egypt to be dominated by hypocritical conservatism furnished with religious colouring.

One of the political forces that supported this shift towards new morality was President Anwar al-Sadat's ambivalent Islamisation policy. In his attempts to diminish the influence of Nasserists and to suppress socialist ideology he silently approved Islamist tendencies and then tried to contain them when he was planning to introduce the Islamic *shari'a* as a major source of legislation, and by promulgating the *al-'aib* (shame) law in 1980 which served at the same time as a convenient way to censor critical ideas. Furthermore, the massive temporary emigration of 4.5 million Egyptians to work in the Gulf States in the early 1980s (from the lower- and middle-class urbanites as well as rural lower classes, prompted by the new regime's loosening of travel permissions for Egyptians) contributed to the new ideology. Confronted with religious and ideological conservatism in their host-countries, the emigrants not only returned with a large amount of hard currency but also more conservative and pro-Islamist worldviews.

In fact, upon a second reading, the narration of the film tackles the issue of social and political freedom in juxtaposition to the radical social changes that have arisen since the 1970s. For this reason, it clearly emphasises the writer's class affiliation along with his ideological orientation. One of the ways it does this is through its characters' dress, behaviour, language, and cultural interests. The citizen is depicted as strongly Westernised in outfit and manners. Not only is his villa furnished with precious antique furniture but he also engages in uncomplicated extra-marital relationships, loves European cuisine and wines, and enjoys classical Western music. This is in contrast to the other protagonists; the detective lives in a small cramped flat on top of a roof in an over-populated lower-class neighbourhood and dresses in the traditional *jalabiyya*, and the thief and the girl, Hayat, dwell in even more informal surroundings, namely in the middle of a deprived shantytown.

The progression of the film shows how the three parties amalgamate and end up wearing the same style dress and living in the same kind of modern villa situated in one of the newly constructed affluent Cairo suburbs. They also arrive to adhere to the same ideas and moral concepts. This is expressed by the citizen's gradual shift to cultural and religious conservatism embodied by his growing beard towards the end of the film, thus indicating the birth of a new brand of conservative Islamic oriented bourgeoisie. Notwithstanding, this development is shown to end up in a fraud. For, despite their respective marriages, the former thief is seen keeping up his relationship with the citizen's wife, Hayat, and the novelist is still courting his former girlfriend, namely the thief's spouse, a matter that explains the two families' heavy objections to their children getting married. The film's finale does not fully explain these objections nor link them in an overt way to the two couples' extra-marital relationships. However, it implies that the parents are not quite sure about their respective paternity, something that stands in overt contradiction to the moral standards promoted by writer and publisher.

Thus, this last twist in the narration represents a disparaging comment on the new bourgeoisie, as does the final scene. At the end, everybody seems to settle into the new cheerful amalgam that is cinematically underlined by a masquerade, namely a masked ball celebrated by the protagonists, in which Abd al-Rihim sings the following lines while everybody joins in dancing:

'Listen to my words: Citizen, detective and thief,

we met, became one and changed names

[...]

I'd like mouse and cat to get along.

If cat loves mouse, how can one scare the other?

I'd like them to be lovers, no strangers any more.

At a nice occasion once I married a sheep off to a wolf.

Dear mouse don't jump! I'll marry you to the cat,

You'll like the marriage and be all right,

no more roaming in the streets, no more sleeping on the walks

[...]

Tomorrow the mouse will carry mousy catties,

mixed all up, a different kind of kiddies,

so that love grows, no hatred anymore,

thanks to sympathy and promise-policies,

why not become just one, with all the difference gone?'

The film does not just portray hypocrisy socially, it sketches the struggle between two parties – one powerful and one weak – without being too clear about who is the mouse and who is the cat and without clarifying who is the winning party at the end. But the course of events have made it clear that there is also a prize to be paid: the application of double standards; the lack of individual freedom and artistic originality; and the onset of depression, as suffered by Hayat. Even with her new social position as the wife of an acclaimed writer, she is repeatedly saved from taking her own life by her family. The reasons are neither explained nor dwelled upon in the film.

As a whole, the ending carries the seemingly positive message that 'all difference is gone', or it signals that the bourgeois character has been liberated from, to cite Pierre Bourdieu's quotation of Proust, 'the infinitely varied art of marking distances'. According to social scientist Bourdieu, classes distinguish themselves not only through their economic capital, but also through their cultural and educational capital. Thus, 'distinction' or better 'class' – the transfigured, misrecognisable, legitimate form of social class – only exist through the struggle for the exclusive appropriation of the signs that make 'natural' distinction. What seems striking in the strategy of 'distinction', as applied to the narration of Citizen, Detective and Thief, is that the mechanism to declassify other cultural protagonists as less cultured and less ethical is as much applied as subverted. Through the motif of the invaded and overrun bourgeois it even sketches out a reversed class-struggle, turning Marxist representations of the proletariat as the victim upside down. This allegorical construction distorts actual social developments. What is represented on the screen as a struggle between bourgeoisie and proletariat was, in Egyptian reality, a struggle between two different types of bourgeoisie: the old and the new, who have been coexisting at times, merging at others, rather than eclipsing each other. The film, in contrast, sets proletariat and bourgeoisie apart on the spatial and temporal level, by depicting how the bourgeois' space is intruded by the lower class and how he then succumbs to intruders from below, in terms of moral standards and cultural values.

This motif of upward class mobility and the depiction of the haunted academic is not new to the work of Daoud Abd El-Sayed. In his first feature film, al-Sa'alik (The Vagabonds, 1983), he dealt with both themes, albeit in a realist style. The film focused on the ascent of two uneducated workers (hereby alluding to the real success-story of the supposedly illiterate Rashad Uthman, who became an influential businessman and member of parliament). The film starts with the two men living on the street and taking in occasional jobs in the Alexandria harbour. Eventually they find a way to start a trafficking business, including drug-dealing, which allows them to become two of the most prosperous businessmen in town. Later, one of them tries to court an academic woman who comes from a traditional, but impoverished, bourgeois family. Through this side story, the film is able to emphasise the gap between the uneducated, quasi-criminal, nouveau riche and the 'respectable' middle-class character, whose family is unable to perform successfully in the new economic system engendered by the open-door policy.

The Vagabonds is based on a typical 'fat cats' plot, which was prevalent in action-films as well as New Realist works in the early 1980s. It was intended as a criticism of the negative social effects of Anwar al-Sadat's *infitah*. The majority of films that featured this theme linked those *nouveau riches* with criminal practices and dismissed them morally by exposing their materialism and lack of traditional sense of community. Quite in line with this logic, *The Vagabonds* closes with a tragic show-down. At the peak of their economic success, the two former tramps, who are closer than brothers, turn against each other because of their business, eventually shooting each other, thus proving the extent to which materialism extinguishes friendship and solidarity.

Despite their loose adaptation of the biographies of some exceptional entrepreneurs of that time, these narratives are mythical. Compared with reality, they exaggerate the span of lower-class mobility and falsify the front line of social struggle, by portraying the middle class as caught between the new bourgeoisie and the urban lower class. In 1973, shantytown dwellers made up 45 per cent of Egypt's urban population. It is hard to imagine that these, to use Saad Eddin Ibrahim's words, 'uneducated, hungry, unhealthy and needy persons, who have few opportunities for socio-economic advancement', could climb up the social and business ladders so quickly, eventually transforming into the country's leading class.

The *infitah* permitted an unprecedented accumulation of wealth and yet, as Malak Zaalouk has proposed, the new ruling class 'is a merger between fractions of the old traditional bourgeoisie' not of the old bourgeoisie and the lower class. She has further described the social origins of the new 'commercial agents' who were thought to represent the *infitah* economy most, as being, for the majority, from traditional trading and industrial bourgeois families, technocrats, managers, senior civil servants, liberal professions or academics.

Ironically, the old elite within the group of commercial agents also liked to distinguish themselves from 'newcomers', who started their activity in the mid-1960s or in the aftermath of 1967. According to the self-selected elitist group, 'outsiders' lacked ethics, finesse and business experience. The elite within the elite voiced exactly the same moral judgement that was made by films against the fat cats, yet they are put forward against members of the same class who have also proven themselves successful.

Citizen, Thief and Detective reflects some of those old strategies of social distinction, presented through the subjective perspective of its author, an intellectual *auteur* coming from an educated, middle-class Cairo family, who comments on the pressures placed upon individual artists in contemporary Egyptian society. However, even though he still fosters the recurrent misconception of the overtaking proletariat on a narrative level, he departs from this concept significantly and proves his sympathies not to be entirely bourgeois; he constantly distances himself from his bourgeois hero through his ironic and satirical style.

Satire works on a number of levels in the film, particularly in its ending and the portrayal of its characters' double standards. Moreover, the plot is intercut with songs performed by the thief, which develop – particularly in the finale – an alienating effect in the way they comment on the ending. The anonymous narrator is a major source of dissociation; a male voice-over that comments on the events presented. For instance, when the detective beats Hayat for the first time to make her return the stolen goods from the citizen's house, she falsely claims to be pregnant in order to make him stop the beating. The narrator comments: 'The citizen's battle was not over yet, by no means could he agree to leave any outreach of himself in this surrounding polluted by ignorance, poverty and corruption; how could he leave his son in Hayat's womb?' Later, he continues: 'What had happened was an experience from which the citizen learned a simple lesson: if a common language and shared values exist, the rules of the game will be known. However when leaving one's own game and playground the outcome will bring about unexpected risks.' In other words, the hero is clearly advised to stay within his own class.

This is how the film ironically recasts the recent radical social change in Egypt, as well as an Egyptian brand of class struggle, in this case evolving around taste, cultural production and censorship. The film alludes to this battle on the narrative level, but also intertextually, by evoking a real-life extra-cinematic debate. It is achieved by casting the *sha'bi* singer Sha'ban Abd al-Rihim in the role of the thief. He was the object of public controversy surrounding the issue of 'taste' due to his allegedly trivial lower-class musical style that seemed to signal a deterioration of musical culture in Egypt. Thus the most important issue raised by singer Abd al-Rihim's presence is the question of social distinction through taste; the differentiation between high- and lowbrow culture. He helps to render hypocrisy, not only in relation to moral values but also in relation to culture, into one of the film's core motifs, depending on the public discourse linked to his on- and off-screen persona.

Abd al-Rihim had become the unexpected star of the season, despite his being linked by audiences with a bourgeois background to the notion of kitsch and the lack of musical culture. This perception is due in part to the social origins of Abd al-Rihim's special brand of *sha'bi* (folk) music, which stems from musical practices and the traditions of urban lower classes and is performed at weddings, saint feasts or, more recently, shop openings.

When Abd al-Rihim eventually made it to the top of the music charts, despite his evident lower-class musical style and origins, it came as a surprise and ignited a fierce debate on cultural standards. Ironically, the illiterate, coarse-looking former laundry-worker was as much blamed for his bad taste and his poor musical talent as much as he achieved with his funny and ironic texts an astonishing popularity among all classes. In particular, his song 'I Hate Israel' made headlines, as did his featuring in a McDonald's television commercial advertising the local falafel as a new dish.

It is not clear to what extent Abd al-Rihim was unwillingly portrayed by the media as the personification of bad taste and to the extent to which he supported this view through conscious self-stylisation. For example, he always wears very colourfully patterned Hawaiian shirts, which are commonly considered unmanly and/or unsuitable for the urban public space. Last but not least, his sense of humour was demonstrated by an anecdote that was circulated by the crew members during the shooting of *Citizen, Detective and Thief*; the singer used to wear two precious and large golden wristwatches – when he was asked for the reason, he replied that one was for himself and the other for anyone who asks him what time it is.

The anecdote conveys much of the ambiguity with which Abd al-Rihim presents himself. Wearing large precious watches is associated with the *nouveau riches*, whilst wearing two of them appears even more pretentious. And yet the singer's own interpretation switches the meaning towards generosity, which fits into the traditional *ibn-balad* concept of the lower classes, or to parody, which seems even more likely, in the light of the wording of some of Abd al-Rihim's songs (usually written by Islam Khalil, a teacher from rural al-Qanatir on the outskirts of Cairo). In some of those texts Abd al-Rihim reproduces the same reproaches that have been raised against him in the media for his low musical and artistic standards, redirecting them against other media stars.

In one song, he alludes to the film, *Hamam in Amsterdam*, which became the box-office hit of 1999–2000, dismissing the music of the comical central character, Muhammad Hinidi (who sings a few songs in the film), as trivial. He begins with the words, 'I am off now to Holland, Amsterdam, leaving my team just like Ibrahim and Husam [soccer players]…', adding several lines on a controversial issue that he thinks 'matters', namely the pollution of the Nile river. He wishes the Nile would look nice, with no garbage, floating paper tissue, and dirty dishes or beasts washed in it.

To blame others for a lack of art, while using a limited range of melodies and rhythms himself, clearly derived from so-called 'wedding' music in every song, seems to add to the irony of the whole Abd al-Rihim phenomenon. And this is exactly the same strategy that Daoud Abd El-Sayed applied in his film, advertising kitsch and simultaneously criticising and deconstructing the preconditions of its emergence. The director establishes the singer's controversial persona as a film star, thus permitting him access to mainstream culture, while at the same time denouncing this very same culture. In this, he departs from the former New Realist concept of the middle class as victims, by turning them into an accomplice in the deformation of their own class.

Viola Shafik

REFERENCES

Bourdieu, Pierre (1984) *Distinction: A Social Critique of the Judgement of Taste.* Cambridge: Harvard University Press.

Ibrahim, Saad Eddin (1977) 'Urbanization in the Arab World', in Nicholas S. Hopkins and Saad Eddin Ibrahim (eds) *Arab Society: Social Science Perspectives.* Cairo: American University of Cairo Press, 123–47.

Zaalouk, Malak (1989) *Power, Class and Foreign Capital in Egypt: The Rise of the New Bourgeoisie.* London: Zed Books.

TEN

ABBAS KIAROSTAMI, IRAN/FRANCE, 2002

Ten (2002) is the first film of Abbas Kiarostami, Iran's most celebrated filmmaker in the West, to feature a woman as the main protagonist. A modern young woman of means (played by Mania Akbari) is behind the wheel in the busy traffic of Tehran. She has several confidants – all female – who join her at different times, and one antagonist, her son, the only male with a speaking role. Unlike post-Revolutionary Iranian cinema, which excluded women or reduced them to faceless non-entities, in this film men are left on the outside. The father of the boy is heard, but not seen. Pedestrians on the road or other drivers (all male) who seem to dominate the outdoor space are simply obstacles to her driving. She tells them, 'Out of the way!' or criticises their parking skills. The big four-wheel-drive vehicle she controls gives her confidence. For one thing, she is at eye level with the people on the street; no one can look down on her. Inside the car, conversation is about men – to buy birthday cakes for them (pampering) or to remark on their infidelity or deceit (weaknesses of immature and insecure characters). It is not surprising then that men in the film are personified by a boy.

Ten is structured into ten episodes of unequal length. Each episode – from ten to one – is introduced with the sound of a bell, almost suggesting a boxing contest (somewhat appropriate for the aggressive verbal banter between mother and son). The leader is included within the body of the film, drawing attention to the 'artifice' of cinema, one of the characteristics of avant-garde filmmaking, although to show the artifice is not a novelty for Kiarostami.

Episode 10 starts with Amin, a boy of around eight or ten years old, entering the car. We hear a woman's voice asking him (twice) to lower the window. 'Let some air', she says instead of 'hello' or 'how are you?' as if his presence stifles her. She then offers him an ice-cream. The boy, who is often one step ahead of his mother, declines. For the next fifteen minutes or so a scene apparently familiar to the duo is repeated. He accuses her of divorcing his father and she tries to ease her mind by trying to convince him that his father was 'destroying' her and he is just like his father. Comparing herself to a stagnant pond when she lived with his father, that has since become a flowing river (a cliché from Persian mystical poetry of the thirteenth century) since her divorce and re-marriage, will not earn his sympathy. As to her motto of not belonging to anyone but oneself, it sounds like self-help psychology, even to Amin, who reminds her that he is only a child. To belong to himself, he has to grow up first. As Amin cannot take the emotional pressure of this unequal match any more, he storms out of the car. It is at this point that the audience first sees the mother. She is a young, attractive and well-attired woman. Her white scarf looks more like an accessory to her outfit than an obligation of *hejab*, the Islamic code of dress enforced on women in Iran. But she does looks troubled.

Episode 9 opens with a modestly-clad woman on the passenger seat picking spots on her face while waiting. Now and then, she lifts her veil to fan her neck and chest (as if testing the limit of the censor's eye). She is the driver's sister, a married woman who is comfortable with her assigned roles in society – wife and mother – and does not feel guilty about leaving her child at day-care when she goes to her teaching job. They discuss husbands' birthdays, Amin's recent irritability and whether the mother should allow him to live with his father. The driver is distracted and somewhat lost.

In episode 8, she gives a ride (it is very common in Tehran for private cars to pick up passengers) to an old woman who has denounced her worldly possessions after having lost her husband and child. The woman visits the local mausoleum three times a day to pray for their souls and tries to convince the driver to go in and pray, but she declines respectfully with the excuse that she is too busy. We are given a glimpse of the old woman through the driver's window before she enters the car but she is never seen inside the car.

Episode 7 is a night scene. A drunk prostitute enters the car when the driver brakes, thinking she is a potential customer. The conversation that ensues reveals more about the personal life and emotional contentment of the driver than the prostitute. The fact that the prostitute is never seen except for her silhouette in the dark gives the impression that perhaps she is real, but that is not the case. When Kiarostami auditioned prostitutes for the role, they refused to appear, apparently on 'moral' grounds. Mania Akbari's sister eventually assumed the role. Kiarostami claims to have kept the faces of the prostitute and the pious old lady of episode 8 (who happens to be a real character unaware she is being filmed) away from the camera because of the private nature of the activities they execute.

In episode 6, the driver is wearing subdued colours and no make-up. She gives a ride to a young woman coming out of the mausoleum and they discuss the significance of prayer. The woman hopes that her prayers will make her fiancé of several years finally marry her. The driver admits that recently she has begun to pray as well to ease her occasional feelings of guilt.

Episode 5 starts with Amin entering the car. This time, the mother says 'Salaam'. He is calmer but does not neglect to point out that she is taking the wrong road to his grandmother's. He casually mentions that his father (with whom he is now living) watches 'sexy' programmes on television at night and repeats to himself, 'sexy, sex, sex', as the prostitute did in episode 7.

Episode 4 takes place at night-time. The driver picks up a female friend or relative, to go to a restaurant. The woman is unhappy because her husband has left her. The advice the driver gives her echoes her argument with her son about not belonging to anyone and loving oneself. Once again, her self-help psychology is unconvincing. The woman objects to her calling 'worthless' a man she has loved for seven years, but it rings true that many men are only interested in 'a big ass, or big tits'. The driver tries to alleviate the pain of her friend by talking about her own sufferings in her first marriage, where her husband and son expected her to be an obedient housewife and not an independent professional – a far cry from the eponymous character of Dariush Mehrjui's *Leila* (1997), also a modern woman, who sacrifices her love and marriage for the sake of her husband's contentment.

In episode 3, the driver is gentle toward her son and, perhaps as a result, he looks happier. She even tells him she missed him. She jokes about finding a wife for his father who may have a suitable daughter for him and they discuss the qualities of an ideal wife. For the boy, the definition is clear – someone whose priority is her family.

Episode 2 opens with the young woman seen in episode 6. Her non-committal fiancé finally left her; she is disturbed but at the same time ready for a new beginning. Somehow, she appears stronger and more in control than when we first saw her coming out of the mausoleum (looking for salvation in forces out of her control). When her scarf slips, her shaven head is exposed. In a moment, referred to by several critics as the 'emotional climax' of the film, everything comes to a halt. The background is motionless. The two women are too overwhelmed by the intensity of the moment to speak. Then the driver encourages the other woman to take off the veil altogether and compliments her on her courage and beauty.

Episode 1 is the shortest. The driver picks up her son who again wants to be driven to the grandmother's. The mother just says 'All right'. The cycle is completed.

Iranian cinema's association with women is complex and layered, although one may find certain trends that follow socio-political developments. The first Iranian film, Ovanes Ohanian's *Abi and Rabi* (1930), had no women in its cast or crew. The second Iranian film, *Brother's Revenge* (1931), introduced two female characters, but they had to be played by non-Muslims. Abdolhossein Sepanta is credited for featuring the first Muslim woman on screen with *Dokhtar-*

e *Lor* (*Lor Girl*, 1933), about a rural girl who sings and dances in the tea-houses and inns to earn her bread. The most popular role designated to the female gender in pre-Revolutionary Iranian cinema was the 'deceived and deserted' woman – victim of male immorality – who inevitably fell into 'bad ways'. During a period of 'new wave' and the promise of a new vision of society and women, family melodramas such as *Tufan-e Zendegi* (*The Storm of Life*, 1948) were made, underscoring the biases of a dominant patriarchal tradition, but following the *coup d'état* of 1953, the general cultural policies of the Shah led to the plethora of song and dance films – *film farsi* – tailored to appeal to the fantasies of sexually deprived men. Avant-garde films of the 1960s, such as *Gheysar* (1969) by Masud Kimia'i, not only pushed women to the margins but also created a distorted image by blaming them for all social evils. *Gheysar* endorsed the values of an andocentric Muslim society and set the precedence for vengeance stories (most of them without the artistic qualities of Kimia'i's work) that showed helpless maidens who could not defend their chastity by themselves, forcing their menfolk to bloodshed to reclaim the lost honour of the family. These films were spiced with sex and nudity to inflate the market. Although the reforms of the 1960s and 1970s gave certain rights to women, cinema chose to present the 'new woman' as corrupt and immoral.

Bahram Bayza'i's *Ragbar* (*Downpour*, 1972) was perhaps the first film to draw a realistic portrait of women. He followed this with other films that were based on the lives of Iranian women, and their feminine and maternal power. Unfortunately, these films were not screened following the the Islamic Revolution of 1979, when it was decreed that there should be restrictions regarding close-ups of women and showing women without the *hejab* on screen. Physical contact with the opposite sex (even between mother and son) was also prohibited unless the actors were related in real life. Women were pushed to the background or assigned the roles of obedient daughters and wives, and suffering mothers (usually of the martyrs of the Iran/Iraq war). Upper-class women were shown as disrespectful, irresponsible and demanding shrews. Under the stifling restrictions of the new regime, several filmmakers left the country; others began to focus on children. One positive reaction of protest was that women started making films themselves; Rakhshan Bani-Etemad and Tahmineh Milani are two good examples.

Abbas Kiarostami began his directing career before the Revolution, but chose to make films with children under the umbrella of the Institute for the Intellectual Development of Children and Young Adults, which he joined at the end of the 1960s and stayed at until 1992. The only film from his pre-Revolution period that does not focus on children is a feature called

Gozaresh (*The Report*, 1977), about a disintegrating marriage in a period of political tension and severe economic crisis.

Kiarostami has customarily been reproached for leaving women out of his films and his answers often point to the restrictions that impose unrealistic ways of presenting women, which he would rather avoid. Women are not totally absent from his films, although their representations are complex and layered. In *Khaneh-ye Dust Kojast?* (*Where is the Friend's House?*, 1987), bogged down by poverty and tradition, the mother is insensitive to the needs of her son. She orders him to do his homework but sends him to do errands each time he sits down. In *Zir-e Darakhtan-e Zeytun* (*Through the Olive Trees*, 1994), young Tahereh, the subject of Hossein's infatuation, is stubborn, pretentious and capricious. The female member of the crew is irritable and cold. In a film with a very adult subject, *Tam-e Gilas* (*Taste of Cherry*, 1996), that won Kiarostami the Palme d'Or, women are not part of the diegis. Although presented as modern and career-oriented – one with a camera, others entering the science museum or studying taxidermy – they appear with the flowers and trees in the landscape, after Badi has arranged the details of his death. In *Bad Ma ra ba Khod Khahad Bord* (*The Wind Will Carry Us*, 1999) women are faceless. They are hidden in the darkness of the pantry, covered with the hay they carry, veiled behind closed doors, a voice on the telephone, a shadow on the wall, or simply too old and too sick to come out. Although the café-owner is outspoken in her complaint about women's three trades – 'by day, they are workers, in the evening they serve and at night they work' – the man has the last word: 'We have a third job, too. If men don't do their third job, they'll be dishonoured.' As the period this film was made was not the darkest for Iranian cinema (restrictions were somewhat eased after the election of moderate Mohammad Khatami as president in 1997), Kiarostami's approach to the female image in this film is almost like beating the censors in their own game.

Ten takes several steps in the opposite direction. The woman is beautiful, stylish and attractive. And she is the protagonist. Furthermore, she is behind the wheel! She can be aggressive with her son, supportive with friends, respectful with the pious old lady (to a limit) and mischievous with the prostitute. However, it is simplistic to consider *Ten* as an exposé on the predicaments of women in contemporary Iran or a celebration of Iranian women's cry for emancipation. The late 1990s and early 2000s display a remarkable number of films on such issues. A documentary, *Divorce Iranian Style* (Kim Longinotto and Ziba Mir Hosseini, 1998) was a candid look at Iranian divorce courts. Tahmineh Milani's *Do Zan* (*Two Women*, 1998) clearly showed that although women's rights to divorce was restored in late 1983, physical cruelty was reason for divorce, but not mental cruelty. Jafar Panahi's *Dayareh* (*The Circle*, 2002) and Rasoul Sadr-Ameli's *Man, Taraneh, Panzdah Sal Darom* (*I, Tareneh, am Fifteen*, 2002) have demonstrated that prostitution exists in Iran, and these are only a few examples from the films that reach the West. Attending the Fajr International Film Festival in Tehran, one comes across several films that discuss (and show) openly, not only divorce and prostitution, but also drug addiction. (The reason why these films do not reach the West is not because of their 'objectionable' content but rather their poor artistic quality.) As for showing a woman's shaven head for the first time (without the *hejab*), credit goes to a young female filmmaker, Maryam Shahriar, with her debut film, *Dakhtaran-e Khorshid* (*Daughters of the Sun*, 2002).

Obviously, Kiarostami is aware of all these new trends in the cinema of his country. *Ten* is not so much about a modern woman with her feet on the ground than about a woman caught between tradition and modernity, and in that sense the protagonist represents the Iranian people in the new millennium, particularly women who are trapped in a false modernity. The driver has had the courage – with the aid of her social status as upper class – to leave a stifling marriage to pursue her dreams – 'photography, painting and travel' – but she cannot rid herself of guilty feelings. During conversations with her son, we learn that she falsely accused her husband of being a drug addict and beating her, to get a divorce. In her battle over independence, she confronts both her internalised traditional thinking and the judgement of others. She is feeling insecure and desperately seeking her son's approval. Her lecturing to others about not belonging to anyone sounds as if she is trying to convince herself. If she wants to be free and independent, why does she get re-married, even to someone who is open-minded and not possessive? She wants to keep the status quo; a married woman is respectable whereas a divorcee can easily become a liability, especially in patriarchal societies. In matters of love, she is not able to discover her individuality in a non-traditional manner outside the established norms.

Kiarostami has already made films where most of the dialogue takes place inside a car or the landscape is fitted inside the frame of a car window. In *Ten*, the car not only serves as a vehicle to accommodate the shooting style of the film – two digital cameras placed on the dashboard – but has another important function. In a culture (and its cinema) where public and private existence is clearly defined, a car is private as far as having conversations in it, but also public because people peer through the windows. In that sense, the car serves as a trope for the driver's liminal state between patriarchal tradition and the challenge of a liberating existence. In the first episode (episode 10), she is wearing bright red clothes and make-up; she is aggressive – with her son, with other drivers on the road – and demands her rights. In episode 8, the old woman she gives a ride to suggests that she should go and pray, but she refuses. In episode 6, however, she appears without make-up and supporting the dark colours of *hejab* – she has come from praying in the mausoleum. It is not accidental that she is often lost and needs others – her sister, even her son – to give her instructions. She keeps asking, 'Is this a dead-end?' She is behind the wheel, but not in total control – not liberated from cultural and societal dichotomy. (Unlike Iran's famous poet and filmmaker Forugh Farrokhzad who had to fight the same battles – divorce, custody, freedom to choose the person she wanted to be – in the 1950s and 1960s, finally finding an outlet in her art.)

The episode with the prostitute is important not so much because the subject is daring for Iranian cinema but because it is an important comment about hypocritical societies, Iran or elsewhere. An upper-class woman thinks she is experiencing something daring and out of the ordinary by quizzing a street prostitute in a non-judgemental manner, when she knows that the next minute she will be home sitting in her comfortable sofa beside her husband. The husbands who visit prostitutes display the same double standards, as the prostitute stipulates: 'They tell their wives on the cellular phone "I love you" while they are in bed with me.'

A life at polar opposition to her own arouses the driver's curiosity. Her comfort, security, visibility, respectability and social acceptance is challenged by the dark world of the prostitute that implies risk, but also adventure and a sense of freedom that comes from nothing left to lose. The expression on her face suggests that she is drawn to the unknown like a moth to the fire, but can only ask the banal question that prostitutes hear over and over again: Why do you do this job? Yet the prostitute, like her son, is one-step ahead of her (and incidentally both call her an idiot), answering: 'Sex, love, sex and I like it.' When the prostitute reverses the question and asks why she does not do it, the driver has no answer. Despite her modernity, total sexual freedom is still something to be experienced vicariously.

We never see the prostitute while she is in the car, but when she steps out, the camera (the gaze of the driver) looks through the windshield to follow her to the curb, until she climbs into another car and is gone. The temptation has passed. The driver can be safe again. The experience has moved her but she is relieved that the prostitute is out of her sight.

The driver is not the only one caught in the rapid Westernisation of Iran, despite the *mullahs*. Her first husband, as we understand, was a traditional man who wanted a traditional wife. However, his tastes seemed to be quite modern, from the car he drives to his satellite TV, where he watches porn films when his son is not around. Amin looks like any Western child his age. He likes to wear T-shirts with logos, watches cartoons, takes computer courses and goes regularly to the swimming pool, but he also believes in the traditional family structure where the wife/mother holds the needs of her family above her own. No wonder he always wants to be taken to his grandmother where he is secure and safe, protected by the good old values of tradition.

This dichotomy is evident in the landscape that rolls outside the windows – a modern city with apartment buildings, offices, small shops, parks. We are taken back when we notice women in *chadoor*, passing by as if to remind us that we are in Iran, where a routine act such as wearing lipstick or nail polish may have severe repercussions for a woman. There is movement and change, however. The woman who desperately wants to marry her fiancé (to be like everyone else and to follow the norms) is somewhat relieved when he deserts her. She shaves her head – the ultimate act of defiance of the male world and their concept of femininity, and a rupture from the dominant traditional codes of behaviour and appearance.

The film sends a few *clin d'oeil* to Iranian cinema and notably post-Revolution strictures. For the first fifteen minutes, the male character talks without giving a chance to the woman (his mother), who is invisible as the censors would like her to be. There is no physical contact in the film except for two instances: when the driver reaches out to the forehead of her son to see if he has fever (and he rejects her) and when the woman who shaved her head removes her veil and the driver's hand enters the frame to wipe away her tears – a playful settling of accounts with the prohibition of touching between opposite sexes on screen, which has often led filmmakers to substitute body parts from someone of the same sex. (In Rakhshan Bani-Etemad's *Banoo-e Ordibehesht* (*The May Lady*, 1998), for example, when the son is taking off his mother's boots, the leg we see on screen does not belong to the actress playing the mother, but to a male substitute.) The 'deceived and deserted' prostitute is a common trope out of the pre-Revolution *faheshe* films (films about prostitutes), but the prostitute in *Ten*, who was also deceived and deserted, seems quite happy to fall into bad ways. With no morals left to lose, she is free of societal impositions. Some critics trace a connection between this scene and the one with the jilted friend – both scenes take place in the dark – and see the prostitute as a warning to the desperate woman. However, all jilted women do not become prostitutes as movies once tried to make us believe. The passenger whose fiancé deserts her does not fall, but instead decides to start a new life, the first manifestation of which is that she shaves her head. As for the driver, despite her uncertainties, she has a mind of her own and if she has to wear different masks, she will. She has crossed over (the boundary) to the other side as her son boldly reminds her although she has not settled there comfortably as yet. She is not above lying when it comes to her needs just like the characters in Kiarostami's other films *Where is the Friend's House?* or *Mashgh-e Shab* (*Homework*, 1989). Deception can be a cultural necessity, and in authoritarian regimes it becomes a mode of survival. (Who knows that better than the post-Revolutionary Iranian cinema that has been trying to get around censorship despite all odds? Did Mohsen Makhmalbaf not don a woman's skirt in *Gabbeh* (1996) when he was prohibited from showing a woman giving birth?) The driver has her doubts and occasional guilty feelings, but the end justifies the means. Given the opportunity, she has no limits. She is the new Iranian cinema itself – pressured, confined, confused, at times naïve, at times running in circles, but open to discourse and never in a dead-end! (Some critics go further and suggest that the driver is a substitute for Kiarostami himself: she wears sunglasses, her occupation with photography, the time she spends in her car, and her inclination to engage passengers in conversation.)

Ten has implications for world cinema as well. It was made practically without the director and definitely without a cinematographer. After meticulous planning, including interviews with many possible candidates for the roles, through which they were asked to speak about themselves and their lives, Kiarostami chose Mania Akbari, a visual artist, as the protagonist and Amin Maher, her son from a previous marriage, as her arrogant, irate, spoiled and somewhat lost son. Kiarostami worked on the dialogue with the actors separately before the shooting. No one knew the other character's dialogue. Placing two digital cameras on the dashboard, Kiarostami stepped aside. At times, he was sitting in the back seat behind the actors (as opposed to the conventional position, in front, which grants the director control), but at other times he was not there at all. Absence of directorial authority or a third party (witness) could render the action a degree of authenticity. The first episode, 10, when the mother drives the son to the swimming pool, had to be shot on the way between their house and the pool, otherwise the boy – who always thought the shooting had not started yet – would not believe they were going there. If they made a detour, he would say that that was not the way to the pool. (His comments are in the film.) All this does not mean that *Ten* is a documentary. What is documentary in the film (according to Kiarostami's comments published as part of the press kit) is 'where people on the street peer inside the car or stop to watch'. The rest is a result of intense editing – 23 hours reduced to 94 minutes.

The formal trope of the film is on-screen figure/off-screen voice recorded by two cameras attached to the dashboard. In several shots, the camera remains on the driver while the passenger is speaking to emphasise listening rather than speaking (a device Jean-Luc Godard employed in

Sympathy for the Devil (1968)). Aided by the confines of the space (a four-wheel-drive vehicle), Kiarostami eliminated everything that could distract the spectator or the players to arrive at a certain minimalism that he has defined in several interviews as his 'résumé of existence'.

The reverse countdown structure emphasises the element of subtraction. In each episode, someone is taken away from someone else. All important happenings – the driver's divorce and re-marriage, the pious woman's loss of husband and child and subsequent renunciation of earthly possessions, Amin's shifts from the mother's to the father's place, the abandonment of the sobbing friend, the jilting of the young woman and the shaving of her head, all happen elsewhere and are reported. At times, the audience has to fill in the gaps, as is often the case with Kiarostami's films.

Ten is different to the other films of Kiarostami, however, as most of the dialogue takes place inside a car. For instance, in *Va Zendengi Edameh Darad* (*Life and Nothing More*, 1992) a filmmaker travels through earthquake-devastated countryside to reach the village of Koker, to find out if the boy who played in *Where is the Friend's House?* has survived, and he shares the journey with his young son. The landscape is integral to the narrative of that film. In *Taste of Cherry* the protagonist goes throw his journey alone, although he picks up different people (strangers) along the way. The landscape – the wasteland that we experience through the driver's gaze, turning to lush green at the end – is also an integral part of that film. In *Ten*, the focus is the human aspect, although the view of Tehran that catches the eye at intervals has a purpose as well. The shooting style is also different. In *Taste of Cherry* the actors were never in the car together; they were only talking to the director. In *Ten*, Kiarostami experiments with the digital medium and by leaving the actors alone with two small cameras, he questions the role of the director and also the cinematographer.

Ten is the second film of Kiarostami (after *ABC Africa*, 2001) to be shot with a digital camera. This was followed by *Five* (2003), a studied minimalist film. He has been quite outspoken in terms of the advantages of the medium, particularly for filmmakers who work with non-professionals in real locations. However, he seems to be weary of the discussions on the subject. During a conversation in Thiruvananthapuram, India in December 2004, he asked, 'Is it so important for a writer to use a pen or the computer? ... The image that remains is the main thing for me.'

Gönül Dönmez-Colin

UZAK DISTANT

NURİ BİLGE CEYLAN, TURKEY, 2002

The film industry has been acquainted with the films of Turkish director Yılmaz Güney for a very long time. However, since 2000, in foreign distribution markets, there has been a marked increase of works by Turkish filmmakers. For example, the films of Fatih Akın, who lives in Germany, and Ferzan Özpetek, who lives in Italy, have attracted large audiences and have been awarded in several international film festivals. *Uzak* (*Distant*, 2002) by Nuri Bilge Ceylan, which was produced and shot in Turkey, has a different style compared to the works of the diaspora filmmakers. Whereas the latter are generally marked by epic or dramatic narrative style, with extensive dialogue and music, Ceylan's is a minimalist art film that favours long takes and a slow rhythm, and was produced on a small budget. Like the director's previous films, *Distant* has been celebrated as a masterpiece, particularly by European audiences. Written, produced, directed, edited and photographed by Ceylan, the film won the Jury Grand Prix and the Best Actor award at the 2003 Cannes Film Festival. Subsequently, the film went on to modest international success, accompanied by very positive responses from critics. In the art cinema category, one may consider Ceylan a 'new wave' filmmaker of contemporary Turkish cinema.

Since the beginning of the 1990s, Turkish cinema has been producing a small number of films (15–25 films per year) that are diverse in style. A comedy like *Gora* (2004), by Ömer Faruk Sorak, has attracted an audience of four million. However, Turkish audiences have not taken much notice of Ceylan's films. While *Distant* sold 150,000 tickets in France, in Turkey the number was around 60,000.

The narrative in *Distant* focuses on people who are on the edge of a precipice, as they try to survive in a metropolis where violence is part of daily life; the characters experience melancholy and grief, caused by this invisible violence. Yusuf leaves his small town to find a job on the ocean liners that dock at Istanbul. He stays with his photographer cousin, Mahmut. Mahmut is not lying when he tells Yusuf, who trusts him, that everywhere is the same. 'Distant' is not only the title of the film; it refers to a place that is either physically or psychologically far away, whether in Turkey or elsewhere. Istanbul, with over ten million people, is an important geographic space between East and West, and conducive to an atmosphere of solitude and loneliness. The film foregrounds abstract subjects such as alienation and lack of communication, as well as various sociological problems, amongst which are the issues of migrant Anatolian workers and rising unemployment.

Ceylan employs a 'mouse' motif to express the loneliness of the two male characters. In the beginning of the film, Mahmut glues a sticky band to the kitchen threshold, to trap the mouse. In the middle, he accidentally sets his foot on the band and finally, in a midnight scene, the mouse is stuck on the band. The two men, the guest (Yusuf) and the host (Mahmut), who are actually trapped inside, hear the squeals of the mouse and find the animal caught in the trap.

We could read the film as an allegorical story of the mice in Aesop's fable: the city mouse (represented by Mahmut) and the country mouse (represented by Yusuf). In the fable, the city mouse visits his cousin, who lives in the country, while in the film the countryman goes to the city where his cousin lives. As they eat the food, the city mouse asks: 'How can you eat such bad food?' These words sound like Mahmut's remarks about Yusuf's cheap cigarettes: 'How can you smoke that shit'? The city mouse who does not like country food invites his cousin to the city to show how he should live and they go to the house of the city mouse and eat delicious food, which is left from a feast. Suddenly, the dogs of the house bark and the mice run away. Finally, the country mouse prefers to eat bad food at peace than eat good food in fear. In fact, Yusuf acts the same way at the end of the film: he prefers to stay unemployed in his small town than live in Istanbul to be accused of stealing.

The relationship between the two cousins is important within the narrative, but the real subject of the film is Mahmut, who has lost his ideals in the city. Yusuf acts as an antagonist, present to help us understand Mahmut. Mahmut, who used to live in Yusuf's small town, works as an art photographer for a tile company. He has alienated himself from his family, his work and even his own self, which has culminated in a kind of depression or angst. He is unhappy in his work and his relationships, because once he longed to be a director like Tarkovsky, but now he is caught in the routine of daily life.

Although Ceylan was viewed as the twin soul – cinematically – of Abbas Kiarostami with his first two features, *Kasaba* (*The Small Town*, 1997) and *Mayıs Sıkıntısı* (*Clouds of May*, 1999), with *Distant* he has been compared to Antonioni and Tarkovsky. He even refers to Tarkovsky in the film. In a humorous scene, Mahmut watches Tarkovsky's *Stalker* (1979) in the hope that Yusuf would be bored and leave. After dozing in his chair for a while, Yusuf asks permission to go to bed. As soon as he does, Mahmut watches a porn film.

Mahmut is divorced from Nazan (played by Zuhal Gencer, the only professional actress in the film) and has sexual intercourse with a married woman. He is reminiscent of Vittoria (Monica Vitti) in Antonioni's *L'eclisse* (*Eclipse*, 1962) who breaks up with the man she loves and begins an affair with another man who lives in a world different from hers. There is a similarity in the melancholy, annoyance and solitude experienced by the two alienated characters.

The relationship between Mahmut and Nazan is complicated. When Mahmut speaks on the phone with Nazan, he wants to say something, but finds he cannot. He says 'Well...' three times and hesitates. The only music that is heard throughout the film, a piece by Mozart, ties Mahmut and Nazan. Once we slightly hear it during their conversation in a pub. In the scenes after Nazan's departure, when Mahmut thinks of her, we hear this grievous soft music suggesting the rekindling of emotions. Mahmut experiences a sense of guilt. In a scene with Nazan, we see him feeling uncomfortable with the memory of her abortion, which he regards as his fault. Although she wants to have a baby in her new marriage, she cannot, perhaps as a result of her abortion. Throughout the rest of the film, the soundtrack features no more than the natural sounds of city life – the passing trains and ships, the television, the birds, the rustling leaves, the whistling wind, the barking dogs or simply the sound of water.

Distant not only foregrounds unsuccessful relationships in the large metropolis, it also focuses on unsuccessful intellectuals who have lost their sense of values. Mahmut usually criticises everything. According to him, out of the fifty television channels, there is not even one worth watching. And yet he always sits in front of the TV. He tries to exist alone, convincing himself that to live, he does not need anyone. He is as lifeless as the characters in Beckett's *Waiting for Godot*. He criticises, but he lacks motivation to change things.

In a sequence when Yusuf and Mahmut take a trip together to take photographs, Mahmut's eye catches an exceptional *mise-en-scène* and for a moment he thinks about photographing it as he would do in the past, but he does not have enough enthusiasm. Yusuf, whose only concern is to do his job as an assistant, tries to encourage him to stop the car but Mahmut uses the opportunity to hurt Yusuf by rejecting his help. In another scene, during a conversation with friends, he is reminded of how they used to try to climb mountains to take photographs and is accused of having changed. Mahmut says: 'Photography is finished.' His hopes and dreams have gone. Likewise, Yusuf's hopes and dreams are about to end.

Gradually, Yusuf begins to resemble Mahmut as he was in the past. He will also lose his dreams like Mahmut. This is best illustrated in a scene in which the two men raise their voices at each other. Mahmut stays over at his sister's to look after his mother, who is hospitalised.

When he returns, he notices that Yusuf has littered his house. In that evening scene, Yusuf stands between the doorframe, with a toy in his hand, like a child. Yusuf's image, seen through the mirror behind Mahmut, is somewhat blurred and outside the frame of his cousin, who stands on the left and in front of the frame. The unclear image on the right, from a distance, looks like Mahmut in his youth; the Mahmut he gave up. The distance between Mahmut and the unclear image in the mirror signifies the distance between him and his ideals, his past and his youth, which is embodied by Yusuf.

This distance between Mahmut and Yusuf widens. At each opportunity, Mahmut literally closes the doors that separate him from Yusuf, or at least tries to. When Yusuf smokes a cigarette on the balcony, Mahmut stays on the other side of the door, slowly closing it. Mahmut has strict rules: he wants Yusuf to use the small toilet and he forbids him to smoke anywhere indoors except the kitchen, finally prohibiting him from smoking even there. As the odour of his shoes and cheap cigarettes annoy him, he constantly reminds Yusuf of the rules of his house.

It is significant that it snows the day after the arrival of Yusuf. The cold atmosphere implies the solitude of the two relatives and prepares a basis for the distance between them. Snowy, gloomy winter and the missing spirit of the characters complement each other. Coldness and rudeness extend everywhere from the dialogue to the film's atmosphere and *mise-en-scène*. For instance, Mahmut forgets the day Yusuf is coming to Istanbul, so Yusuf has to wait for him in the lobby of the building until the evening. From beginning to end, Mahmut treats Yusuf poorly, maintaining his distance from him. Mahmut asks him repeatedly: 'How many days before you find a job?', 'What happened with the ship job?', 'When will you know for sure?' and 'So what are your plans?' His questions suggest that he wants his guest to leave as quickly as possible. Hospitality is generally shown as a basic part of Turkish culture in many popular narratives and is one of the most important characteristics of national identity, but Mahmut is unusual – he does not like his guest.

When his friend calls him for a get-together, Mahmut says: 'I'll come. The thing is, I'm coming with someone. No. He is someone from a distant place.' Disenchanted as he is, Mahmut refuses to be of any help to Yusuf. He has becomes 'distant' to his roots and alienated from most other things, though he does not notice it. As he keeps himself away and keeps everybody away from himself, he eradicates his origin and identity, instead hiding himself. As he selfishly keeps himself at a distance, even from his past, he places himself into nothingness.

During their first dialogue, Mahmut asks Yusuf several questions about his plans. In this scene, Ceylan's frame squeezes them into the kitchen door. The edges of the doors have a compressive effect on the characters. Mahmut feels uncomfortable with Yusuf's existence in his home. Yusuf, who stands behind Mahmut's armchair, is redundant in the room when Mahmut watches television. Mahmut waits for a while, then turns round and gazes at him, until he is forced to leave.

A number of metaphors suggest the besiegement of the characters. The fish out of water, the stuck mouse and the capsized ship indicate the circumstances of Yusuf, Mahmut, or sometimes both. When Mahmut accuses Yusuf of stealing the silver pocket-watch, in spite of his cousin's innocence, he besieges Yusuf, who is caught in a trap, like the mouse. The two events, trapping the mouse and accusing Yusuf, occur on the same day. The next morning, Yusuf leaves the house after Mahmut drives to the airport to secretly see Nazan for the last time, as she leaves for Canada with her new husband.

Distant has more intense conflicts than the other films of Nuri Bilge Ceylan. Each of his stories are tightly interwoven. It is the third film of a trilogy, which could be viewed as one long film. Therefore, to understand *Distant*, we should look to the other two parts for similarities. He describes in detail the tranquil life in the village in *The Small Town* and focuses on the desire to leave the small town in *Clouds of May*. *Distant* completes this physical, psychological and emotional journey, as the man travels from the small town to the big city, only to face unemployment, resentment and solitude. The characters are almost the same in each film. In *The Small Town* and *Clouds of May*, Ceylan's real cousin, Mehmet Emin Toprak, as Saffet, wants to go far away. In *Clouds of May*, the film director Muzaffer (Muzaffer Özdemir, Ceylan's architect friend) promises Saffet, his cousin, to find a job in Istanbul. Saffet trusts his cousin and gives up his factory job in the small town, but Muzaffer does not keep his word. Yusuf (Toprak) in *Distant* once more trusts his cousin Mahmut, now a photographer (Özdemir) and comes to Istanbul with the hope of working on the ocean liners.

The films of Ceylan are personal and, to a degree, autobiographical. Just like the characters in his first two feature films, he had lived in a small town during his childhood. In *Distant*, the apartment and the car of the main character (Mahmut) belong to Ceylan. A poster of *Koza* (*Cocoon*, 1995), Ceylan's short film, hangs on the wall of Mahmut's house. And the director is also a photographer, like Mahmut. Ceylan has stressed the autobiographical aspect of his film during almost every interview given on the film's release. He not only narrates a story of solitude and alienation in Turkey, but also holds a mirror to himself. Therefore, this film can be interpreted as the auto-analysis of the director to solve the conflicts and contradictions in his life.

The conflict between the city (represented by Mahmut) and the country (represented by Yusuf) is at the centre of *Distant*. No doubt, the behaviour of city people and country people are quite different. In rural areas, people still have a sense of solidarity and hospitality. They are always ready to lend others a helping hand and they know how to live together with others. Generosity and solidarity, which are the characteristics of country life, do not exist in the city. According to Yusuf, the reason for the change in Mahmut is the city. There is peace and silence in rural areas, which is depicted in the other films of Ceylan, while the city, where people experience poverty and unemployment, is a place of intolerance, cruelty and violence.

The film thus juxtaposes the binaries of ideals and reality, country and city, traditional and modern, tolerance and intolerance. The ideals of Yusuf, who bears all the purity of traditional life, are still alive. However, Mahmut loses his ideals and inspiration while living the cruel modern life of the big city. In addition, the way the characters use space displays sharp contrasts. To drink tea, Yusuf goes to a traditional coffeehouse, where ordinary men play cards and chat with each other. But Mahmut goes to a pub at night and drinks beer alone. Turkish coffeehouses are cheaper than bars, of course, and the type of music played in these two places is very different. It is meaningful that when Yusuf enters the coffeehouse, he can sit at the table of a stranger and warmly begin to chat. But Mahmut cannot communicate with the other people in the pub.

The difference between them in the film is made obvious in the locations in which they are shot. Yusuf is often filmed outdoors, whereas Mahmut mostly stays indoors. Yusuf, who comes from a small town, is closer to nature than Mahmut. Meanwhile, Mahmut always sits in his big comfortable armchair at home. Yusuf sits there only when Mahmut goes out.

They react differently in their relations with their mothers. Mahmut cannot call his mother, and does not want to speak to her, whereas the first sentence in this film belongs to Mahmut's mother on the answering machine: 'This is mom. I called earlier, but you were out.' Mahmut also listens to his mother's words, but does not pick up the phone to answer her. In a later scene, Mahmut's sister sounds angry on the answering machine because of Mahmut's indifference to their mother's illness. She leaves a message: 'You're so irresponsible! Call me, immediately.' By contrast, Yusuf is always worried about his mother's health.

The two male characters exhibit several opposing traits, but they have one common attitude: their relationships with women exhibit not only a lack of communication but also a certain crisis of masculinity, and no matter how much distance Mahmut puts between Yusuf and himself, they look like the two faces of the same man.

As Roger Horrocks and many feminist theorists suggest, sex identity (the male/female distinction) is to be distinguished from gender identity (the masculine/feminine distinction). Our sex identity comes by birth, whereas the gender identity is a mixture of collective attitude, fantasies and roles. According to certain research, macho traditions are important in some cultures, where a man is expected to father many children and earn money for his family, usually by working extremely hard. He is also expected to protect his family against dangers. Masculinity myths are generally concerned with the assertion of toughness, stoicism and courage. Therefore, the man naturally conceals his weakness, his tears, his fears and his love for others. Horrocks claims that the feminist movement that rose in the 1960s has led to a crisis of masculinity. The movement arrived in Turkey only in the early 1980s, and in the big cities where traditional values were steadily eroding and men's roles constantly changing has had adverse effects on a large number of men who felt alienated. Mahmut is a good example.

The anti-heroes of the film show their weakness to each other and us. Their weakness and anxiety can be read from their faces and behaviour. For example, Yusuf returns as soon as Mahmut's mistress has left and Mahmut begins to scold him because the house is dirty. In fact, he is angry because he has had a bad night with his mistress and they broke up. Both men conceal their emotions in their relations with women. They treat their problems this way because they are hopeless, not powerful. Mahmut stands silently near women and cannot explain his emotions. Yusuf does not know how to act or what to do. He harasses a young girl on the bus by touching her leg. When Mahmut answers his friend's invitation, he asks: 'Are any girls coming?' On the one hand, they want to communicate with women, but on the other, they do not know how to.

The crisis of masculinity is everywhere. There is the absence of a father. Both Mahmut and Yusuf have a mother whom we see or hear, but where are their fathers? We only know Yusuf's father is unemployed, so he has no power. We do not know where Mahmut's father is. Perhaps he is dead. In this sense, is Mahmut's camera a symbol of power (like a phallus)? If it is so, Mahmut with his machine (and his armchair…) has power over Yusuf, but this actually suggests the weakness of Mahmut. His camera has not given pleasure to himself yet. He wants to seem powerful but in fact he is not so. Although he is an intellectual and he has a job, a house, a car and friends, unlike Yusuf, he is still unhappy; he has lost his ideals, his dreams and his soul. He cannot express his emotions to women; he is powerless, fragile. In a certain scene he admits that he has many problems himself and he does not want to have to deal with Yusuf.

Their weak masculinities are bound together in two shots. The two men are in different places, but they watch beautiful women, on a fashion channel, at the same time, and these images are juxtaposed. They always gaze at all women. A real woman/man relationship is lacking because the male gaze is everywhere. Laura Mulvey has claimed that the male gaze (of a director, cameraman and a hero – in other words, a spectator who identifies with the male character in the film) on the passive and powerless woman is active and powerful in the mainstream Hollywood film. However, Yusuf's gaze is timid and Mahmut's implies regret and guilt. Employing psychoanalysis, Mulvey shows that the woman has two functions in the patriarchal unconscious. She is a symbol of castration threat for men in the films because she lacks a penis, and she symbolically bears her child. Men have two types of solutions to this castration anxiety: firstly, devaluation or punishment of the woman, or saving her; secondly, making a sexual object of her, or fetishising her. But neither Mahmut nor Yusuf use these defence mechanisms. Moreover, Yusuf is devalued because he has limited opportunities and he is unemployed. Mahmut may have been punished because he loses his ex-wife and his mistress, and moves away from his ideals, youth, relatives, friends and job. And we could say that the longest takes support the fetishistic images of Mahmut's loneliness.

Mahmut's watching a pornographic film is very significant in this context. Feminists argue that pornography represents violence for women, as well as causing violence against women. As Roger Horrocks points out, porn not only shows the female body, it also shows male loneliness and inadequacy. And pornography does not lead to contact with women, sexual or otherwise. The crisis of masculinity becomes clearly visible in this scene, which implies Mahmut's loneliness and inadequacy. Horrocks argues that the male is both an 'object' of oppression under patriarchal capitalism and a 'subject' over the female. Some writers claim that pornography has a negative impact on men's sexuality and male sexuality is alienated under patriarchy. It is possible to understand Mahmut in this frame. As a man, he has experienced a bad marriage and he does not have a successful relationship with another woman, and as an artist, he has to work for a big commercial company for a living.

Some writers regard men's use of pornographic fantasy as a compensation for their powerlessness in the real world. In contrast, Harry Brod assumes pornography is both an expression of men's public power (in other words, the powerful rapist using pornography to consummate his sexual violence) and an expression of their lack of personal power (the shy recluse using pornography to consummate his masturbatory fantasies). It is obvious that

Mahmut, who lacks power, is a shy recluse and he uses pornography for his fantasies, not violence. Nevertheless, he uses the language of violence against Yusuf.

We see Mahmut watching a porn film and Yusuf worrying about his mother at the same moment. The contradictions and differences between these two men are very sharp, but it should be remembered that when Yusuf phones his mother to learn about her health, he does not ask Mahmut's permission. The two men perform these secret acts simultaneously. Moreover, they both secretly listen to each other when one of them is on the phone. Hence they resemble each other.

As was discussed earlier, despite various opposite characteristics between the two men, Yusuf represents Mahmut's youth. Consequently, one (Mahmut) is the other (Yusuf). They are only one man who is represented by two different persons in the film. One of them desires to leave his ideals and youth; to distance himself from his dreams and hopes. The other desires to go abroad and distance himself from his provincial troubles; from unemployment and limited opportunities.

The only scene in the film where Mahmut metaphorically opens his door for Yusuf is in the final sequence. On a bench at the seaside, Mahmut smokes one of Yusuf's cigarettes, which he had scorned before: they once stayed in a hotel during their trip and Yusuf offered a cigarette to Mahmut: 'Have one of these sailor cigarettes?' Mahmut replied, 'Fuck off!' Yusuf was offended at his remarks and went to sleep. Finally, Mahmut smokes the cigarette that he rejected at first. He may be beginning to understand Yusuf, which creates a sense of sympathy, but unfortunately, Yusuf is now distant from him.

With this final sequence, Mahmut will be reconciled with his past. When he met Yusuf, he remembered his youth and the ideals he wanted to forget. That is why he was angry and nervous. However, at the end of the film, while smoking one of Yusuf's cheap cigarettes, he confronts himself. The last shot in the film implies the beginning of a change in him.

S. Ruken Öztürk

REFERENCES

Brod, Harry (1990) 'Pornography and the Alienation of Male Sexuality', in Jeff Hearn and David Morgan (eds) *Men, Masculinities & Social Theory*. London: Unwin Hyman, 124–39.

Horrocks, Roger (1995) *Male Myths & Icons: Masculinity in Popular Culture*. London: Macmillan.

Mulvey, Laura (1975) 'Visual Pleasure and Narrative Cinema', *Screen*, 16, 3, 6–18.

Un film de Samir

FORGET BAGHDAD
Juifs et Arabes ١ نسي بغداد
שכח מבגדד

Avec Shimon Ballas, Moshe Houri, Sami Michael, Samir Naqqash, Ella Habiba Shohat, une co-production de Dschoint Ventschr Filmproduktion avec Tag Traum Filmproduktion Cologne, SF DRS, WDR et Teleclub, Directeur de la Photographie Nurith Aviv, Philippe Bellaiche, Montage Nina Schneider, Samir Musique

FORGET BAGHDAD: JEWS AND ARABS – THE IRAQI CONNECTION

SAMIR, SWITZERLAND/GERMANY, 2003

In his film *Forget Baghdad: Jews and Arabs – The Iraqi Connection* (2003) director Samir aims to compensate for the historical 'abyss of abandonment' (to use the expression of the poet Amira Hess) that looms between the official Zionist story of Israel and its Iraqi chapter, through the intimate and poignant reminiscences of five individuals of Baghdadi origin. He does this in part by closing in on the faces of the five 'actors' – Shimon Ballas, Moshe Moussa Houri, Sami Michael, Samir Naqqash and Ella Habiba Shohat – for whom the film is a vehicle for their return to their ancestral homeland and, to a certain extent, to their selves. What have been, in the Israeli rhetorical climate, spurned fragments in a linear journey – a one-way ticket to the Promised Land – are transformed into a roundtrip journey, characterised by endless loops and coils.

The film opens with a view of a man's suited legs walking through an airport; in the background is heard an announcement of the imminent departure of an El Al flight to Tel Aviv. Airport sounds merge, giving way to Lebanese composer Rabih Abou-Khalil's multicultural jazz instrumental, 'Got to Go Home', reminiscent of Henry Mancini's 'Pink Panther' theme song. Both the music and the film's title and credits, by way of typewritten font, sum up both the investigative narrative and documentary style of Samir's nearly two-hour film.

It is one thing to return to a place that is associated with violence – collective or personal – but another to return to the place that was forsaken in the hope of a better one. The viewer quickly discovers that Baghdad is a place that invokes both trauma and solace. The trauma of Baghdad lies its exile from Israeli memory. But, as the film underscores, it is only through memory that Baghdad can be recuperated and reclaimed as part of Israeli cultural history. Baghdad appears in the film as a place of origin; of cultural reference and genealogy. However, the film is not so much about Baghdad and everyday life prior to emigration, but about the memory of the city as it is informed by the experience of being Israeli today, more than fifty years later. The idea of 'going back', therefore, is part of a wider discussion of discursive legitimacy and recently invented strategies to effectively participate in the public debates on ethnicities and cultures of origin. Another occasion for remembering Baghdad was 'Remember

Baghdad', a conference organised in Vienna in July 2004 whose aim was to remember history, historiography and collective memory, and to rethink the contribution of such a potential community to the future of the Middle East, especially Iraq, Israel and Palestine. With *Forget Baghdad*, the key questions are what kinds of narratives are produced from this film, and what is the nature of the memory retrieved? The main issues at stake are not only in gaining permission to go back, in conjunction with the nostalgic and sentimental value inherent in going back, but more critically, the broader matter of how the film engages its participants – and viewers – in a continual negotiation of Iraqi-Jewish and Arab-Jewish identities, beyond permitted gendered, ethnic and national discursive limits.

Returning to Baghdad might well be an easy act if not for the troubling nature of the departure of Jews from Baghdad, which is recounted in two conflicting scenarios. 'Ezra and Nehemia' was the Bible-derived name given to the Zionist-orchestrated emigration (or expulsion) of Iraqi Jews to Israel in 1950–51. The official story of this operation dealt with another successful Zionist mission to rescue a Jewish community that was, in this case, 120,000 strong. Later in the 1960s, several journalists conjured up the theory that Zionists and not Arabs/anti-Zionists were responsible for planting the bombs targeting Iraqi Jews and their religious institutions, which convinced them of the wisdom of settling in Israel. If one subscribes to the logic of this theory, then if not for the Farhud of 1941, the violent attack on Jews and their property by young, pro-Nazi Iraqis, Iraqi Jews could reflect on their life in the old country with much less ambivalence. Consequently, these contested scenarios have generated impressions of Baghdad as, on the one hand, a site of violence and betrayal, and on the other, a site of wistful longing. Samir does not use the film to support one or the other thesis; he, like his interlocutors, was partial to the latter theory. For the Jews who left Iraq in the 1950s, Baghdad appears in the film as a resurrected place of affective attachment. *Forget Baghdad* itself offers to the five interlocutors an opportunity to reclaim Baghdad as an integral part of their personal and collective biography through mind-travel back to the point of departure.

The film is a montage crafted in part from vignettes of the four male and one female interlocutors who neither appear together nor interact with each other. They converse exclusively with Samir or speak to the camera. The males are Iraqi-born and of the same generation as Samir's father; the one exception is Ella Shohat, who was born in Israel and is a generation younger. Each in their own way is deeply committed to their Iraqi identity and to its expression through their personal, political, pedagogical, literary and scholarly engagements. Prominent in their professional work and evident in the film is their struggle with the subject of representation and especially with the relationship of Hebrew to their Arab-Jewish identity. As Shimon Ballas has expressed elsewhere, even though he is a Hebrew writer, he does not identify himself as part of Hebrew literature. His writing, as he claims in a 1996 interview with Ammiel Alcalay, strives to approach Hebrew without mystification and without what he perceives as the Judeocentrism that has characterised Hebrew literature. The late Samir Naqqash chose to eschew Hebrew altogether.

The choice of interlocutors, introduced briefly below, was influenced by Samir's desire to meet his father's old Communist Party comrades. The four men were all active figures in the Iraqi Communist Party and were regular contributors to its press. They also participated in major demonstrations and strikes, and several were sentenced to time in prison. Although avowedly not Zionists, they nevertheless opted to emigrate to Israel and continued their commitment to the Israeli Communist Party and to leftist parties in general. Shohat is present as a theorist and scholar who creates links between Samir's personal past, Iraqi Jewish ancestry and the ethnic politics of culture in Israel today.

Shimon Ballas, a major novelist, translator and scholar of Arabic language and literature, is a graduate of the Alliance School in Baghdad, where he immersed himself in Arabic, French and English literature. Ballas was exposed to Hebrew and to a normative Jewish education only after his arrival in Israel in 1951. He is currently active in the pro-Palestinian peace and civil rights movement, and devotes much of his recent writing to that subject.

Moshe (Moussa) Houri is an affluent building contractor who began his vocational career as a kiosk owner. He likes to think about himself as both a 'simple man' and a peace-seeker. He still votes for the Communist Party. He grew up in Bacham-bar-Ali in the western part of Baghdad, and today lives in Ramat Gan, a city east of Tel Aviv with a relatively large population of Iraqi Jews.

Sami Michael is one of Israel's most renowned authors and a visible public intellectual who broke with the Israeli Communist Party in the mid-1950s. Michael's political activism forced him underground and even, in 1948, to self-imposed exile in Iran. He subsequently emigrated to Israel, where he felt for a long time like an outsider, as he neither spoke Hebrew nor shared the Zionist ideology.

Samir Naqqash was one of the most important writers and intellectuals of his generation. Born in Baghdad, Samir lived in Teheran and Bombay before his arrival in Israel, where he spent most of his life in Petach Tikva. As noted earlier, he chose to write in Arabic exclusively as an act of political resistance to the totalising assimilation practices of the Israeli state. Naqqash inhabited the tense space in Israel, and as a Jew who wrote in Arabic felt discriminated against. Although his work is well known in the Arab states, and doctoral theses have been written on his books in Italy, the United States, England and Arab countries, his literary achievements remain, for the most part, ignored by the Israeli (Hebrew-speaking) readership.

Ella Habiba Shohat is a professor at New York University and a prolific writer, whose work on film, literature, third world feminist and postcolonial theory has been translated into several languages, including Arabic. Her first book, *Israeli Cinema: East/West and the Politics of Representation*, to which she alludes in the film, established her as an astute analyst of ethnic identity politics in Israeli popular culture. As noted earlier, Shohat was born in Israel and, with her natal family, emigrated to New York in her early adulthood where they have lived ever since. She identifies herself as a leading Mizrahi activist, a political commitment that informs her scholarship.

The five actors collectively reaffirm the historical and cultural integrity of their Iraqi ancestry and expose the unnaturalness of the exclusionary Zionist category of 'Oriental Jews'. Their individual voices converge to tell the story of a community and the vanished vibrant world of Baghdadi Jews. The vivid collage of their voices contrasts starkly with the mono- chrome footage composited from archival photographs, historical newsreels and 'Orientalist' feature films produced in studios from Hollywood to Cairo and Herzelia (in Israel). This use of montage enables Samir to graphically demonstrate the disparaging ways in which Iraqi Jews were (and are) represented in Zionist intertexts.

The film has a personal emotional value for me as it provides a vivid portrait of my father's generation. I grew up in Ramat Gan, where my maternal grandfather, Gorgy Kor, like Mussa, would spend many hours sitting on one of the benches in the local park, socialising with his fellow Baghdadis. My autobiography also has some points of overlap with that of Ella Shohat. Our parents came to Israel from Baghdad in the same immigration wave in 1950/51. We were both born in Israel, in the *ma'abarah* (the transit or refugee camps of the early 1950s), which represents an important moment in the history of Israel, characterised by post-war austerity and newly constructed hierarchies of ethnicity, ancestry and class. In the ironically Eurocentric Zionist social scheme, Iraqi Jews as a category, simply by virtue of their 'Oriental' Middle Eastern ancestry, were locked into a subordinate position relative to the Ashkenazi elite. For Iraqi Jews, the *ma'abarah* was the place where the open sky of the Promised Land sunk to the height of the canvas walls of the winter rain-soaked tent.

Samir's self-conscious engagement with his Iraqi ancestry motivated him to produce this film. How could Samir, a Swiss national, do what so many Israelis have failed to do, namely to engage on an intimate level with Israeli ethnic identity politics? From an Israeli perspective the fact that Samir is an outsider – he is neither Jewish nor Israeli, nor is he embroiled in the politics of Middle Eastern culture – makes him especially well-suited to undertake such a challenge. He introduces new variables to the representation of Iraqi Jews that hitherto were not available in the film medium. A comparison with Sasson Somekh's recently published memoir, *Baghdad, Yesterday* (2003) is instructive in this regard. First serialised for two years in *Ha'aretz*, a leading daily Israeli newspaper, where it enjoyed an enthusiastic reception, the book is a rich personal testimony of Iraqi-Jewish life in Baghdad before emigration. However, unlike the voices of Samir's interlocutors, Sasson's book, coming from within the culture, as a legitimate stage of representation, does not have an obvious critical edge. Sasson gained admission to Israeli public discourse via his academic achievements: he is a top scholar of modern Arabic literature. Memory, he claims, is non-political; he does not write as a sociologist or as a historian or as a folklorist. It is as if his memory itself has written the narrative.

Samir's own nostalgia feeds the spirit of the recuperation: his imagined community of childhood includes Jews as well as Muslim and Christian minorities. As an outsider, his very person blurs the national and religious boundaries that otherwise dominate the conflicted discourse of Zionism and Mizrahim in Israel. Moreover, the cinematic invitation that he extends to Israeli Iraqi Jews helps to create a novel cultural space in which he and the participants insist on continuing a disrupted conversation about the multicultural space of mid-twentieth-century Baghdad. In the multiethnic society of Israel, the highly hierarchical and selective mechanism of the system of social codes determines the parameters of inclusion and exclusion, controlling who can speak and from which cultural location. *Forget Baghdad* explores another dimension of minority discourse by introducing a new context for framing the key questions of to whom one speaks and to whom one's narrative is addressed. In this context, travelling through memory is a potentially radical psychological act with its own trajectory. Memory precedes both the intellect and the language; and yet, in itself, is more than an emotional attachment to places infused with nostalgia – rather, it can often constitute a political act that enables one to reposition oneself within history, in this case, Israeli cultural history.

Samir travelled from Switzerland to Israel in making his film about Baghdad. Incidentally, it is only as a European passport holder that non-Jewish Iraqis can even enter Israel. It was in the relaxed atmosphere of Israeli and American living rooms that he and his interlocutors could slip into the Iraqi dialect of Arabic and savour Iraqi cuisine. The body postures of Ballas and Michael are revealing; instead of their usual edginess, they appear relaxed and comfortable with themselves. The conversations in Arabic are friendly and flow easily as the five earnestly recount their personal stories. From the privileged position of remembering, they are able to focus not only on the memory of life in Baghdad but on the very nature of the colonising encounter between Baghdad (Iraq) and Israel. Their candid demeanour allows them to be both more trenchantly critical when discussing ethnic and cultural politics.

Samir's quest for the missing Jewish links of his childhood maps onto a more inclusive cultural terrain that extends beyond the limited Israeli frames of reference; beyond the ethnocentric localism of canonical Zionist conventions to embrace the forgotten 'ethnoscape', or landscape of ethnicity, of Baghdad. Israel, from his perspective, is but one diasporaic destination, albeit an important one, for Iraqi emigrants. New York (Shohat) and Switzerland (Samir) are two others.

On the cultural map of Jewish experience, Baghdad (Iraq) has long been caricatured in opposition to Israel: it is Arab, it is the enemy, it is backward and modern Israel is moving forward. Consequently, over the last fifty years, the discourse about Iraq and Iraqis has tended to be stereotypically reductive. The canonical Jewish narrative of the Babylon of antiquity, of the time of the Talmud and later of the Geonim instead is highlighted and contemporary ethnic differences are underplayed in favour of promoting a singular common Jewish identity. This discourse conforms to the basic premise of Zionism: what Jews around the globe share in common is much more substantial than what any one group of Jews share with their neighbours in the diaspora. In other words, a Jew from a small Russian village and a Jew from Cairo or San'a share deeper historical roots and future aspirations than they do with Russians, Egyptians or Yemenites. The logic of this premise is being challenged now in the wake of a massive wave of Russian immigrants of 'dubious Jewishness' and by the visible presence of foreign workers from Thailand, Nigeria and elsewhere.

Forget Baghdad redefines the relationship of Israelis to Iraq by presenting Baghdad as another home (land). Home is a contested construct; it can even be regarded as the place where one can exercise the very privilege and legitimacy to remember. If the question was once, 'Where is the home (land)?' it is now, 'What does it mean to go home?' Is it Israel, where the Law of Return, predicated on the ideal of a Jewish state for the Jewish people, automatically grants every Jew the right of citizenship upon arrival? Is it Baghdad? Which Baghdad? Babylonian Baghdad? British Baghdad? Ba'athist Baghdad? The bombed-out Baghdad now occupied by the

American army? Or, the Baghdad wistfully remembered and imagined as an intimate city with fluid boundaries among religions, nationalities and languages?

The collective return of Samir and his five interlocutors exposes the Baghdadi experience not as a reified category, but as an accumulated consciousness that ruptures the dominant Israeli cultural codes of rejection, intimidation and humiliation. From this position, the hybrid, hyphenated identity of Iraqi-Jew, or Arab-Jew, is carefully crafted by the five, adding new stories to the general Jewish archive of personal narratives, along with those contributed by Polish Jews, Ethiopian Jews and Sephardic Jews.

True, threaded throughout the film is a melancholic tone, symptomatic of mourning for the past, so strikingly highlighted by the intellectual isolation of each of the speakers and his or her sense of lost community. In the 1930s and 1940s, communism and Zionism were the two totalising movements in which the young, educated Jewish people of Baghdad could participate. In an Iraqi-Jewish context, communism was largely a radical movement of enthusiastic young intellectuals who felt that they could change their world. They read Marx in English, a colonial language under the British Mandate, and at times supported anti-Nazis and anti-Arab government positions; at other times, they adopted an anti-colonial stance against the British. Most important for them was the notion that to be communist was to believe in the solidarity of Jewish and Arab intellectuals striving together for a common social cause. As Sami Michael asserts in the film, communism was the main ideology of the twentieth century. And to be an intellectual in Baghdad at that time meant to be a communist. In many ways, this political affiliation amplified Iraqiness by assuming membership in an intellectual community so desperately missing in Israel. Like Zionism, Marxism also offered a manifesto of belonging, politically and intellectually, in the face of the destabilising processes (for Jews) of pan-Arabism and forced emigration. Ironically, in Israel of the early 1950s, communism, which attracted members of the newly lower-class emigrants of the *ma'abarah*, was invested with an edge of resistance as the young men of Iraqi ancestry organised protest marches, demonstrating for jobs and bread.

Beyond their nostalgic, sentimental value, these individual yet generalisable narratives of return have socio-political value in generating the alternative space for new modes and subjects of communication. They provide an opportunity for the speakers and viewer alike to rethink, in different languages and contexts, the histories and realities of ethnic differences, and those posed by Baghdadis (Iraqis) in particular.

In many ways, the film enables its participants to come out of their ethnic closets by giving an ostensibly unfiltered personal account of their experiences as Baghdadi or Iraqi

Jews in Israel, especially in the early years of the state. Their stories of oppression lie in the shadow of the Shoah, or the Holocaust, the dominant public discourse of Jewish victimisation. The over-determined discursive space of Israeli wars and national defence, together with the brittle political economy of ethnic identity continuously agitated by exigencies of immigration, labour needs and religious dogmatism, diminish, disable and trivialise the versatility and multi-dimensionality of the story of Iraqi Jews. In this context, the inclusion of Ella Shohat in the film is crucial, and not just because she represents a largely absent female – and feminist – perspective. Her postcolonial meta-narrative of Israeli ethnicity helps to place the other personal narratives within a wider context of third world politics, racism and female experience with its specific vocabulary and language. But Shohat's presence in the film is not limited to her status as a scholar. Some of the most evocative passages in the film are of her girlhood memories of the internalised humiliation of ethnocentric discrimination in the immigrant enclave of Petach Tikvah. It is in this film that she narrates publicly for the first time her painful experience of racism and its impact on her life and work.

I have commented at length on the virtues and power of *Forget Baghdad*. In conclusion, I would like to draw attention to what I perceive to be an ironic oversight. In a film that seeks to recuperate the vitality of Jewish individuals of Iraqi ancestry, it is curious that the literary and academic achievements of the five interlocutors are not fully incorporated into the cinematic montage. Especially because the integrity and dynamism of the Iraqi-Jewish community is at issue in this film, the exclusion of their actual literary productions is both perplexing and a missed opportunity to educate viewers. Nor do the five interlocutors incorporate their work, with all of its textured and nuanced complexity, into their monologues and interviews.

In this instance, the case of the late Samir Naqqash is particularly relevant. As a Jewish novelist who wrote exclusively in Arabic and who is celebrated in the Arab literary world, his work remains relatively inaccessible to Israeli and American readers. Naqqash is often acknowledged as an important writer but without any engagement with his body of work. In the film, it is his physical body that is present in his role as Samir's interlocutor. I would like to conclude this consideration of *Forget Baghdad* by remembering Naqqash's literary body. Two short paragraphs from his short story 'Prophesies of a Madman in a Cursed City' are especially evocative of the way Naqqash articulated 'presence' in literature as the ultimate testimony of his credo:

> Many tasks await me, but my only skill is in following the command and uttering 'here
> I am' [in Arabic, the original, *ha-ana-dha*, and in Hebrew, its intertext, *hinneini*]. And

I have nothing in my dominion but this covert mission that fills my very being, measureless and without colour, but whose weightlessness already makes it like lead. And if I dare to rebel against its voice, it will transgress and put me to death – if I do not say 'Here I am'. Yet it is my most prized possession, even though people refer to it as a mental defect and even distance themselves, and utterly convinced, call it insanity.

...As for me, I have my tears, my flesh, and my suffering. I quickly learned that shedding tears and expressing grief are but the other face of revolution and rebellion. They are the resistance of an important madman from who, in every syllable of the words flowing from his mouth, can be heard that here is his sole of only possession: 'Here I am'.

Ruth Tsoffar

REFERENCES

Ballas, Shimon (1996) 'At Home in Exile: An Interview with Shimon Ballas', in Ammiel Alcalay (ed.) *Keys to the Garden: Israeli Writers in the Middle East*. San Francisco: City Lights Books, 62–9.

Naqqash, Samir (1993) 'Prophesies of a Madman in a Cursed City', trans. by Ammiel Alcalay, Joseph Halibi and Ali Jimale Ahmed in A. Alcalay in *Keys to the Garden: Israeli Writers in the Middle East*. San Francisco: City Lights Books, 111–32.

Shohat, Ella (1989) *Israeli Cinema: East/West and the Politics of Representation*. Austin: University of Texas Press.

Somekh, Sasson (2003) *Bagdad 'Etmol* ('Baghdad, Yesterday'). Tel Aviv: ha-Kibbutz ha-Me'uchad.

FILMOGRAPHY

GHAZAL AL-BANAT CANDY FLOSS 1949
Director: Anwar Wagdi
Production Company: Sharikat al-aflam al-muttahida
Screenplay: Badi' Khayri, Nagib al-Rihani
Photography: Abd al-Halim Nasr (b&w)
Editing: Kamal El-Cheikh
Music: Layla Murad
Designer: Antoine Boliseuz
Producer: Anwar Wagdi
Cast: Layla Murad (Pasha's daughter), Nagib al-Rihani (Hamam), Anwar Wagdi (Officer), Yusuf Wahbi
Running time: 120'

BAB EL-HADID CAIRO STATION 1958
Director: Youssef Chahine
Production Company: Al Ahram Studios
Screenplay: Muhammad Abu Yusuf; Abdel Hay Adib
Photography: Alvise Orfanelli (b&w)
Editing: Kamal Abu al-'Illa
Music: Fy'ad al-Zahiri
Art Direction: Gabriel Karraze
Designer: Abbas Hilmi
Sound: Aziz Fadel
Producer: Gibra'il Talhami
Cast: Farid Chaouqi (Abu Seri'), Hind Rostom (Hanouma), Youssef Chahine (Kenaou), Hassan el Baroudi (H. el Baroudy), Naima Wasfy (Naima Wasfi), Abdel Aziz Khalil
Running time: 98'

AL MOMIA THE MUMMY 1969
Director: Shadi Abdel Salam
Production Company: General Film Organisation
Screenplay: Shadi Abdel Salam
Photography: Abd al-Aziz Fahmi (Eastmancolour)
Editing: Kamal Abu al-'Illa
Music: Mario Nachimbini
Designer: Salah Marei
Sound: Nasri Abd al-Nur
Cast: Ahmed Marei (Wanis), Ahmad Hegazi (Brother), Zouzou Hamdy El-Hakim (Mother as Zouzou El-Hakim), Nadia Lutfi (Zeyna), Abdelazim Abdelhack (Uncle), Abdelmoniem Aboulfoutouh (Uncle), Ahmad Anan (Badawi), Gaby Karraz (Maspero), Mohamed Khairi (Kamal), Mohamed Morshed (Stranger), Mohamed Nabih (Murad), Shafik Noureddin (Ayoub)
Running time: 102'

UMUT HOPE 1970
Director: Yılmaz Güney
Production Companies: Lale Film, Güney Filmcilik
Screenplay: Yılmaz Güney and Şerif Gören
Photography: Kaya Ererez (b&w)
Editing: Celal Köse
Music: Arif Erkin
Light: Ender Işık Service
Set: Nizam Ergüder
Synchronisation: Mustafa Kurt
Sound: Necip Sarıcıoğlu
Producer: Yılmaz Güney
Cast: Yılmaz Güney (Cabbar), Gülsen Alnıaçık (Cabbar's wife), Tuncel Kurtiz (Hasan), Osman Olyanak (Hodja)
Running time: 100'

GELIN THE BRIDE 1973
Director: Lütfi Ö. Akad
Production Company: Erman Film
Screenplay: Lütfi Ö. Akad
Photography: Gani Turanlı (c)
Editing: Ismail Kalkan
Music: Yalçın Tura
Art Design: Nejat Buvan
Sound: Marco Buduris, Faruk Ören
Producer: Hürrem Erman
Cast: Hülya Koçyiğit (Meryem), Kerem Yılmazer (Veli), Kamran Usluer (Hıdır-brother-in-law), Aliye Rona (Mother-in-law), Nazan Adalı (Naciye-sister-in-law), Ali Şen (Hacı İlyas-father-in-law), Kahraman Kıral (Osman-son), Seden Kızıltunç (Güler)
Running Time: 92'

TABIAT-E BIJAN STILL LIFE 1974
Director: Sohrab Shahid Saless
Production Companies: Telfilm, Progressive Film Union
Screenplay: Sohrab Shahid Saless
Photography: Hushang Baharlu (c)
Editing: Ruhollah Emami
Art Direction: Morteza Momayez, Hushang Baharlou, Sohrab Shahid Saless
Sound: Sadeq Alemi, Ahamad Khanzadi
Producer: Parviz Sayyad, Maleksaan Veisi
Cast: Zadour Bonyadi (Mohamad Sardari), Zahra Yazdani (his wife), Mohammed Kani (Inspector)
Majid Baghai, Hedayatollah Navid, Noor Mohamad Guglani, Hossein Ali Bidgoli, Khoswrow Zandi, Habibollah Safaryan
Running time: 93'

TRAVERSÉES CROSSING OVER 1982
Director: Mahmoud Ben Mahmoud
Production Companies: SATPEC, Marisa Films
Screenplay: Mahmoud Ben Mahmoud and Philippe Lejuste
Adaptation & Dialogue: Mahmoud Ben Mahmoud and Fadhel Jaziri

English Dialogue: John Boyle
Photography: Gilberto Azevedo (c)
Editing: Moufida Tlatli
Music: Francesco Accolia
Art Design: Maryse Houyoux
Sound: Fawzi Thabet and Hechmi Joulak
Producer: Selma Baccar
Cast: Fadhel Jaziri (Youssef Kouraichi), Julian Negulesco (Bogdan Merovitch), Eva Darlan (Vera), Vincent Grass (English policeman), Christian Maillet (Purser), Jean-Pierre Dauzin (Officer)
Running Time: 95'

DAVANDEH THE RUNNER 1984
Director: Amir Naderi
Production Company: Centre for the Intellectual Development of Children and Young Adults
Screenplay: Amir Naderi, Behruz Charib
Photography: Firuz Malekzadeh (c)
Editing: Bahram Baiza'i
Sound: Nezamodin Kiai
Producer: Fathola Dalili
Cast: Majid Nirumand (Amiro), Abbas Nazarnik, Musa Torkizadeh (Musa)
Running time: 94'

LO SAM ZAYIN I DON'T GIVE A DAMN 1987
Director: Shmuel Imberman
Production Company: Roll Films/Gelfand Films
Screenplay: Hanan Peled (based on a novel by Dan Ben-Amotz)
Photography: Nissim Leon (c)
Editing: Atara Horenstein
Music: Benny Nagari
Producer: Israel Ringel, Yair Pradelsky
Cast: Ika Zohar (Rafi), Anat Waxman (Nira), Shmuel Vilozhny (Eli), Shlomo Tarshish (Amnon), Liora Grossman (Maya)
Running time: 90'

NUJUM AL-NAHAR STARS IN BROAD DAYLIGHT 1988
Director: Oussama Mohammad
Production Company: National Film Organisation for Cinema
Screenplay: Oussama Mohammad
Photography: Abdel-Kader Shurbagi (c)
Editing: Antoinette Azrie
Art Direction: Hala Abdallah
Artistic Collaboration: Mohamad Malas
Set Design: Rida Hushus
Sound: Hassan Salem, Emile Saadeh, Ahmad Kaouk
Producer: Housni el-Barem
Cast: Abdel-Latif Abdulhamid (Khalil Ghazi), Zouheir Ramadan (cousin Tawfiq Ghazi), Zouheir Abdel-Karim (Kasser Ghazi), Maha el-Saleh (Hasna, Khalil Ghazi's wife), Saba al-Salem (Sana), Saadeddine Baqdounes (Grandfaher), Susanne el-Saleh (Mayada, Kasser Ghazi's bride-to-be)
Running time: 115'

DOCHARKHEH SAVAR THE CYCLIST 1988

Director: Mohsen Makhmalbaf

Producers: Institute for the Cinematographic Affairs of Janbazan Foundation, Seyyed Jamaleddin Hosseini Cultural Foundation

Scriptwriter: Mohsen Makhmalbaf

Editor: Mohsen Makhmalbaf

Photography: Ali-Reza Zarrindast (c)

Music: Majid Entezami

Cast: Moharram Zaynalzadeh (Nasim), Esmail Soltanian, Mohamed Reza Maleki, Mahshid Afsharzadeh, Firooz Kiyani, Samira Makhmalbaf (fortune-teller's daughter)

Running time: 83'

BAB AL-SAMA MAFTOUH A DOOR TO THE SKY 1989

Director: Farida Benlyazid

Production Companies: SATPEC (Tunisia), France Media SA (France), Interfilm (Maroc), Ministry of External Affairs (France), Ministry of Culture (France), Centre Cinématographique Marocain, Rabat (Morocco)

Screenplay: Farida Benlyazid

Photography: Georges Barsky (c)

Editing: Moufida Tlatli

Music: Anouar Braham (and J. S. Bach, St Mathew's Passion; Andalusian music by Ba Jeddour; Berber songs by Mohamed Damou and Najet Aatabou; Abdelbasset Abdessamed's voice; Fez AISSOUA group)

Art Direction: Georges Barsky

Designer: Khadija Lahman and Latifa Amor

Sound: Faouzi Thabet

Producers: Farida Benlyazid and Mohamed Belkziz

Cast: Zakia Tahiri (Nadia), Eva St. Paul (Leyla); guest actors: Chaibia Aadroui, Bachir Skirej, Ahmed Bouanani; reading of the Koran by Aziza Tazi.

Running time: 107'

YOUCEF OU LA LÉGENDE DU SEPTIÈME DORMANT YOUSSEF OR THE LEGEND OF THE SEVENTH SLEEPER 1993

Director: Mohamed Chouikh

Production: CAAIC/ENPA (Algeria)

Screenplay: Mohamed Chouikh

Photography: Allel Yahiaoui (c)

Editing: Yamina Chouikh

Music: Khaled Barkat

Art Direction: Ahmed Kobbi

Sound: Rachid Bouaffia

Cast: Mohamed Ali Allalou (Youssef), Shiraz Selma (Aïcha), Youcef Benhadouda (Amin), Dalila Helilou (Fatima), Mohamed Benguettaf (Ali), Azzedine Medjoubi (Lyes), Abdenor Chelouche (Athmane), Ahmed Fillali (Hadj Lakhdar), Baaziz (Singer), Yamina Medjoubi (Woman from the South)

Running Time: 105'

SAMT AL-QUSUR SILENCES OF THE PALACE 1994

Director: Moufida Tlatli

Production Companies: Cinetelefilms, Magfilm, Mat Film, French Ministry of Foreign Affairs, Tunisian Ministry of Culture

Screenplay: Moufida Tlatli and Nouri Bouzid

Photography: Youssef Ben Youssef (c)

Editing: Moufida Tlatli
Music: Anouar Brahem
Designer: Claude Bennys
Set Design: Fawzi Thabet
Sound: Faouzi Thabet
Producer: Ahmed Baha Eddine Attia and Richard Magnien
Cast: Amel Hedhili (Khedija), Hend Sabri (Young Alia), Najia Ourghi (Khalti Hadda), Ghalia Lacroix (Adult Alia), Kamel Fazaa (Sidi Ali), Hishem Rostom (Si Bechir), Helene Catzaras (Fella), Sonia Meddeb (Jneina)
Running time: 127'

KAN YA MAKAN BAYRUT ONCE UPON A TIME, BEIRUT 1994
Director: Jocelyn Saab
Production Companies: Balcon, Arte, Aleph
Screenplay: Philippe Paringaux, Roland-Pierre Paringaux, Jocelyn Saab
Photography: Roby Breidi (c/b&w)
Editing: Dominique Auvray, Isabelle Dedieu
Art Direction: Seta Khoubesserian
Sound: Pierre Bouvier
Producer: Hessischer Rundfunk
Cast: Myrna Maakaron (Leila), Michele Tyan (Yasmine), Emile Accar (Monsieur Farouk) Khaled El Sayed (Driver), Pascal Faugeras (Officer), Ziad Makhoul (Gardner), Khodr Ala' Ed-Din (Chouchou), Pierre Chamassian
Running time: 107'

SEGELL IKHTIFA CHRONICLE OF A DISAPEARANCE 1996
Director: Elia Suleiman
Production: Asaf Amir
Screenplay: Elia Suleiman
Photography: Marc-Andre Batigne (c)
Editing: Anna Ruiz
Art Direction: Samir Srouji, Hans Tel Elst
Sound: Jean-Paul Mugel
Cast: Elia Suleiman (himself), Olan Tabari (Adan), Nazira Suleiman (Mother), Fuad Suleiman (Father), Jamal Daher (Jamal, owner of the Holyland), Juliet Mazzawi (Aunt), Fawaz Eilemi (Abu Adnan), Leonid Alexeenko (Priest), Taha Mohammed (Writer)
Running time: 88'

EŞKİYA THE BANDIT 1997
Director: Yavuz Turgul
Production Companies: Filma-Cass/Artcam International/Geopoly
Screenplay: Yavuz Turgul
Photography: Uğur İçbak (c)
Editing: Onur Tan, Selahattin Turgut
Music: Erkan Oğur
Art Direction: Mustafa Ziya Ülkenciler
Producer: Mine Vargi
Cast: Şener Şen (Baran, the Bandit), Uğur Yücel (Cumali), Kamran Usluer (Mahmud/Berfo), Sermin Sen (Keje), Yesim Salkim (Emel), Kayhan Yıldızoğlu (Artist Kemal), Şermin Şen Hürmeriç (Kece), Necdet Mahfi Ayral (Andref Miskin), Melih Çardak (Demircan)
Running time: 212'

BEYROUTH ALGHARBIYYA WEST BEIRUT 1998

Director: Ziad Doueiri

Production Companies: 3B Productions, Cine Libre, Doueiri Films, Exposed Film Productions, La Sept ARTE

Screenplay: Ziad Doueiri

Photography: Ricardo Jacques Gale (c)

Editing: Dominique Marcombe

Music: Stewart Copeland

Art Direction: Hamzi Nasrallah

Costume Designer: Pierre Matard

Sound: Nicolas Canton and Thierry Sabatier

Producer: Rachid Bou Chareb and Jean Brehat

Cast: Rami Doueiri (Tarek), Mohamad Chamas (Omar), Rola Al Amin (May), Carmen Lebbos (Hala), Joseph Bou Nassar (Riad), Lialiane Nemri (Neighbour), Laila Karam (Brothel Madam), Hassan Farhat (Roadblock Militiaman), Mahmoud Mabsout (Baker), Fadi Abou Khalil (Bakery Militiaman), Aida Sabra (School Principal)

Running time: 108'

KIKAR HAHALOMOT CIRCLE OF DREAMS 2000

Director: Beni Torati

Production Companies: The Israeli Film Foundation, Reshet

Screenplay: Beni Torati

Photography: Dror Moreh

Editing: Yosef Grinfeild

Art Direction: Dalit Inbar

Sound: David Lies

Cast: Yona Elian (Seniora Mandabon), Muhammad Bakri (Avram Mandabon), Yosef Shiloah (Yisrael 'the Indian'), Uri Gavrieli (Aron 'Gabardine'), Nir Levi (Nissim Mandabon), Tamara Dayan (Plump Sara), Sharon Rajuan (George Mandabon), Ayelet Zorer (Gila, the waitress), Uri Ran-Klauzner ('Jellyfish' David), Shlomi Sarenga (Yudakis, the singer), Yonatan Dani (Yonatan), Baruch Sason (Baruch)

Running time: 95'

KIPPUR 2000

Director: Amos Gitai

Production Companies: Agav Hafakot, ARTE France Cinema, Canal Plus, Eldan/MP Productions, R & C Produzioni, Telad, Tele Plus

Screenplay: Amos Gitai and Mary-Jose Sanselma

Photography: Renato Berta (c)

Editing: Monica Coleman and Kobi Netanel

Music: Jan Garbarek

Art Direction: Miguel Markin

Sound: Eli Yarkoni

Producers: Michel Propper and Amos Gitai

Cast: Liron Levo (Weinraub), Tomer Ruso (Rousso), Uri Ran Kaluzner (Doctor), Yoram Hattab (Pilot), Guy Amir (Gadassi), Juliano Merr (Officer), Ran Kauchinsky (Shlomo), Kobi Livne (Kobi), Liat Glick Levo (Dina), Pini Mittelman (Hospital doctor), Shai Gani (Army doctor), Noach Faran (Rescue Commander), Keren Gitai (Soldier)

Running time: 123'

MUVATIN WA MUKHBIR WA HARAMI CITIZEN, DETECTIVE AND THIEF 2001

Director: Daoud Abd El-Sayed

Production Company: Société arabe pour la production et la distribution cinématographique Diogène
Screenplay: Daoud Abd El-Sayed
Photography: Samir Bahzan (c)
Music: Ragueh Daoud
Set Designer: Onsi Abou Seif
Producer: Ihab Ayoub
Cast: Khaled Abol Naga (Selim), Salah Abdallah (Fathi, the detective), Shabaan Abdel Rehim (Harami), Hend Sabri (Hayat), Rola Mahmoud (Madiha)
Running time: 135'

TEN 2002
Director: Abbas Kiarostami
Production Company: MK2 Productions
Screenplay: Abbas Kiarostami
Photography: Abbas Kiarostami (c)
Editing: Abbas Kiarostami
Music: Peyman Yazdanian, closing song Howard Blake
Sound: DTS
Producer: Abbas Kiarostami and Marin Karmitz
Cast: Mania Akbari (Driver), Amin Maher (Amin), Roya Arabshahi (Roya), Katayoun Taleidzadeh, Mandana Sharbaf, Amene Moradi (other passengers)
Running time: 94'

UZAK DISTANT 2003
Director: Nuri Bilge Ceylan
Production Companies: NBC Film/Özen Film
Screenplay: Nuri Bilge Ceylan
Photography: Nuri Bilge Ceylan
Editing: Nuri Bilge Ceylan and Ayhan Ergürsel
Art Direction: Ebru Ceylan
Designer: Ebru Ceylan and Ebru Yapici
Sound: Ismail Karadaş
Producer: Nuri Bilge Ceylan
Cast: Muzaffer Özdemir (Mahmut), Mehmet Emin Toprak (Yusuf), Zuhal Gencer Erkaya (Nazan), Nazan Kırılmış (Lover), Feridun Koç (Janitor), Fatma Ceylan (Mother), Ebru Ceylan (Young girl)
Running time: 105'

FORGET BAGHDAT: JEWS AND ARABS – THE IRAQI CONNECTION 2003
Director: Samir
Production Companies: Dschoint Ventschr Filmproduction, TAG/TRAUM Filmproduction/SRG-SSR idée suisse/SF DRS Teledub AG, WDR Westdeutscher Rundfunk
Screenplay: Samir
Photography: Nurith Aviv and Philippe Bellaiche (c)
Editing: Samir and Nina Schneider
Sound: Tully Chen
Sound Editor: Alexander Weuffen
Music: Rabih Abou-Khalil
Producer: Samir, Karin Koch, Gerd Haag
Cast (playing themselves): Sami Michael, Moshe (Moussa) Houri, Samir Naqqash, Shimon Ballas, Ella Habiba Shohat
Running time: 112'

BIBLIOGRAPHY

GENERAL

Ahmed, Leila (1992) *Women and Gender in Islam: Historical Roots of a Modern Debate*. New Haven: Yale University Press.

Amilcar, Cabral (1973) *Return to the Source*. New York: Monthly Review Press/Africa Information Service.

Anderson, Benedict (1983) *Imagined Communities: Reflections on the Origin and Spread of Nationalism*. London: Verso.

Appadurai, Arjun (1996) *Modernity at Large: Cultural Dimensions of Globalization*. Minneapolis: University of Minnesota Press.

Appiah, Kwame Anthony and Henry Louis Gates Jr (eds) (1995) *Identities*. Chicago and London: University of Chicago Press.

Arab Cinema and Culture: Round Table Conferences (1965) Beirut: Arab Film and Television Centre.

Arasoughly, Alia (ed. and trans.) (1998) *Screens of Life: Critical Film Writing from the Arab World*. St. Hyacinthe: World Heritage Press.

Armbrust, Walter (ed.) (2000) *Mass Mediations: New Approaches to Popular Culture in the Middle East and Beyond*. Berkeley: University of California Press.

Armes, Roy (1987) *Third World Film Making and the West*. Berkeley: University of California Press.

____ (1996) *Dictionary of North African Film Makers/Dictionnaire des cinéastes du Maghreb*. Paris: Editions ATM.

____ (2005) *Post-Colonial Images: Studies in North African Film*. Bloomington: Indiana University Press.

Asfour, Nana (2000) 'The Politics of Arab Cinema: Middle Eastern filmmakers face up to their reality', *Cineaste*, 26, 1, 46–8.

Ashcroft, Bill, Gareth Griffiths and Helen Tiffin (2001) *The Postcolonial Studies Reader*. London & New York: Routledge.

Bakari, Imruh and Mbye Cham (eds) (1996) *African Experiences of Cinema*. London: British Film Institute.

Barlet, Olivier (1996) *Les Cinémas d'Afrique noire: Le regard en question*. Paris: Harmattan.

Bataille, Maurice-Robert and Claude Veillot (1956) *Caméras sous le soleil: Le Cinéma en Afrique du nord*. Algiers: V. Heintz.

Bazin, Andre (1967-71) *What is Cinema?*, trans. Hugh Gray. Berkeley: University of California Press.

Benali, Abdelkader (1998) *Le Cinéma colonial au Maghreb*. Paris: Cerf.

Benshoff, Harry M. and Sean Griffin (2003) *America on Film: Representing Race, Class, Gender, and Sexuality at the Movies*. Oxford: Blackwell.

Bernstein, Matthew and Gaylyn Studlar (eds) (1997) *Visions of the East: Orientalism in Film*. London: I.B. Tauris.

Berrah, Mouny, Victor Bachy, Mohand Salama and Ferid Boughedir (1981) 'Cinemas du Maghreb', *CinemAction*, 14.

Berrah, Mouny, Jacques Levy and Claude-Michel Cluny (1987) 'Les cinemas arabs', *CinemaAction*, 43.

Bhabha, Homi K. (1992) 'The World and the Home', *Social Text*, 31/32, 141–53.

____ (1994) *The Location of Culture*. London: Routledge.

Bossaerts, Marc and Catherine Van Geel (eds) (1995) *Cinéma d'en Francophonie*. Brussels: Solibel Édition.

Boughedir, Ferid (1987) *Le Cinéma africain de A à Z*. Brussels: Éditions OCIC.

____ (1995) 'African Cinema and Ideology: Tendencies and Evolution', unpublished paper presented at 'Africa and the History of Cinematic Ideas', British Film Institute, London.

Boulanger, Pierre (1975) *Le Cinéma colonial*. Paris: Seghers.

Bouzid Discacciati, Leyla (2000) 'The Image of Women in Algerian and Tunisian Cinema'. On-line; available at http://www.library.cornell.edu/colldev/mideast/cinmwmn.htm.

Bouzid, Nouri (1995) 'New Realism in Arab Cinema: The Defeat-Conscious Cinema', trans. Shereen-el Ezabi, *Alif: Journal of Comparative Poetics*, 15, 242–50 (English section), 199–200 (Arabic section).

Brahimi, Denise (1997) *Cinémas d'Afrique francophone et du Maghreb*. Paris: Nathan.

Carr, Steven Allan (2001) *Hollywood and Anti-Semitism: A Cultural History up to World War II*. Cambridge: Cambridge University Press.

Cham, Mbye 'Globalizing African Cinema?' On-line; available at http://www.africanfilmny.org/network/news/Acham4.html.

Cham, Mbye and Imruh Bakari (eds) (1996) *African Experiences of Cinema*. London: British Film Institute.

Cheriaa, Tahar (1979) *Ecrans d'abondance ... ou cinémas de libération en Afrique?* Tunis: STD.

Chomsky, Noam (2003) *Middle East Illusions: Peace, Security and Terror*. New Delhi: Penguin Books India.

Cluny, Claude-Michel (1978) *Dictionnaire des nouveaux cinémas arabes*. Paris: Sindbad.

Colla, Elliot (2000) 'Shadi Abd el Salam's al-Mumiya: Ambivalence and the Egyptian Nation State', in Ali Abdullatif Ahmida (ed.) *Beyond Colonialism and Nationalism in the Maghreb: History, Culture and Politics*. New York: Palgrave.

Davies, Miranda (ed.) (1983) *Third World-Second Sex*. London: Zed.

Deeley, Mona (2003) 'Overview of Arab Cinema', Zenith Foundation. On-line; available at http://www.library.cornell.edu/colldev/mideast/arbcinem.htm.

Diawara, Manthia (1992) *African Cinema: Politics and Culture*. Bloomington: Indiana University Press.

Di Martino, Anna, Andrea Morini and Michele Capasso (eds) (1997) *Il cinema dei paesi arabi*, quarta edizione/*Arab Film Festival*, fourth edition. Naples: Edizioni Magma.

Downing, John D. H. (ed.) (1987) *Film and Politics in the Third World*. New York: Praeger.

Dönmez-Colin, Gönül (2004) *Women, Islam and Cinema*. London: Reaktion Books.

_____ (2006) *Cinemas of the Other: A Personal Journey with Filmmakers from the Middle East and Central Asia*. Bristol: Intellect.

_____ (2007) 'Cinemas of Islam', in Andrew Rippin (ed.) *The Islamic World*. London: Routledge.

El Saadawi, Nawal (1980) *The Hidden Face of Eve, Women in the Arab World*. London: Zed Books.

Fanon, Frantz (1970) *Toward the African Revolution*, trans. Haakon Chevalier. London: Pelican.

Fawal, Ibrahim (2000) 'Three Perspectives on Arab Cinema', *Edebiyat: The Journal of Middle Eastern Literatures*, 11, 2, 275–82. Online; available at http://www.gbhap.com:80/journals/393/393 top.htm.

FEPACI (1995) *L'Afrique et le centenaire du cinéma/Africa and the Centenary of Cinema*. Paris: Présence Africaine.

Gabriel, Teshom H. (1982) *Third Cinema in the Third World: The Aesthetics of Liberation*. Ann Arbor: UMI Research Press.

Gabriel, Teshome H. and Hamid Naficy (1993) *Otherness and the Media: The Ethnography of the Imagined and the Imaged (Studies in Film and Video)*. Chur, Switz.: Harwood Academic Publishers.

Gariazzo, Giuseppe (1998) *Poetiche del cinema africano*. Turin: Lindau.

_____ (2001) *Breve storia del cinema africano*. Turin: Lindau.

Ghareeb, Shirin (1997) 'An Overview of Arab Cinema', *Journal for Critical Studies of the Middle East*, 3, 11, 119–27.

Ghazoul, Ferial J. (ed) (1995) 'Arab Cinematics: Towards the New and the Alternative', *Alif: Journal of Comparative Poetics*, 15.

Givanni, June (ed.) (2000) *Symbolic Narratives/African Cinema: Audiences, Theory and the Moving Image*. London: British Film Institute.

Graves, Benjamin (1998) 'Homi K. Bhabha: an Overview', On-line; available at http://www.scholars.nus.edu.sg/landow/post/poldiscourse/bhabha/bhabha1.html.

Gresh, Alain and Dominique Vidal (2004) *The New A-Z of the Middle East*. London: I.B. Tauris.

Guneratne, Antony R. and Wimal Dissanayake (eds) (2003) *Rethinking Third Cinema*. New York and London: Routledge.

Haffner, Pierre (1978) *Essai sur les fondements du cinéma africain*. Dakar: Nouvelles Éditions Africaines.

Hamzaoui, Hamid (1997) *Histoire du Cinema Egyptien*. Marseille: Editions Autres Temps.

Harrow, Kenneth W. (ed.) (1999) *African Cinema: Postcolonial and Feminist Readings*. Trenton: Africa World Press.

Holmes, Winifred (ed.) (1959) *Orient: A Survey of Films Produced in Countries of Arab and Asian Culture*. London:

British Film Institute.

Jameson, Fredric (1986) 'Third World Literature in the Era of Multinational Capitalism', *Social Text*, 15, 65–88.

_____ (1992) *The Geopolitical Aesthetic: Cinema and Space in the World System*. Bloomington: Indiana University Press/ London: British Film Institute.

Jayawardena, Kumari (1986) *Feminism and Nationalism in The Third World*. London: Zed Books.

Kaplan, E. Ann (1996) *Looking for the Other: Feminism, Film, and the Imperial Gaze*. New York and London: Routledge.

Khatib, Lina (2003) 'Communicating Islamic Fundamentalism as Global Citizenship', *Journal of Communication Inquiry*, 27, 4, 389–409.

Khayati, Khémais (1996) *Cinémas arabes: Topographie d'une image éclatée*. Paris: L'Harmattan.

Khelil, Hédi (1994) *Résistances et utopies: Essais sur le cinéma arabe et africain*. Tunis: Édition Sahar.

Lanza, Federica (1999) *La donna nel cinema maghrebino*. Rome: Bulzoni Editore.

Landau, Jacob M. (1958) *Studies in the Arab Theater and Cinema*. Philadelphia: University of Pennsylvania Press.

Laroui, Abdallah (1976) *The Crisis of the Arab Intellectual: Traditionalism or Historicism?* Berkeley: University of California Press.

Leaman, Oliver (ed.) (2001) *The Companion Encyclopedia of Middle Eastern and North African Film*. London and New York: Routledge.

Les cinemas d'Afrique: Dictionnaire. Paris: Éditions Karthala/Editions ATM.

Malandrin, Stephane (1995) 'Cinéma Arabe, Souviens-toi de Carthage!', *Cahiers du Cinéma*, 487, 75–81.

Malkmus, Elizabeth and Roy Armes (1991) *Arab and African Film Making*. London: Zed Books.

Mansouri, Hassouna (2000) *De l'identité, ou Pour une certaine tendance du cinéma africain*. Tunis: Éditions Sahar.

Mayne, Judith (1990) *The Woman at the Keyhole: Feminism and Women's Cinema*. Bloomington: Indiana University Press.

Mernissi, Fatema (1996) *Women's Rebellion and Islamic Memory*. London: Zed Books.

Michalek, Laurence (1989) 'The Arab in American Cinema: A Century of Otherness', *Cineaste*, 17, 1, 3–9.

Mikhail, Mona N. (1985) *Images of Arab Women: Fact and Fiction*. Washington, DC: Three Continents Press.

Mir-Hosseini, Ziba (1999) *Islam and Gender: The Religious Debate in Contemporary Iran*. Princeton: Princeton University Press.

Moore-Gilbert, Bart (1997) *Postcolonial Theory: Context, Practices, Politics*. London: Verso.

Morini, Andrea, Erfan Rashid, Anna Di Martino and Adriano Aprà (eds) (1993) *Il cinema dei paesi arabi*. Venice: Marsilio Editori.

Naficy, Hamid (ed.) (1999) *Home, Exile, Homeland: Film, Media and the Politics of Place*. London and New York: Routledge.

_____ (2000) 'Self Othering: A Postcolonial Discourse on Cinematic First Contact', in Fawiza Afzal-Khan and Kalpana Seshadri-Crooks (eds) *The Pre-Occupation of Post Colonial Studies*. Durham: Duke University Press, 292–310.

_____ (2001) *An Accented Cinema: Diasporic and Exilic Filmmaking*. Princeton: Princeton University Press.

Nichols, Peter M. (2001) 'Middle East, Elusive on Film', *New York Times*, 12 October, E28.

Pakzad, Bahram (1993) 'Arab Cinema in Crisis', *International Film*, 1, 1, 33–7.

Pines, Jim and Paul Willemen (eds) (1989) *Questions of Third Cinema*. London: British Film Institute.

Rony, Fatimah Tobing (1996) *Third Eye: Race, Cinema and Ethnographic Spectacle*. Durham: Duke University Press.

Russell, Catherine (1999) *Experimental Ethnography: The Work of Film in the Age of Video*. Durham: Duke University Press.

Saadawi, Nawal El (1980) *The Hidden Face of Eve: Women in the Arab World*. London: Zed Books.

Sadoul, Georges (1966) *The Cinema in the Arab Countries; anthology prepared for UNESCO*. Beirut: Interarab Centre of Cinema & Television.

_____ (1968) *The History of Cinema in the World*, trans. I. Kilani and F. Naqsh. Beirut: Manshurat 'Uwaydat wal-Bahr al-Mutawasit.

Said, Edward W. (1978) *Orientalism*. New York: Vintage Books.

_____ (1979) *The Question of Palestine*. New York: Times Books.

_____ (1981) *Covering Islam: How the Media and the Experts Determine How We See the Rest of the World*. New York: Pantheon Books.

_____ (1983) *The World, the Text and the Critic*. Cambridge: Harvard University Press.

_____ (1992) *Culture and Imperialism*. New York: Knopf.

_____ (1999) *Out of Place: A Memoir*. London: Granta Books.

_____ (2001) *Reflections on Exile and Other Literary and Cultural Essays*. London: Penguin Books.

Saliba, Therese, Carolyn Allen and Judith A. Howard (2002) *Gender, Politics, and Islam*. Chicago and London: University of Chicago Press.

Salmane, Hala (1976) *Algerian Cinema*. London: British Film Institute.

Serceau, Michel (ed.) (2004) 'Cinémas du Maghreb', *Corlet/Télérama/CinémAction*, 111.

Shafik, Viola (1996) *Arab Cinema: History and Cultural Identity*. Cairo: American University in Cairo Press.

Sherzer, Dina (1996) *Cinema, Colonialism, Postcolonialism: Perspectives from the French and Francophone Worlds*. Austin: University of Texas Press.

Shiri, Keith (ed.) (1992) *Directory of African Film-makers and Films*. London: Flicks Books.

Shohat, Ella (1985) 'The Cinema After Babel: Language, Difference, Power', *Screen*, 26, 3/4, 35–58.

_____ (1997a) 'Gender and Culture of Empire: Toward a Feminist Ethnography of the Cinema', in Matthew Bernstein and Gaylyn Studlar (eds) *Visions of the East: Orientalism in Film*. London: I.B. Tauris, 19–66.

_____ (1997b) 'Framing Post-Third-Worldist Culture: Gender, Nation and Diaspora in Middle Eastern/North African Film and Video', *Jouvert: A Journal of Postcolonial Studies*, 1, 1, On-line; available at http://www.social.chass.ncsu.edu/jouvert/v1i1/shohat.htm.

Shohat, Ella and Robert Stam (1994) *Unthinking Eurocentrism: Multiculturalism and the Media*. London and New York: Routledge.

_____ (eds) (2003) *Multiculturalism, Postcoloniality and Transnational Media*. New York: Rutgers University Press.

Slemon, Stephen (1988) 'Magic Realism as Post-Colonial Discourse', *Canadian Literature*, 116, 9–24.

Spass, Lieve (2000) *The Francophone Film: A Struggle for Identity*. Manchester: Manchester University Press.

Spivak, Gayatri Chakravorty (1999) *A Critique of Postcolonial Reason: Toward a History of the Vanishing Present*. Cambridge and London: Harward University Press.

Stam, Robert (1989) *Subversive Pleasures: Bakhtin, Cultural Criticism, and Film*. Baltimore: Johns Hopkins University Press.

_____ (1992) *Reflexivity in Film and Literature*. New York: Columbia University Press.

Thoraval, Yves (1998) 'West Asia: Wars and Much More', *Cinemaya*, 41, 30–5.

_____ (2000) *Les cinémas du Orient, Iran, Egypte, Turquie*. Paris: Séquier.

_____ (2003) *Les Ecrans du Croissant fertile, Irak, Liban, Palestine, Syrie*. Paris: Séquier.

Vasudev, Aruna, Latika Padgaonkar and Rashmi Doraiswamy (eds) (2002) *Being and Becoming: The Cinemas of Asia*. New Delhi: Macmillan India.

Wassef, Magda (2000) 'Three Arab Women Documentary Filmmakers', *Documentary Box*, 16, 28–32.

Winston, Brian (1995) *Claiming the Real: The Documentary Film Revisited*. London: British Film Institute.

Zuhur, Sherifa (ed.) (1998) *Images of Enchantment: Visual and Performing Arts of the Middle East*. Cairo: American University in Cairo Press.

ALGERIA

Allouche, Merzak (1987) *Omar Gatlato* (script). Algiers: Cinematheque Algerienne/Editions LAPHOMIC.

_____ (1996a) *Salut cousin!* (script). Paris: L'Avant-Scene du Cinema.

_____ (1996b) *Bab el-Oued*. Paris: Seuil and Casablanca: Editions le fennec.

Arasoughly, Alia (ed. and trans.) (1998) *Screens of Life: Critical Film Writing from the Arab World*. Quebec: World Heritage Press.

Armes, Roy (1998) *Omar Gatlato*. Trowbridge: Flicks Books.

_____ (1999) *Omar Gatlato: Film-clef du cinema algerien*. Paris: Editions L'Harmattan.

_____ (2001) 'Cinema in the Maghreb: Algeria', in Oliver Leaman (ed.) *The Companion Encyclopedia of Middle Eastern* and *North African Film*. London and New York: Routledge, 420–517.

Brossard, Jean-Pierre (ed.) (1981) *L'Algérie vue par son cinéma*. Locarno: Locarno International Film Festival.

El Kenz, Nadia (2003) L'Odysée des Cinématheques. La Cinématheque Algerienne à la recherché d'une mémoire perdue (de Meliès à Lakhdar Hamina). Rouiba: Editions ANEP.

Farzanefar, Amin (2005) 'Interview with Yamina Bachir-Chouikh: No Freedom of Expression without Funds', *Quantara*. On-line; available at http://www.qantara.de/webcom/show_article.php/_c-310/_nr-155/i.html.

Hennebelle, Guy, Mouny Berrah and Benjamin Stora (eds) (1997) 'La Guerre d'Algérie à l'écran', *Télérama/CinémAction*, 85.

Images et Visages du Cinéma Algérien (1984). Algiers: ONCIC/Ministry of Culture and Tourism.

Maherzi, Lotfi (1980) *Le Cinéma algérien: Institutions, imaginaire, idéologie*. Algiers: SNED.

Megherbi, Abdelghani (1982) *Les Algériens au miroir du cinéma colonial*. Algiers: SNED.

____ (1985) *Le Miroir aux alouettes*. Algiers and Brussels: ENAL/UPU/GAM.

Mimoun, Mouloud (ed.) (1992) *France-Algérie: Images d'une guerre*. Paris: IMA.

Où va le cinéma algérien? (2003) Paris: *Cahiers du Cinéma*: hors-série.

Quarante Ans de Cinéma Algérien (2002). Algiers: Dar Raïs Hamidou.

Salmane, Hala, Simon Hartog and David Wilson (eds) (1976) *Algerian Cinema*. London: British Film Institute.

Simarski, Lynn Teo (1992) 'Through North African Eyes', On-line; available at http://www.africa.upenn.edu/Audio_Visual/North_African_10051.html.

Taboulay, Camille (1997) *Le Cinéma métaphorique de Mohamed Chouikh*, Paris: K Films Editions.

Tamzali, Wassyla (1979) *En attendant Omar Gatlato* Algiers: EnAP.

Vautier, René (1998) *Caméra citroyenne: Mémoires*. Rennes: Editions Apogée.

EGYPT

Abu-Lughod, Lila (1995) 'Movie Stars and Islamic Moralism in Egypt', *Social Text*, 42, 53–67.

Abu Shadi, Ali (1996) 'Genre in Egyptian Cinema', in Alia Arasoughly (ed. and trans.) *Screens of Life: Critical Film Writing from the Arab World*. Quebec: World Heritage Press, 84–129.

____ (1998a) *al-Sinima wa-al-Siyasah (Cinema and Politics)*. Cairo: Dar Sharqiyat lil-Nashr wa-al-Tawzi'.

____ (1998b) *A Chronology of the Egyptian Cinema in Hundred Years, 1896–1994*, trans. Nora Amine. Cairo: al-Majlis al-A'la lil-Thaqafah.

Al-Obaidi, Jabbar A. (2000) 'Egyptian Film: Gender and Class Violence Three Cycles', *International Journal of Instructional Media*, 27, 3, 261.

Armbrust, Walter (1995) 'New Cinema, Commercial Cinema, and the Modernist Tradition in Egypt', *Alif: Journal of Comparative Poetics*, 15, 81–129 (English section), 191–2 (Arabic section).

____ (1996) *Mass Culture and Modernism in Egypt*. Cambridge: Cambridge University Press.

____ (2000) 'The Golden Age before the Golden Age: Commercial Egyptian Cinema before the 1960s', in Walter Armbrust (ed.) *Mass Mediations: New Approaches to Popular Culture in the Middle East and Beyond*. Berkeley: University of California Press, 292–327.

____ (2002) 'The Rise and Fall of Nationalism in the Egyptian Cinema', in Fatma M. Göçek (ed.) *Social Constructions of Nationalism in the Middle East*. Albany: State University of New York Press, 217–50.

Armes, Roy (1987) 'Youssef Chahine', in *Third World Film Making and the West*. Berkeley: University of California Press.

Baker, Raymond (1995) 'Combative Cultural Politics: Film Art and Political Spaces in Egypt', *Alif: Journal of Comparative Poetics*, 15, 6–38.

Bindari, Mona Mahmud Qasim and Ya'qub Wahbi (eds) (1994) *Mawsu'at al-Aflam al-'Arabiya (Encyclopedia of Arab Cinema)*. Cairo: Bayt al-Ma'rifa.

Bosseno, Christian (ed.) (1985) *Youssef Chahine l'Alexandrin*. Paris: CinemAction.

Chmeit, Walid (2001) *Youssef Chahine: The Life of Cinema*. Beirut: Riad el-Rayyes Books.

Culhane, Hind Rassam (1995) *East/West, an Ambiguous State of Being: The Construction and Representation of Egyptian Cultural Identity in Egyptian Film*. New York: Peter Lang.

Daney, Serge and Serge Toubiana (1990) 'Alexandrie, parce que', *Cahiers du Cinéma*, 431–2, 44–50, 52.

Darwish, Mustafa (1998) *Dream Makers on the Nile: A Portrait of Egyptian Cinema.* Cairo: American University in Cairo Press.

Davis, Eric (1983) *Challenging Colonialism: Bank Misr and Egyptian Industrialization 1929–1941.* Princeton: Princeton University Press.

Doran, Michael (1999) *Pan-Arabism before Nasser: Egyptian Power Politics and the Palestine Question.* Oxford: Oxford University Press.

Ehrenstein, David (1991) 'Alexandria Again and Forever', *The Advocate*, 580, 89.

Gaffney, Jane (1987) 'The Egyptian Cinema: Industry and Art in a Changing Society', *Arab Studies Quarterly*, 9,1, 53–75.

Gershoni, Israel and James P. Jankowski (1986) *Egypt, Islam and the Arabs: The Search for Egyptian Nationhood 1900–1930.* New York: Oxford University Press.

Gordon, Joel (2000) '*Nasser 56/Cairo 96*: Reimaging Egypt's Lost Community', in Walter Armbrust (ed.) *Mass Mediations: New Approaches to Popular Culture in the Middle East and Beyond.* Berkeley: University of California Press.

____ (2001) 'Class-Crossed Lovers: Popular Film and Social Change in Nasser's New Egypt', *Quarterly Review of Film & Video*, 18, 4, 385–96.

____ (2002) *Revolutionary Melodrama: Popular Film and Civic Identity in Nasser's Egypt.* Chicago: Middle East Documentation Centre.

Hamzaoui, Hamid (1997) *Histoire du cinema Egypt.* Marseille: editions autre temps.

Kehr, Dave (1996) 'The Waters of Alexandria: the Films of Youssef Chahine', *Film Comment*, 32, 6, 23–25.

Khan, Mohammad (1969) *An Introduction to the Egyptian Cinema.* London: Informatics.

Khatib, Lina (2004a) 'The Politics of Space: The Spatial Manifestations of Representing Middle Eastern Politics in American and Egyptian Films', *Visual Communication*, 3, 1, 69–90.

____ (2004b) 'The Orient and its Others: Women as Tools of Nationalism in Political Egyptian Cinema', in Naomi Sakr (ed.) *Women and Media in the Middle East.* London: I.B. Tauris, 72–88.

Khayati, Khémais (1990) *Salah Abou Seif: Cineaste Egyptien.* Cairo: Sinbad.

Kiernan, Maureen (1995) 'Cultural Hegemony and National Film Language: Youssef Chahine', *Alif: Journal of Comparative Poetics*, 15, 130–52.

Klawans, Stuart (2000) 'Nine Views in a Looking Glass: Film Trilogies by Chahine, Gitai, and Kiarostami', *Parnassus: Poetry in Review*, 25, 2, 231–2.

Landau, Jacob (1958) *Studies in the Arab Theater and Cinema.* Philadelphia: University of Pennsylvania Press.

Le Péron, Serge and Serge Daney (1980) 'Le syndrôme Alexandrie.: Entretien avec Youssef Chahine', *Cahiers du Cinéma*, 310, 18–25.

Malkmus, Lizbeth (1988) 'The "New" Egyptian Cinema: Adapting Genre Conventions to a Changing Society', *Cineaste*, 16, 3, 30–3.

Malkmus, Lizbeth and Roy Armes (1991) *Arab and African Film Making.* London: Zed Books.

Massad, Joseph (1999) 'Art and Politics in the Cinema of Youssef Chahine', *Journal of Palestine Studies*, 28, 2, 77–93.

Nazarenko, J. M. (1990) 'Alexandrie, toujours', *Cahiers du Cinéma*, 427, 9.

Qasim, Mahmud (1998) *al-Sinima al-Misriyah wa-al-Itharah (Egyptian Cinema and Sexual Provocation).* Cairo: al-Dar al-Thaqafiyah.

Ramzi, Kamal (1992) *Amina Rizq.* Cairo: Cultural Development Fund.

____ (1994) 'Les sources litteraires dans le cinéma égyptien', in Magda Wassef (ed.) *2e Biennale des cinemas arabes a paris.* Paris: Institut du Monde Arabe, 111–20.

Richter, Erika (1974) *Realistischer Film in Agypten.* Berlin: Henschel Verlag.

Salah al-Din, Muhammad (1998) *al-Din wa-al-'Aqidah fi al-Sinima al-Misriyah (Religion and Faith in the Egyptian Cinema).* Cairo: Maktabat Madbuli.

Shafik, Viola (1998) *Arab Cinema: History and Cultural Identity.* Cairo: American University in Cairo Press.

____ (2001a) 'Prostitute for a Good Reason: Stars and Morality in Egyptian Cinema', *Women's Studies International*

Forum, 24, 6, 711–25.

____ (2001b) 'Egyptian Cinema', in Oliver Leaman (ed.) *The Companion Encyclopedia of Middle Eastern and North African Film*. London and New York: Routledge, 23–129.

Stollery, Martin (2004) *Al-Muhajir/L'émigré*. Trowbridge: Flicks Books.

Thabet, Madkour (1998) *Industrie du Film Egyptien*. Guizeh: Ministère égyptien de la culture.

Thoraval, Yves (1975) *Regards sur le cinema egyptien*. Beirut: Dar el-Machreq.

Tignor, Robert (1984) *State, Private Enterprise, and Economic Change in Egypt, 1918–1952*. Princeton: Princeton University Press.

Toufic, Jalal (ed.) (1999) 'The Night of Counting the Years (aka *The Mummy*): A Screenplay by Shadi Abd al-Salam', *Discourse*, 21, 1, 88–126.

Vatrica, Vincent (1995) 'Le terre des pharaons', *Cahiers du Cinéma*, 489, 28–33.

Vitalis, Robert (2000) 'American Ambassador in Technicolor and Cinemascope: Hollywood and the Revolution on the Nile', in Walter Armbrust (ed.) *Mass Mediations: New Approaches to Popular Culture in the Middle East and Beyond*. Berkeley: University of California Press.

Wassef, Magda (ed.) (1995a) *Egypte: 100 ans de cinema*. Paris: Institute du monde Arabe.

____ (1995b) 'Egypt through the looking-glass', *UNESCO Courier*, 4, 49.

Wassef, Magda and Salah Marei (eds) (1996) *Chadi Abdel salam: Le Pharaon du cinema egyptien*. Paris: Institite Monde Arab.

Yari, Abbas (1993) 'Out of History: Tawfik Saleh', *Film International*, 1, 3, 51–3.

Zuhur, Sherifa (ed.) (1998) *Images of Enchantment: Visual and Performing Arts of the Middle East*. Cairo: American University in Cairo Press.

IRAN

Afkhami, Mahnaz and Erica Friedl (eds) (1994) *In the Eye of the Storm: Women in Post-Revolutionary Iran*. London and New York: I.B. Tauris.

Akrami, Jamsheed (1987) 'The Blighted Spring: Iranian Cinema and Politics in the 1970s', in John D. H. Downing (ed.) *Film and Politics in the Third World*. New York: Praeger, 131–44.

Amiel, Vincent (2002) '*Ten*, Voyage autour du monde', *Positif*, 499, 15–16.

Andrew, Geoff (2002) '*10*: Drive, He Said', *Sight and Sound*, 12, 10, 30–2.

____ (2005) *Ten*. London: British Film Institute.

Aufderheide, Pat (1995) 'Real Life is More Important Than Cinema: an interview with Abbas Kiarostami', *Cineaste*, 21, 3, 31–3.

Bahari, Maziar and Carla Power (2001) 'Freedom for Film', *Newsweek International (Iran)*, 5, 28, 56.

Bluin, Patrice and Olivier Joyar (2002) 'Dix Raisons d'aimer *Ten*', *Cahiers du Cinéma*, 6, 28–9.

Bouruet-Aubertot, Veronique (1999) 'Abbas Kiarostami', *Beaux Arts Magazine*, 187, 54–7.

Bradshaw, Peter (2002) '*Ten*', *Guardian*, 27 September.

Chaudhuri, Shohini and Howard Finn (2003) 'The Open Image: Poetic Realism and the New Iranian Cinema', *Screen*, 44, 1, 38–57.

Cheshire, Godfrey (1996) 'Abbas Kiarostami: a Cinema of Questions' *Film Comment*, 32, 4, 34-40.

____ (1997a) 'Makhmalbaf: The Figure in the Carpet', *Film Comment*, 33, 4, 62–8.

____ (1997b) '*Taste of Cherry*: Journey to the End of Night', *Film International*, 5, 1, 25–8.

____ (1997c) 'The Iranian who won the world's attention' (profile of Abbas Kiarostami), *New York Times*, 147, 2, 9, 28.

____ (2000) 'How to Read Kiarostami', *Cineaste*, 25, 4, 8.

Ciment, Michel and Stéphane Goudet (2002) 'Entretien: Abbas Kiarostami, des femmes réelles et non de cinéma' *Positif*, 499, 17–21.

Dabashi, Hamid (1999) 'Mohsen Makhmalbaf's *A Moment of Innocence*', in Rose Issa and Sheila Whitaker (eds) *Life and Art: The New Iranian Cinema*. London: National Film Theatre.

____ (2001) *Close Up: Iranian Cinema, Past, Present, and Future*. London: Verso.

____ (2002) 'Persian Blues', *Sight and Sound*, 12, 1, 32–4.

Dehbashi, Ali (ed.) (1999) *Yadnameh-ye Sohrab Shahid Saless*. Tehran: Entesharat-e Sokhan and Entesharat-e Shabab-e Saqeb.

Della Nave, Marco (1999) *Abbas Kiarostami*. Milano: Editrice Il castoro.

Ditmars, Hadani (1996) 'From the Top of the Hill', *Sight and Sound*, 6, 12, 10–13.

Dönmez-Colin, Gönül (1996) 'Portrait of the Revolutionary as an Artist: Two Interviews with Mohsen Makhmalbaf', *Blimp: Film Magazine*, 35, 33–8.

____ (1999a) 'Rakhshan Bani-Etemad: Unveiling Iranian Cinema' (interview), *Blimp*, 40, 14–20.

____ (1999b) 'Abbas Kiarostami: Life is Nothing But…' (interview), *Celluloid*, 21, 1, 8–11.

____ (2002) 'Refugees in Love and Life: Interview with Majid Majidi', *Asian Cinema Studies*, 13, 1, 87–92.

Elena, Alberto (2005) *The Cinema of Abbas Kiarostami*, trans. Belinda Coombes. London: Saqi.

Eslami, Majid (1999/2000) 'The Freshness of Repetition: *Where is the Friend's Home?* 13 Years Later', *Film International*, 7, 2/3, 108–14.

Fahdel, Abbas (1990) 'The Versatile Cinema of Sohrab Shahid Saless', *Cinemaya*, 9, 9.

Giardina, Sonia (2002) 'Another Look at *Homework* by Abbas Kiarostami: An Investigation of a Pedagogic and Social Drama', *Film International*, 3, 35, 33.

Jenkins, Mark (2002) 'Iranian Cinema: New Directors, New Directions', *Washington City Paper*, 1, 18, 88.

Golmakani, Houshang (1996) 'Dreams Gone With the Wind: Kiarostami Meets his Actor in *The Traveller* After 20 Years', *Film International*, 4, 3, 40–5.

____ (1999) 'The Tide Turns', *Cinemaya*, 45, 4–7.

____ (2000) 'The Makhmalbafs in Long Shot', *Film International*, 8, 1, 9–10.

____ (2000/2001) 'The History of Iranian Cinema', *Film International*, 30/31, 42–54.

____ (2002) 'A Review of *Ten*, Kiarostami's Latest Film: The Lies He Utters', *Film International*, 9, 3, 30–2.

Graffy, Julian (2002) '*Ten*', *Sight and Sound*, 12, 10, 57–8.

Haghighat, Mamad (1999) *Histoire du cinema iranien 1900–1999*. Paris: Centre Georges Pompidou.

____ (2000) 'After the Revolution: The Cinema Will Carry Us', *UNESCO Courier*, 10, 26.

Hamid, Nassia (1997) 'Near and Far', *Sight and Sound*, 7, 2, 22–4.

Hamid, Rahul (2001) 'Films by and about Mohsen Makhmalbaf', *Cineaste*, 27, 1, 40–1.

Ishaghpour, Youssef (2001) *Le reel, face et pile: le cinema d'Abbas Kiarostami*. Tours: Farrago.

Issa, Rose and Sheila Whitaker (eds) (1999) *Life and Art: The New Iranian Cinema*. London: National Film Theatre.

Issari, Mohammad Ali (1989) *Cinema in Iran, 1900–1979*, Metuchen: The Scarecrow Press.

Jousse, Thierry and Serge Toubiana (1999) 'Un film n'a pas de passeport: entretien avec Abbas Kiarostami', *Cahiers du Cinéma*, 541, 30–3.

Kakhi, Morteza (2000) 'Flight of Fancy in Kiarostami's Poetry', *Film International*, 8, 1, 11.

Kéy, Hormuz (2000) *Le Cinema Iranien, l'Image d'une Société en Bouillonnement, de 'La Vache' au 'Gout de la Cerise*. Paris: Karthala.

Khoshchereh, Mahmood (2002) 'The Bounteous Rain of Life: Baran', *Film International*, 3, 35, 34–8.

____ (2003/04) '10. Kiarostami: The Man with the Digital Camera', *Film International*, 10, 2, 56–63.

Klawans, Stuart (2000) 'Nine Views in a Looking Glass: Film Trilogies by Chahine, Gitai, and Kiarostami', *Parnassus: Poetry in Review*, 25, 2, 231–2.

Lopate, Phillip (1996) 'Kiarostami close up' (interview), *Film Comment*, 32, 4, 37–41.

Maghsoudlou, Bahman (1987) *Iranian Cinema*. New York: New York University Press.

____ (1991) 'Amir Naderi: Images Bitter and Sweet', *Cinemaya*, 11, 32–5.

Makhmalbaf, Mohsen (1991) 'Mirror Images', *Cinemaya*, 13, 18–20.

____ (1993) 'The Unbearable Lightness of Determinism', *Film International*, 1, 3, 44–50.

Mohammadi, Ali (2001) 'Cinema in Iran: Culture and Politics in the Islamic Republic', *Asian Cinema*, 12, 1, 14–28.

Moruzzi, Norma Claire (2001) 'Women In Iran: Notes on Film and from the Field', *Feminist Studies*, 27, 1, 89–100.

Mosleh-Heidarzadeh, Ali (2004) '*10 on Ten*: an attempt to return the auteur to the text', *Film International*, 10, 4, 60–1.

Mulvey, Laura (1998) 'Kiarostami's Uncertainty Principle', *Sight and Sound*, 8, 6, 24–7.

Najafi, Behrad (1986) *Film in Iran, 1900 to 1979: A Political and Cultural Analysis*. Stockholm: University of Stockholm.

Naficy, Hamid (1990) 'The Aesthetics and Politics of Iranian Cinema in Exile', *Cinemaya*, 9, 4–8.

____ (1998) 'Shohrab Shahid Salesss's Accented Films and Claustrophobic Spaces', *Film International*, 6, 1, 53–8.

____ (2001) 'Iranian Cinema', in Oliver Leaman (ed.) *The Companion Encyclopedia of Middle Eastern and North African Film*. London and New York: Routledge, 130–222.

Nayeri, Farah (1993) 'Iranian Cinema: What Happened in Between', *Sight and Sound*, 3, 12, 26–8.

Negar Mottahedeh (2000) 'Bahram Bayzai's *Maybe … Some Other Time*: The un-Present-able Iran', *Camera Obscura*, 15, 1, 162–91.

Neudeck, Rupert (1975) 'Review of *Far From Home*', *Film-Korresponenz*, 5.

Omid, Ruhani (1992) 'Khab dar Cheshme Taram Mishekanad', *Kelk*, 40.

Rahmati, Shahzad (1997) 'The Story of Victory', *Film International*, 5, 1, 22–5.

Rahmati, Shahzad and Majid Sedqi (1998) 'A Nest for the Different Ones: A Glance at the Center for Intellectual Development of Children and Young Adults', *Film International*, 5, 2, 14–19.

Rastin, Shadmehr (1999/2000) 'Kiarostami: Simple and Complicated. Part Two', *Film International*, 7, 2/3, 104–7.

Ridgeon, Lloyd (2001) *Makhmalbaf's Broken Mirror: The Socio-Political Significance of Iranian Cinema*. Durham: Middle East Papers.

____ (2003) 'The Islamic Apocalypse: Mohsen Makhmalbaf's Moment of Innocence', in S. Brent Plate (ed.) *Representing Religion in World Cinema: Filmmaking, Mythmaking, Culture Making*. New York: Palgrave Macmillan, 145–58.

Rosen, M. (1992) 'The Camera of Art: An Interview with Abbas Kiarostami', *Cineaste*, 19, 2/3, 38–40.

Rosenbaum, Jonathan (2000) 'Short and sweet', *Film Comment*, 36, 4, 26–7.

Rosenbaum, Jonathan and Mehrnaz Saeed-Vafa (2003) *Abbas Kiarostami*. Urbana: University of Illinois Press.

Roth, Laurent (1995) 'Abbas Kiarostami, le dompteur de regard', *Cahiers du Cinéma*, 493, 68–73.

Sadr, Hamid-Reza (1998) '…and the World Became His', *Film International*, 5, 3/4, 50–5.

Saeed-Vafa, Mehrnaz (1998) *A Simple Event*. Tehran: Ney Publishing House.

____ (1999) 'Sohrab Shahid Saless: A Cinema of Exile', in Rose Issa and Sheila Whitaker (eds) *Life and Art: The New Iranian Cinema*. London: National Film Theatre, 135–44.

Saffarian, Nasser (1999/2000) 'A Dream and a Fantasy, a Lure and a Flash: A Glance at the Script of Mohsen Makhmalbaf's *Silence*', *Film International*, 7, 2/3, 115–7.

Scott, A. O. (2002a) 'An Afghan Boy Cheated of Childhood', *New York Times*, 3, 30, A24.

____ (2002b) 'A Darkness Cast Upon Childhood: *ABC Africa*', *New York Times*, 5, 3.

Siavoshi, Sussan (1997) 'Cultural Policies and the Islamic Republic: Cinema and Book Publication', *International Journal of Middle East Studies*, 29, 4, 509–30.

Sterritt, David (2000) 'With borrowed eyes', *Film Comment*, 36, 4, 20–2, 25–6.

Tapper, Richard (ed.) (2002) *The New Iranian Cinema: Politics, Representation and Identity*. London: I.B. Tauris.

Tayab, Manouchehr (1998) 'Sohrab Shahid Saless: An Innovator in Iran's Contemporary Cinema', *Film International*, 6, 1, 59–60.

Thoraval, Yves (1999) 'Before the Revolution: Iranian Cinema 1900–1979', *Cinemaya*, 44, 53.

Thrupkaew, Noy (2003) 'Will and Testament: What Iranian Filmmakers are Showing the Wider World', *American Prospect*, 6, 14, 6–45.

Totaro, Donato (2000) 'Reflexivity in Recent Iranian Cinema: The Case of Mohsen Makhmalbaf', *Asian Cinema*, 11, 2, 32–46.

Whatley, Sheri (2003) 'Iranian Women Film Directors: A Clever Activism', *Off Our Backs: The Feminist Newsjournal*, 33, 3/4, 30–2.

Williamson, Casey (1999) 'Art Matters: The films of Abbas Kiarostami', in Rose Issa and Sheila Whitaker (eds) *Life and Art: The New Iranian Cinema*. London: National Film Theatre, 90–104.

Zahedi, Hassan S. (1993) 'Mohsen Makhmalbaf: In Search of the Lost Horizon', *Film International*, 1, 3, 36–9.

IRAQ

Braude, Joseph (2003) *The New Iraq: Rebuilding the Country for its People, the Middle East, and the World*. New York: Basic Books.

Kennedy-Day, Kiki (2001) 'Cinema in Lebanon, Syria, Iraq and Kuwait', in Oliver Leaman (ed.) *The Companion Encyclopedia of Middle Eastern and North African Film*. London and New York: Routledge, 364–405.

Mufarriji, A. F. (1981) *Masadir dirasat al-nahat al-sinimai fi al-Iraq, 1968–1979*. Beirut: al-Muassasah al-Arabiyah li-Dirasah wa-al-Nashr.

Nuri, Shakir (1986) *A la recherché du cinema irakien: histoire, infrastructure, filmography (1945–1985)*. Paris: L'Harmattan.

ISRAEL

Avisar, Ilan (1988) 'National Fears, Personal Nightmares: The Holocaust Complex in Israeli Cinema', in Nurith Gertz, Orly Lubin and Judd Ne'eman (eds) *Fictive Looks: On Israeli Cinema*. Tel Aviv: Open University of Israel.

_____ (1996) 'Israeli Cinema and the Ending of Zionism', in Fred Lazin and Greg Mahler (eds) *Israel in the Nineties*. Tallahassee: Florida State University Press, 153–68.

Ben-Shaul, Nitzan (1997) *Mythical Expressions of Siege in Israeli Films*. New York: Edwin Mellen Press.

Burstein, Igal (1990) *Face as Battleground*. Tel Aviv: Hakibbutz Hame'uchad.

Chetrit, Sami (2004) 'The Desperation and the Dream of Beni Torati', On line; available at http://www.kedma.co.il.

_____ (2004) *The Mizrahi Struggle in Israel: Between Oppression and Liberation, Identification and Alternative 1948–2000*. Tel Aviv: Am Oved.

Dolev, Aharon (2000) 'Israeli Cinema: The Collapse of the Frameworks of Cultural Sanity', *Nativ*, 13, 3, 74. On-line; available at http://www.acpr.org.il/NATIV/2000-3/dolevxs.htm.

Fainaru Edna and Dan Fainaru (eds) 'A Hundred Years of Life and Cinema in the Holy Land', special supplement of *Cinematheque*, 1, 7.

Gertz, Nurith (1993) *Motion Fiction: Israeli Fiction in Film*. Tel Aviv: Open University of Israel.

_____ (1997) 'Historical Memory: Israeli Cinema and Literature in the 1980s and 1990s', in Kevin Avruch and Walter Zenner (eds) *Critical Essays on Israeli Society, Religion, and Government*. Albany: State University of New York Press, 209–26.

_____ (1998) 'From Jew to Hebrew: The 'Zionist Narrative' in the Israeli Cinema of the 1940s and 1950s', *Israel Affairs*, 4, 3, 175–200.

_____ (1999) 'The Medium That Mistook Itself for War: *Cherry Season* in Comparison with *Ricochets* and *Cup Final*', *Israel Studies*, 4, 1, 153–74.

_____ (2003) 'Gender and Space in the New Israeli Cinema', *Shofar: An Interdisciplinary Journal of Jewish Studies*, 22, 1, 110–16.

_____ (2004) *Holocaust Survivors, Aliens and Others in Israeli Cinema and Literature*. Tel Aviv: Am Oved.

Gross, Nathan and Ya'acov Gross (1991) *The Hebrew Film*. Jerusalem: privately published.

Halachmi, Joseph (1995) *No Matter What: Studies in the History of the Jewish Film in Israel*. Jerusalem: Steven Spielberg Jewish Film Archive and the Central Zionist Archives.

Israeli Film Academy (1990–present) Catalogues.

Israel Film Centre (1972–present) Information Bulletins.

Jerusalem Film Festival (1992–present) Catalogues.

Klawans, Stuart (2000) 'Nine Views in a Looking Glass: Film Trilogies by Chahine, Gitai, and Kiarostami', *Parnassus: Poetry in Review*, 25, 2, 231–2.

Kronish, Amy (1996) *World Cinema: Israel*. Trowbridge: Flick Books/New Jersey: Associated University Press.

Loshitzky, Yosefa (2001) *Identity Politics on the Israeli Screen*. Austin: University of Texas Press.

Naaman, Dorit (2001) 'Woman/Nation: Orientalism as Alterity in Israeli Cinema', *Cinema Journal*, 14, 4, 36–54.

Neeman, Y. Judd (1995) 'The Empty Tomb in the Postmodern Pyramid: Israeli Cinema in the 1980s and 1990s', in Charles Berlin (ed.) *Documenting Israeli Cinema: A Case Study*. Cambridge: Harvard College Library, 117–51.

_____ (1998) 'Popular Israeli Cinema and its Social realism', in G. Ballas (ed.) *Social Realism in the Fifties, Political Art in the Nineties*. Haifa: Haifa Museum exhibition catalogue.

____ (1999) 'The Death Mask of the Moderns: A Genealogy of New Sensibility Cinema in Israel', in Ilan Troen (ed.) *Israel Studies* 4, 1, 100–28.

____ (2001) 'Israeli Cinema', in Oliver Leaman (ed.) *The Companion Encyclopedia of Middle Eastern and North African Film*. London and New York: Routledge, 223–363.

O'Brien, Conor Cruise (1986) *The Siege*. New York: Simon and Schuster.

Rosenberg, Joel and Stephen J. Whitfield (2002) 'The Cinema of Jewish Experience: Introduction', *Prooftexts*, 22, 1–2, 1–10.

Schnitzer, Meir (1994) *The Israeli Cinema*. Jerusalem: Kineret Publishing House.

Shohat, Ella (1987a) 'The Return of the Repressed: The "Palestinian Wave" in Recent Israeli Cinema', *Cineaste* 15, 3, 10–17.

____ (1987b) 'Israeli Cinema', in William Luhr (ed.) *World Cinema Since 1945*. New York: Ungar Publishing, 330–46.

____ (1988) 'Sepharadim in Israel: Zionism from the Stand Point of its Jewish Victims', *Social Text: Theory, Culture and Ideology*, 19/20, 1–35.

____ (1989) *Israeli Cinema: East/West and the Politics of Representation*. Austin: University of Texas Press.

Tryster, Hillel (1995) *Israel Before Israel: Silent Cinema in the Holy Land*. Jerusalem: Steven Spielberg Film Archive.

Willemen, Paul (ed.) (1993) *The Films of Amos Gitai: A Montage*. London: British Film Institute.

Yosef, Raz (2004) *Beyond Flesh: Queer Masculinities and Nationalism in Israeli Cinema*. London: Rutgers University Press.

LEBANON

Arabi, Afif (1996) *The History of Lebanese Cinema 1929–1979: An Analytical Study of the Evolution and the Development of Lebanese Cinema*. Unpublished doctoral thesis, Ohio State University.

Bitton, Simone (1995) 'Cinéma libanais: La releve des militants', *Le Monde Diplomatique*, 1, 21.

Kennedy-Day, Kiki (2001) 'Cinema in Lebanon, Syria, Iraq and Kuwait', in Oliver Leaman (ed.) *The Companion Encyclopedia of Middle Eastern and North African Film*. London and New York: Routledge, 364–406.

Ra'ad, Walid (1996) '*Beyrouth ya Beyrouth*: Maroun Baghdadi's *Hors la vie* and Franco-Lebanese History', *Third Text* 36, 65–82.

Saab, Jocelyn (1976) *Paroles … elles tournent!* Paris: Editions des femmes.

Suwayd, Muhammad (1996) *Ya Fu'adi: sirah sinama'iyah can salat Bayrut al-rahilah*. Beirut: Dar al-Nahar.

Thoraval, Yves (1994/95) 'A World in Microcosm; Jocelyne Saab's Beirut', *Cinemaya*, 25/6, 14–16.

Zaccak, Hady (1997) *Le Cinéma Libanais, Itinéraire d'un cinema vers l'inconnu (1929–1996)*. Beyrouth: Dar el-Machreq Sarl.

MOROCCO

Araib, Ahmed and Eric de Hullessen (1999) *Il était une fois … Le cinéma au Maroc* Rabat: EDH.

Armes, Roy (2001) 'Cinema in the Maghreb: Morocco', in Oliver Leaman (ed.) *The Companion Encyclopedia of Middle Eastern and North African Film*. London and New York: Routledge, 420–517.

Cinquante ans de courts métrages marocains 1947–1997 (1998). Rabat: CCM.

Dwyer, Kevin (2002) *Moroccan Cinema in the Global Marketplace*. Berkeley: Berkeley University Press.

____ (2004) *Beyond Casablanca: M. A.Tazi and the Adventure of Moroccan Cinema*. Bloomington: Indiana University Press.

Elkhadi, Khalid (1989) *La literature marocaine et le cinema*. Rabat: Edition Maktabat.

____ (2000) *Guide des réalisateurs marocains*. Rabat: El Maarif Al Jadida.

Jaïdi, Moulay Driss (1991) *Le Cinéma au Maroc*. Rabat: Collection al majal.

____ (1992) *Public(s) et cinema*. Rabat: Collection al majal.

____ (1994) Vision(s) de la société marocaine à travers le court métrage. Rabat: Collectional majal.

____ (1995) *Cinégraphiques*. Rabat: Collection al majal.

____ (2000) Diffusion et audience des médias audioivisuels. Rabat: Collection al majal.

Regard sur le cinéma au Maroc (1995). Rabat: CCM.

Souiba, Fouad and Fatima Zahra el Alaoui (1995) *Un siècle de cinéma au Maroc*. Rabat: World Design Communication.

PALESTINE

Gertz, Nurith (2004) 'The Stone at the Top of the Mountain: The Films of Rashid Masharawi', *Journal of Palestine Studies*, 34, 1, 23–36.

Khalidi, Rashid (1997) *Palestinian Identity: The Construction of Modern National Consciousness*. New York: Columbia University Press.

Khalidi, Walid (1991) *Before Their Diaspora*. Washington DC: Institute for Palestine Studies.

_____ (1992) *All That Remains: The Palestinian Villages Occupied and Depopulated by Israel in 1948*. Washington DC: Institute for Palestine Studies.

Khalidi, Walid and Jill Khadduri (eds) (1974) *Palestine and the Arab-Israeli Conflict*. Beirut: Institute of Palestine Studies.

Hennebelle, Guy and Khemà Khaayati (eds) (1977) *La Palestine et le cinema*. Paris: E. 100.

Masalha, Nur (2003) *The Politics of Denial: Israel and the Palestinian Refugee Problem*. London: Pluto Press.

_____ (1997) *A Land Without a People: Israel, Transfer and the Palestinians, 1949–96*. London: Faber and Faber.

Said, Edward (1979) *The Question of Palestine*. New York: Vintage Books.

Shafik, Viola (2001) 'Cinema in Lebanon, Syria, Iraq and Kuwait', in Oliver Leaman (ed.) *The Companion Encyclopedia of Middle Eastern and North African Film*. London and New York: Routledge, 23–129.

Shohat, Ella (1989) 'The Return of the Repressed: The Palestinians in Israeli Cinema', in *East/West and The Politics of Representation*. Austin: University of Texas Press.

SYRIA

Aliksan, Jan (1987) *Tarikh al-sinima al-Suriyah, 1928–1988*. Damascus: Wizarat al-Thawafah, al-Jumhuriyah al-Arabiyah al Suriyah.

Comolli, Jean-Louis and Serge Daney (1978) 'Interview With Omar Amiralay', *Cahiers du Cinema*, 290–1, 79–89.

Darraj, Marwan (1995) 'Omar Amiralai: The Cinema I make is Disturbing', *Alif: Journal of Comparative Poetics*, 15, 138–47.

Dehni, Salah (1991) 'Highs and Lows of Syrian Cinema', *Cinemaya*, 13, 25.

El-Raheb, Waha (2001) *Surat al-Mara'a fi al-Sinama al-Suriya* (*Representation of Women in Syrian Cinema*). Damascus: National Organization for Cinema Publications.

Ibrahim, Bashar (2003) *Alwan al-Sinama al-Suriya* (*The Colours of Syrian Cinema*). Damascus: National Organization for Cinema Publications.

Kennedy-Day, Kiki (2001) 'Cinema in Lebanon, Syria, Iraq and Kuwait', in Oliver Leaman (ed.) *The Companion Encyclopedia of Middle Eastern and North African Film*. London and New York: Routledge, 364–406.

Thoraval, Yves (1993/94) 'Syrian Cinema: A Difficult Self Assertion', *Cinemaya*, 22, 48–50.

Wedeen, Lisa (1999) *Ambiguities of Domination: Politics, Rhetoric and Symbols in Contemporary Syria*. Chicago: University of Chicago Press.

TUNISIA

Armes, Roy (2001) 'Cinema in the Maghreb: Tunisia', in Oliver Leaman (ed.) *The Companion Encyclopedia of Middle Eastern and North African Film*. London and New York: Routledge, 420–517.

Bachy, Victor (1978) *Le cinéma de Tunisie*. Tunis: Société Tunisienne de Diffusion.

Ben Aissa, Anouar (ed.) (1996) *Tunisie: Trente and de cinema*. Tunis: EDICOP.

Chamkhi, Sonia (ed.) (2002) *Cinéma Tunisien Nouveau*. Tunis: Sud Editions.

Gabous, Abdelkrim (1998) *Silence, elles tournent! Les femmes et le cinéma en Tunisie*. Tunis: Cérès Editions/CREDIF.

Khelil, Hédi (2002) *Le Parcours et la trace: Témoignages et documents sur le cinema tunisien*. Salambo: MediaCon.

Khlifi, Omar (1970) *L'Histoire du cinema en Tunisie*. Tunis: STD.

Mansour, Guillemette and Samama Chikly (2000) *Un tunisien à la rencontre du XXIème siècle*. Tunis: Simpact Editions.

Moumen, Touti (1998) *Films tunisiens: Longs métrages 1967–98*. Tunis: Touti Moumen.

Salah, Rassa Mohamed (1992) *35 ans de cinéma tunisien*. Tunis: Éditions Sahar.

Stollery, Martin (2001) 'Masculinities, generations, and cultural transformation in contemporary Tunisian cinema', *Screen*, 42, 1, 49–63.

TURKEY

Abisel, Nilgün (1994) *Türk Sineması Üzerine Yazılar*. Ankara: İmge Kitapevi.

Armes, Roy (1981) 'Yılmaz Güney: The Limits of Individual Action', *Framework*, 15, 17, 9–11.

Bayrakdar, Deniz (ed.) (2001/04) *Türk Film Araştırmalarında Yeni Yönelimler 1–4*. Ankara: Bağlam Yayıncılık.

Basutçu, Mehmet (ed.) (1996) *Le cinema turc*. Paris: Centre George Pompidou.

Ceylan, Nuri Bilge (1999) 'Ordinary Stories of Ordinary People', *Cinemaya*, 43, 22–3.

____ (2004) *Uzak*. İstanbul: Norgunk.

Daldal, Aslı (2003) *Art Politics and Society*. Istanbul: The Isis Press.

____ (2003/04) 'Gerçekçi Geleneğin İzinde: Kracauer, Basit Anlatı ve Nuri Bilge Ceylan Sineması', *Doğu Batı*, 25, 255–73.

Dorsay, Atilla (1985) *Sinema ve Çağımız-2*. Istanbul: Hil Yayın.

____ (1987) 'An Overview of Turkish Cinema from its Origins to the Present Day', in Günsel Renda and Max Kortepeter (eds) *The Transformation of Turkish Culture: The Atatürk Legacy*. Princeton: Princeton University Press, 113–29.

____ (1989) *Sinemamızın Umut Yılları: 1970–80 Arası Türk Sinemasına Bakışlar*. Istanbul: İnkilap Kitabevi.

____ (1991/92) 'Against All Odds', *Cinemaya*, 14, 10.

____ (1994/95) 'Before Tomorrow After Yesterday', *Cinemaya*, 25/26, 56–8.

____ (1999) 'The Young Turks are Here', *Cinemaya*, 43, 18–19.

____ (2000) 'Journey to the Future', *Cinemaya*, 47/48, 92–4.

Dönmez-Colin, Gönül (1993a) 'Contre l'heritage de Kemal Atatürk: Cinema et morale Islamiste', *Le Monde Diplomatique*, 16 October.

____ (1993b) 'Images of a Vertical Dichotomy', *Cinemaya*, 21, 55–7.

____ (1993c) 'Cinema turc: Reflets d'une culture duale', *Cinebulles*, 13, 3, 14–15.

____ (1994) 'Reflections of a Culture in Conflict – Turkish Cinema of the Nineties', *Blimp*, 27/28, 15–19.

____ (1994/95) 'Contending with an Alien Land: Sema Poyraz', *Cinemaya*, 25/26, 60–1.

____ (1995) 'Yeşim Ustaoğlu: Personal Stories Need Not be Autobiographical' (interview), *Cinemaya*, 30, 30–2.

____ (1996) 'Filmmaker in Strife' (Ali Özgentürk interview), *Cinemaya*, 33, 42–6.

____ (1996) 'Auf Der Suche Nach Vielfalt', in Bogdan Grbic, Gabriel Loidoit, Rossen Milev (eds) *Die Siebte Kunst Auf Dem Pulverfass: Balkan Film*. Graz: edition blimp.

____ (1997) 'Dans les bidonvilles d'Istanbul: *Le Bandit* – un film de Yavuz Turgul', *Le Monde Diplomatique*, 9 July.

____ (1998) *Paylaşılan Tutku Sinema (Cinema: A Passion to be Shared)*. Istanbul: Cumhuriyet Kitapları.

____ (1999) 'The Journey Must Go on', *Cinemaya*, 44, 4–6.

____ (2000) 'New Turkish Cinema: The Young Turks Have Arrived', *Blimp*, 42, 84–109.

____ (2001a) 'Esthetiek van het minimalisme: de Jonge Tukse Film', *Film & Televisie*, *Video*, 512, 10–1.

____ (2001b) 'Nuri Bilge Ceylan Bespreking, *Clouds of May*', *Film & Televisie*, *Video*, 512, 12–3.

____ (2003) 'New Turkish Cinema: Individual Tales of Common Concerns', *Asian Cinema*, 14, 1, 138–45.

____ (2004) *Women, Islam and Cinema*. London: Reaktion Books.

____ (2006) *Cinemas of the Other: A Personal Journey with Filmmakers from the Middle East and Central Asia*. Bristol: Intellect.

____ (2007) *Turkish Cinema and Politics of Identity*. London: Reaktion Books.

Erdoğan, Nezih (1994a) 'Das Fernsehen in der Türkei' (Television in Turkey), in Zafer Senocak (ed.) *Gebrochene Blick nach Westen: Positionen und Perspektiven türkischen Kultur*. Berlin: Babel Verlag, 281–92.

____ (1994b) 'Das Neue türkische Kino' (The new Turkish cinema), in Zafer Senocak (ed.) *Gebrochene Blick nach*

Westen: Positionen und Perspektiven türkischen Kultur. Berlin: Babel Verlag, 293–302.

_____ (1998) 'Narratives of resistance: national identity and ambivalence in the Turkish melodrama between 1965 and 1975', *Screen*, 39, 3, 259–69.

_____ (2001) 'Mute Bodies, Disembodied Voices: Notes on Sound in Turkish Popular Cinema', *Screen*, 43, 3, 233–49.

Esen, Şükran Kuyucak (2002) *Sinemamızda Bir 'Auteur': Ömer Kavur*. Istanbul: Alfa.

Evren, Burçak (1990) *Türk Sinemasında Yeni Konumlar*. Istanbul: Broy Yayınları.

Giles, Denis and Haluk Şahin (eds) (1982) 'Revolutionary cinema in Turkey: Yılmaz Güney', *Jump Cut*, 27, 35, 7.

Göktürk, Deniz and Nezih Erdoğan (2001) 'Turkish Cinema', in Oliver Leaman (ed.) *Companion Encyclopedia of Middle Eastern and North African Film*. London and New York: Routledge, 533–73.

Göktürk, Deniz (2001) 'Turkish Delight – German Fright: Migrant Identities in Transnational Cinema' in Karen Ross and Deniz Derman (eds) *Mapping the Margins: Identity Politics and the Media*. Cresskill: Hampton Press, 177–92.

Güçhan, Gülseren (1992) *Toplumsal Değişme ve Türk Sineması*. Ankara: İmge Kitabevi Yayınları.

Güney, Yılmaz (1975) *Arkadaş* (script). Istanbul: Güney Filmcilik Sanayi ve Ticaret A.Ş.

_____ (1994) *Sürü* (script). Istanbul: Yılmaz Güney Kültür ve Sanat Vakfı.

Kahraman, Ahmet (1999) *Yılmaz Güney*. Istanbul: Civiyazıları.

Kalkan, Faruk (1988) *Türk Sineması Toplum Bilimi*. Izmir: Ajans Tümer Yayınları.

Kandiyoti, Deniz and Ayşe Saktanber (eds) (2002) *Fragments of Culture: The Everyday of Modern Turkey*. London: I. B. Tauris.

Kayalı, Kurtuluş (1994) *Yönetmenler Çerçevesinde Türk Sineması*. Ankara: Ayyıldız Yayınları.

Kinzer, Stephen (2001) *Crescent & Star: Turkey Between Two Worlds*. New York: Farrar, Straus and Giroux.

Onaran, Alim Şerif (1994) *Türk Sineması I and II*. Istanbul: Kitle Yayınları.

Onaran, Ozlem, Seçil Büker and Ali Atif Bir (1998) *Eskişehir'de Erkek Rol ve Tutumlarına İlişkin Alan Araştırması*. Eskişehir: Anadolu Üniversitesi.

_____ (2004) 'Sinemada Müzik Kullanımı ve Bir Örnek: *Uzak*', in Cem Pekman and Barış Kılıçbay (eds) *Görüntünün Müziği Müziğin Görüntüsü İçinde*. Istanbul: Pan, 11–21.

Özgüç, Agah (1990) *Bütün Filmleriyle Yılmaz Güney*. Istanbul: Afa Sinema.

_____ (1995) *Türk Film Yönetmenleri Sözlüğü*. Istanbul: Afa.

Özkaracalar, Kaya (1999) 'Aksiyon Filmleri', *Sinema Dergisi*. On line; available at http://www.aykatili.sitemynet.com.

Özön, Nihat (1985) *Sinema Uygulayımı Sanatı Tarihi*. Istanbul: Hil Yayınları.

_____ (1995) *Karagözden Sinemaya: Türk Sineması ve Sorunları*. I & II. Ankara: Kitle Yayınları.

Öztürk, Mehmet (2004) 'Türk Sinemasında Gecekondular', *European Journal of Turkish Studies*. On-line; available at http://www.ejts.org/document94.html.

Saktanber, Ayşe (2002) *Living Islam: Women, Religion and the Politicization of Culture in Turkey*. London: I.B. Tauris.

Scognamillo, Giovani (1998) *Türk Sinema Tarihi*. Istanbul: Kabalcı Yayınevi.

Suner, Asumen (2004) 'Horror of a Different Kind: Dissonant Voices of the New Turkish Cinema', *Screen*, 45, 4, 305–23.

Sönmez, Necati (2000) 'Co-productions, Looking West, Looking East', *Cinemaya*, 47/48, 95–6.

Türk, İbrahim (2001) *Düşlerden Düşüncelere Söyleşiler*. Istanbul: Kabalcı.

Türkali, Vedat (2001) *Yeşilçam Dedikleri Türkiye*. Istanbul: Gendaş Kültür.

Woodhead, Christine (ed.) (1989) *Turkish Cinema: An Introduction*. London: SOAS/Turkish Area Study Group Publications.

Yağız, Nebihat (1998) 'Zihniyet ve Toplumsallık İlişkilerinin Türk Sinemasındaki Yansımaları', unpublished Master's thesis, Dokuz Eylül University. On-line; available at http://www.sinemasal.gen.tr/umutfilmi.

INDEX